Dedication

This book is dedicated to my family for their constant support and encouraging words over the years.

This book is also dedicated to mi amore Jeannie for her love and support. You have made me the happiest man alive for the last eleven years. Here's to many, many more years to come.

And of course, this book is dedicated to you, the musician. Your enthusiasm for music technology is what makes books like this possible. Thank you very much for letting me share some time with you. And now, go make music!

Acknowledgments

As always, my first thank you goes out to Course Technology for the continuing opportunities to share my printed thoughts and views with musicians everywhere. Thank you twelve times (one thank you for every chapter of this book) to Mr. Mark Garvey for his editing expertise. As always, you are a constant source of creative inspiration for my books. My thanks to Stan Dudinsky and Jenny Davidson for their editing help as well. Thank you to Russ Jones and Brent Hoover of audioMIDI.com for the wonderful drum tuning content. Thank you to my friends Greg Ripes for the microphones, Neal Acree (**www.nealacree.com**) for the killer GigaStudio tips, and Adam Howe of Nimbus (**www.nimbusmusic.net**) for loaning me himself and his guitars for the sampling chapter. A big thank you to Shubert Avakian for studio time and thank you to the Sepulveda Unitarian Society for letting me photograph and sample their piano. Above all, thank you to the software companies who make books like this possible: Native Instruments, Tascam (Pete Snell, you rock), Arturia, Steinberg, Cakewalk, Emagic, Camel Audio, and VirSyn.

About the Author

Michael Prager has been involved with music technology for more than ten years. As a graduate of many fine technology-driven campuses, Michael has had the privilege of working with such companies as Cakewalk, Steinberg, Spectrasonics, Sony Classical, Q Up Arts, *Keyboard Magazine*, ArtistPro, audioMIDI.com, the Columbia College of Hollywood, and Disney Interactive. Michael currently resides in Chatsworth, CA and is the author of *Reason 2.5 Power!*, *Reason CSi Starter*, *Reason CSi Master*, and the co-author of *Mac Home Recording Power!*.

TABLE OF Contents

Introduction

Welcome to the exciting world of sampling and software synthesis. Since the late '90s, soft synths have taken the music industry by storm. Gone are the days of racks and racks of hot and heavy studio gear (samplers, synthesizers, keyboards). Instead, you can now run your studio virtually from your own computer. All you need to start is a MIDI keyboard, a computer, your favorite DAW application such as Pro Tools or SONAR, and a few good soft synths and samplers. The sounds and textures that excite you and haunt your dreams are now available in a matter of mouse clicks with the help of sampling and synthesizing in the virtual studio!

In this book, you'll learn all there is to know about programming today's hottest soft synths and samplers, including the synthesis fundamentals that drive them and how to unleash their creative potential. You'll also learn the basics of recording techniques and how to use them when recording your own samples.

What You'll Find in This Book

Throughout this book, you'll find a wealth of information about sampling, soft synthesis, and related technology, including:

- Introductions to sampling and software synthesis
- Guidance on selecting the right gear for your soft synth studio
- In-depth tutorials on recording and editing your samples
- Close-up looks at various types of synthesis and how to program them

Who This Book Is For

This book is for musicians interested in integrating software-based synthesizers and samplers into their music. Whether you're a synthesizing expert or a complete novice, you will find valuable information within this book that will help you realize the potential these software wonders are capable of. The incorporated tutorials are laid out in easy-to-understand terms, and in many cases include supplementary content, which can be downloaded from the Course Technology Web site (**www.courseptr.com**).

Above all, this book focuses on software-based synthesizers and samplers available for both the PC and Mac platforms, including any relevant information and keyboard commands. This ensures that the information contained within these pages can be applied to both platforms from start to finish.

How This Book Is Organized

This book is divided into twelve chapters and two additional appendixes, including:

- **Chapter One, "An Introduction to Sampling**"—This chapter introduces you to the world of sampling, including the history of sampling, digital audio fundamentals, and how samples can be used to create your own realistic "virtual band."
- **Chapter Two, "Configuring a Soft Synth Studio"**—Consider this chapter your "shopping list," as I help you think about software and hardware for your soft synth studio. You'll find recommendations for computers, speakers, mixers, and software.
- **Chapter Three, "Recording Your Samples"**—Let's get down to business and start recording our samples. This chapter focuses on getting the best sounds possible from your piano, guitar, and drums.
- **Chapter Four, "Advanced Sampler Techniques"**—When a sampling session is finished, there's still a lot left to do. This chapter will give you some great ideas to make your samples shine in both GigaStudio and Kontakt.
- **Chapter Five, "Audio Editors—Close Up"**—No sampling studio would be complete without the help of a dedicated audio-editing application. This chapter will help you get to know Sony's Sound Forge for the PC and Bias Peak for the Mac.

- **Chapter Six, "GigaStudio 3"**—GigaStudio is the most widely used PC software sampler. This chapter introduces GigaStudio and guides you through the latest and greatest version of this sampling monster, including the incredible GigaPulse reverb. You'll also learn how to create your own sample instruments.
- **Chapter Seven, "Kontakt Tutorial"**—Kontakt, by Native Instruments, has become a software sampling platform of its own for Mac and PC users alike. This chapter provides an in-depth tour and teaches you how to construct your Kontakt instruments.
- **Chapter Eight, "An Introduction to Software Synthesis"**—This chapter introduces the topic of the second half of this book, software synthesis. In this chapter, you'll get a brief introduction to the subject that will be expanded on in the following four chapters.
- **Chapter Nine, "Subtractive Synthesis—Close Up"**—Subtractive synthesis is the granddaddy of synthesis. This chapter acquaints you with its fundamentals and provides insight into such subtractive soft synths as the Native Instruments Pro-53 and the Arturia Moog Modular.
- **Chapter Ten, "FM Synthesis—Super Freq"**—Get out your spandex and mullet wigs—this chapter will help you get to know our old friend FM synthesis. Responsible for several key albums of the '80s, FM synthesis is considered a soulful, yet complicated form of synthesis. However, this chapter will help it all make sense and give you a close-up look at the fantastic FM7 by Native Instruments.
- **Chapter Eleven, "Additive Synthesis—Sine of the Times"**—Imagine building complex waveforms one sine wave at a time. Additive synthesis is the soft synth for you. This chapter sheds some light on this extremely versatile, yet mysterious form of synthesis with a little help from the Cameleon 5000 by Camel Audio.
- **Chapter Twelve, "RAM Synthesis"**—Ever feel the need to just load up a good sound and write music quickly? RAM synthesis is right up your alley, and to show you how cool it is, we've selected SampleTank 2 Free (a free soft synth) as our RAM synth of choice.

Keeping the Book's Content Current

Everyone involved with this book has worked hard to make it complete and accurate. But as we all know, technology changes rapidly, and a small number of errors might have crept in. If you find any errors or have suggestions for future editions, please contact Course Technology at this Web site:

www.courseptr.com

You can also find updates, corrections, and other information related to the content of the book at this site.

1 An Introduction to Sampling

Sampling is one of the most widely used technologies in the music-making process. Developed in the late 1970s, sampling enabled musicians to create short digital recordings of real-world sounds and instruments, which could then be stored in the memory of a hardware-based synthesizer to be edited, manipulated, and played back from its piano keyboard interface. In recent years, sampling has undergone a transition from the hardware environment to the virtual studio as software-based instruments, which has made it all the more popular. This chapter is designed to help familiarize you with the fundamental concepts of sampling and how it is used to create music in a virtual studio environment. Whether you are a beginner to music technology or a seasoned veteran of hardware-based studios, this is a good place to begin your education in this truly exciting field of the electronic music world.

In this chapter, we'll cover the following topics:

- Defining sampling and samplers
- Digital audio fundamentals
- Sampling terms and fundamentals

What Is Sampling?

In a single sentence, *sampling* could be defined as "the act of recording, editing, and playing back small digital audio recordings known as samples." This is a valid definition for either the hardware or software environments, as they both require the involvement of an instrument known simply as the *sampler*.

A sampler is the instrument that's used to create, manipulate, and play samples. The idea behind samplers is to imitate the sounds and performance characteristics of various instruments, such as flutes, guitars, and vocals, in order to introduce those sounds into a piece of music that would otherwise require the hiring of real players. This was a revolutionary idea, as it enabled keyboardists to re-create sounds that would otherwise be unavailable to them due to their lack of experience with those other instruments. If you're writing a piece of music that requires a guitar chord progression, but you don't know how to play the guitar, you can use a sampler to record the performance of an experienced guitar player, edit the performance, and play it back from a keyboard, thus bringing your musical ideas to fruition. (Or, even more likely today, you can easily purchase, load up, and play from your keyboard one of hundreds of commercially available guitar sample collections.)

Of course, this is just a basic overview of samplers and sampling. Once the ball starts bouncing, sampling goes from zero to complicated in a matter of minutes, which is the reason books like this exist.

History of Samplers

The history of sampling goes back further than you might think, well before digital recording was around in any form. Back in 1946, an organ player named Harry Chamberlin came up with the idea of recording individual notes from other musical instruments and playing those notes like an instrument. From this idea spawned the development of the Model 100 Rhythmate, a machine that would loop the playback of recorded drum patterns to be used as a rhythm accompaniment device. In essence, it was the first drum loop machine!

The initial success of this instrument led to the development of integrating taped recordings into a keyboard-driven instrument. After many initial attempts on his own, Chamberlin found that his designs were a good idea, but utterly unreliable, as there were many problems to be solved, including maintenance and mass production. At that point, a sales associate of Chamberlin took the idea to the UK to see if the problems could be solved abroad. Without getting into the melodrama of this story (it's a pretty long one), these issues were indeed resolved, and the Mellotron was born in 1966.

The Mellotron was a keyboard-driven instrument that played back recorded performances of various instruments, including flutes, trumpets, and others. Each of these recordings was approximately eight seconds long and would begin to play whenever a key was depressed on the keyboard and stop when the key was released, at which point the tape would return to its beginning position.

The Mellotron was a good idea and was used on many signature recordings, such as "Strawberry Fields Forever" and "Stairway to Heaven." However, the 70s were right around the corner, and times were about to change.

Introduced in 1979, the Fairlight CMI was the first digital sampler. This was the first instrument to introduce the analog-to-digital (A/D) audio conversion process, which is the converting of an actual sound, such as a person's voice, into digital information, represented in binary ones and zeros. With a "blistering" sample rate of 24kHz (the standard sampling rate of a CD is 44.1kHz) and a price tag that was a far cry from chump change (about $60,000), the CMI was not quite a household name in sampling. On the plus side, it did bring a lot of new ideas and concepts to the table, such as A/D conversion, looping, and digital audio editing.

From this point on (late 70s to early 80s), other keyboard companies, such as EMU, Ensoniq, and Akai, saw the creative potential in sampling technology and proceeded to develop samplers that were faster, more portable, and, most importantly, cheaper. This resulted in some of the most revered developments in sampling technology of the 80s with the introduction of samplers such as the Emulator series (EMU), the Mirage (Ensoniq), and the Akai S series, in addition to several popular sample-driven drum machines, which included the classic EMU Drumulator and the Linn drum machines. These floppy disc-driven samplers supported higher sampling rates and larger bit depths, making for better-sounding samples, but due to space restrictions they could hold only a maximum of 12 seconds worth of sampling data per floppy disc. Not only that, but the user interfaces were difficult to understand and navigate, making for a rather confusing sampling experience. Most of these issues were resolved by hardware revisions throughout the late 80s and early 90s in samplers such as the Akai S3000 and the Emulator III, as well as by improvements in computer technology, which allowed users to expand the sampling memory and integrate peripherals such as CD-ROM drives into the setup.

VINTAGE INFO

If you'd like to know more about vintage synthesizers and samplers, I recommend checking out the book *Vintage Synthesizers: Pioneering Designers, Groundbreaking Instruments, Collecting Tips, Mutants of Technology* by *Keyboard* staff writer Mark Vail.

Samplers in the Now

This brings us to the mid-90s, at which time computers were becoming faster, more reliable, and extremely chic with musicians and the general public. It seemed only a natural evolution in sampling that it would find its way into the virtual environment. That day finally came in the late 90s when a small software company called Nemesys released a Windows-based sampling program called GigaSampler. This program was, in essence, a sample playback instrument, as it did not actually record audio as a standard hardware sampler does. Rather, GigaSampler used a groundbreaking streaming technology that enabled it to play large samples from a computer's hard drive. This technology will be discussed further in Chapter 6, "GigaStudio 3," when we look at the latest incarnation of GigaSampler, called GigaStudio 3.

Once the technology and potential of GigaSampler were realized by composers and musicians the world over, competing software companies began to develop their own lines of Mac- and Windows-based software samplers, such as Steinberg's HALion (see Figure 1.1), the Emagic EXS24 (see Figure 1.2), Native Instruments' Kontakt (see Figure 1.3), and, most recently, the MOTU Mach 5 (see Figure 1.4). While each of these samplers serves the same purpose, which is to play back samples, they have their own unique feature sets and graphic interfaces. The second sampler we'll be working with in this book is Native Instruments' Kontakt, which we'll cover in Chapter 7, "Kontakt Tutorial."

Figure 1.1
The HALion by Steinberg is a VST Instrument for use in Cubase or Nuendo.

Figure 1.2
The EXS24 is a software sampler made for use in Logic.

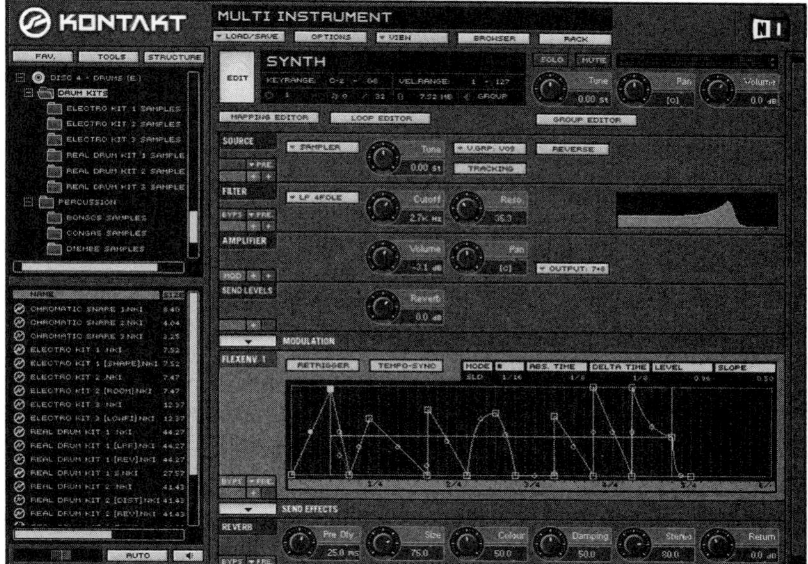

Figure 1.3
Kontakt by Native Instruments is a software sampler that can be used in many different music applications.

Sound Fundamentals—Frequency and Amplitude

What is sound? A "sound" can simply be defined as a vibration that is capable of being detected by a human ear. When our eardrums vibrate, we are hearing a sound. The rate at which our eardrums (and the sound-producing object) vibrate is called the vibration's *frequency*, which is measured in units called *Hertz*.

Figure 1.4
The Mach 5 by MOTU is a complex software sampler that supports extremely high sampling rates (up to 192kHz).

Frequency also has a counterpart element, called *amplitude*, which is simply the volume of the sound and is measured in units called *decibels*. Every sound has a frequency and an amplitude that are measured over a period of time, which is then plotted on an XY graph and is known as a *waveform*.

DIFFERENT SPACE—DIFFERENT SOUND

Space can be thought of as a counterpart to amplitude, as it is space that defines the amplitude of a recorded sound through time. For example, let's say you are recording a handclap in a medium-size room with the microphone placed near your hands. The recorded sound will be very loud and present, as there is very little space between your hands and the microphone. Next, try recording the handclap again in the same room, but standing much farther from the microphone. The recorded sound will be much different from before, not only in amplitude, but also in character.

For certain instruments, a specific amount of space is needed in order to capture its audible characteristics accurately. A good example of this is a recording of an orchestral ensemble within a large auditorium, where the microphones are typically placed a good distance from the instruments.

For other instruments, such as drums or acoustic guitars, very little or no space is ideal for accurately capturing its frequency range. We'll be exploring some of these recording techniques later in Chapter 3, "Recording Your Samples."

Digital Audio Fundamentals—Bit Depth and Sampling Rate

Whether you're recording a sound in the analog or digital domain, you'll find that they both depend on the same common fundamentals (frequency and amplitude). However, unlike analog recordings, capturing sounds digitally is fundamentally based upon the properties of bit depth and sampling rate.

In 1928, an engineer named Harry Nyquist theorized that he could accurately record a sound's waveform by sampling its frequency and amplitude electronically twice in one cycle and then play those samples back perfectly replicated. Although this theory was the foundation of today's digital audio, at the time Nyquist didn't have the available technology to prove his theory. All the same, the Nyquist theory has been accurately proven, and it is this theory that makes it possible to record audio digitally.

The process of recording digital audio would follow as such:

1. Amplitude is measured as voltage values and then captured as numeric data called *bits*.
2. These bits are read as binary data comprised of ones and zeros, each one representing "on," and each zero representing "off." Although bits can represent large values (16-bit, 24-bit), in computer terms these values translate into long strings of ones and zeros.
3. The more bits, the more possible measurements of amplitude. This means more volume potential to musicians.
4. The rate at which these bits are captured is noted as a frequency measured in kilohertz (kHz). This is called the *sampling rate*, and it is responsible for capturing both the frequency and the amplitude of a sound.
5. The higher the sampling rate, the better the clarity of the captured bits.

> **AUDIO CDs = 16/44.1k**
> The bit depth and sampling rate of a standard audio CD are 16 bits and 44.1kHz, which are sometimes labeled as 16/44.1k in books and magazines.

Bit Depth

Bit depth refers to the number of data bits used to capture analog signals (both amplitude and frequency) digitally. The bits are represented in the simple binary language of zeros and ones. For example, an 8-bit recording could have approximately 256 amplitude levels that would be represented as a rather long string of zeros and ones in binary (for example, 00001100, 10100010). A standard 16-bit recording would have nearly 65,535 amplitude levels that would be represented in a virtually endless string of zeros and ones. So in essence, a greater bit depth equals more volume.

Although a commercial audio compact disc has a standard bit depth of 16 bits, the professional recording studio typically records audio at a much higher bit depth, usually 24. This is to ensure that the recorded audio is being captured at its highest potential. The more bits available to digitally capture a sound, the more accurate that captured sound will be in terms of dynamic range (see Figure 1.5).

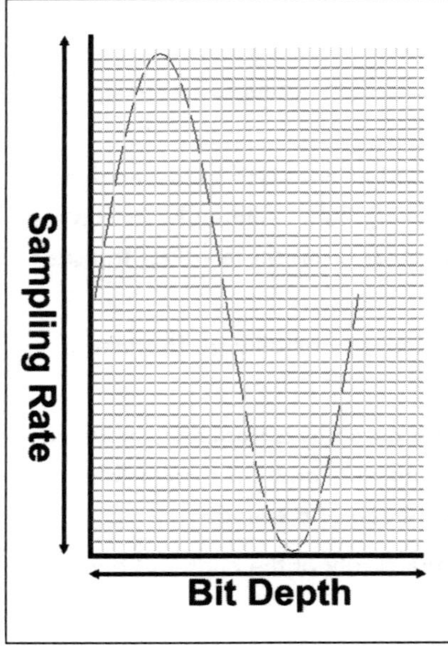

Figure 1.5
This diagram graphically plots both bit depth and sampling rate in digital recording.

Sampling Rate

While bit depth is responsible for the amplitude side of digital recording, *sampling rate* describes the speed of capture, or sampling, of a signal. The rate of capture, or frequency, is measured in units called Hertz (Hz), named after the German scientist Heinrich R. Hertz. A *Hertz* is defined as the unit of measurement to determine the number of vibrational cycles that a sound produces in one second. Therefore, the sampling rate is simply the rate at which "digital snapshots" are taken of the sound you're sampling, expressed in Hertz. Some of the more commonly known sampling rates include 44,100Hz, or 44.1 kilohertz (kHz), 48kHz, and 96kHz.

Okay, this is all fine and good, but what does sampling rate mean to you in digital recording terms? In a word, clarity. Higher sampling rates make it possible to capture a signal's entire frequency range accurately, which in turn results in a captured waveform that is more true to the original signal, as shown in Figure 1.7. For example, let's suppose we wanted to sample a crash cymbal on a drum kit, which generates a very broad frequency range. Using the standard 44.1kHz sampling rate associated with standard audio CDs, the captured sample would sound good and clear, but it would sound even better with a sampling rate of 96kHz, which is quickly becoming a standard sampling rate in most studios. Think of it in photographic terms: When you take a picture with a digital camera, you are "sampling" an image, and capturing pictures using a higher "resolution" or sampling rate will result in a clearer, higher-quality image.

Mapping and Sample Manipulation

After an audio signal has been recorded and stored onto your computer's hard drive, you're in position to use that recording as a sample. In this section, we're going to introduce you to the basic terms that describe the process of sampling, including mapping and manipulation.

A WORD ABOUT MIDI

The world of sampling and soft synths intersects broadly with the world of MIDI (Musical Instrument Digital Interface) technology, and we'll touch on MIDI throughout this book. If you're unfamiliar with MIDI, it would be a good idea to learn at least the fundamentals before getting too deep into this book. You can learn the essentials of MIDI in almost any good introductory book about computer music. A more in-depth treatment is available in *Robert Guérin's MIDI Power!*

Mapping and Multisampling

Mapping describes the process of importing and placing samples along the virtual keyboard of the sampler. It's a fundamental procedure that needs to be explained and demonstrated in great detail, as it has a direct impact on the realism of your samples. For example, let's say you're going to sample an acoustic guitar and import it into either GigaStudio or Kontakt. Conceivably, you could sample one single note of that guitar and import it into the sampler, at which time the sample will be mapped out over the entire range of the virtual keyboard of the sampler (see Figure 1.6). The sampler will then stretch and shrink the sample accordingly in order to interpolate and approximate the pitch differences from one key to the next. The problem with doing this is that the guitar sample will not retain its natural characteristics as you play the sample further away from the sample's original pitch. Rather, the sample will contain several unpleasant digital noises and artifacts, which is not very usable at all. To keep the imported sample sounding as real and natural as possible, we must use another sampling function called *multisampling*.

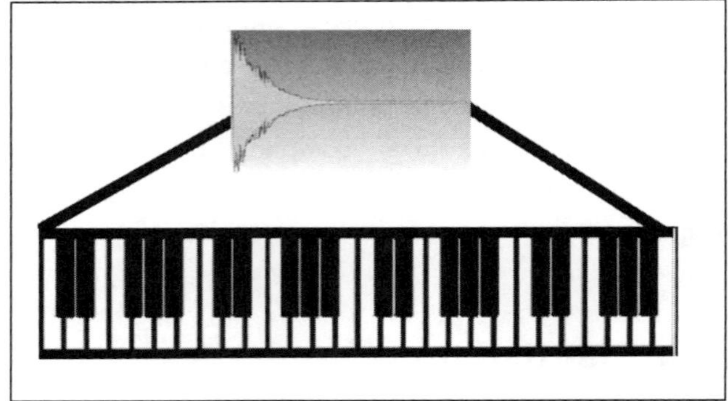

Figure 1.6
Importing a single sample and mapping it over the entire range of a keyboard doesn't quite make the cut for realism.

Multisampling plays a key role in retaining the intended realism of a sampled instrument. It's a process that involves importing numerous samples of an instrument—samples representing the entire tonal range of the instrument—and mapping those samples along the virtual keyboard of the sampler. Have a look at Figure 1.7, and let's discuss an example of multisampling a guitar.

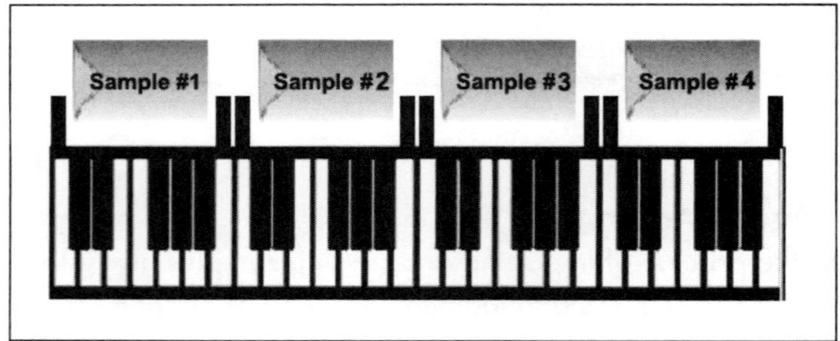

Figure 1.7
If you intend to sample real instruments, multisampling is a good way to go.

1 First, I'll start by importing a sample of a low E string on a guitar. I'll then map that sample across seven notes, ranging from D1 to G#1.
2 Second, I'll import a sample of a low A string on a guitar and map it across five notes from A1 to C#2.
3 Third, I'll import a sample of a low D string on a guitar and map it across five notes from D2 to F#2.

4. Fourth, I'll import a sample of a low G string on a guitar and map it across four notes from G2 to A#2.
5. Fifth, I'll import a sample of a low B string on a guitar and map it across five notes from B2 to D#3.
6. Sixth and last, I'll import a sample of a high E string on a guitar and map it across six notes from E3 to A3.

Multisampling may sound complicated, but once you grasp a few of the key terms involved, it's not that tough. Three terms related to multisampling are *roots, zones, and velocity mapping.*

Roots and Zones

The term *root* identifies the original pitch of a recorded sample. For example, if you sample a piano playing middle C, the root of this sample would also be middle C, or C3 as it is also commonly called. Once the root of a sample has been established, that sample can then be imported into the sampler and mapped to a specific range of keys based around the root note, which is known as a *zone*.

A zone is an assigned portion of the virtual keyboard to which a defined range of notes can be mapped, which relates to the idea of multisampling. For example, a zone can have an assigned low note of C3 and a high note of E3, giving you a range of five notes to import and map a sample to (see Figure 1.8). Additionally, a sample that has a root note within this five-note range (such as C3) can then be loaded into this zone and, when played within this zone, will sound very natural.

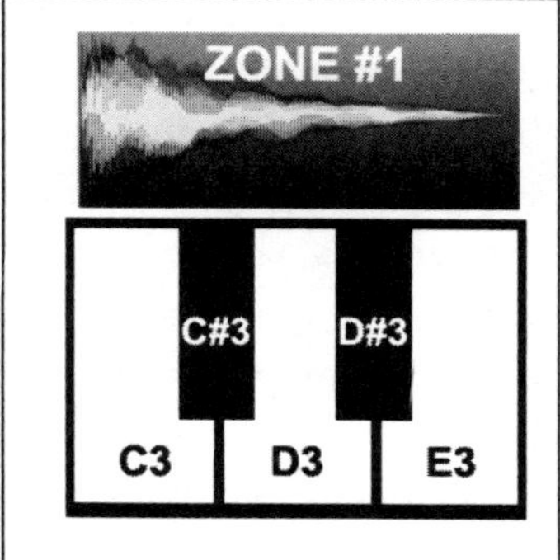

Figure 1.8

Zones are used to assign a specific note range to a sample. Notice in this figure that we have a five-note range from C3 to E3 with a root note of C3.

MISSING ROOTS

When you are importing samples into your sampler, the sampler will usually attempt to determine the root note of the imported sample. At times you may encounter samples for which the root note cannot be determined by the sampler. This is not a problem because there are many fine audio-editing applications such as Steinberg's Wavelab that will determine the root for you (see Figure 1.9). Furthermore, it will embed that information within the digital audio file, which can then be read by the sampler. This feature can also be found in different sampling applications as well. Check the manual of your sampler for more information.

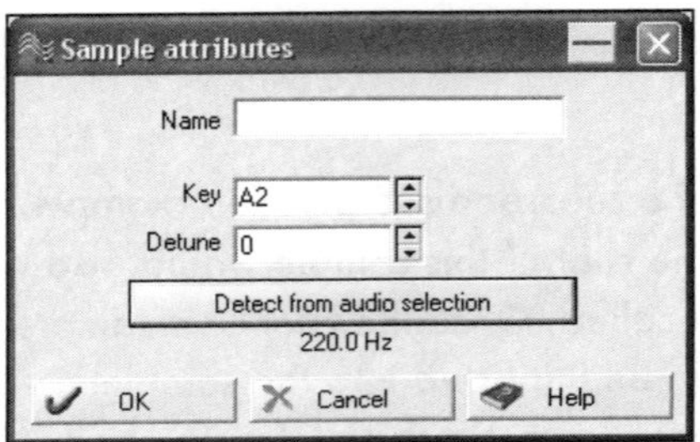

Figure 1.9
Steinberg's Wavelab contains a sampling function that determines the root of a sample. This is especially helpful when the root is unknown.

Velocity Mapping

Another advantage to multisampling is the ability to layer samples with different velocities on the same key of the virtual keyboard. If your MIDI keyboard is capable of transmitting varying velocities (the force with which you hit the key), this makes it possible to imitate the behavior of an instrument according to the velocity at which it is played. This is known as *velocity mapping.*

Consider this scenario: You're sampling a snare drum, which is a dynamically versatile instrument that sounds very different depending on the velocity (the amount of force) with which it's struck. In order to imitate the dynamic behaviors of the snare, you sample it several times, each time at a different velocity, ranging from soft to very hard. After recording, editing, and naming the samples, you can assign all of them to one key on your keyboard. Then you can assign a velocity range to each snare sample so that when the assigned key on the MIDI keyboard is played at a particular velocity, the corresponding sample will play back. Strike the key softly and the snare plays quietly; strike it hard and the snare plays loudly. See Figure 1.10 and the following list to get a better idea of how this works.

Snare_Low.aif—Low Velocity 1, High Velocity 32

Snare_Mid.aif—Low Velocity 33, High Velocity 64

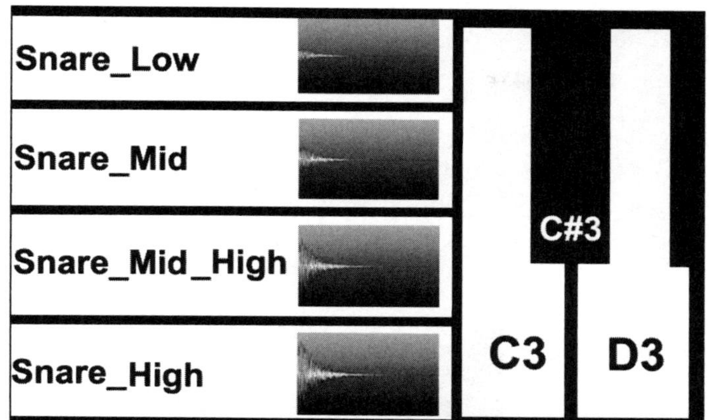

Figure 1.10
In this diagram, I have sampled a snare drum playing at four different velocities, and I have velocity mapped the sample on the D3 key of the keyboard. When I play that key at different velocities, the corresponding samples will play back.

Snare_Mid_High.aif—Low Velocity 65, High Velocity 99

Snare_High.aif—Low Velocity 100, High Velocity 127

Manipulation

Of course, the best part of sampling (besides the playing) is the ability to twist, turn, shape, and contort your loaded samples in ways that just can't be imagined. This gives you a virtually endless assortment of creative possibilities in sound design. Let's get you acquainted with some of the terms used in today's sampling environment.

Looping

Looping is an essential editing function of a sampler that gives the illusion that a loaded sample is sustaining. Looping is commonly used on samples such as pianos or guitars to make the patch sound more like the actual instrument. When you press a key on a piano, that note sustains for a long time if you hold the key down or press the sustain pedal. Creating a loop within a piano sample simulates this sustaining effect by having the sample play through to a specific point called the *loop end* and then jump back to an assigned position in the sample, called the *loop start* (see Figure 1.11). Once the corresponding MIDI note is released, the sample plays through to the absolute end (the loop end).

Let's explore this function by assuming we have a guitar sample loaded and use the following example:

1 Examine the latter half of the sample and find a place where there is visually and audibly a steady rate of amplitude between two points (see Figure 1.12).

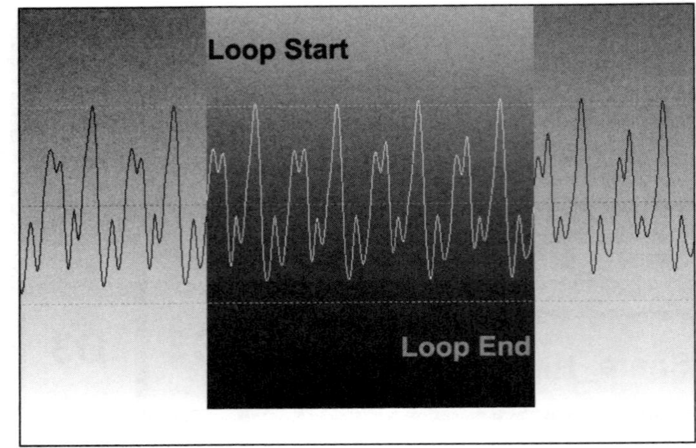

Figure 1.11
Looping a sample gives the illusion of sustain by repeating all of the digital content between the loop start and end points until the corresponding MIDI note is released.

2 Now we'll zoom into this section of the sample and locate a proper point to insert a loop start point.

3 Once a loop start has been established, we'll find an appropriate location to insert a loop end point. Ideally, this point should not be too far from the start point, as this will introduce a difference in amplitude.

4 Once the points have been established, you can hold the corresponding MIDI note, and the sample will loop continuously until the note has been released.

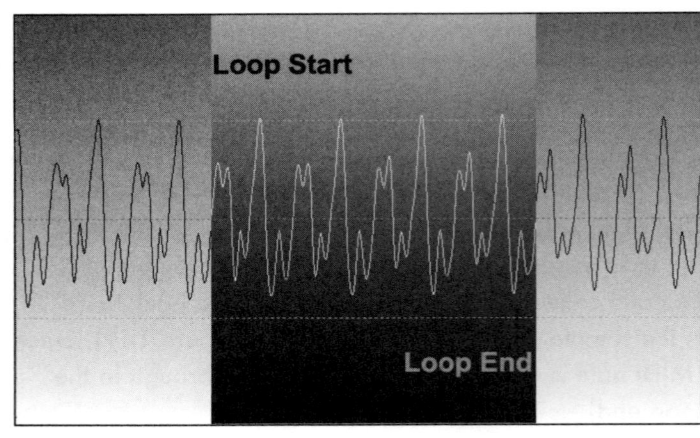

Figure 1.12
This diagram shows a close-up view of a digital audio file. Using the latter half of a sample is a good place to find a suitable region to loop.

MORE LOOPING LATER

Looping, like sampling, is an art form that requires plenty of practice. We'll revisit this in Chapter 3 when we begin our first sampling session.

Reversing

If you're old enough to remember using record players, my bet is that you were one of those kids who loved to spin records in reverse to hear what sort of subliminal messages and sounds you could pull out (oh, the things the Beatles told me to do). Seriously, though, reversing samples is a way of life in the digital age. It's a great effect to use on percussion instruments in particular, as reversing makes it possible to take a cymbal crash and reverse it to use as a filler or intro to a song (see Figure 1.13). Combine that with some flanger and a dab of reverb, and you get some tasty samples!

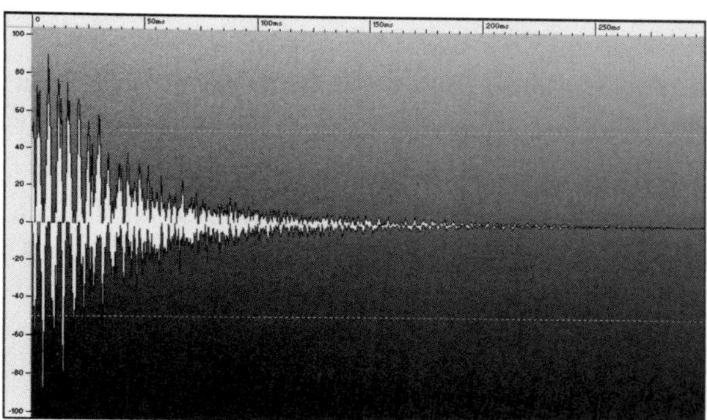

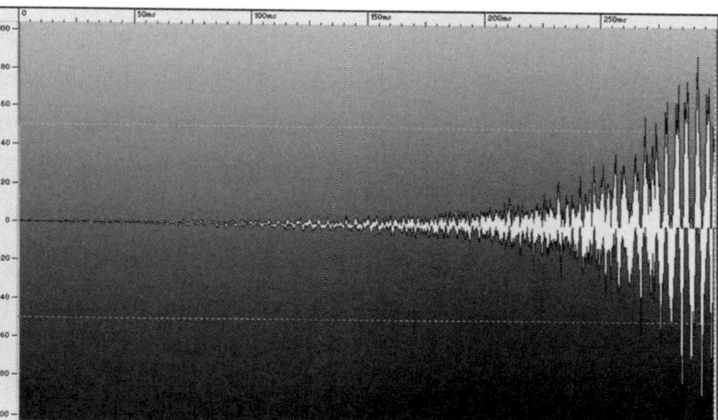

Figure 1.13

The waveform on the left is a cymbal sample that is playing forward. The waveform on the right is that same sample playing in reverse.

Filters and Envelopes

Filters and *envelopes* are a couple of normal modules found within the circuitry of any standard synthesizer, and no sampler would be complete without them, software or otherwise. These modules are solely responsible for shaping the timbre and character of a signal by altering the frequency range and the dynamics of the samples. Let's begin by discussing the properties of the filter module.

Filters

By centering in on a specific range within the frequency spectrum of a sample and either cutting or boosting that range, a filter can create the popular sweeping effect that we hear so often in dance and electronic music. This is made possible by manipulating two main filter parameters: resonance and cutoff frequency.

The cutoff frequency specifies where the filter will function within the frequency spectrum. When the cutoff frequency alters a filter, it opens and closes the filter within a specific frequency range. For example, if the cutoff frequency of a filter is set to the highest possible value, the entire frequency spectrum will pass through unaffected. Likewise, if the cutoff is set to a lower value, the resulting sound will contain a majority of low-end signal because only the lower end of the frequency spectrum can pass through.

Resonance is a parameter that modifies the filter's sound. It emphasizes different frequencies around the set value of the cutoff frequency. When used in different positions, the resonance slider can filter out different frequencies, resulting in tones and textures that ring like bells. For example, if the cutoff frequency is set to the maximum value and the resonance is set to a minimal value, the resulting sound will be extremely treble heavy with minimal bass. However, if the resonance is set to its highest value while the cutoff is set to its lowest value, the resulting signal will be extremely bass heavy. As the cutoff frequency increases, the bass frequencies will be dynamically enhanced by the resonance, and the resulting sound will be loud and clear to anyone within earshot.

DIFFERENT FILTER MODES

Filters are not always used to alter the low end of a sample's frequency range. They can also be used to make slight or drastic changes to the mid-to-high frequency range as well, by using two additional filter modes called the *band pass* and the *high pass*, found on most synths and samplers.

Band pass mode filters out both the high and low frequencies, leaving the mid frequencies unaltered. It can be used effectively on samples that live in the mid frequency range of a mix, such as guitars and certain percussion instruments.

High pass mode filters out the low frequencies while letting the high frequencies pass through. It is especially useful with treble-heavy instruments, such as hi-hats or maracas. High pass filters can also be used in more creative ways with instruments that dominate the low frequencies of a mix, such as a bass guitar or a kick drum.

Envelopes

An envelope alters the dynamic characteristics of a sample (see Figure 1.14). For example, if you have a violin sample that has a very abrupt or short attack, you can use an envelope to manipulate the speed of the sample's attack in order to create a slower bowing action of the instrument. Likewise, if you have a pad sample, such as a string or horn section that has an abrupt release that you want to fade away gradually, an envelope can be used to alter the release of the sample so that it fades away more slowly. This is commonly known as an *amplitude envelope.*

Another common use for an envelope is to manipulate the dynamic characteristics of a filter. For example, if you have a sample that is being processed by a low pass filter, you could use an envelope to prolong the filter effect on the sample by applying a slow attack in order to create the popular sweeping effect that you hear so often in electronic music. This kind of envelope is called a *filter envelope.*

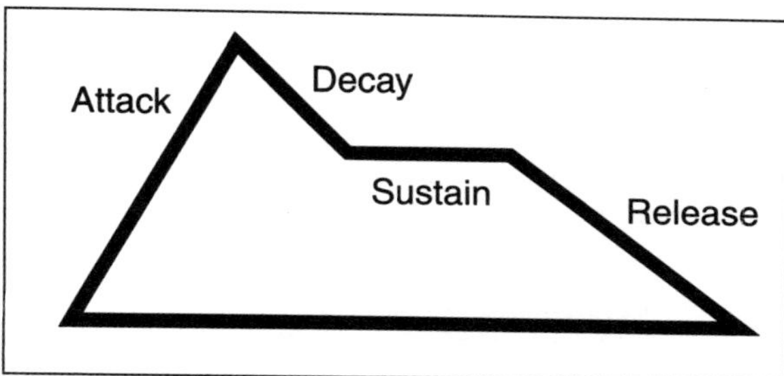

Figure 1.14
An envelope, such as the one shown here, alters the dynamic behaviors of a sample by adjusting its attack, decay, sustain, and release.

An envelope has four basic parameters:

Attack—When a sound's envelope is triggered, the *attack* parameter determines the length of time before the envelope reaches its maximum value (see Figure 1.15).

Decay—Once the maximum amplitude is reached, the *decay* parameter determines the length of time until the volume begins to drop.

Sustain—After the volume begins to drop, the *sustain* parameter determines at which volume the amplitude should remain.

Release—Once the value has been set at its rested value, the *release* parameter determines how long it will take until the value will fade out after releasing the key (see Figure 1.16).

I'm sure by now you are starting to see the potential in this technology and what it can do for you. In the next chapter, I'll provide an overview to choosing the right gear for your soft synth and sampling studio.

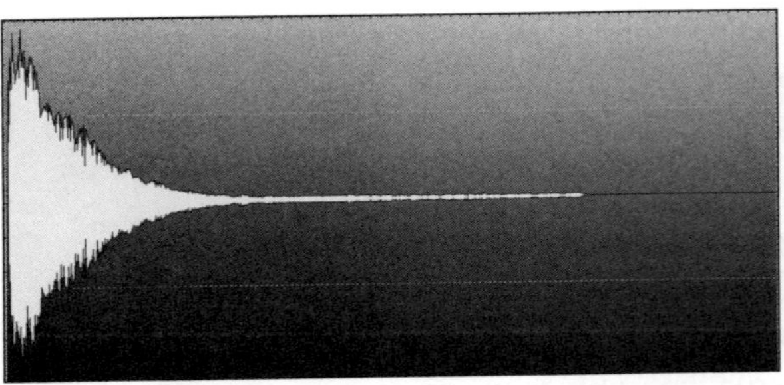

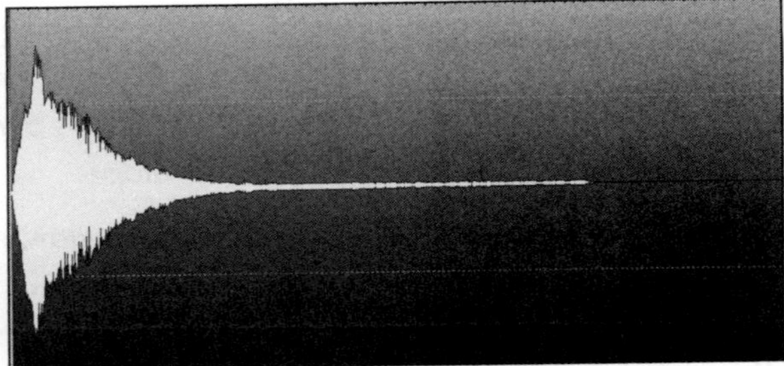

Figure 1.15

On the left, we have a piano sample, which inherently has a very abrupt attack. If the attack parameter of the sample's envelope is adjusted to produce a slower attack, we get a sample that looks like the one displayed on the right.

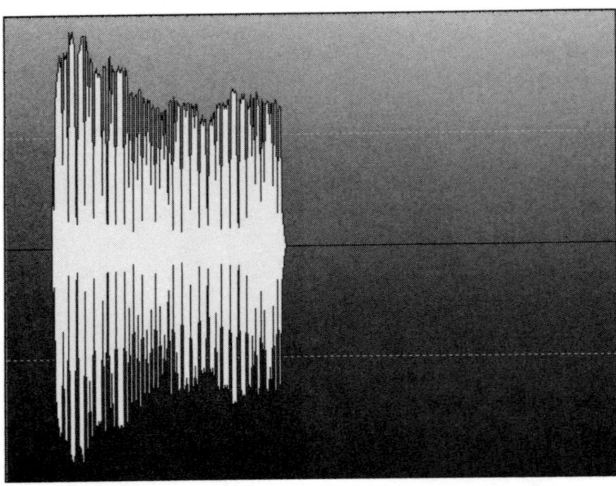

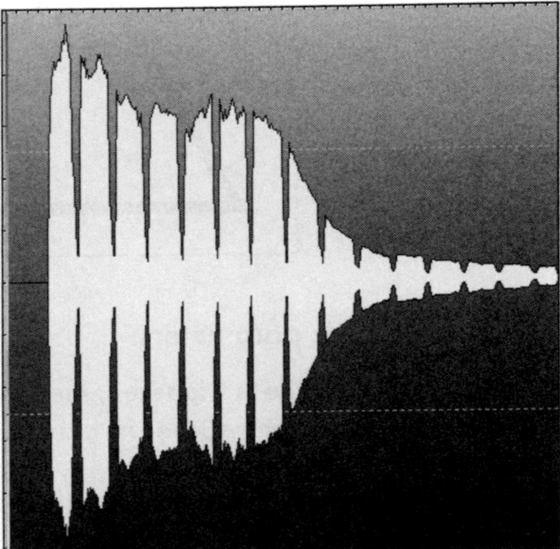

Figure 1.16

On the left, we have a horn stab, which has an abrupt cutoff. If the release parameter is adjusted to produce a slower release after the corresponding MIDI note has been released, we get a sample that looks like the one displayed on the right.

Configuring a Soft Synth Studio

If you're new to all this modern music technology, it can sometimes be confusing and frustrating. I vividly recall my first foray into computer music back in the "dark ages" of the early 1990s, when hard disk recording was something I could only dream about, as it was entirely too expensive for a student to afford.

Today, the cost of setting up a software-based studio is within the reach of just about any budget. Computers are cheaper, software is cheaper, and the accompanying hardware is cheaper. The challenge today is in knowing what to buy, how much to spend, and most importantly, how to put it all together.

Throughout this chapter, we'll consider all the steps you'll need to take in assessing, purchasing, and installing your virtual studio, samplers, and soft synths.

Elements of the Virtual Studio

Let's begin by listing all of the gear needed to get you started.

- **Computer**—This is the brain of the studio.
- **Software**—If the computer is the brain, the software is the heart of the studio. This includes a sequencing application in addition to the soft synths and samplers.
- **Computer Add-Ons**—These include a sound card and MIDI keyboard.
- **Mixing Board**—This is an important tool for recording and playing back digital audio.
- **Microphones**—In order to sample, you need a means to capture the sounds.
- **Speakers**—You can't hear your synthesized bliss without a pair of these.

- **External Hardware**—This would include microphone preamps and DAT recorders. Please note that these are not required to get started, but it would be a good idea to consider them.

So why all the hardware? After all, aren't we talking about putting together a *virtual* studio? Well, yes. This book specifically concentrates on the use of software sequencers and synthesizers, but in order to realize the full potential that a virtual studio offers, some hardware will be required. This is not to say that there aren't a few shortcuts around some of these components, but you will need more than just software in order to record and play back your samples.

Computer

The hub of your virtual studio is your computer. Aside from the software, this is the single most important investment that you will make in order to take advantage of today's soft synths and samplers. Whether you intend to buy a ready-made computer system or have one built to your specifications, you've come to the right place. In this section of the chapter, we'll look at the specific requirements that will help your computer make the most of soft synths and samplers.

Three Key Computer Requirements

When it comes to the computing needs of a virtual studio, there are three key requirements:

- A fast CPU
- Lots of RAM
- A fast hard drive

CPU (Central Processing Unit)

The CPU is where all of the real-time processing for your computer takes place. Installed on the computer's motherboard, the CPU handles and regulates the flow of information throughout the entire computer and, most importantly, gives you the power to use soft synths and samplers in real time within your computer.

When it comes to processors, there are a few notable brands and models to choose from and others that you should steer clear of. Having built and maintained music computers for various clients, I present the following list of approved processors for the PC and Mac platforms.

- **Intel** has developed and released a long line of CPUs for the Windows platform called the *Pentium* series. At the time of this writing, the Pentium IV processor is the most current and ranges in speeds from 2.8GHz (gigahertz) to a blistering 3.4GHz. Embedded within most of the faster Pentium IV processors is a unique "Hyper-Threading" technology, which, when used with a program that supports it, splits its various processes into a series of parallel functions, enabling the CPU to process faster than ever. What does that mean to you? Better overall performance and more soft synths!
- **AMD** is another company that has developed many CPUs for the Windows platform. The currently available Athlon XP 64 series can run at speeds up to 2.4GHz, which is more than adequate for soft synthesizing.
- **Apple** has two available processors: the G4 and the new G5. These can be found in all of the current Apple systems, including the iBook, iMac, and Power Mac computers. While the G4 is a good, solid CPU for making music, the G5 is a much more robust and stout processor, with speeds up to 2.0GHz, which can be further enhanced by using two processors at once.

RAM (Random Access Memory)

Computers use two kinds of memory: permanent and temporary. Permanent memory can save and store data when the computer is powered down; temporary memory (called RAM, for random access memory) stores and processes data only when the computer is turned on. When it comes to RAM-based soft synths and software samplers, the primary function of RAM is to store the compilation of digital samples included within a soft synth or sampler patch.

It's best to purchase and install as much RAM as you can afford, especially if you plan to use RAM-based soft synths, large sampler patches, or a lot of digital audio tracks. As a minimum, 512MB of RAM will get you started, but if you can afford it, 1GB of RAM will offer better performance.

THINK ABOUT THE FUTURE

I am often asked how to save money when building a computer system for music. For most musicians, dropping over a thousand bucks for a new computer is a big financial strain, so it's a reasonable question. But remember, the computer is the most important part of your virtual studio, so it should be given the priority it deserves in your studio budget. Buy as much RAM and CPU power as you can afford. Buy a CD burner to back up your data easily. The bigger the system is, the better your performance will be.

If you buy as much computer as you can afford now, you can keep it longer and get maximum use from it before needing to upgrade.

Hard Drives

Your computer's hard drive is your medium for permanent data storage. Among other things, it holds your operating system, your applications, and above all your samples and patches. The hard drive is also where the digital audio files will be recorded.

When shopping for a hard drive, there are four main points to consider.

- **Brand Name**—Be sure to purchase a hard drive from a well-known manufacturer with a good reputation. This lowers the odds of experiencing hard drive crashes, resulting in a loss of data and hair on your head. Western Digital, Seagate, Samsung, and Maxtor are good choices.
- **Transfer Rate**—This specifies how fast the hard drive transfers data. Make sure the hard drive has a transfer rate of at least 10 megabytes per second or higher.
- **Seek Time**—This specifies how fast the hard drive accesses information. The hard drive must have a seek time of 10 milliseconds (ms) or less to be used for digital audio.
- **Rotation Speed**—This specifies how fast the hard drive rotates. Many hard drives have a rotation speed of 5,400 rotations per minute (RPM), but this generally won't cut it for digital audio. Look for a hard drive with a rotation speed of 7,200 RPM or better.

> **BACK IT UP**
>
> Hard drive crashes are nearly impossible to predict. But they happen, and in all likelihood your hard drive will crash one day, no matter how well you care for your computer. But there's an easy and affordable remedy: Back up your hard drive to CD frequently, weekly if possible. Almost any new computer purchased today will come with a CD burner. If yours doesn't, you should plan to purchase one as soon as possible.

Getting a Second Hard Drive

While you're in the planning stages of configuring your computer, you might want to consider purchasing a second hard drive for use with music applications. A second hard drive is especially useful if you plan to use a lot of samples and digital audio tracks, as having a second drive will help your computer perform more efficiently (see Figure 2.1). If this sounds like a bit of a stretch, let me justify this suggestion by presenting the following reasons.

- **Your main drive works hard enough**—A computer's main hard drive is responsible for administering both the operating system and any actively running software, which in turn limits its bandwidth. This makes the simultaneous playback and recording of samples and digital audio files difficult to accomplish.
- **Samples take up a lot of room**—As you begin to accumulate your growing library of samples and digital audio files, you will find yourself running out of space quickly. Having a second hard drive will help to relieve this problem.

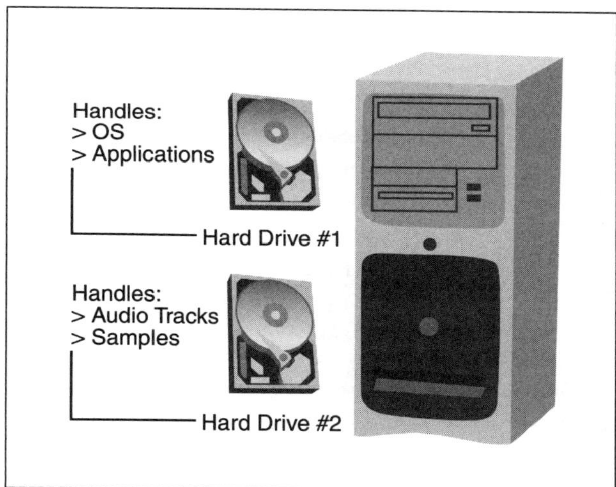

Figure 2.1
This diagram shows the data flow architecture of a music computer with two hard drives. Hard drive one is used for running the operating system and programs, while hard drive two is responsible for handling digital audio playback and recording.

PARTITION IS NOT THE SAME

Partitioning is the process of virtually splitting the empty space of a hard drive into two separate empty spaces. Once done, the computer views these two separate empty spaces as separate hard drives and will assign an identifying device letter to each partition (for example, C drive = partition 1, D drive = partition 2). This may sound like a good way of getting around the purchase of a second hard drive, but it's not the case. A partitioned hard drive will not perform as efficiently as two separate hard drives. While the computer may see the second partition as a separate hard drive, all the work (recording, playback) is still being done on one drive.

BUYING A LAPTOP

Laptop computing has come a long way in recent years. Today's laptop is faster, reliable, and extremely portable (see Figure 2.2). While laptops are a fantastic tool (I wrote my last three books on one), they may not live up to your needs as a soft synth user.

Let's look at the pros and cons. First, the pros:

- **Portability**—You can take them anywhere.
- **Compatibility**—There are many portable solutions for laptops, such as removable hard drives, external sound cards, and portable MIDI keyboards.

And now, the cons:

- **Speed**—Although laptops are much faster than they used to be, they are by no means as fast as most newer desktops. The hard drives are especially slower.
- **Limited Expandability**—Laptops are more limited than desktop computers when it comes to expanding and upgrading components such as RAM, hard drives, and sound card options.
- **Limited Reliability**—When a laptop crashes, it crashes *hard.* There are quite literally a thousand things that could go wrong with a laptop when using it as a music computer. As a recent victim of data loss due to a hard drive crash, I can tell you that it wasn't easy or cheap to fix.

So you see, while laptop computing may be a good temporary solution for the traveling musician, it may not meet all of your needs as a computer musician.

Figure 2.2
While a laptop may work well for the traveling musician, it may not be powerful enough for all of your music computing needs.

Software

After you get your computer configuration sorted out, the next step you're going to want to take is selecting the various software titles to install into your virtual studio, which of course is the focus of this book. Throughout this section, I will introduce you to the various software titles that will be used throughout this book, including:

- Sequencing software
- Soft synths and samplers

Sequencing Software

A sequencer can be thought of as the brain of the entire virtual studio. It is the compositional tool that makes it possible to record your MIDI performances, edit them, and then play them back with accuracy and precision. A sequencer can also be used to record and edit digital audio files, making it the most important tool in your studio (aside from your creativity, of course). Most importantly, a sequencer is used to host and trigger the soft synths and samplers that we will be discussing throughout this book.

In this section, I will introduce you to the sequencers we will be using throughout this book. If you're using a sequencer that differs from the ones I'm using, don't worry. Many of the terms and concepts we'll be discussing can most likely be applied to your own sequencer easily.

SEQUENCER, A.K.A. DAW

At times throughout this book, I may refer to sequencers as DAWs. The term DAW is short for *digital audio workstation*, a term that describes the hardware and software combination of computer, sound card, and sequencing software.

SONAR 3 for Windows XP

SONAR is a fine choice for sequencing soft synths/samplers and hard disk recording (see Figure 2.3). Its interface is organized and easy to understand, making it our sequencer of choice for this book.

Logic 6 for Mac OSX

Logic 6 is a Mac-based sequencer that goes above and beyond the call of duty when it comes to feature sets (see Figure 2.4). It was the first software to integrate the Core Audio engine of Mac OSX and is a solid music-making application.

Figure 2.3
SONAR 3 by Cakewalk is a fantastic sequencing and hard disk recording solution for the Windows platform.

OTHER PC SEQUENCERS

If you don't own a sequencer yet and want some good PC alternatives to SONAR, you might consider one of the following applications.

- Steinberg Cubase SE/SL/SX
- Adobe Audition
- Magix Samplitude
- Pro Tools LE

For more information on these and other DAWs, visit your local music dealer, such as Guitar Center or Sam Ash, or check them out via the Web at online stores such as Sweetwater.com and audioMIDI.com

Figure 2.4
Logic 6 by Emagic is the signature sequencer/hard disk recording software for the Apple platform.

OTHER MAC SEQUENCERS

If you don't own a sequencer yet and want some good Mac alternatives to Logic, you might consider one of the following:

- Steinberg Cubase SE/SL/SX
- Mark of the Unicorn Digital Performer
- Pro Tools LE

For more information on these DAWs, visit your local music dealer, such as Guitar Center or Sam Ash, or check them out via the Web at online stores such as Sweetwater.com and audioMIDI.com.

CHOOSING A SEQUENCER

With the number of sequencers there are to choose from, how can you pick the one that's best for you?

Choosing a sequencer really comes down to a few key issues:

- **Feature set**—When shopping for a sequencer, you want to make sure that you are getting the most bang for your buck. You should look for a sequencer that includes the features you want, such as soft synth support, plug-in support, and so forth.
- **Ease of use**—How easily can you find the transport controls to stop and start the sequencer or the virtual mixing board of the audio recording side of the sequencer? How easily can you load a virtual effect or soft synth device? Most importantly, does the graphic layout of the sequencer make sense? You usually can answer these questions simply by experimenting with the software in a music store or at home with a downloadable demo version.
- **Is it compatible?**—Is the sequencer compatible with the soft synths and samplers that you want to use? Does the sequencer support 24-bit recording? What kind of audio interfaces is the sequencer compatible with?
- **Technical support**—After you buy the sequencer, it's guaranteed that you will need some help from time to time to solve technical issues, which is where a sequencer company's technical support department comes into play. Visit each company's Web site, where you are sure to find a message board full of opinions by current customers.
- **What do the professionals say?**—Let's suppose that you have gone through all of these steps and there are still too many sequencing candidates to choose from. Grab a copy of *Keyboard, Electronic Musician, EQ,* or *Computer Music* magazine and see what their reviewers think of these titles. As a freelance writer for one of these magazines myself, I can tell you that the opinions you will find in these trades can be as unbiased as they come. If the sequencer is hard to use or completely useless, a reviewer will let you know this without hesitation.

Without a doubt, it will take a bit of time and research to come to a decision. Just remember to be patient and be confident that you will know when you have found the right sequencer for you.

Software Samplers

By musical instrument standards, a sampler is a piece of hardware capable of recording and playing back selected bits of digital audio called samples. No studio would be complete without a sampler, as it is a key instrument used to introduce "real" sounds, such as guitars, basses, and voices.

Today, software-based samplers are incredibly popular and versatile when it comes to creating either very realistic or intentionally unrealistic sounds in electronic music. The resulting audio creations can be anything from mock-ups for film scores to music for recording sessions or just for generating ambient noises and textures. In short, you're going to learn a lot in these next few chapters.

Now let's get to know our software samplers a little better, starting with GigaStudio 3.

GigaStudio 3

GigaStudio is *the* standard in software sampling for film composers and electronic musicians alike (see Figure 2.5). It integrates such features as hard disk streaming and on-board DSP (Digital Signal Processing) effects. New to version 3, Giga is now capable of actually recording digital audio samples without the need for additional software, making it a true sampler among samplers.

Figure 2.5
GigaStudio 3 is the latest in software sampling from Tascam.

Kontakt

Kontakt by Native Instruments is a software sampler with a feature set so large that it rivals most DAWs (see Figure 2.6). Like GigaStudio, it supports hard disk streaming and DSP effects, but it also supports a wide variety of platforms, such as VST, Audio Units, DXi, and RTAS. These features, combined with an audio engine with limitless creative possibilities, make Kontakt a giant in software samplers.

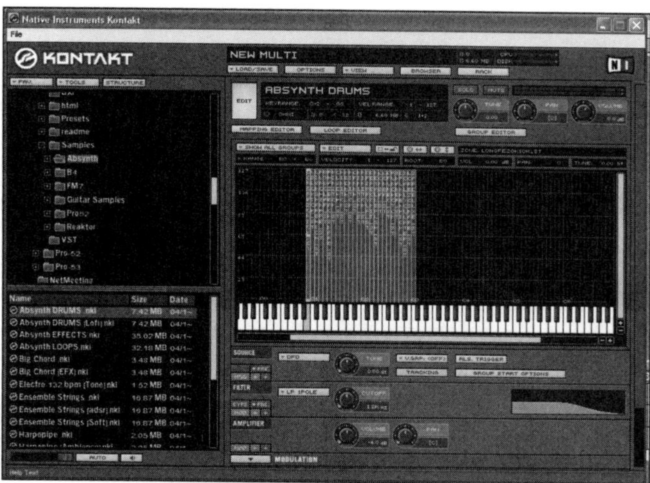

Figure 2.6

Kontakt 1.5 is a software sampler with enough features to satisfy the most demanding electronic musician.

Software Synthesizers

Throughout this book, I'll be covering every category of synthesis that's been integrated into the virtual environment. If you're familiar with the status quo of soft synths, this might seem like a pretty tall order, as there are so many to choose from. However, after searching high and low, I have selected a list of soft synths that will clearly demonstrate each form of synthesis, and you'll learn easy, creative ways to get the most out of them.

> **TRIAL VERSIONS**
>
> Most of the soft synths I have selected for this book can be downloaded from the manufacturers' Web sites in trial versions, which allow you to explore the creative potential of the software before you actually plunk down the cash to buy it.
>
> But even if you don't own some of the soft synths found in this book, you'll still benefit from the content within, as it covers the basic concepts that encompass each synthesis style.

Moog Modular

The Moog Modular is a soft synth emulation of the hardware counterpart of the same name, which played a pivotal role in the development of electronic music in the mid-to-late 1960s (see Figure 2.7). Like the hardware model, the Moog Modular is a modular subtractive synthesizer, which generates sound by linking several devices called modules by way of virtual patch cables. This in turn opens up several creative sound design possibilities.

Figure 2.7
The Moog Modular is a soft synth that emulates the behaviors of the vintage Moog Modular hardware synth.

Reaktor

Reaktor by Native Instruments is the "Ubersynth" of the virtual environment (see Figure 2.8). It's quite simply the most complete soft synth package around, as it includes 31 uniquely individual soft synths and effects. Reaktor is built on a modular scheme and can be used to construct customized soft synths by piecing together the individual device modules. For example, you could construct a simple synthesizer based on the principles of frequency modulation, or FM, and then introduce elements that wouldn't normally be found on an FM synth, such as filters or LFOs. Reaktor also offers the ability to create virtual effects, which can be used in a sequencing program such as Cubase or Pro Tools, or alone.

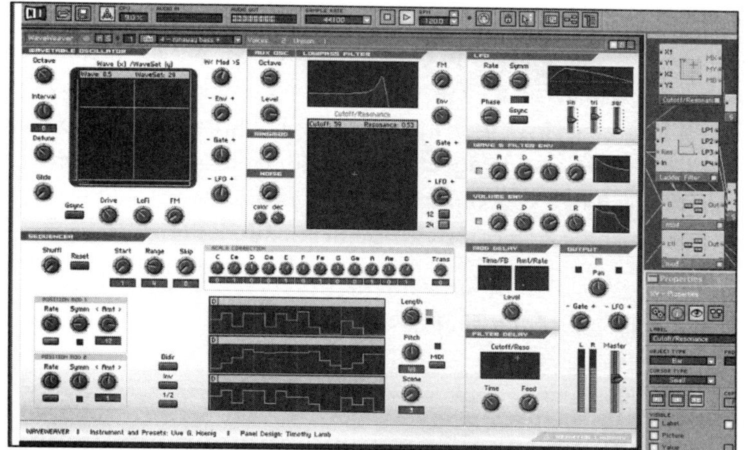

Figure 2.8

Reaktor is a soft synth that meets the needs of gearheads and tweakers alike.

FM7

The FM7 is another soft synth by Native Instruments, but unlike Reaktor, the FM7 is a software emulation of the classic Yamaha DX-7 (see Figure 2.9). Back in its heyday, the DX-7 was the catalyst that single-handedly launched the trend of FM synthesis. Every feature of the DX-7 has been reproduced here in explicit detail, including a lot of additional features that make the FM7 a unique synth in its own right.

You'll get a close-up look at the FM7 when we cover FM synthesis in Chapter 10, "FM Synthesis—Super Freq."

Figure 2.9

The FM7 is a software emulation of the classic Yamaha DX-7, but with a lot of extra features.

Cameleon 5000

When it comes to synthesis, additive is by far the most complex and misunderstood style around. Fortunately, the Cameleon 5000 by Camel Audio is a soft synth that lays it down in a straight and easy manner (see Figure 2.10). The Cameleon also integrates a supplementary synthesis model called *resynthesis,* which lets you import a digital audio file or digital photo, analyze it, and generate a completely original sound.

Get ready for a lot of fun with the Cameleon 5000 in Chapter 11, "Additive Synthesis—Sine of the Times."

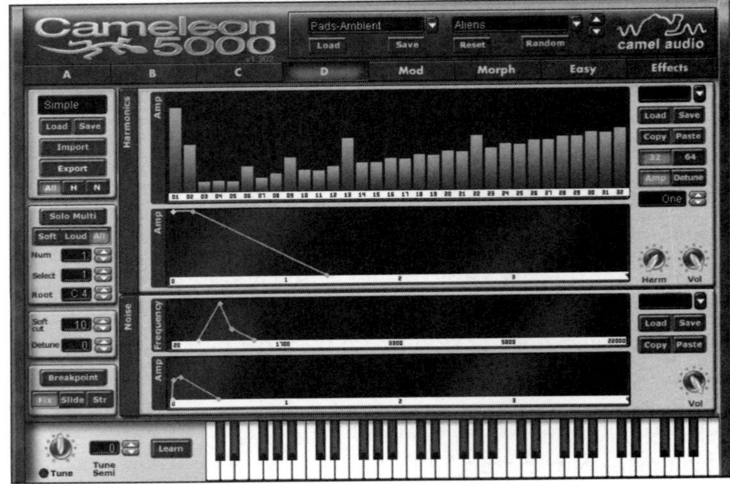

Figure 2.10

The Cameleon 5000 is additive synthesis in a user-friendly environment.

SampleTank 2 Free

SampleTank is a RAM-based soft synth that loads its sounds into your computer's installed RAM (see Figure 2.11). It also includes a variety of professional synthesis parameters, which help shape its character and timbre.

Computer Hardware

Your choices of sound card and MIDI keyboard are important considerations for your virtual studio. Your computer's sound card is the bridge between the analog and digital worlds. It works by translating analog signals into digital information and vice versa. The MIDI keyboard sends data to your soft synths and samplers via a computer language known as MIDI, which allows you to play the soft synths.

Let's take a closer look at both of these components.

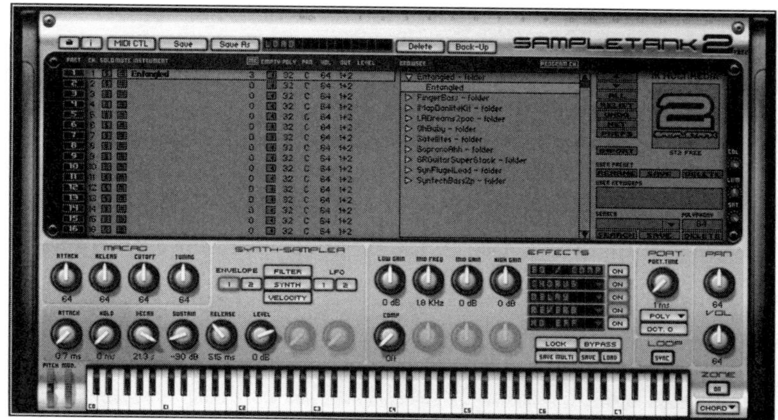

Figure 2.11

SampleTank 2 Free is a freeware RAM-based soft synth.

Choosing a Sound Card

On the recording side of things, a sound card is responsible for translating an analog signal, such as voice or guitar, into digital information. The sound card is also responsible for both playing back digital audio and providing the capability to create real-time performances with soft synths and samplers while using a sequencer. To put it simply, the sound card is one of the most important links in your virtual studio chain.

If you go to your local music instrument store and look around, you'll find a wide variety of sound cards that cater to just about every kind of musician. There are basic PCI sound cards, which install directly into your computer. There are PCI sound cards that include an additional piece of hardware with audio inputs and outputs called a "breakout box." There are also sound cards that operate via USB or FireWire, which are great for portable recording solutions. In short, there's *a lot* to choose from.

Since there are so many sound cards available, you need to make sure yours supports the formats specified by your sequencer application. A sound card's *driver* is software that comes with the card and closely integrates it with your computer's operating system. When active, a driver makes it possible to record and play back digital audio in real time with low latency.

When shopping for a sound card, you'll find that there is a variety of different driver formats that each card supports in order to be used within specific software titles, which we'll be discussing in a moment. Let's discuss these different formats in more detail, beginning with DAE.

LATENCY EXPLAINED

Latency is the time lag between striking a note on your instrument and hearing that note played back through your studio speakers.

For example, on the Fourth of July, you see the fireworks explode in mid-air, but you have to wait almost a full second before you hear the explosion, depending on the distance between you and the fireworks. That is latency, plain and simple. But fireworks latency is a result of distance. In computer synthesis, the latency effect occurs because the instructions from your MIDI keyboard have to be processed inside your computer before your speakers can generate the sound.

The same can also be said of recording digital audio. The latency effect can be heard when a recorded audio signal is captured, processed inside your computer, and then sent back out through the speakers.

Although latency is something to be concerned with when using soft synths and audio recording software, it can be greatly improved by configuring your hardware and software components efficiently.

DAE

A long time ago in a DAW far, far away...Digidesign exploded onto the scene with its introduction of the virtual studio program called Pro Tools. Embedded within this program was the DAE (Digidesign Audio Engine), which is the driver that bridges the gap between Pro Tools and the installed audio hardware.

ASIO Drivers

Steinberg developed and released a driver format called ASIO, or Audio Stream Input/Output, which was also embedded in its flagship application, Cubase VST. ASIO started a trend in digital audio technology by introducing an affordable way to use both the processing power of the computer's CPU and the DSP (Digital Signal Processing) of the sound card to produce real-time audio performance in both PCs and Macs. To make things even better, Steinberg made the ASIO source code available to any company that wanted to write and design ASIO drivers for its audio cards and programs. Currently, there are well over 100 audio cards on the market that support ASIO, as well as many sequencing applications that support it.

WDM Drivers

In 2001, Microsoft released yet another driver format: Windows Driver Model (WDM). Built from the technology in the Windows NT operating system and supported in Windows 98/Me/XP, the WDM format is a popular format for sequencing applications such as Project 5 and SONAR.

CoreAudio Drivers

In 2002, Apple announced its own audio driver technology called CoreAudio, which essentially performs the same tasks as ASIO or WDM, except that it was designed and optimized for OSX 10.2. As this is basically the only solution for Mac owners using OSX, many audio card manufacturers have written drivers to support the CoreAudio platform.

Choosing a MIDI Keyboard

It's important to have a MIDI keyboard of some kind to trigger your soft synths and samplers. It could be a keyboard with its own built-in sounds, such as a Yamaha or Roland, or you could choose a MIDI controller keyboard, which is simply a MIDI keyboard without built-in sounds. If you have not purchased a keyboard yet but are intending to, I recommend purchasing one without built-in sounds. Why? Think of it this way; once you start using soft synths and samplers, are you really going to need additional sounds from another keyboard? Probably not, as the soft synths will certainly provide the sound sets that you will need to get the job done.

Here are a few additional pros to controller keyboards:

- **Cost**—Controller keyboards cost far less than keyboards with built-in sounds. A standard 25-key controller can be purchased for well under $200.
- **Variety**—Controller keyboards come in a wide variety of sizes and configurations. Classically trained piano students can use controller keyboards with weighted keys. Traveling musicians can buy a very small controller keyboard to hook up to a laptop.
- **Compatibility**—Most modern controller keyboards support the USB (Universal Serial Bus) standard, which is great because there is no need for any additional hardware, such as a MIDI interface.
- **Expandability**—Many controller keyboards come with knobs and sliders that send out MIDI controller messages. These knobs and sliders can be assigned to specific soft synth editing parameters, enabling you to record very alive and creative performances into your sequencer.

SOME MIDI RECOMMENDATIONS

Let's take a look at some of the most popular and capable MIDI controller keyboards.

The Oxygen 8 by M-Audio is a compact and versatile controller keyboard that is perfect for the traveling musician or hobbyist (see Figure 2.12). It includes USB and MIDI output ports and assignable knobs for controlling the parameters of your soft synths. At around $129, it's a real bargain.

For the more demanding electronic musician, the Remote 25 by Novation offers a variety of knobs and sliders (see Figure 2.13). With semi-weighted keys and a sporty look, the Remote 25 may not be too cheap ($399 street price), but it will certainly do the trick.

One of the biggest disadvantages of being a classically trained pianist turned computer musician is the lack of weight-sensitive keys in most controller keyboards. Weighted keys are MIDI keyboards that simulate the action and control of a standard piano. To the trained pianist, it makes all the difference in playing style and performance. The fact is that there aren't many weighted controller keyboards on the market, but the Keystation Pro 88 by M-Audio is a good start (see Figure 2.14). At $499, this controller is a sure bet.

Figure 2.12
The Oxygen 8 by M-Audio is a good, versatile MIDI controller.

Figure 2.13
The Novation Remote 25 is a MIDI controller that can be used in numerous ways, including mixing and editing soft synths.

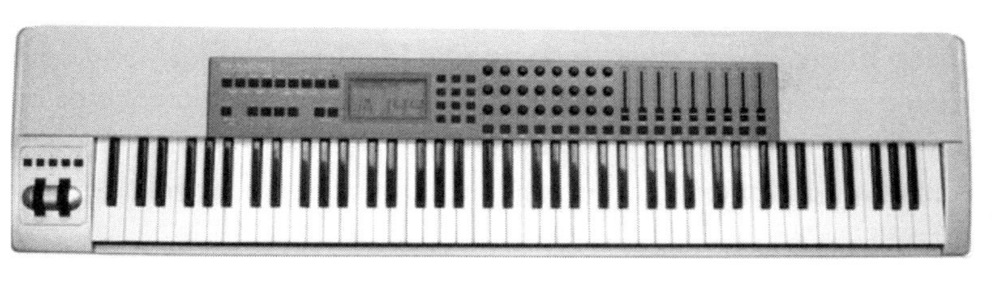

Figure 2.14

The Keystation Pro 88 is the ideal MIDI controller for a classically trained musician who wants to retain the weighted key action of a piano to trigger soft synths.

THE MOOG PIANOBAR

Conceived by renowned synth designer Don Buchla, the Moog PianoBar (see Figure 2.15) is a unique MIDI controller that is installed on a standard acoustic piano. The package includes a strip of sensors that is installed just above the keys of a piano and a pedal used for expression and *portamento* (sliding between notes).

The concept of the PianoBar is simple: It gives classically trained musicians the ability to incorporate their beloved acoustic piano into the MIDI environment. The installed sensors receive note information from the piano keys and send that data to a controller module, which translates it to note on/off and velocity MIDI messages. Those messages can then be used to trigger any of the built-in sounds of the controller module or sent via MIDI to a sequencing program, which can be routed to a soft synth or sampler.

More information on the PianoBar can be found by visiting the Moog Music Web site at **www.moogmusic.com**. Also, be sure to check out my interview with the man himself, Bob Moog, in Chapter 9, "Subtractive Synthesis—Close Up."

Figure 2.15

The Moog PianoBar is a combination of sensors used to transform an acoustic piano into a MIDI controller.

The Mixing Board

A mixing board is a hardware component that no studio should be without. Its main purpose is to combine signals from various audio sources and provide a means of adjusting each source's attributes, including equalization and panning assignments. The resulting sum of audio signals from these adjustments is commonly known as the *mix*.

A mixer is an important piece of hardware for sampling. It's used to input, amplify, and route the signals you want to sample to the computer. In addition, a mixer makes it easy to introduce external effects such as compression and reverb into the signal. In short, a mixer would be a wise investment for your studio.

The good news is that you don't have to buy a large, complicated mixer to do the job. A very simple $300 mixer will be more than adequate for most electronic musicians. A couple of great budget mixers are those made by Mackie and Behringer. Both of these companies offer every kind of mixer you could want, from the simple to the very complicated (see Figures 2.16 and 2.17).

Figure 2.16
The Mackie 1202VLZ is a good, basic mixer for the virtual studio and costs around $399.

> **LOOK FOR INSERT POINTS**
>
> Choose a mixer that has built-in insert points. This will allow you to easily integrate external audio effects such as compressors and limiters into the signal flow. This will be explained in more detail in Chapter 3, "Recording Your Samples."

Figure 2.17
The Behringer UB2442FX Pro EuroRack is slightly more complicated and costs around $339.

Microphones

A good selection of microphones is a key element to a proper sampling setup. Microphones are the first step towards capturing and transmitting sounds to a recording system. It's easy to be overwhelmed by the wide variety—in terms of price and quality—of microphones available today. In this section, we'll discuss two main types of microphones, and I'll offer some recommendations.

And hey, if you really want to impress your friends, call the microphone a "transducer" once in while. Just a little tip in "Geek Speak."

MIC PLACEMENT

While a high-quality microphone is a good start down the path of quality sampling, good microphone placement is the key to sampling accuracy. We'll discuss this at length in Chapter 3.

Dynamic Microphones

Dynamic microphones are the most common of all mic varieties. This is primarily due to the fact that they are self powered, can accept a very wide range of amplitude (hence "dynamic"), and have an affordable price tag. Dynamic mics are also the most durable, which makes them good candidates for stage shows. Whenever you see a live band playing at a club and the singer decides to get "a little physical" with the mic, you can be sure it's dynamic.

The inner workings of a dynamic microphone (or any microphone for that matter) are similar to that of the human ear. The main element of a dynamic microphone, called the *diaphragm*, is the "eardrum" of the microphone. Just like the eardrum found in your ear, the mic diaphragm is the element that picks up the vibrations, which then stimulate the other functioning parts of the microphone, namely a magnet and a coil of copper wire, which is why a dynamic microphone is also referred to as a "moving-coil" mic. These vibrations are converted to electrical impulses, which are then output and routed to the inputs of a mixer.

While dynamic mics are extremely durable, due to the simplicity and ruggedness of their construction, there is a price to pay in terms of audio quality. Dynamic microphones have an inherent high-end roll-off around 12–14kHz, which basically means they are incapable of capturing the highest frequencies of instruments that can produce them. For example, a crash cymbal on a drum kit has a very wide frequency range, but when recorded with a dynamic microphone, it can sound somewhat muddy, as the higher frequencies above 14kHz are gone (see Figure 2.18).

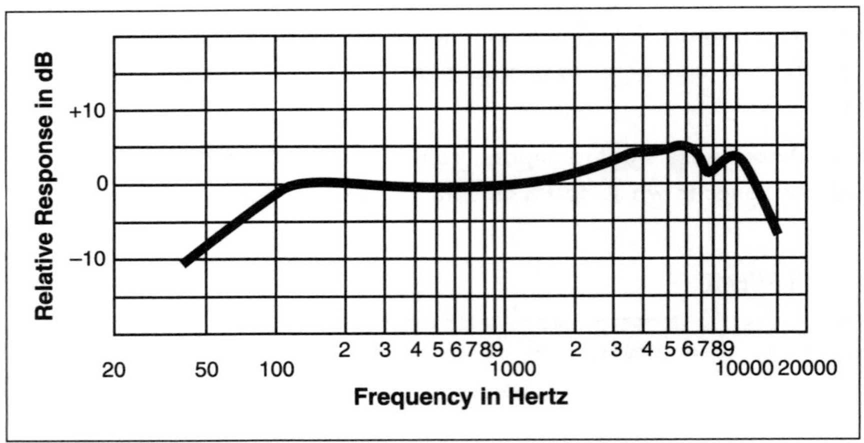

Figure 2.18
This diagram represents the frequency response of a Shure SM58 dynamic microphone. Note the high-end and low-end roll-offs.

But don't let this deter you from considering the purchase of a dynamic microphone. Remember, when first born, a human ear can perceive frequencies up to 22.05kHz. Heck, you can practically hear the air molecules bouncing off each other while lying in your crib as a baby. But as a human ear develops and matures over a lifetime of loud CDs and concerts, the perception of frequency range diminishes somewhat, meaning that your ear is more likely able to hear up to 21kHz on a good day. So what may sound muddy to one engineer may not sound that way to another.

If you are planning to record loud guitars and bass pumped through stacks of amplifiers, then a good solid dynamic microphone is your best bet, as it can accept a wide range of amplitude. What's a good dynamic microphone to purchase? A sure bet would be the trusty SM57 or SM58 series by Shure (see Figure 2.19). At under $100, they don't cost too much, and they produce great results.

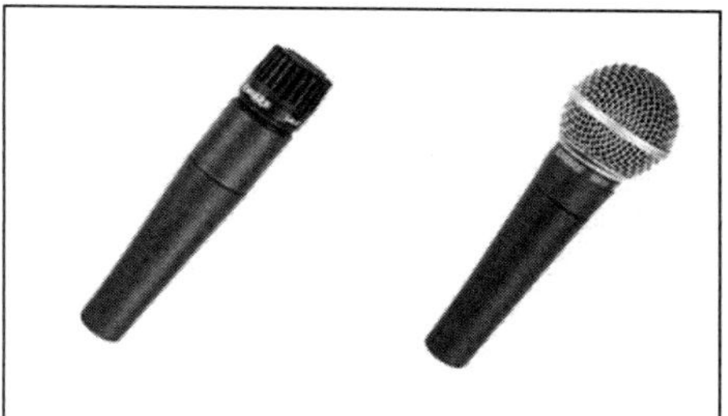

Figure 2.19
The SM57 and SM58 dynamic microphones by Shure are the best bang for the buck.

RIBBON MICROPHONES—DYNAMICS IN DISGUISE

Like a moving-coil dynamic mic, a ribbon mic is also based on the stimulation of a diaphragm by sound waves. But unlike a moving-coil mic, a ribbon mic uses an ultra-thin sheet of metal instead of a coil, which produces a much richer tone. However, this apparatus is much more delicate than your standard moving-coil mic, so they're not often used in stage performances.

In Figure 2.20, you can see that the frequency response of a ribbon microphone differs greatly from that of a moving-coil mic. It is capable of capturing more frequencies than a moving-coil, making it a better solution for picking up both high frequencies and ultra-low bass frequencies.

But if ribbon mics are so great, why don't we use them more often? Well, there are a couple of reasons.

- **Wind**—Due to their design, ribbon microphones are extremely sensitive to external wind. Placing them directly in front of speaker cones or in the bells of brass instruments, as you would with moving-coil mics, is not the best idea. That's not to say you can't do this, but a little more time and adjustment is needed to get a good sound.
- **Amplification**—Moving-coil dynamic mics can self-generate a decent amount of electricity, but ribbon mics do not. Therefore, a ribbon mic requires a good, solid microphone preamp, which boosts the output of the mic to realize its audible potential.

A ribbon microphone would be a great solution for your sampling setup. If you're looking for a few recommendations, you might try the R-121 by Royer Labs (see Figure 2.21).

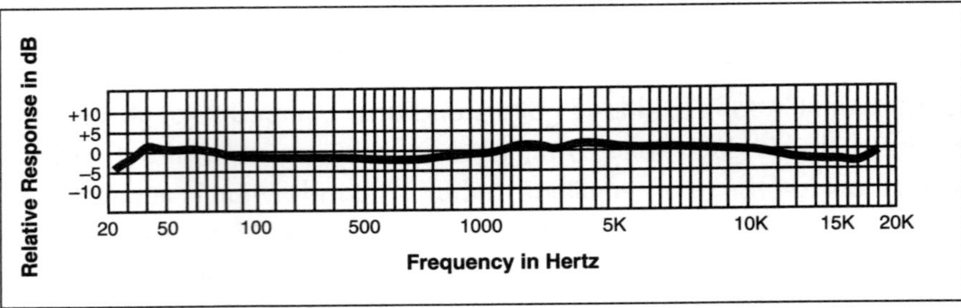

Figure 2.20
This diagram represents the frequency response of a Royer R-121 ribbon microphone. Note that the R-121 has a much smoother response than the SM58. Also note the expanded frequency range, which is much better than that of a moving-coil mic.

Figure 2.21
The Royer R-121 ribbon microphone. It isn't cheap, but it's got quality written all over it.

Condenser Microphones

Now that you're thoroughly versed on the "yin" of dynamic microphones, let's talk about the "yang"—condenser microphones. Condenser microphones are very different from dynamic microphones in both functionality and audio quality. A condenser microphone is composed of a diaphragm and two tiny thin metal plates, which are placed close together. One of these plates is solid, meaning it doesn't move, while the other is looser and therefore able to vibrate. When these plates receive a sound wave, the vibrations cause an electrostatic charge to build, which results in the signal that is sent to the mixing board.

As the space between the two metal plates is small, so is the output potential of a condenser microphone. This requires the introduction of an additional source of power (called *phantom power*) to boost the electrostatic charge.

Phantom power can be supplied by either batteries or a mixer with a phantom power feature. Condensers are frequently thought of as the "studio microphone," as their sensitivity to sound makes them ideal for accurately capturing vocals and acoustic instruments (piano, guitar, choirs). It is rare to find them used in live performance, with the exception of acoustic guitars and such.

However, due to their sensitive nature, even in a studio environment, condensers should not be used in certain methods of recording or with specific instruments, such as drums. A dynamic microphone is a much better choice for drum miking.

Condensers usually cost more than other kinds of microphones, but their prices have dropped significantly in recent years, making them easily accessible for most studio budgets. They start around $100 and work their way up to $2,000 pretty quickly. Of course, the sound quality varies according to the price. However, I have found a couple of exceptions to this rule. For example, I own a Carvin CM90E, which I often use as a voice-over mic. It costs around $100, and I have been quite happy with it.

A couple of other choices are the M-Audio Nova at $130 a pop and the Baby Bottle by Blue Microphones, which is around $500.

POP OFF

In addition to the purchase of a condenser mic, do yourself a favor and pick up a pop filter, which deflects extra wind noises from the microphone (see Figure 2.22). This will result in a cleaner recording. In Chapter 3, I'll show you how to make a cheap but effective pop filter with just a wire coat hanger and a pair of panty hose.

Figure 2.22

The add-on purchase of a pop filter will make for a much cleaner recording.

MIC MODELING

When setting up a studio budget, microphone budgeting often seems to get the short end of the stick. While we might fantasize about buying really first-rate condenser microphones, the hefty price tag that accompanies them often leaves us looking for a cheaper alternative.

Antares Audio Technologies feels our pain and has produced a virtual solution called the Microphone Modeler (see Figure 2.23). The Microphone Modeler is a plug-in that reproduces the sonic characteristics of a wide selection of classic and cult classic microphones and processes any digitally recorded audio track with it. It supports all of the popular plug-in formats, including VST, MAS, RTAS, and DirectX.

For example, say you have recorded a series of acoustic guitar samples with a Shure SM80, which is a decent but inexpensive condenser microphone. Upon listening to the samples, you decide you'd like them to sound as though they were recorded with a vintage Neumann U87, which is a microphone that is not only difficult to find but is also extremely pricey. The Microphone Modeler can reproduce the sonic qualities of the U87 and embed them onto your recorded samples with very authentic results. In addition, the Microphone Modeler supplies a tube saturation effect to warm up the recording even more.

For more information on the Microphone Modeler, visit the Antares Web site at **www.antarestech.com**.

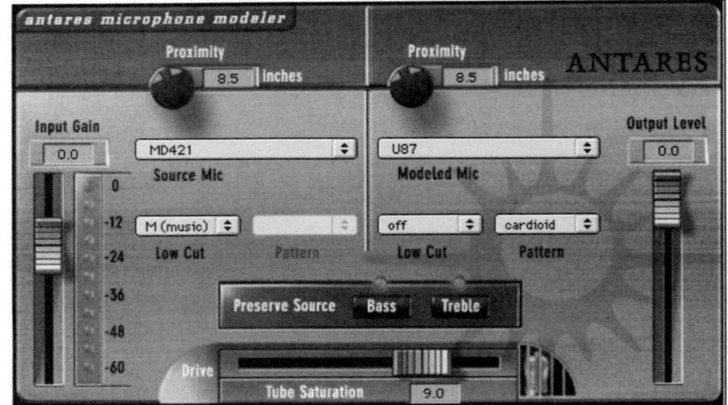

Figure 2.23
The Antares Microphone Modeler embeds the sonic qualities of vintage microphones into your audio tracks.

Speakers—Sounds Good

I like to think of speakers as musical instruments. Selecting and using them efficiently requires practice and patience, just as using your trusty guitar, piano, or drums does. Speakers come in a wide variety of brands, sizes, and quality, and you can bet it will take a bit of budgeting, researching, and auditioning before you're ready to make your final purchase decision.

POWERED AND NON-POWERED SPEAKERS

There are two types of speakers available for your studio: non-powered and powered. A non-powered speaker requires an external amplifier in order to be heard, while a powered speaker includes its own built-in amplification.

Bang for the Buck

No matter what anyone (including me) tells you, the most important factor in selecting a pair of speakers will ultimately be the price tag, so you'll need to decide how much you are going to spend on a new pair of speakers. These days, you can pay anywhere from $200 to $2,000 for a decent pair. Just keep in mind the classic saying, "You get what you pay for," and plan to spend more than $200 for best results.

CYBER-SOUND RECOMMENDATIONS

There are lots of good Internet sources for information on musical gear of all sorts. Harmony Central (**www.harmony-central.com**) is one such Web site; it's full of information and advice. That said, I present the following three speaker recommendations to satisfy a variety of budget ranges.

On a beginner's budget, the BX8 near-field speakers by M-Audio are a good value at around $299 a pair (see Figure 2.24). These self-powered speakers have a frequency response of 56Hz to 20kHz and offer up to 75 watts of amplified action.

If you are looking to drop a little more cash, the RP8 speakers by KRK are a great buy at around $800–900 per pair (see Figure 2.25). These speakers have a frequency response of 45Hz to 20kHz and offer a nice tight low end.

Finally, if you are prepared to go all out Donald Trump style, you might want to check out the 2920B series by Genlec (see Figure 2.26). At around $1,500 per pair, the 2920B features a great sound and digital inputs that can be used to make a straight digital connection to your sound card.

Go online and see these speakers for yourself, or better yet call your local music instrument store to see if they carry them so you can preview them in the flesh, so to speak.

Figure 2.24

The BX8 near-field speakers by M-Audio are good solid speakers with an affordable price tag to boot.

Figure 2.25
The RP8s by KRK have a tight and punchy low end.

Figure 2.26
The 2920B series by Genlec aren't cheap, but they have superior sound quality.

Playing the Field

So how big should your speakers be? This decision should largely be based on the size of the room you'll be working in; the room's dimensions will determine how the room responds to different frequencies. Once the room dimensions are found, you can then make an educated choice between two kinds of speakers:

- **Near-field**—Near-field speakers are used in small-size rooms that are not adequately treated acoustically. They are useful for reducing the perception of unwanted frequencies or reflections, as they are meant to be used in close proximity to your head. They sound best when placed 3 to 4 feet away from your seated position.

- **Mid-field**—Mid-field speakers are used in mid to large rooms. Ideally, these speakers are much larger than near-fields, and they work well in rooms that have been adjusted or acoustically treated to allow for the best sound possible. This is accomplished by using acoustic foam or baffles, which are used to reduce any unwanted frequencies. As they are meant to be used in a large room, mid-field speakers sound their best when placed 6 to 12 feet from your seated position.

Hearing Is Believing

Call me a kid at heart, but the best part of shopping for new gear is actually cruising down to the local music store and auditioning each pair of speakers that sparks your interest. Most of these stores have a specific, isolated room—away from the guitar department and any musicians trying to play "Stairway to Heaven"—in order to give you an honest representation of each speaker's capabilities.

Here are a couple of tips to make the most of your time.

- **Find the "Sweet Spot"**—When auditioning speakers, try to find the *sweet spot* between the pair. This is the point in space at which the mix sounds properly balanced, not too heavy to either the left or the right side. Read the following Note for more information.
- **Use Recorded Music**—Bring along a CD or two of source music to audition through different speakers. The kind of music you bring should best represent the style of music you plan to create in your studio. Since this book deals with sampling and synthesis, some good techno, R&B, or even progressive rock would be good choices.

> **HOW SWEET IT IS**
>
> How do you find the sweet spot between a pair of speakers? It comes down to a matter of measurement between you and the two speakers. Fundamentally, the three of you must be at equal distances from each other in a triangular arrangement, otherwise known as an "equilateral triangle" (see Figure 2.27). In addition, your head must be at monitor level. Although this may take a few extra minutes to accomplish, doing this will ensure that you find the sweet spot quickly and select the right pair of speakers for you.

Rest assured that finding the right pair of speakers for you may very well take more than a day at the music store, so prepare to spend some time doing this.

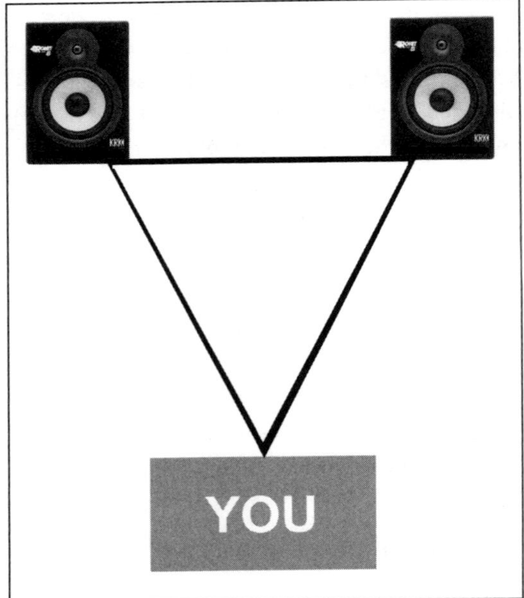

Figure 2.27
The diagram demonstrates the location of the sweet spot in a typical studio setup. Be sure to refer to this figure again when you set up your speakers.

USING HEADPHONES

When recording on a small budget, headphones are a great solution for most musicians, as they provide an inexpensive way of monitoring your audio. As an added bonus, headphones allow you to work late at night without disturbing friends, neighbors, or pets.

If you're sampling, they offer a good alternative to closely monitoring every nuance of an instrument being recorded. Every pop from a string and every breath from a voice or woodwind instrument can be heard with breathtaking clarity. Acoustic guitars, for example, sound fantastic through a good set of headphones.

Look for a pair of headphones with a nice, smooth frequency response, or in other words a pair that doesn't contain any thin-sounding high frequencies or overdriven thumping bass. That said, it would be a good idea to stay away from headphones that offer features such as "Mega Bass" or 3D surround, as this will not give you a clear, objective representation of the entire mix.

But you should be aware that using headphones is *not* an ideal way to *mix* your audio, since listening that way doesn't accurately represent the natural stereo field. Sure, there are ways around this if you absolutely must mix with headphones, but I'd take a mix made with speakers any day of the week.

For more detailed information on headphones, check out the HeadWize Web site at **www.headwize.com.**

Additional External Hardware

In this section, we are going to look at some additional hardware to add to your studio setup, including various types of processors and an external recording device for safeguarding your work.

Processors

External processors are necessary for enhancing an audible signal before sending that signal off to the computer to be recorded. Although a lot of these processors can be simulated through software, there is still a need to have a couple of external effects like compressors and microphone preamps to ensure that the recording you make is as clean as possible.

Later in this section, I will cover using a microphone preamp and a compressor, but you might consider the following additional effects:

- **Noise Gate**—A noise gate blocks unwanted noise by establishing a set level (called a *threshold*) of audio input, which "opens up" to allow a signal to pass through the processor. Once the signal's audio level falls below the threshold, the noise gate closes.
- **De-esser**—This processor reduces the amount of sibilance (very high-frequency noise heard on some "s" sounds) in a vocal performance.
- **Equalizer**—This processor enhances a signal by cutting and boosting various frequencies.

MULTI-EFFECTS

If you're working on a shoestring budget but still need to purchase an external effect processor of some kind, you might consider a multi-effect processor. This provides a variety of different effects (compressor, EQ, mic pre) in one compact unit.

Microphone Preamp

The microphone preamp is a piece of external gear that boosts the output of a microphone to "line" level, which is the standard amplification level for the rest of the gear in your studio, including mixers, sound cards, and speakers. Although many mixers include built-in mic preamps, they can sometimes produce questionable results. For that reason, I recommend you consider buying a decent mic pre, such as the DMP3 by M-Audio for $159 (see Figure 2.28).

Of course, there are many different configurations and brands of mic pres, so you might want to schedule a trip to the music shop to check them out.

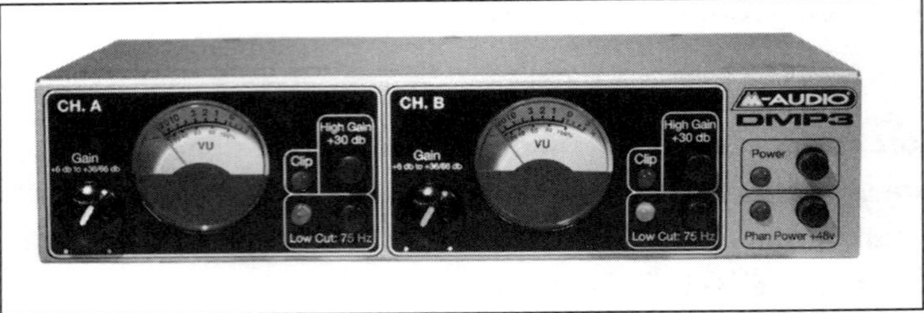

Figure 2.28

The DMP3 by M-Audio is a dual-channel microphone preamp.

NO MIXER REQUIRED

If you're planning to do very basic recordings for your sampling sessions that require only a microphone or two, you might want to consider not using a mixer at all. Just plug your microphones into the mic pre and send those outputs to the inputs of the sound card, bypassing the mixer altogether (see Figure 2.29). This lowers the risk of introducing any extra external noise that might be caused by the mixer.

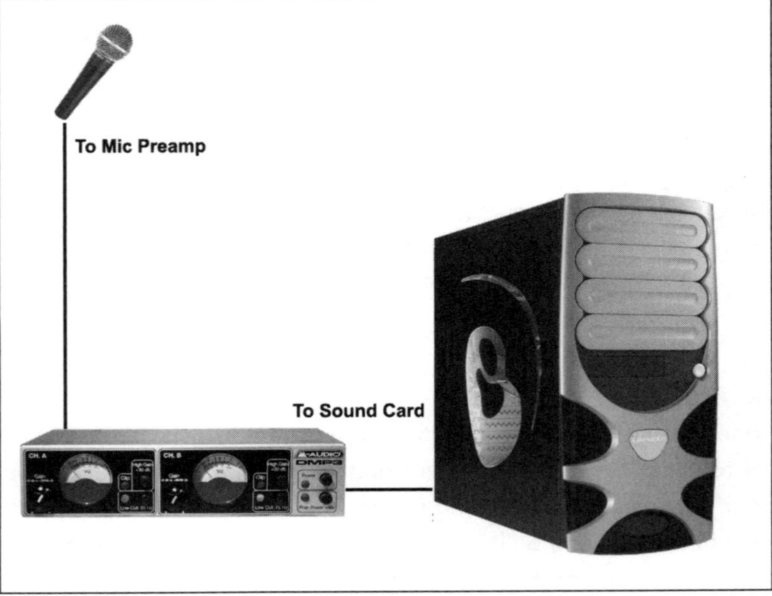

Figure 2.29

This diagram represents how to route your audio signal to the computer without using a mixer.

Compressors

The compressor is quite possibly one of the most important pieces of external hardware you'll purchase for your studio. A compressor evens out the dynamics of a performance by altering its loud and soft qualities. If, for example, you have a singer who likes to sing quiet one minute and then let loose the next, a compressor can boost the signal during the quiet parts of the performance and hold back the signal on the louder parts, thus reducing the chance of distorting your signal when recording. Take it from me, digital distortion sounds horrible!

There are many varieties of compressors, from the inexpensive guitar pedal to the tube warming saturation king. It's a good idea to do some research when shopping for a compressor. My advice is to get a good middle of the road compressor that sounds good but won't put too big a dent in your pocketbook. For 120 bucks, the Behringer AutoCom Pro XL is a good bet (see Figure 2.30). Plus, it is a dual-channel effect, meaning that you can use it on two separate signals at one time.

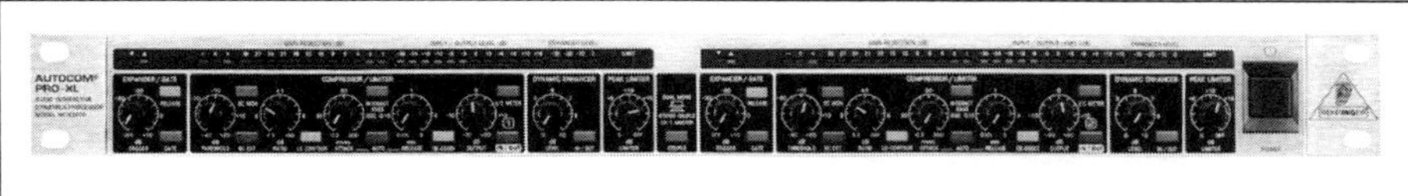

Figure 2.30
The Behringer AutoCom Pro XL is an inexpensive but effective compressor.

DAT Recorder

The lights are low, your recording session is smoking great, when all of a sudden you get an error message on your computer informing you that your recording program has unexpectedly quit. This is the point at which your reputation as a cool, calm producer is put to the test. Confidently, you look down at the warm glow of your backup DAT recorder, which is still recording audio, knowing that both the session and your reputation are safe.

It's a fact that hard drives will crash, and programs will quit without warning. Truthfully, it rarely happens, but that is the price we pay for doing the entire recording process on computers. This is why I recommend purchasing an additional, inexpensive backup recording device to save your session, not to mention your sanity.

DAT (digital audio tape) recorders are a great way of doing this. All the rage back in the 90s, DAT recorders were once thought of as the new format to replace the household tape deck. However, due to the DAT tape's sensitivity to the outdoor elements of life, namely dust particles, DAT recorders eventually found their niche in the recording studio. Since then, they have become somewhat obsolete, as most studios prefer to put all their trust into DAW systems. But this is a great advantage for you as a "Sampling Guru in Waiting," as a DAT recorder makes the perfect companion for your sampling sessions.

- **Affordability**—DAT recorders can be bought used for around $300–500.
- **Reliability**—Provided the DAT recorder you choose is in great shape, they are virtually crash proof.
- **Portability**—Using a DAT recorder allows you to travel off site to record your sounds in different locations. Even better, you can find DAT recorders that are battery driven for complete portability.

There's a good chance that you've already dropped a lot of money for all the other gear that you plan to use in your recording studio, so a DAT recorder is really just kind of a bonus purchase. But in the long run, it's a smart investment. If you are in the market for one, I suggest looking for Panasonic or Tascam machines, as they really are the best in quality and design.

MINIDISCS

If you want something a little more modern, you might consider picking up a MiniDisc recorder. As was the case with DAT recorders, the MiniDisc was poised to be the replacement format for the standard compact disc. Once again, this was not the case, and the MiniDisc found its way into the recording studio. These days, you can find several varieties of MiniDisc recorders, including home decks, field recorders, and portable Walkman-style recorders, such as the Sony MZ-NF610 (see Figure 2.31).

Putting It All Together

We've finally left our "virtual shopping mall" and now come to the last hurdle to jump, which is making sense out of all this technology and putting it all together. This is where the fun really begins, as assembling a studio allows you to customize your working and creative environment to reflect the kind of work you want to do in your virtual studio.

For this last part of this chapter, I'm going to take you through the steps of making the proper connections for your studio, including some tips and tricks I've picked up after doing this more than a few times.

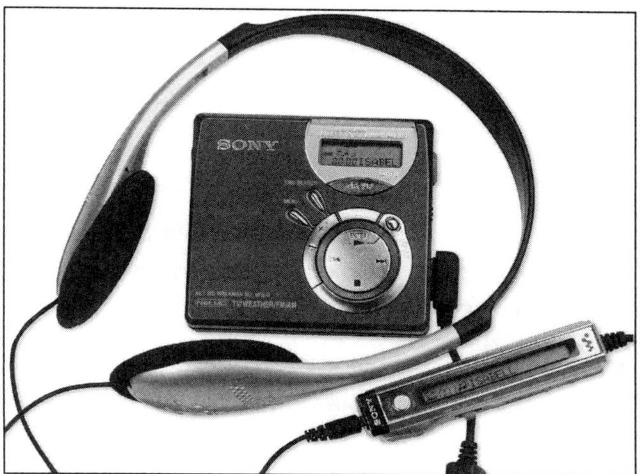

Figure 2.31
The Sony MZ-NF610 MiniDisc recorder is a good solution for field recordings.

From the Ground Up

The first component to evaluate in the virtual studio is your source of electricity. Electrical circuits in and around the studio can be a great cause of frustration and confusion by introducing additional noise into your signal path. This is usually caused by inadequate grounding and cross connections. The point of this section is to help you evaluate your workspace and learn how to keep it as noise free as possible.

The term "ground" refers to a conducting connection that is made between an electrical circuit and Earth, or between an electrical circuit and a conducting object that represents Earth. It's a necessary connection made to safely dispose of hazardous electrical charges caused by lightning or static discharge. In short, it's a safety measure to ensure you don't electrocute yourself when using your household appliances.

In the studio, grounding your equipment is essential not just for your personal safety but also to avoid any unwanted noise that may occur due to a single power source regulating various equipment operating at different voltages. This is commonly known as "ground looping."

Without getting technical (we're musicians, not electricians, right?), ground loops are something you want to try to avoid at all costs. If you encounter any ground loop noise in your studio setup, first look at how your equipment is connected electrically, and make sure that all of the equipment shares a common grounded power socket. Also make sure that your audio cables are not crossing with the electrical, as this will also cause unwanted noise.

If you have tried these remedies and you are still encountering noise, then you may want to consider a few other options, such as a voltage regulator or an isolation transformer, both of which can be found at just about any electrical equipment store.

Basic Audio Connections

With all the electrical mumbo-jumbo out of the way, you're now ready to connect your gear. I'll take you step by step through the process, starting with the mixer and speakers.

First, the Mixer and Speakers

Connecting the mixer and speakers is the first item on your "to do" list. It's a relatively simple connection, but this places you in a good spot to start experimenting with speaker placement in your studio and finding that sweet spot we've talked about in this chapter. To make the connection between the mixer and the speaker, you will need two cables with quarter-inch connections, or *jacks*, on both ends. Connect the outputs of the mixer, which are typically labeled either main out or monitor out, to the inputs on the speakers. When doing this, make sure that you are connecting the left output to the left speaker and likewise for the right.

The next step is to make sure the outputs of your speakers are set to the same value, which is handled by a volume knob on the back of each speaker (if your speakers are powered). This is to ensure that you will get a balanced stereo mix and is probably covered in greater detail in the speaker's manual.

GET THE BALANCE RIGHT

Using balanced cables in your studio will help in the quest to avoid potential noise problems created by external elements such as radio transmissions and fluorescent lighting. A balanced cable makes use of three internal conductors: a positive, a negative, and a ground connection. When a signal is sent through a balanced cable, it's split into two separate signals, which run along the positive and negative conductors. These two signals are 180 degrees out of phase with each other. Any noise interference that the cables pick up will be picked up equally by both the positive and negative conductors. When the signals reach the other end of the cable, the positive and negative signals are put back into phase, and any noise that's been picked up along the way will be thrown 180 degrees out of phase, effectively eliminating it.

Balanced cables come in two varieties: Tip/Ring/Sleeve (also known as TRS) and XLR, which is the standard mic cable connection (see Figure 2.32). Balanced cables cost a little more than unbalanced cables, but it's a higher-quality cable.

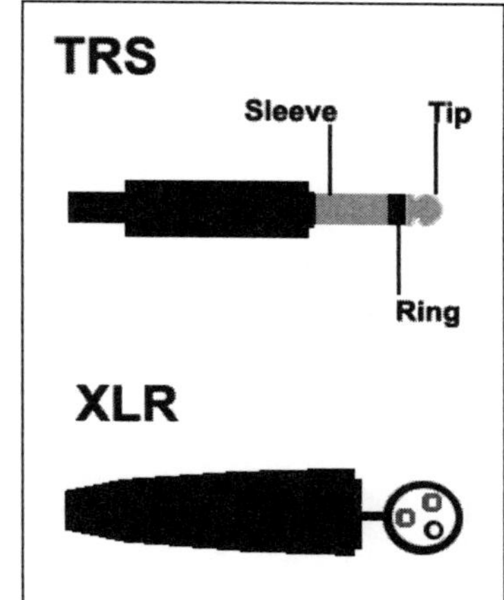

Figure 2.32
Balanced cables such as the ones displayed here help to reduce the risk of exposure to external noises.

Connecting the External Processors

Connecting external processors such as compressors or equalizers can be done by making use of the mixer's insert points. These are commonly found on the back of the mixer, as on the Mackie 1202VLZ, which I will refer to throughout the rest of this chapter. In order to connect an external effect to an insert point of the mixer, you will need a cable with a quarter-inch TRS jack on one end and two mono quarter-inch jacks on the other. In such a cable, the tip and ring of the TRS connection are split up to each of the mono quarter-inch jacks on the other end of the cable. In other words, the "tip" of the TRS connection is connected to one mono jack, while the "ring" is connected to the other jack.

Here's how to connect the processor.

1. Plug the stereo TRS jack into an insert point. Make sure it inserts all the way.
2. Plug the "tip" jack (see Figure 2.33) into the input of the compressor.
3. Plug the "ring" jack into the output of the compressor.

When you're finished, you should get a connection like the one shown in Figure 2.33. Now that the connection is complete, you can plug in a guitar or microphone to the channel that corresponds to the insert point and apply the effect before the signal is sent to the EQ or gain section of the mixer.

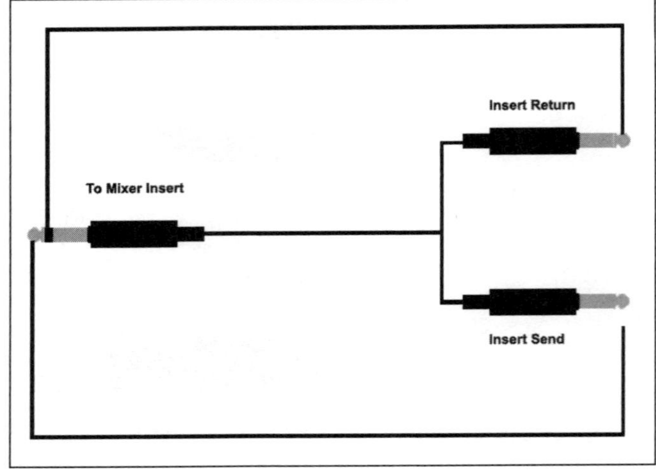

Figure 2.33
This diagram demonstrates how to connect an external effect to an insert point.

Connecting the DAT Recorder

If you followed my advice from the previous section and got yourself a DAT recorder or a backup recording device of some kind, here is where you'll learn how to hook it up. There are typically two ways to do this, via the main outs (if the monitor outs are connected to the speakers) or the tape monitor outputs if your mixer has them. Both of these outputs will work equally well. For example, I own a Tascam DA20-MkII, which has RCA jacks for inputs and outputs. Therefore, I tend to use the tape monitor outputs of the mixer, since these tend to be RCA jacks as well. However, if I used a Panasonic SV3700, which has XLR jacks, then I would use the main outs of the mixer, since they are also XLR.

Once you have made the connections, your studio setup should look like Figure 2.34.

Connecting the Sound Card

Connecting your sound card to your mixer is a two-step process. First, you need to connect the outputs of the sound card to your mixer. Second, you need to connect an output from your mixer to your sound card. The complexity of this process really depends on how many inputs and outputs your sound card and mixer have. In our example here, we will connect a sound card that has two inputs and two outputs.

Connect the outputs of your sound card to the first two inputs of your mixer. If this is your first time making this connection, I recommend using the line inputs on your mixer, just to keep it simple.

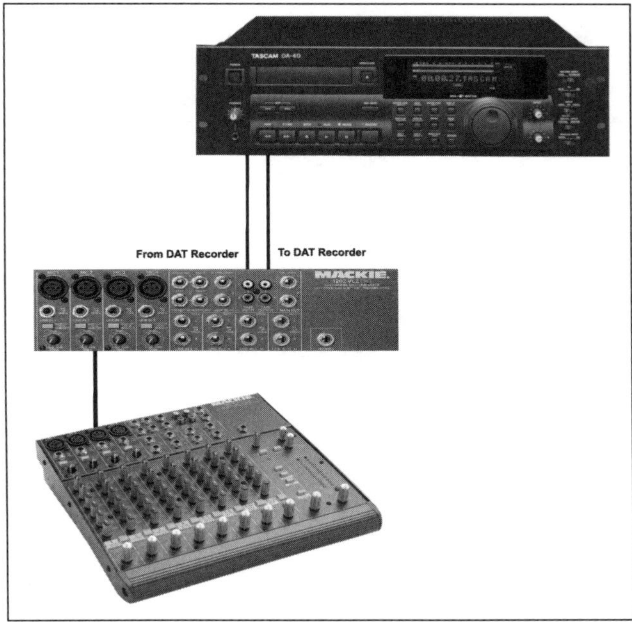

Figure 2.34

Our DAT recorder is now hooked up, and we can record our sessions with more confidence.

PAN THOSE INPUTS

Remember to pan the inputs on your mixer appropriately when monitoring your audio from the computer. This means that the first input should be panned hard left, while the second input should be panned hard right. This will ensure that you are monitoring in true stereo from your computer.

Connecting the outputs of the mixer to your sound card might get a little more complicated, depending on what kind of mixer you have. In the example shown in Figure 2.35, I'm using a Mackie 1202VLZ as my reference mixer. Looking at the back panel, you can see the main outputs, which are XLR connections, and a pair of alternate outputs. While the main outputs can go to your speakers, the four connections at the right can be used as outputs to be connected to your sound card inputs. Another possibility is the alt 3/4 outputs as well. Keep in mind that there is more than one way to do this, so read your mixer's manual for more information.

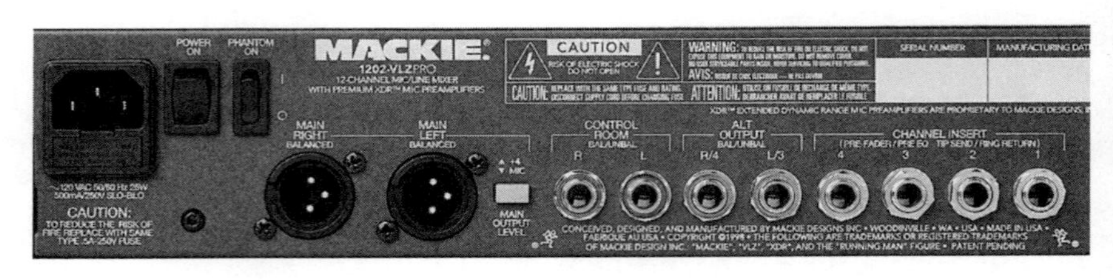

Figure 2.35

The output connections on the back of the Mackie 1202VLZ include the main outputs, the alt outputs, and the insert points to send to your sound card.

Connecting the MIDI Keyboard

The final step is to connect your MIDI keyboard to the computer. This will enable you to control and sequence your soft synths and samplers. This is commonly done in one of two ways:

- MIDI interface
- USB port

If you are using an older MIDI keyboard as your controller, you will need to purchase a basic MIDI interface. There are several to choose from, such as the MIDIsport 2×2 by M-Audio, or perhaps the Fastlane USB by Mark of the Unicorn. Just remember that the MIDI OUT on your keyboard goes to the MIDI IN on the interface, and vice versa (see Figure 2.36).

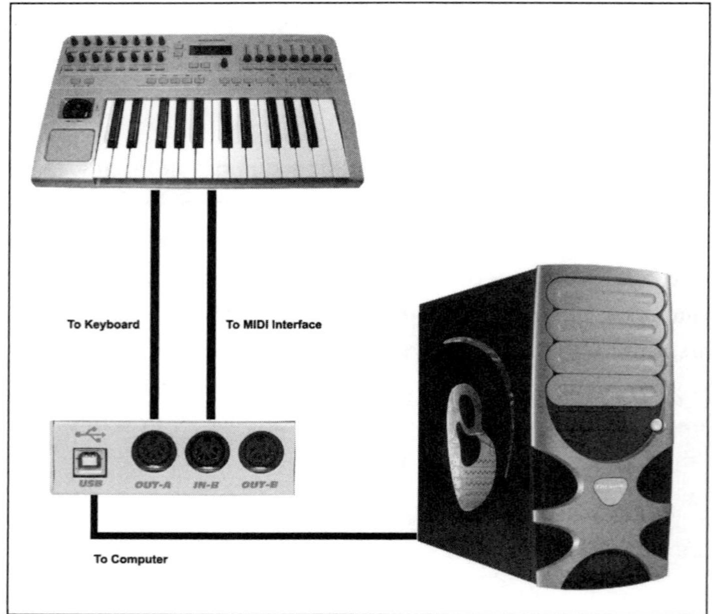

Figure 2.36

This diagram shows the proper way to hook up a MIDI interface to your keyboard.

SOUND CARDS WITH MIDI

There are several sound cards that have a MIDI I/O port integrated into the interface. This is a great way to go, as it will save you the trouble and expense of getting another MIDI interface.

If you are using a MIDI keyboard with a USB port, then it's smooth sailing. Just connect a USB cable from the MIDI keyboard to the computer. Assuming you have installed the drivers for the MIDI keyboard, your computer should see the MIDI keyboard and make it available to use right away.

Okay, we've come to the end of our setup for your studio. Give yourself a pat on the back, take a picture for posterity, and get ready to head in hard and heavy for the rest of this book as I take you through soft synths and sampling.

3 Recording Your Samples

Today's sampling musicians generally come in two types: those who use only store-bought samples and those who record and use their own samples. While there is nothing wrong with purchasing and using commercially made samples, it can become an excessively expensive habit. On the other hand, when time is a consideration, as it is with many film and television composers, conceiving and creating one's own samples from the ground up can be prohibitively time consuming, which makes commercial samples more attractive.

There's something truly exciting about recording your own samples. It presents several creative opportunities to try different combinations of microphones, playing styles, and of course experimentations in sound design. The purpose of this chapter is to introduce you to the process of recording your own samples. This includes such topics as these:

- Preparing to record
- Mic placement for guitar, drums, and piano
- Recording your samples

Preparing to Record

Before taking the plunge into making your first sample recordings, it would be beneficial to take a few minutes to cover the guidelines of working in a recording situation. While I'm sure that many of you reading this book have had your own experiences in this field, I find that covering the basics helps to avoid confusion and frustration in the recording studio.

Space Considerations

Selecting an ideal location for recording your samples should be the first item on your "to do" list of preparations. For most of us, this means either making use of an extra room in the house or converting the garage into a dedicated home studio. Either of these locations will work just fine for the purpose of recording samples, as long as your selected space meets the basic recording requirements:

- **Is it quiet?**—Close all the doors and windows in the room and listen closely. Can you easily hear your neighbors? Can you hear external noises such as cars or jets? If the answer is yes, this space may not work to your best advantage, but don't worry, there are ways of fixing noise leakage problems with soundproofing materials found at your local hardware store.
- **Does it sound good?**—Aside from noise isolation, how does the room actually sound? Clapping your hands inside the room and listening for any unwanted sound elements, called "reflections," can answer this question. Many of these issues can be resolved by using acoustic foam and other sound-absorbing materials.

HOME RECORDING POWER

For more in-depth information on the dynamics of the home studio environment, have a look at *Home Recording Power* or *Mac Home Recording Power*. Both are available at **www.courseptr.com**.

THE IMPORTANCE OF ISOLATION

Remember that *everything* in your studio can make noise, so it's important to take the proper steps to isolate the musician from the gear in order to avoid recording any unwanted background noise.

I recall working on a project years ago in which the musician and I had an operating computer in the same room as we were recording. As the song being recorded was an acoustic ballad consisting of just guitar and voice, we took steps to ensure that the microphones would not pick up noise from the computer fan by surrounding the computer with Styrofoam, and at the time this seemed to do the trick. However, upon listening back to the recording later that week (after I had applied reverb and delay to the guitar), I was able to hear the rotation of the hard drive buzzing away faintly in the background of the recording after each verse of the song. To make matters even worse, the buzzing sound was also accompanied by the ghost reflections of the reverb and delay effects, which created a lot of unwanted ambience in the mix.

Routing Audio

Aside from the selection of a space in which to record your samples, understanding the routing and mixing of audio signals is very important. You can have the best equipment money can buy in your studio, but if you don't understand these basic concepts of routing audio, you might as well record your samples with a wax cylinder.

There are two rules to remember when recording samples:

- **Keep It Clean**—A dirty or noisy recording is an unusable recording, so it's imperative that you record your samples as clean as possible. Check the connections between your signal and the destination. Are they dusty or damaged? If yes, either clean the connections with some contact cleaner (available at any electronics store such as Radio Shack) or replace the cables entirely.
- **Keep It Simple**—When recording your samples, try to use as few add-ons as possible, such as external equalizers or effect processors. Remember that once a sample has been recorded into a computer program such as Sound Forge or Peak (see Chapter 5, "Audio Editors—Close Up"), you can add all the effects you like. But starting with a dry, un-effected recording will simply give you more options later. Of course, this doesn't mean that you can't record effects with your samples; you should just use them sparingly. It's sometimes necessary to record using a compressor, since they help smooth out the wide dynamic swings in instruments such as drums and percussion.

Let's map out a basic audio routing scheme using a single microphone, mixer, and computer system. This kind of setup is good for use with a vocal sample or recording an acoustic guitar playing various rhythms. Use Figure 3.1 as a reference while reading the list.

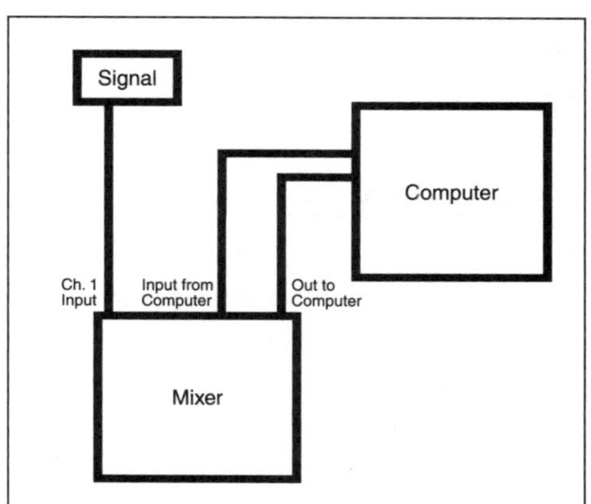

Figure 3.1

This diagram represents a basic recording setup with a single signal to be recorded.

1 The microphone is routed to the first input of a mixer. Since this is a mono recording, the mixer input should be panned dead center.
2 The mixer input is bussed or routed internally to a single output, which is routed to the audio input of the computer.
3 The computer uses either a DAW application or an audio editor to record the audio. Note that the program should be set up to make a mono recording.
4 As the signal is being recorded, the outputs of the computer's audio card are fed back to the mixer as a way of monitoring the signal as it's being recorded.

If you plan to make a stereo recording, the setup is quite similar. See Figure 3.2 to get a better idea of how this is done.

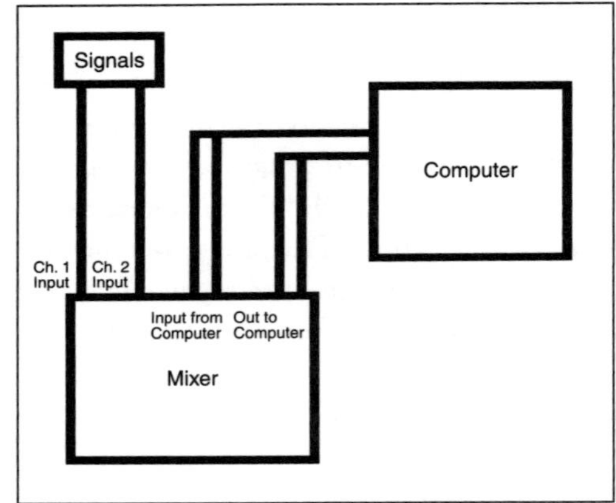

Figure 3.2
This diagram represents the audio setup for creating a stereo recording. Make sure that your audio recording application is set up to create a stereo recording.

PANNING STEREO SIGNALS
When making a stereo recording of a sample, such as a piano or vocal choir, remember to pan your first input hard left and the second input hard right. This is necessary to maintain the stereo field between the two inputs.

Sampling Your Instruments

Your studio is set up, the microphones are hot, and you've just put on a fresh pot of coffee. At long last, it's time to go to work and record your samples. Throughout this section of the chapter, we'll discuss the process of sampling guitars, drums, and piano, which involves a little mic technique and a lot of experimenting.

Remember, the whole point of sampling is to capture the performance and nuance of a selected instrument accurately, edit it, and then use it in a musical way. Make sure that you do your best to make the sample sound as authentic as possible and leave the electronic sound design stuff for later.

Sampling Guitars

The first instrument we're going to sample in this chapter is the guitar. With today's much-improved recording and sampling capabilities, creating stunning and expressive guitar samples is easier than ever. All that is needed to start is a working knowledge of the fundamentals of recording guitars, which primarily focuses on microphone placement.

Sampling Acoustic Guitars

Sampling an acoustic guitar takes a bit of time and experimentation, depending on how complicated you want to get with the sound. The biggest hurdle to jump when recording acoustic guitars is the sound hole, which defines the timbre of the guitar and is the primary source of amplification. With that in mind, the trick is to capture as much natural amplification as possible without introducing too many mid to low frequencies, which can easily happen. Furthermore, you want the microphone to be positioned in such a way that it captures the playing dynamics of an acoustic guitar, such as harmonics, finger picking, and fret noise.

GET IN TUNE

Before you begin recording, take a minute to make sure your guitar is in tune, with the help of an electronic tuner. While it's true that a sample's pitch can be corrected after recording, it's better to get it right the first time!

Mic Placement

Acoustic guitar mic placement can be an interesting process as there are several different playing styles and guitar types to keep in mind when setting up. In this section, I'll show you a few different approaches to miking acoustic guitars that will help complement the unique characteristics of that instrument.

Let's start with the most basic of all mic setups, which is the steel-string guitar played strumming style. Since this style of guitar playing requires a lot of room for dynamics, especially in rock and country music, it's important to closely monitor the distance between the guitar and the microphone; you don't want to run the risk of clipping your signal. Looking at Figure 3.3, you can see that for this setup we have opted to use a single condenser microphone, which has been placed approximately 12 inches from the guitar and aimed where the neck meets the body. This will produce a good solid tone, perfect for recording a guitar chord progression to be looped.

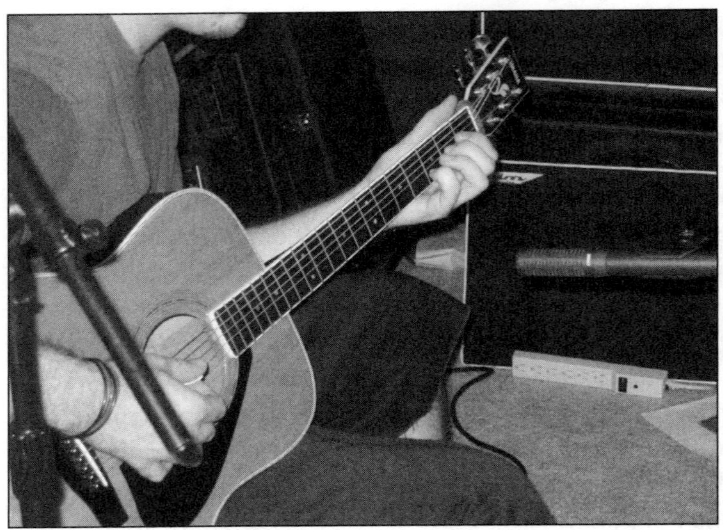

Figure 3.3
Placing the microphone 12 inches from the guitar and aiming it at the neck-body joint creates a good solid sound.

DYNAMIC MICS

You may want to try using a dynamic mic in place of the condenser, depending on how hard you intend to play the guitar, since dynamic mics are less likely to distort.

The next mic setup we'll look at is good for use with steel-string acoustics played finger picking style. Since this is a live playing style that calls for a lot more single note action than strumming, more attention needs to be paid to the intimacy of the mic placement. In this case, a pair of microphones would be ideal for accurately capturing the full frequency spectrum. In Figure 3.4 you'll see that we have kept the microphone placement from the previous example, but this time we have moved it closer to the guitar and introduced a second microphone, which has been placed to the player's right side and aimed at the bridge. This produces a much more "in your face" tone that allows a player to really give expression to the performance.

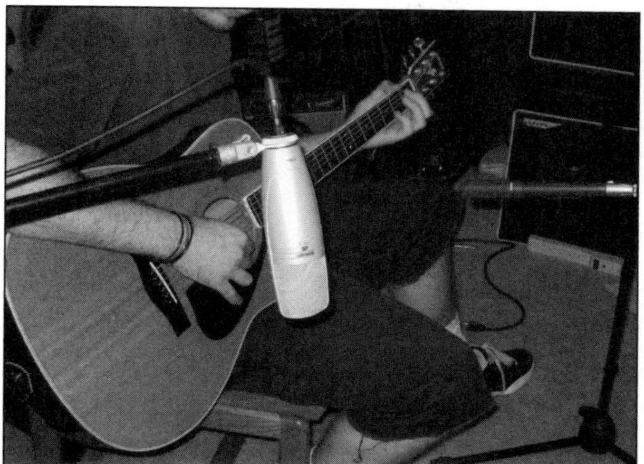

Figure 3.4

For finger picking style guitar, a second microphone has been placed to the player's right side and aimed at the bridge.

Our last mic setup is the distinguished nylon-string classical guitar. Like the finger picking style, a classical guitar requires a generous amount of intimacy in order to capture its full frequency spectrum. However, unlike a finger picked guitar, great care must be paid to distance and placement to ensure that the captured sound is not muddy or "boomy." The best rule of thumb to follow here is to place a condenser microphone (no dynamic mics please) about 9 to 12 inches away from the guitar and aim it between the neck-body joint and the sound hole (Figure 3.5). This should adequately capture the performance characteristics of the guitar, while avoiding a muddy tone. An additional condenser microphone placed a couple of feet away from the guitar and aimed at the neck might also work nicely.

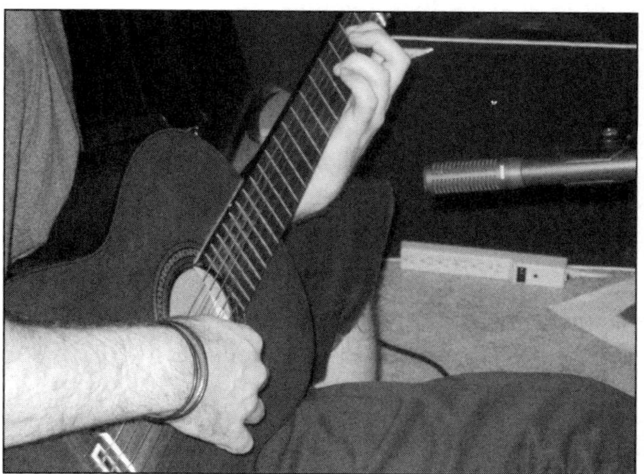

Figure 3.5

For classical guitar, a single condenser microphone has been placed 9 inches away and aimed between the neck-body joint and the sound hole.

EXTERNAL GEAR

While it's not a good idea to use effects such as delays and reverbs, a good solid microphone preamp and compressor/limiter such as the ones discussed in Chapter 2, "Configuring a Soft Synth Studio," would be a good addition to this setup.

Going Direct

These days, most acoustic guitars include an on-board pickup, which can provide a sufficient direct connection between the acoustic guitar and the mixing board without the need of using microphones at all. This offers a good solution for those of you trying to record in a less than noise-free situation. On the other hand, the downside to going direct is losing the aural characteristics that come with recording an acoustic with microphones.

Just keep in mind that there are no "rules" when it comes to recording (aside from the fundamentals of microphone placement); the whole point is to find a sound that you're happy with. There's really no reason why you can't use a combination of microphones and pickup to create a multifaceted sound. It's really up to you and how much time you're willing to put into sound experimentation.

Make the Recording

Once you have made the proper mic adjustments for your acoustic guitar setup and have volume levels you're happy with, the final step is to start your recording. Assuming that you're using an audio editing application such as Sound Forge or Peak (see Chapter 5) to make your recordings, let's have a look at some audio examples.

For our first example, I have recorded a strummed acoustic guitar playing an E major chord. Looking at Figure 3.6, you can see that it contains a great deal of amplitude, which is good.

NORMALIZATION

Once you are finished recording, you may find that the samples sound very soft and not quite as loud as you would like. This is where normalization comes in. Normalization is a function that finds the peak amplitude within an audio file, boosts it, and finally alters the amplitude of the remaining audio data proportionately.

We'll take a closer look at this process in Chapter 5.

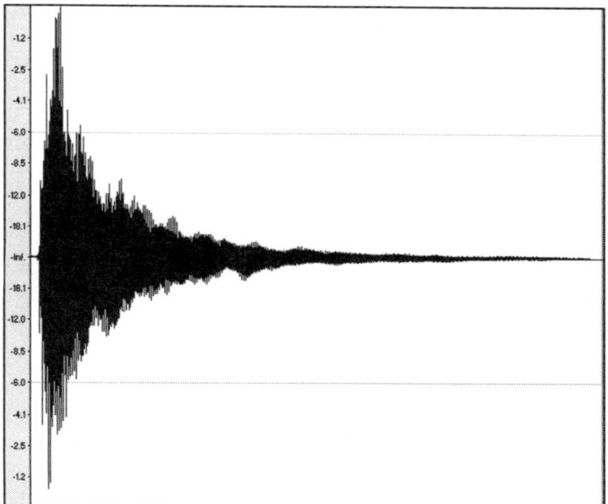

Figure 3.6

In this example, the recorded guitar is quite full and loud.

In the next example, I have recorded a single note sample of a guitar low E string played *forte* and, as you can see in the left side of Figure 3.7, it's not all that loud. In this case, it would be a good idea to normalize the audio, but not too much. This results in a sample as seen in the right side of Figure 3.7.

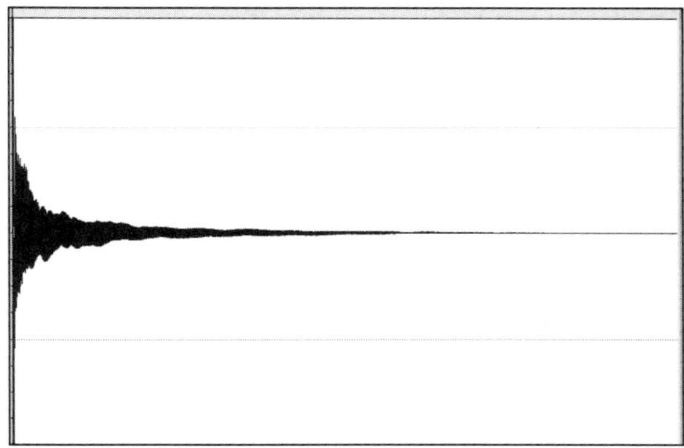

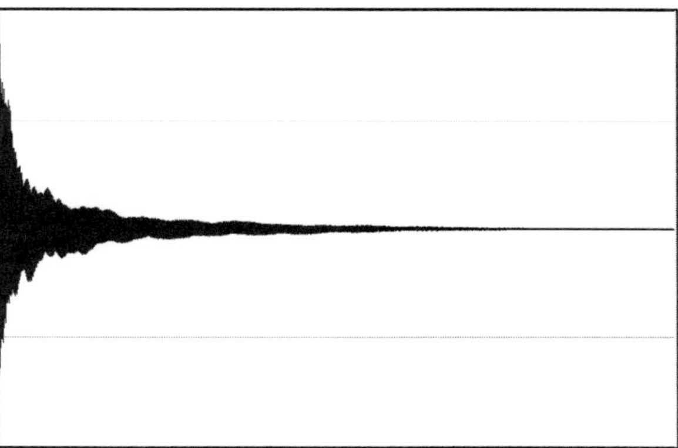

Figure 3.7

In the left figure, I have recorded a single note of an acoustic guitar, but it sounds a little quiet. This is fixed by normalizing the sample, which results in a much louder sound, as shown in the figure on the right.

Multisampling an Acoustic Guitar

Multisampling plays a key role in retaining the intended realism of a sampled instrument. It's a process that involves importing numerous samples of an instrument—samples representing the entire tonal range of the instrument—and mapping those samples along the virtual keyboard of the sampler.

When recording single-note acoustic guitar samples, multisampling is essential if you intend to make the guitar sound as real as possible when playing it from a sampling program such as GigaStudio or Kontakt. Although we are going to discuss multisampling at great length in Chapters 6, "GigaStudio 3," and 7, "Kontakt Tutorial," look at Figure 3.8 and read the caption to get a better idea of this concept.

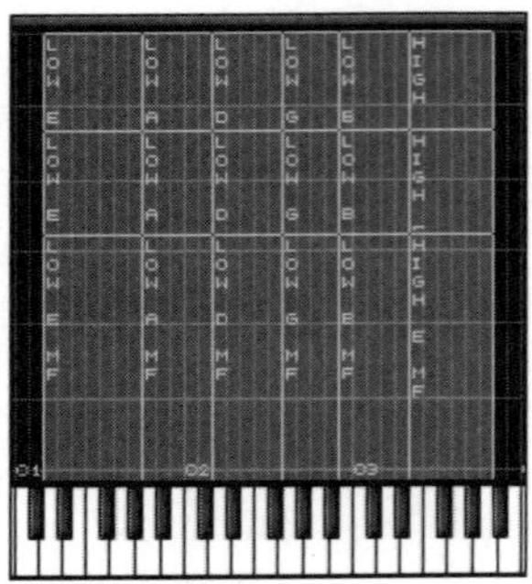

Figure 3.8
In this diagram, the individual notes of an acoustic guitar have been mapped across a keyboard interface.

Sampling Electric Guitars

Although not as complicated as recording acoustic guitars, sampling an electric guitar opens up myriad creative possibilities. This is mainly due to its wide range of tones and additional effects such as distortions and wah-wah pedals, which give the electric guitar its characteristic sound. The fact that it's also an electrically powered instrument makes way for many imaginative sound design possibilities, which we'll discuss at the end of this section.

Mic Placement

In both live and recording situations, proper mic placement with an electric guitar rig is pretty straightforward, as it is simply a matter of recording the speaker of the amp. All that is needed to start is a short mic stand and a dynamic microphone, such as the Shure SM57. The most important aspect of miking an amp is, well, the amp—and the speakers. Here are some general tips to follow:

- With most amps, the volume should be as high as you can get it, depending on the style of guitar you are sampling. Generally speaking, the hotter the amp, the more consistent and warmer its output, and you can add a bit of compression to smooth things out during recording.
- Keep the mic angled at an acute angle to the grill cloth—not perpendicular—and generally about 1 to 3 inches away. Direct the mic into the cone but not right on the center.

- As a general rule, plan on recording the guitar dry and adding your effects during mixdown.

Going Direct

Recording and sampling electric guitars directly without using a microphone is another option for the home studio, and with the right setup, you can achieve some interesting and desirable guitar sounds. The Pod guitar preamp from Line 6 (**www.line6.com**) is one of the solutions for this task. It features 16 different amp speaker models, from a Small Tweed vintage Fender amp to Rectified, the Mesa Boogie Dual Rectifier. The back panel features stereo inputs and outputs along with MIDI in and out. The Pod also provides some good, basic functions, including output level, EQ, reverb, and gain.

CREATIVE ELECTRIC GUITAR

Here's a neat electric guitar sample trick I've used over the years. Find any mechanical device in your house that's powered by batteries, such as an electric razor or toothbrush. Turn it on and hold it over the pickups of a guitar without touching the strings. This will create a magnetic field between the device and guitar pickups, which in turn creates a controlled feedback impression of the device.

To give you a better idea of this concept, I've created and uploaded a few samples of my electric toothbrush (see Figure 3.9) and mini tape recorder (see Figure 3.10) to the Course Technology Web site (**www.courseptr.com**).

Figure 3.9
Who knew that brushing your teeth could sound so cool?

Sampling Drums

Let's face it–drums and percussion are probably the most popular of all sampled instruments. As most electronic musicians are not drummers by trade, they're always on the prowl for good drum samples and of course, an endless assortment of drum loops that seem to go on forever.

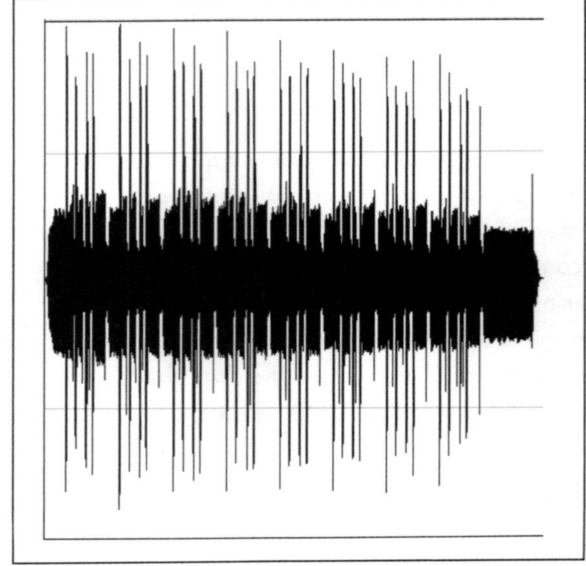

Figure 3.10
In this figure, I have used a mini tape recorder as a rhythmic device by having it stop and start in tempo.

With all these drum samples readily available at your local music store, why should you want to create your own drum samples? From an artistic perspective, recording and editing your own drum samples and loops allows you to dip your big toe into the creative sampling pool of using different mic setups and drums in order to create your own ultimate sampled set of drums. From a financial perspective, creating your own drum samples is a surefire way to keep your wallet happy!

Working with Individual Drums

In the first half of our drum sampling tutorials, we are going to look at sampling individual drums, sometimes called *hits.* After these individual hits have been recorded, edited, and assigned a new file name (such as snare_drum.wav), they can then be imported, mapped, and compiled into a single sampler preset in either GigaStudio or Kontakt. This way, you can trigger the hits of an entire drum kit from one preset, then play and sequence them in real time.

Mic Placement

Like all sampled instruments, recording drum hits requires both time and patience, since there are many possible mic and mic placement combinations. However, if you came to this chapter looking for some good solid

DRUM TUNING 101

To help your drum samples sound their best, it's important to take the time to tune drums properly. This involves tightening the drumheads and then making the proper adjustments to each drum to achieve the tone, pitch, and performance you want your drums to have. Drummer Brent Hoover of audioMIDI.com offers some theory on this subject.

"The basic idea behind tuning any drum is that you want the tension to be even over the entire surface of the head. Take a drumstick and tap near the lug (those are the screws that hold the head on) and listen for the pitch. Then, using a drum key, tighten the other lugs so that they are the same pitch."

Brent offers the following advice for tuning the snare:

- You can normally tune the ring out of a snare by carefully making the tension equal. But for some reason, sometimes this doesn't work. Try tapping around each lug until you hear the part of the drum that sounds most like the note of the ring, and try changing that lug (and then even out the others).
- Tighten the bottom head very tight (being careful again to keep the tension even) so as to make the snares as responsive as possible. Tighter snares will give you a faster attack and decay.
- The style of music that is being played is important in determining how tight the top head needs to be. Drummers who play rock will need to keep the head somewhat loose so that they can hit hard. Funk and jazz players will need the head pretty tight so that they can get the proper response for things like "ghost notes" and press rolls.

Brent also offers the following advice for tuning the kick drum:

- How you tune the kick really depends on what sort of sound you want. I like to tune it as low as possible until it becomes "flabby" and then tighten it back up a little. This gives you a very deep sound.
- If you want a little more "click," you can try placing a piece of duct tape right where the batter meets the head and tuning the head up a little.

For more information on this subject, visit the "Classroom" section at audioMIDI.com.

drum mic placement fundamentals, you came to the right place. Let's begin this section with the kick drum.

For rock and pop music, the kick drum is the most important percussion element in a mix. It's responsible for establishing the low end of a mix and supplying rhythmic patterns for the bass guitar to follow, which in essence locks in the rhythmic backbone of any good song. It's fairly important to make sure that you're using the right mic and placement to accurately capture the dynamic characteristics of the kick drum.

To begin, a good dynamic microphone, such as the Senheiser 421, will do just fine as a kick microphone. Although it's a bit on the pricey side (around $300), its vast frequency range of 30 to 17,000Hz makes it a good solution.

Proper mic placement for recording a kick drum involves getting the mic as close to the beater as possible (without touching it, of course). The best way to go about this is to position the microphone inside the kick drum as shown in Figure 3.11. This will produce a nice low-end kick sound to record. Note that you can either use a short boom stand, or just lay the microphone directly on the pillow.

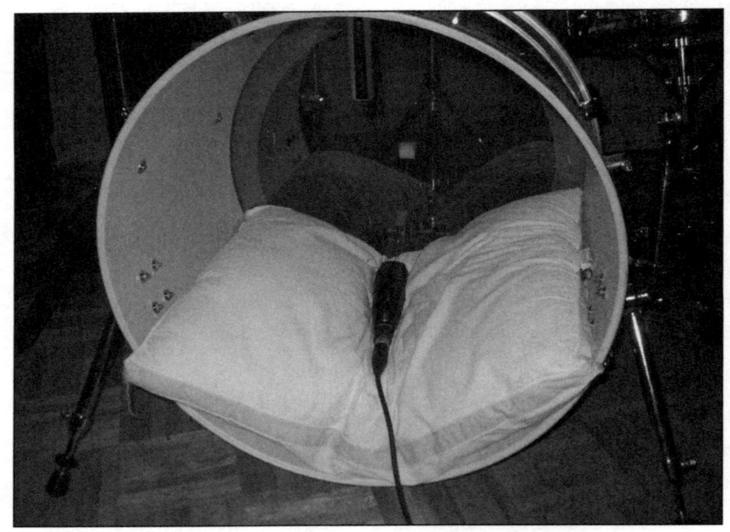

Figure 3.11

To get the best sound from a kick drum, place a dynamic microphone as close to the beater as possible. If your kick drum head has a hole in the front, use a boom stand to insert and position the mic. If your kick drum head does not have a hole in the front, then you may want to remove the head entirely (as shown here).

DAMPEN THE KICK

Make sure to use a pillow or a couple of heavy blankets to dampen the kick drum. This will reduce the risk of capturing unwanted low frequencies.

When it comes to the snare and hi-hat, the Shure SM57 will do just fine as your dynamic microphone. As was the case with the kick drum, the secret to getting a good snare and hi-hat sound is to get close to the point of contact between the tip of the stick and the instrument itself. However, you also want to make sure that the microphone doesn't get in your way or in the way of your drummer's playing style, so a little distance is needed. Looking at the left side of Figure 3.12, you can see that the microphone has been placed about five inches from the top half of the hi-hat and is aimed in parallel fashion. This will ensure a true and bright hat sound without running the risk of capturing any puffs of air caused by the opening and closing of the hi-hat while in play. On the right side of the same figure, our microphone has now been placed approximately eight inches above the snare rim and aimed down at the head. This generates a snare sample that is full bodied and includes a touch of room ambience. As a creative tip, you might also place a second mic in similar fashion underneath the snare to thicken up the sound.

Figure 3.12
When recording a hi-hat, it's a good idea to place the microphone five inches away from the instrument and aimed parallel to it (left). When recording a snare, place the mic eight inches above the rim and aim it toward the skin of the drum (right). This is also a good mic placement idea for toms.

WATCH YOUR LEVELS

Keep a close eye on your input levels when recording your drums, as you can easily clip the signal. If you have a compressor handy, use it sparingly to establish a limiting effect on the input.

When compared to the mic placements we've just looked at, miking cymbals is pretty much a walk in the park. In this case, a condenser mic placed one or two feet above the instrument will not only capture the essence of a cymbal, but it will also introduce some ambient space into the sound.

Make the Recording

You're now ready to start recording your drum hits. Let's now take a look at some sound examples. In Figure 3.13, I have recorded a kick drum using the mic placement shown earlier. As you can see, this produces a nice, solid-sounding kick. Note, though, that I used a little compression in order to avoid the risk of distorting.

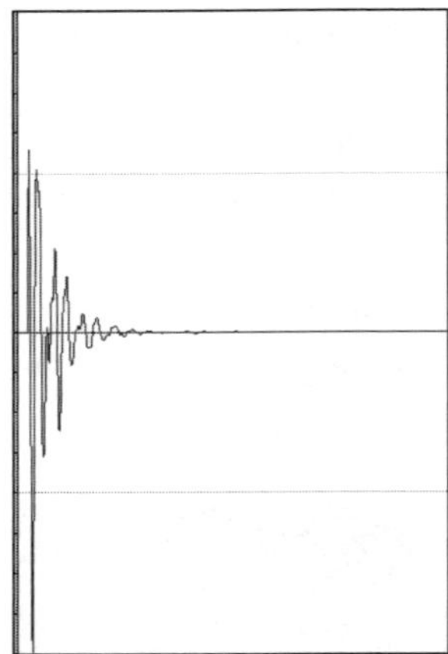

Figure 3.13
The kick drum sample was made using the mic placement shown earlier in this section and a Senheiser 421 dynamic microphone with a little bit of compression to avoid distorting.

In Figure 3.14, I have created two separate samples of the hi-hat in order to show the importance of mic placement. In the figure on the left, the mic has been intentionally positioned too low, which captures the wind of the hi-hat opening and closing. The figure on the right demonstrates the results of better mic placement, where the microphone is aimed across the top of the hi-hat. This produces a hat sample that is both solid and clean.

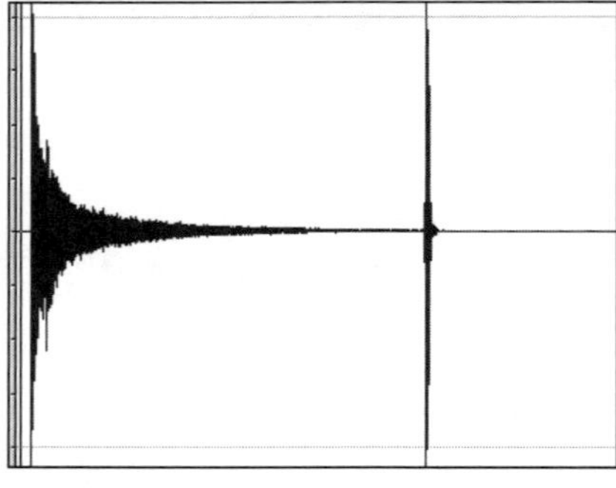

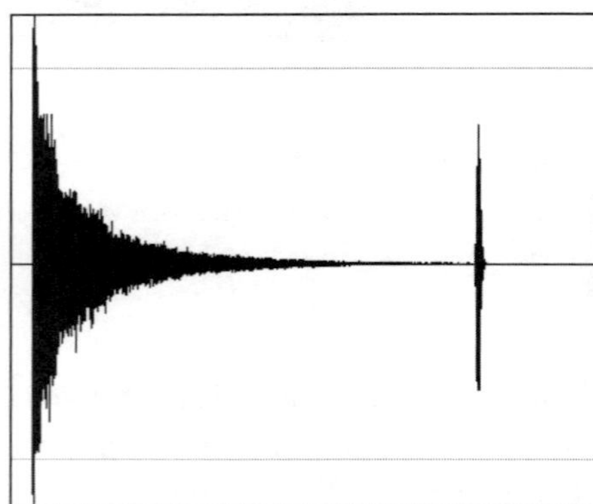

Figure 3.14
These waveforms demonstrate bad mic placement versus good mic placement. The left waveform represents a recording made with bad mic placement, in which the microphone has captured the wind noise of the hi-hat opening and closing. The right waveform represents a recording made with good mic placement, which looks and sounds as wind free as possible.

Creating Drum Loops

The other side to recording drums for the purpose of sampling is to conceive and create *drum loops,* or tempo-based drum patterns. A drum loop can be useful for establishing an overall feel and rhythm for a song by being used in a repetitive way over a desired number of measures in a song. For example,

> **CREATIVE PERCUSSION**
>
> Although recording acoustic drums and percussion is a fun challenge, sampling technology teaches us to not limit ourselves by recording "traditional instruments" exclusively. Expanding your creative potential and finding other objects or actions to use as percussive elements make for an interesting take on the traditional drum kit. Take a look around your home or studio, and you're sure to find a few abnormal sounds that would work great when used as percussion samples. A creaky door, for example, could be a great "record scratch" sound, while a bouncing basketball could be used as kick drum. Likewise, a push broom or aerosol can of hairspray could work as hi-hat sounds, and the crushing of a soda can makes for a perfect snare drum.
>
> To help you along your path to creativity, I have sampled a few of these elements and uploaded them to the Course Technology Web site (**www.courseptr.com**) for you to download and enjoy.

the drum loop shown in Figure 3.15 displays a simple drum loop, which was recorded at a tempo of 80 beats per minute and covers a distance of two measures. Once captured, these loops can be edited, tweaked out using real-time effects with your audio editing program, and then imported into a sampling program such as Kontakt or GigaStudio.

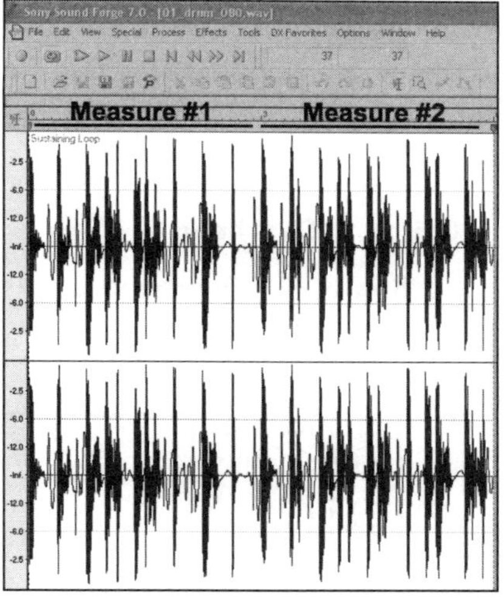

Figure 3.15
The drum loop shown here was recorded at 80 beats per minute and covers a musical distance of two measures.

These days, it seems that drum loops make the world turn, as you hear them so often on television, CDs, and of course movie soundtracks. And why not? They offer both a great-sounding and time-saving solution to musicians who need to work fast (not to mention that they are also much cheaper than hiring a drummer to play on each session). Don't get me wrong, there's definitely a time and place to hire a real drummer when you're going after a specific sound on a piece of music, but drum loops are here to stay, no matter what.

So why not throw your hat in the circle and take a stab at creating your own drum loops? It's a lot of fun and can end up being a creative and rewarding experience, as you'll see throughout this section.

Creating a Drum Mix

Like mixing an entire song, mixing drums is a purely subjective process, since there are so many different combinations relating to mic placement and placing drums in the stereo field. Some engineers prefer the "more is better" approach, which involves using several mics to adjust the amplitude and panning assignments for each drum. This method is good for big-budget professional recording situations, where money and time are of little consequence. Other engineers (like me) tend to go for a simpler approach and use fewer microphones to achieve a similar, yet not as complex, sound. This entails using a single microphone to capture and mix two or more drums, with the exception of the kick drum. While not as exact as the previously described method, I find that it gets the job done adequately.

With this concept in mind, let's have a look at how to use four microphones to create a full-bodied mix. Use Figure 3.16 for reference while reading the corresponding list.

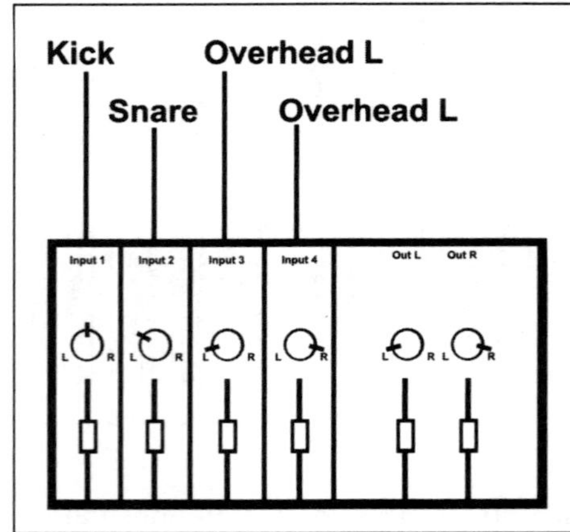

Figure 3.16
In this diagram, I have opted to use four microphones to record an entire drum kit for the purpose of creating a solid stereo mix.

- **Kick Drum**—Recording the kick in a drum kit mix should not differ from recording it as an individual hit, which was discussed earlier in this chapter. Use the same mic placement as previously described and pan it dead center.

- **Snare and Hi-Hat**—Recording both the snare and hi-hat with a single mic is a little tricky to master, and it requires a little bit of experimentation. I suggest positioning the microphone 5 to 6 inches above the rim of the snare and aimed slightly between the two instruments, with an emphasis on the snare, as it is more important in the mix than the hi-hat. After positioning the mic, pan it slightly left or right to place it in the stereo field, according to either the player's perspective (on the left) or the listener's perspective (on the right).
- **Toms and Cymbals**—Recording the toms and cymbals should be done with two condenser microphones, which are positioned 1 to 2 feet above the player and aimed in an X/Y or criss-cross pattern. After positioning the microphones, pan them hard left and right to create a full stereo image.

Once you have positioned your mics and created a suitable mix, you should plan to enhance its dynamic character with amplitude adjustments and a bit of tweaking with an equalizer or two in order to bring out the tonal colors of each drum. Assuming that you're using one of the hardware mixers described in the previous chapter, this should not be difficult, since most mixers provide an equalizer for each channel. However, in the case of amplitude adjustments or any other external hardware you choose to incorporate, your ears are the best judges, so my best advice would be to tinker with the mix until you find a sound you like.

KEEPING TIME

In addition to the sound of a recorded drum kit, the next issue to be aware of is the importance of a good sense of tempo. Whether you're the performer, the producer, or both, tempo and timekeeping is a topic not to be taken lightly, as it will dictate how well your recorded loops will fit into your music. A small investment of $20 in a metronome will help avoid any tempo or timing issues. Just make sure it includes an earphone jack, so the microphones won't pick it up while recording.

Sampling Pianos

The piano is considered by most musicians to be the most time-consuming and complicated of instruments to record. There are several reasons for this. For one, a piano is a huge and heavy instrument that doesn't exactly stand up to the test of time without constant maintenance. So it is fair to assume that like an old car, a piano begins to develop creaks and rattles. And of course, pianos constantly fall out of tune.

However, rolling up your sleeves and digging into sampling a piano is great experience, and it can be accomplished with some imagination.

Mic Placement

When setting up to record a piano, there are typically two different microphone setups to choose from: close miking and pulled-back miking. While the difference between these setups is pretty obvious, the one you choose is dependent primarily on the room in which you are recording. If you are recording in a room with bad acoustics, such as your living room or den (not acoustically treated), close miking is preferable. On the other hand, if you are recording a piano in a more acoustically friendly environment, such as a recital hall, you can use the pulled-back miking technique to capture some of the natural ambience of the room. In either case, the microphone placements are quite different.

For the time being, let's assume that you're recording in a not so acoustically happy environment. This will be the case for most musicians on a budget (myself included). Looking at Figure 3.17, you can see that I've opted to use a two-condenser mic setup, which will create a very full sound. Each mic should be approximately 12 inches above the strings and should be a good distance apart from each other. Since this is a stereo recording, the mics should be panned hard left and hard right to take full advantage of the stereo field.

Figure 3.17

In a close-miking situation, a two-mic setup is preferable.

Make the Recording

Now that you have found a piano sound you're happy with, it's time to jump in and get down to recording. Let's look at some recording examples. In Figure 3.18, I have recorded a single note played *forte* on the piano using the mic placement shown earlier. In addition, I have also recorded an A chord played *forte*, as you can see in Figure 3.19. This mic placement setup produces a nice, solid sound, which is enhanced even more when normalized.

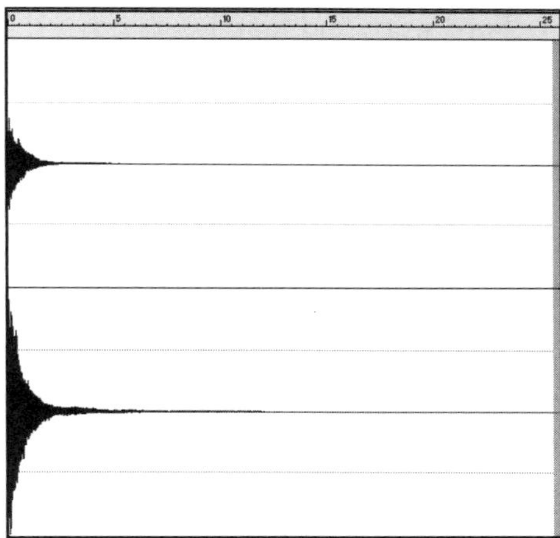

Figure 3.18

This is a recording of a C2 note played *forte*. Note the lengthy recording time of nearly 26 seconds, which indicates a long sustain time. Sampling individual notes is a time-consuming process, since you must sample at least five notes from every octave if you intend to retain the realism of an acoustic piano.

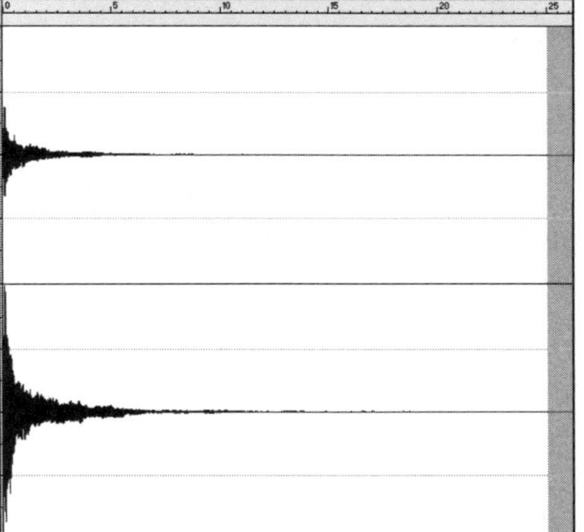

Figure 3.19

This is a recording of an A chord played *forte* using the same mic placement.

DON'T LOSE YOUR TAIL

The most important aspect to recording and sampling a piano is to let the played note sustain completely; it is imperative to capture the tail end of the note. Make sure to leave long gaps of empty space between each note sampled to make sure you don't lose your tail!

CREATIVE SAMPLING—STRUM YOUR PIANO

If you're sampling a baby grand piano, try slowly strumming the piano strings with a guitar pick. This will create interesting, slightly creepy sounds similar to an out-of-tune autoharp.

When You're Finished Recording

Completing your first recording session always feels like a triumph, as all of the hard work and long hours pay off tenfold when you listen back to the recordings. You should now begin making plans for what comes next in the sampling process.

- Backing up your work
- Splitting up the audio files
- Importing them into your sampler

Since the last two items of this list are covered extensively throughout Chapters 5, 6, and 7, let's take just a moment to cover the backup procedures for the Mac and Windows platforms.

Backing up, of course, means to create a duplicate volume of data that can be used as a means of recovery, should an unforeseeable accident occur with your computer, such as a hard drive crash. Let's face it, you never know when a computer crash may occur, and establishing a consistent backup schedule is a good idea to avoid the loss of your data. The easiest way to do this is to burn your data onto a blank CD or DVD, and I will show you how this is done on both the Mac and PC.

WINDOWS AND MAC CAN BURN CDs!

Both Windows XP and Mac OSX have the capability to burn CDs without the need for an additional program.

Through the rest of this section, I will use screen shots from these burning programs, rather than the optional Roxio or Nero software, so that you can become more familiar with these little-known wonders in your operating system.

To be fair to Roxio and Nero, I should point out that these programs come with many extra features, such as backup programs and the capability to create many different types of discs. If you have the means, pick them up. You won't regret it.

THE FOUR FLAVORS OF BLANK MEDIA

There are four types of blank disc media available.

- **CD-R**—This is the standard blank media used to burn music and data CDs. These blank CDs can be burned only one time. This is also called "disc at once." I recommend using this media.
- **CD-RW**—This is the next level up from the CD-R. These discs can be burned and erased several times, making them very useful for backing up files on your computer.
- **DVD+/-R**—These blank discs are for use with DVD players and burners. They hold incredibly large amounts of data—up to 4GB, in fact. However, as with CD-RWs, these discs are not compatible with most home and car stereo systems. Please note that there are two formats of blank DVDs, called DVD+R and DVD-R. DVD+Rs are used with Windows-based machines, unless otherwise specified by the DVD burner; and DVD-Rs are used with Mac-based machines exclusively.
- **DVD+/-RW**—These blanks are the same as DVD-Rs, but they can be used over and over again, just as with CD-RWs. They carry the same restrictions as DVD-Rs.

Burning CDs with Windows XP

Burning CDs with Windows XP is simple and easy, since the burning application is embedded within the operating system. Read below and use the included figures as references.

1. Start by placing a blank CD in your burner and closing it. Once the blank CD starts to spin, Windows will detect it as a blank and open a window that has a few options, as shown in Figure 3.20.
2. Choose the Open Writable CD Folder Using Windows Explorer option by clicking it and clicking OK. Windows will create an open window into which you can simply drag your files.
3. Drag and drop your data into the open window, which will create a temporary file on the CD drive, which means that the data is ready to be burned to CD.
4. At the left side of the open window is an option called Write These Files to CD. Click on it, and this will start up the CD Writing Wizard.
5. Assign a name to your CD to be burned and click the Next button to begin the burning process (see Figure 3.21). Once finished, the CD Wizard will close and eject the newly burned CD automatically.

Figure 3.20
As soon as Windows detects a blank CD, it will give you a few options. Choose Open Writable CD Folder Using Windows Explorer.

Figure 3.21
The CD Writing Wizard is the program that burns data onto blank CDs and DVDs.

Burning CDs with Mac OSX

Mac OSX provides an equally easy process to burn several different CD formats. Read below and use the included figures as references.

1. Begin by first inserting a blank CD into your CD burning drive. OSX will detect it as a blank and will open a window that has a few options that can be selected via a pull-down menu. Select Open Finder, name the disc, and click OK (see Figure 3.22).

2 The CD icon with the assigned name will appear on the desktop. From here, it's just a matter of dragging and dropping folders and files onto the CD icon, at which point they will be "virtually copied" onto the CD. Mind you, this doesn't mean it's been written to the CD just yet.

3 With the CD icon highlighted, select Burn Disc from the File pull-down menu. You can also click and drag the CD icon into the Trash Can to perform the same task.

4 A new window will pop up and ask you to select a burn speed (see Figure 3.23). The default setting of Maximum will work fine in most cases, so just click the Burn button, and the CD should be ready shortly.

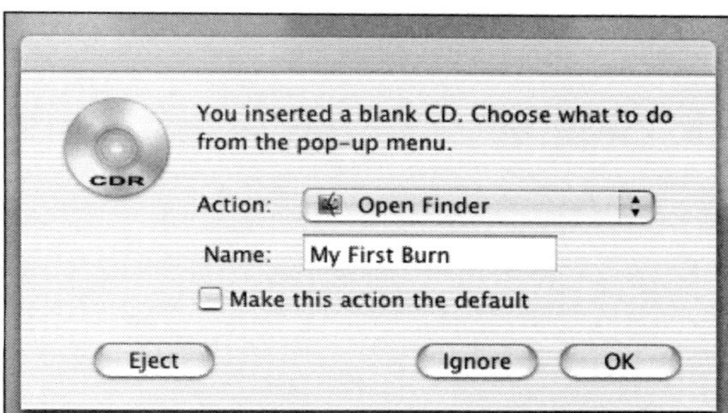

Figure 3.22

Once a blank disc is inserted into the CD burning drive, the Mac will ask you to name the CD.

Figure 3.23

Upon starting the burning process, a new window will ask you to assign a burn speed. Note that Maximum is selected by default, and this will work fine.

Advanced Sampler Techniques

After sampling an instrument, the next step is importing the samples into a soft sampler and then enhancing them with the sampler's built-in parameters. This can involve something as simple as adding a little modulation for vibrato or something a little more complicated, such as using LFOs or programming filters. Throughout this chapter, I'll discuss various advanced sampling techniques and functions that can be used to enhance the aural qualities of your newly created samples.

READ THIS FIRST

In this chapter, we'll be discussing various sampling procedures that pertain to the embedded functions of Kontakt and GigaStudio. Therefore, it would be a good idea to familiarize yourself with the basic functions of these two applications by reading Chapters 6, "GigaStudio 3," and 7, "Kontakt Tutorial."

Using Modulation for Vibrato

The integration of vibrato in samples of string, brass, and woodwind instruments is a crucial element of their realism. Vibrato is a slight wavering modulation of pitch used for expression that occurs with wind or bowed instruments when playing long, sustained notes. Vibrato is also a frequently used singing technique in numerous classical, pop, and jazz tunes.

For this example, I'll use a Kontakt instrument to program a vibrato by way of the modulation wheel. Note that this tutorial can be used on any Kontakt instrument that includes a sustaining element, such as pad sounds. If you don't have any string, brass, or woodwind samples readily available, locate and load the nearest pad instrument and follow along.

1 With the instrument loaded, click on the Edit button to expose all of the available modules.

2 Navigate to the Source module and click on the plus button to the right of the Mod button, located in the lower-left corner. A pop-up menu listing all of the available sources of modules will appear. Select LFOs > Sine to create an LFO module (see Figure 4.1).

3 A small sub module will appear just below the Source that lists the modulation source (LFO#1), amount (100%), and destination (Pitch). Adjust the Amount slider to 0.

4 Navigate to the LFO 1 module, which should now be located just below the Amplifier module (see Figure 4.2). Set the Frequency parameter to approximately 5Hz. This will create a steady rate of modulation for our vibrato effect.

5 While still using the LFO module, click on the plus button located to the right of the Mod button to assign a controller source to the LFO. Select External Sources > MIDI CCs (see Figure 4.3).

6 Once the MIDI CC option is selected, a numeric dialog box will appear to the right. This assigns a MIDI controller number to the appropriate external source, which for this tutorial is the modulation wheel, which is Controller #1. Enter 1 into this dialog box either by clicking and dragging upward in the dialog or by double-clicking in the dialog and typing in the number.

7 To the right of the modulation source is the Amount slider. Set this to approximately 1.2.

8 To the right of the amount is the Smoothness dialog, which smooths out the transition between a non-modulated and a modulated signal. Set this dialog to 250.

9 Finally, set the modulation destination of the LFO to Intensity (ADD).

Figure 4.1

Click on the plus button to the right of the Mod button to assign an LFO as the source of modulation. The LFO module will appear below.

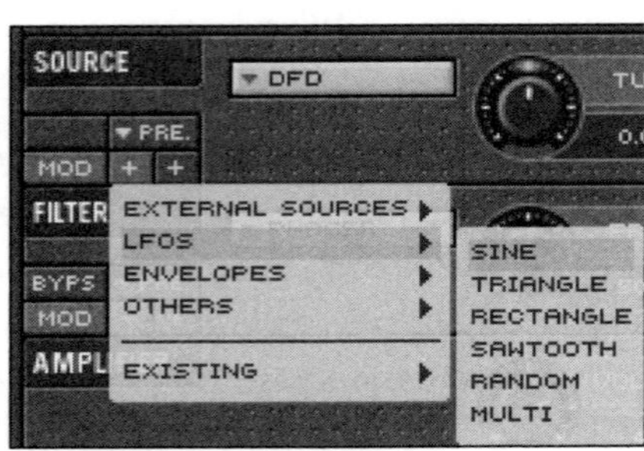

Figure 4.2

The Frequency parameter of the LFO module assigns a rate of modulation to the instrument pitch. Set this to a value of 5Hz to create a smooth and steady modulation speed.

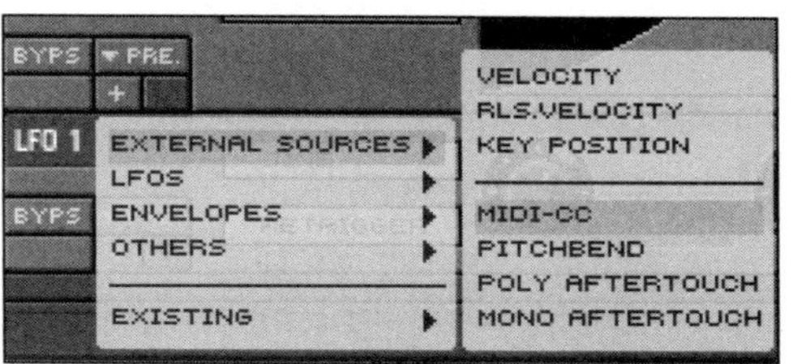

Figure 4.3

Assign an external source of MIDI CCs (continuous controllers) as modulation for the LFO module.

Now play the Kontakt instrument and use the modulation wheel to hear the vibrato effect transition in smoothly.

Using Filters for Brass

When composing music for film or television, realistic horn sections can help set the overall tone, complementing the film's visuals. Creative horn arrangements can even be used to paint musical pictures of explosions in space, animated high jinks, and dramatic situations.

While this book can't teach you how to be an orchestral arranger (there are plenty of books on that subject), we can teach you how to alter the timbre of your horn samples to emulate the natural playing personalities of those instruments through real-time filter adjustments. Take for example the trumpet, which is capable of producing several natural timbres or tones. When played softly, a trumpet has a very warm and mellow tone with little or no high frequencies. However, when played with more force of air, the tone of the instrument changes drastically, and several high frequencies are introduced to the signal. This effect is perhaps heard best when playing a sustained crescendo from *mezzo forte* to *double forte*. The brassy tone of the trumpet seems to creep out from within the louder it gets.

This effect can be replicated through your software sampler by using a combination of a low pass filter and a modulation wheel. Here's how this is accomplished using the GigaStudio Editor program included with GigaStudio 3.

1 Launch the GigaStudio Editor and open a brass preset.

2 Click and drag a box around all of the regions within the preset to select them all (see Figure 4.4).

3 Use the Parameter Edit section in the lower-right corner and select Filter from the supplied list of available pages.

4 Once the Filter page is available, set the Filter Type parameter to Lowpass and set the Cutoff Controller parameter to Modulation Wheel. See Figure 4.5 for reference.

5 Select Save from the File pull-down menu to save the changes to the preset and then close the program.

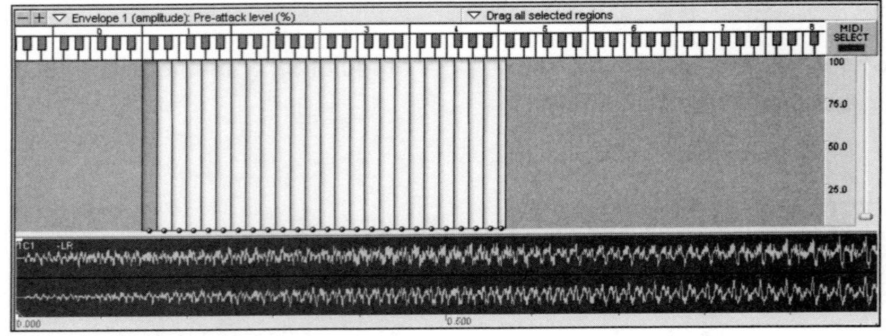

Figure 4.4
Click and drag a box around all of the regions in a preset to select them all.

Filter	
Filter type	1 - Lowpass
Turbo LPF	0 - Off
Cutoff freq (0-127)	
Cutoff controller	(1) Mod wheel
Control invert	0 - No
Minimum cutoff	60
Resonance (0-127)	0
Dynamic resonance	
Resonance controller	None
Key tracking	0 - No
Keytrack breakpoint	0
Velocity curve	0 - Nonlinear
Velocity range	4 - Med low

Figure 4.5
After selecting the Filter page of the GigaStudio Editor, set the Filter Type to Lowpass and set the Cutoff Controller to Modulation Wheel. This will enable you to open and close the filter as you increase and decrease the amount of modulation by way of the modulation wheel.

After making the changes to the preset, load it into GigaStudio 3, play the instrument, and use the modulation wheel to open and close the filter. To add even more expression to this effect, try using a volume/expression pedal to attenuate the volume of the brass preset.

CONTROLLING FILTERS WITH KONTAKT

It is also possible to create this same filter effect within Kontakt. Load an instrument of brass sounds and do the following:

1. Navigate to the Source module and click on the right plus button to list all of the available insert effects (see Figure 4.6).
2. Select the 1 Pole Low Pass (6dB) filter from the Sample Filters subdirectory. This will place the Filter module directly under the Source module.
3. Now all that is needed is to assign your modulation wheel to the Filter Cutoff parameter. Right-click (Ctrl+Click for the Mac) on the Cutoff knob and select Automation (see Figure 4.7) to activate the Automation pop-up window (see Figure 4.8).
4. The last step is to assign the modulation wheel (MIDI Controller #1) to the Cutoff parameter, which is easily done by adjusting the modulation wheel on your MIDI keyboard. Once you do, the Automation window should automatically close, and you can now control the Cutoff parameter with your modulation wheel.

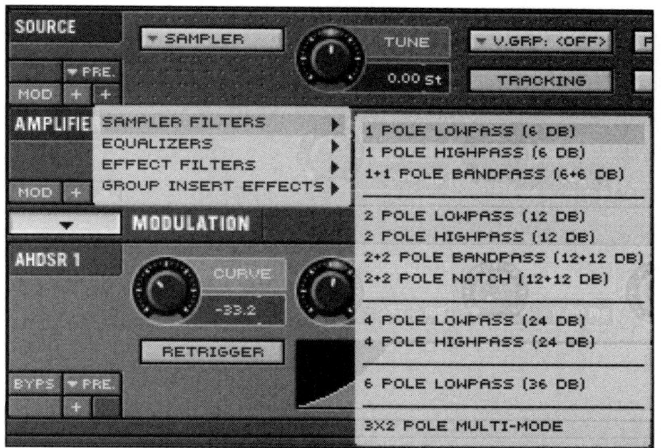

Figure 4.6
Locate the Source module and click on the right plus button to list the available group insert effects. Select the 1 Pole Low Pass (6dB) filter from the Sample Filters subdirectory.

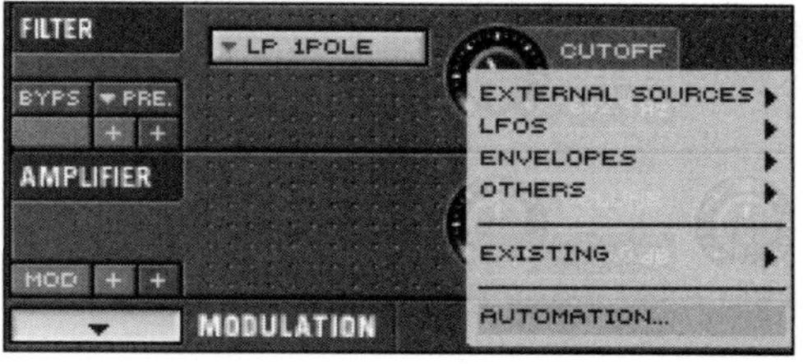

Figure 4.7
Right-click (Ctrl+Click for Mac) on the Cutoff parameter of the Filter module and select Automation to assign it to a MIDI controller.

Figure 4.8

The Automation window assigns MIDI controllers, such as the modulation wheel, to any Kontakt parameter.

Randomly Triggered Samples

One of the greatest obstacles to overcome in sampling is repetition. Repeating the same sample over and over risks making your music sound stale and uninspired. Think of a guitar player repeatedly strumming a chord. Although the rhythm and resonance between each strum sound identical, there are subtle but noticeable variations in each strum, such as strength and presence. This is what gives a real guitar performance its charm and personality, so the ultimate goal in sampling is to re-create that charm by creating variations within your samples.

Both GigaStudio and Kontakt include two functions that accomplish this: Round Robin (Cycle Round Robin in Kontakt) and Random (Cycle Random in Kontakt). Both of these functions involve importing several samples to a single key on a sampler and then switching between each sample every time the related sampler key is played. That way, there is an audible variation between each sample trigger. The way GigaStudio and Kontakt switch between these samples differs greatly between the (Cycle) Round Robin and (Cycle) Random modes.

(Cycle) Round Robin will switch between each sample in uniform order. For example, if you import four samples of a guitar strum (such as strum01.wav, strum02.wav, strum03.wav, strum04.wav), (Cycle) Round Robin will start with strum01.wav and continue to strums 2, 3, and 4, after which it will start back at strum01.wav. So while it does give some variation to your sampler parts, there is still some repetition.

(Cycle) Random differs from (Cycle) Round Robin in that it will randomly trigger any of the same four samples each time the sampler key is played. Since it's random, you cannot predict which sample will play next.

And now, let's see these functions in action, starting with Round Robin.

Using Round Robin with GigaStudio

The first tutorial in this section involves setting up Round Robin on GigaStudio. Start by launching GigaStudio Editor and creating a new instrument.

1. With our new instrument created, right-click along the gray area below the virtual keyboard and select New Region (see Figure 4.9).
2. Next, import your samples into the instrument by clicking and dragging them into the Sample Group section, located in the lower-left side of the Editor interface. Release the mouse, and the samples will copy into the Default Sample Group tree (see Figure 4.10).
3. Navigate to the Dimension section of the Editor interface and click on the Click to Assign button of the first dimension on the left. This will open the Dimension Controller window (see Figure 4.11).
4. Set the Controller Source to Round Robin. Note that doing this will place an additional split in the Split Name section of this window.
5. For this tutorial, I am using three drum samples, so we'll need to create an additional split, which will give us one split per sample. Click on the Add button to add a split. Then use the Rename button to rename each split. By the time you're finished, your Dimension Controller window should look like Figure 4.12. Click OK to close the window and get back to the Editor interface.
6. Looking at the Editor interface now, you can see that the upper-left dimension contains three splits, with the first split on the left selected and colored bright orange. We're now ready to import our samples. Click and drag the first drum sample into the blank Velocity region, which is just to the left of the Dimension section.
7. After importing the first drum sample, click on the second dimension split and then click and drag the second drum sample into the second blank Velocity region.
8. Next, click on the third dimension split and then click and drag the third and final sample into the third blank Velocity region. By the time you're done, you should have an instrument that looks similar to Figure 4.13.

At this point, you are ready to save your edits as a Giga instrument. Click on the Save button, name the instrument, and save it. After this, activate GigaStudio, import your newly created instrument, and try out the Round Robin function in action by playing it with your MIDI keyboard or just using the virtual keyboard of the GigaStudio interface. You should hear the drum samples alternate each time the related MIDI note is triggered.

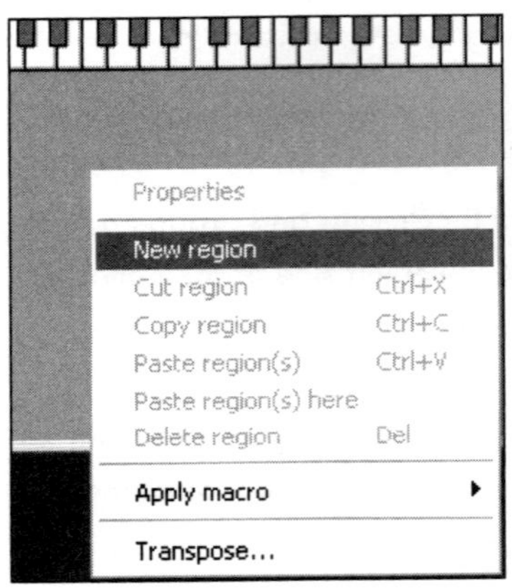

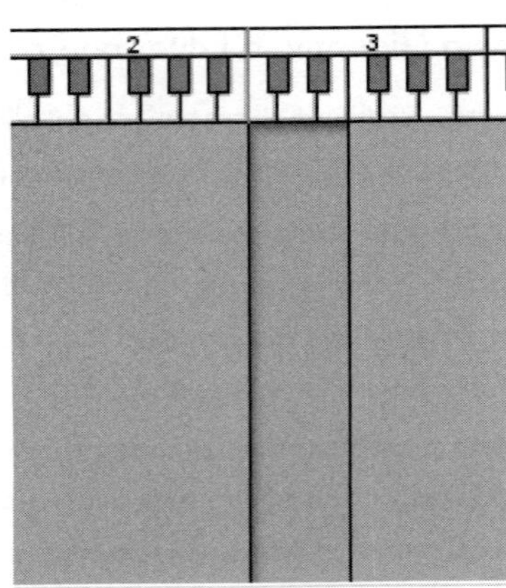

Figure 4.9

Begin by creating a new blank region.

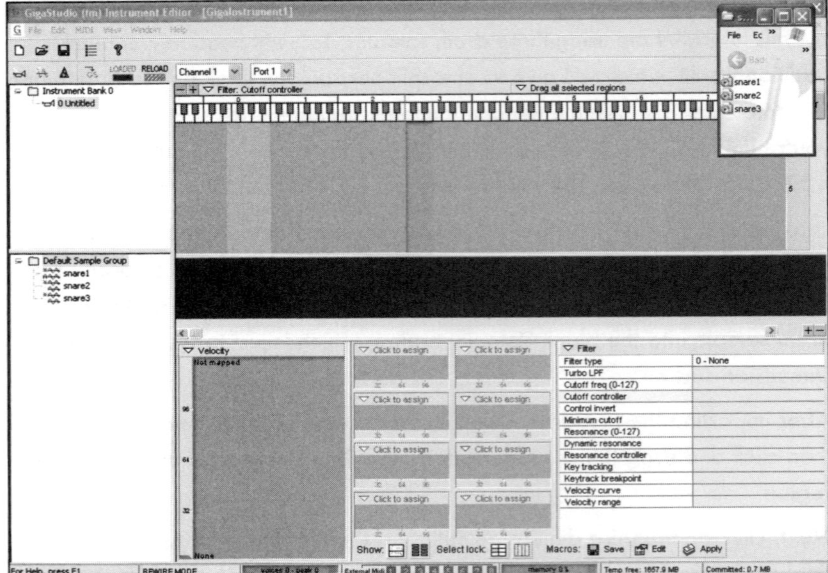

Figure 4.10

Next, copy the samples into the Default Sample Group tree.

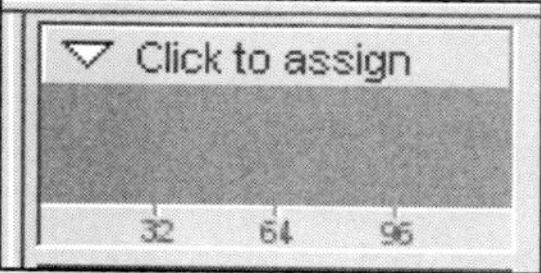

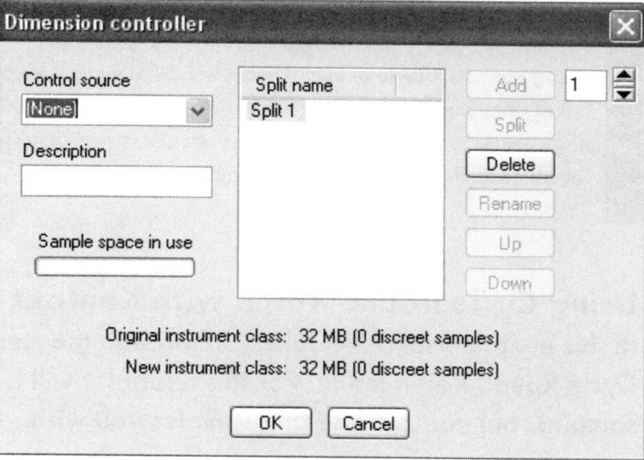

Figure 4.11

Click on the first dimension button in the upper-left corner of the Dimension section (left) to launch the Dimension Controller window (right).

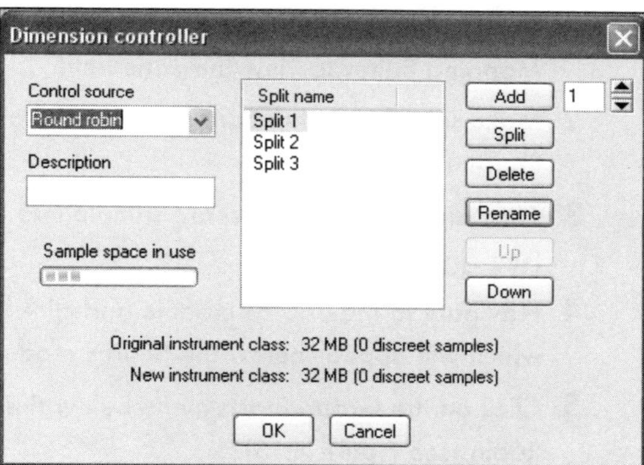

Figure 4.12

Our Round Robin splits are now all set up.

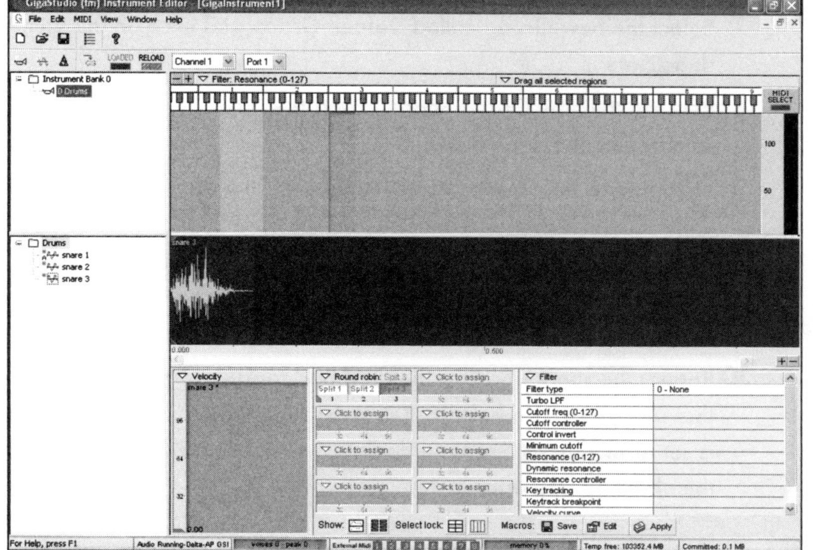

Figure 4.13

And now, all of the drum samples have been imported into our instrument. Note that I have changed the name of the Bank and Group trees to Drums.

> **USING RANDOM WITH GIGASTUDIO**
>
> Using Random instead of Round Robin with GigaStudio is simply a matter of selecting it from the list of Controller Sources in the Dimension Controller window. Then create the splits and import the samples to each split. Save the instrument and open it in GigaStudio, and the samples will alternate each time the related MIDI note is triggered.

Using Cycle Round Robin with Kontakt

In this next tutorial, I will take you through the steps of setting up Kontakt for Cycle Round Robin mode. For this tutorial, I will be using four snare drum samples, but you can use any samples you wish.

1. Create a new instrument by selecting it from the Load/Save menu. Click on the Edit button to expand the instrument interface and then click on the Mapping Editor to view the zone field.
2. Make sure the Group Editor is activated and rename the Default Group to Snare 1.
3. Click and drag the first snare sample into the zone field and release it at C3 (see Figure 4.14).
4. Navigate to the Source module and click on the Group Start Options button, which will appear below the Source module.
5. Click on the Group Starts menu below the Source and select Cycle Round Robin (see Figure 4.15).
6. Select Create Empty Group from the Edit menu of the Mapping Editor.
7. Select the new Group called Default Group and click on the Edit All button to deactivate it.
8. Rename the new Group Snare 2, and then click and drag the next snare sample into the zone field.
9. Navigate to the Group Starts menu below the Source module and select Cycle Round Robin. But this time, set the Position in Round Robin Chain dialog to 2. This will tell Kontakt to play the first snare sample when first triggered, follow by the second snare sample the next time the same key is triggered.
10. Repeat the same steps for the third and fourth snare samples. Just make sure that the third snare is set to 3 in the Round Robin Chain and the fourth snare is set to 4. This will create a cycling chain of snare one, two, three, four, and then back to one again.

Figure 4.14
The first snare sample has been imported into the zone field.

Figure 4.15
After selecting Cycle Round Robin, note that the Position in Round Robin Chain dialog is set to 1, which means that the first time this key is triggered, the sample residing on Group 1 will trigger first.

USING CYCLE RANDOM WITH KONTAKT

To use the Cycle Random function instead of Cycle Round Robin, just select each group and change its Group Starts menu from Cycle Round Robin to Cycle Random (see Figure 4.16). After this, play the samples again, and Kontakt will play each sample back randomly.

Figure 4.16
Select each group of your Kontakt instrument and change its Group Starts option from Cycle Round Robin to Cycle Random.

Using LFOs

The first sample parameter we're going to tweak is the LFO, or Low Frequency Oscillator. This is an additional oscillator found on all standard synth interfaces. Recall that LFOs generate waveforms with a low frequency, hence the name LFO, in order to modulate a parameter, such as a filter or another oscillator. That means that the LFO itself is never actually heard, just its effect on other synth parameters.

Let's see and hear the LFO in action, starting with Kontakt.

Using LFOs with Kontakt

Setting up an LFO in Kontakt is very simple. You first need to decide which synth parameter you wish to modulate. In our example this will be the Cutoff parameter of a two-pole low pass filter. Applying an LFO to this parameter will cause the filter to open and close as the loaded Kontakt instrument plays back. For this example, I will be using a drum loop as my instrument.

1. With the instrument loaded, navigate to the bottom-left side of the Source module and click on the right plus button to view a pop-up menu of all the available group insert effects. Select 2 Pole Lowpass (12dB) from the Sample Filters subdirectory. This will place the filter directly under the Source module (see Figure 4.17).
2. Next, navigate to the lower-left corner of the Filter module and click on the left plus button to select an LFO as the filter modulation source. Select Sine from the LFO subdirectory to assign the sine waveshape to the LFO module, which will appear just below the Amplifier module (see Figure 4.18).

Figure 4.17
Select the two-pole low pass filter from the Group Insert subdirectory. This will activate and place it just underneath the Source module.

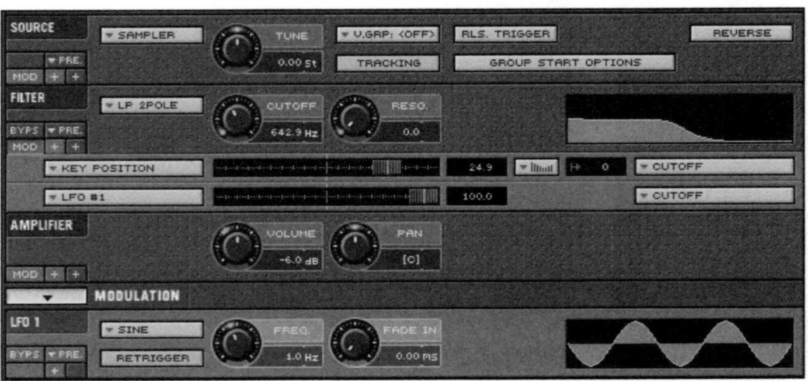

Figure 4.18
The LFO module has been selected as the modulation source for the filter.

At this point, it's simply a matter of making adjustments to the various parameters of the low pass filter and the LFO to create an effect you like.

THE TIME MACHINE

You can change the timbre of the loaded instrument by selecting an alternative source algorithm, which is done by selecting one from the menu located in the upper-left corner of the Source module. The Time Machine and Time Machine II in particular are fantastic algorithms to apply to drum loops, since they both pair granular synthesis with intuitive time-stretching features. Read more about these algorithms in Chapter 7.

Using LFOs with GigaStudio

Setting up LFOs in GigaStudio can be done either from the GigaEdit program or by using the QuickEdit window within the GigaStudio application itself. For this tutorial, I'll show you how to set up an LFO with QuickEdit to modulate the Cutoff parameter of a low pass filter.

Before starting this tutorial, make sure that you have a Giga instrument loaded into the first instrument slot. Once this is done, click on the Q button to activate the QuickEdit interface (see Figure 4.19).

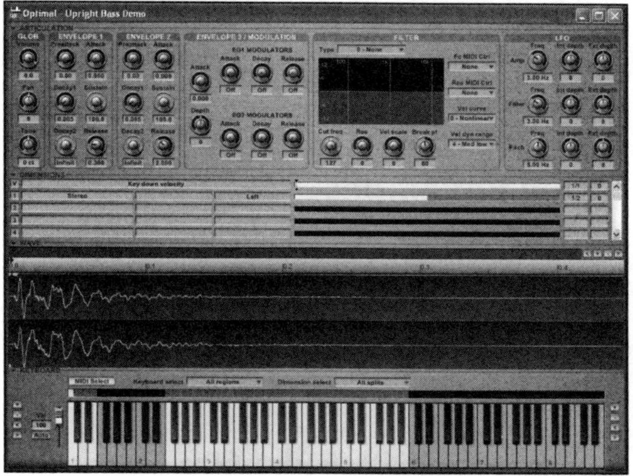

Figure 4.19
Applying synth parameters such as filters, LFOs, and envelopes in GigaStudio 3 is easily done with QuickEdit.

1 Navigate to the Filter section of the QuickEdit interface and select the low pass filter from the Type menu.

2 Make adjustments to the Cutoff Frequency and Resonance parameters to create a deep, resonating filter effect. As a suggestion, try setting the Cutoff Frequency to 39 and the Resonance to 68. As you make these parameter adjustments, you will see those adjustments reflected in the filter graph.

3 Now that the filter has been activated, navigate to the LFO section of the QuickEdit interface, which is located just to the right of the Filter section. You will notice that it is split into three destinations: Amp, Filter, and Pitch. For this tutorial, we will use the Filter destination, as we intend to modulate the filter to open and close it. Set the Frequency parameter of the Filter destination to a value of .50Hz to create a slow modulation of the filter. Note that as you make adjustments to the Frequency parameter, they are reflected in the waveform display below (see Figure 4.20).

4 If you play the Giga instrument now, you will not hear the LFO effect yet. This is because a depth has not been assigned yet, which in this case is handled by the Internal Depth parameter. Use this knob to assign a depth value of 3000, which will create a strong LFO modulation of the filter.

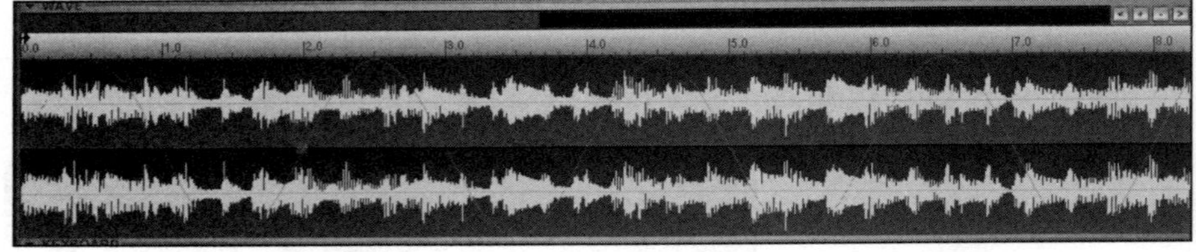

Figure 4.20
The QuickEdit waveform display reflects any LFO or Envelope parameter adjustments.

Using Envelopes

For our final batch of tutorials, I will introduce you to using envelopes with GigaStudio and Kontakt. As you will find throughout this book, envelopes are an important piece of the synthetic pie, as they are used to alter the dynamics of filters and amplifiers. Through the magic of soft synths, envelopes can also be used to produce several creative possibilities.

Using Envelopes with Kontakt

Kontakt's envelopes allow you to create some interesting modulation possibilities in addition to all the standard envelope uses. For this example, we are going to use an envelope to modulate the Amplifier module. This will affect the amplitude of the loaded Kontakt instrument. For this example, I will be using a drum loop as my instrument.

1 Navigate to the Amplifier module and click on the left plus button to list all modulation sources. Select Envelopes, Flexible Envelope. This will place the envelope directly below the Amplifier module (see Figure 4.21).

2 As you can see, the Flexible Envelope has the ability to create numerous breakpoints along the envelope timeline, which in turn creates an extremely complex envelope curve. A breakpoint can be added by simply right-clicking (Ctrl+Click for Mac) anywhere along the envelope timeline, which can then be dragged up/down/left/right. To give you a better idea of its capabilities, let's select an envelope preset by clicking on the Pre button of the Envelope module and selecting the Rhythmic Four 01 preset (see Figure 4.22).

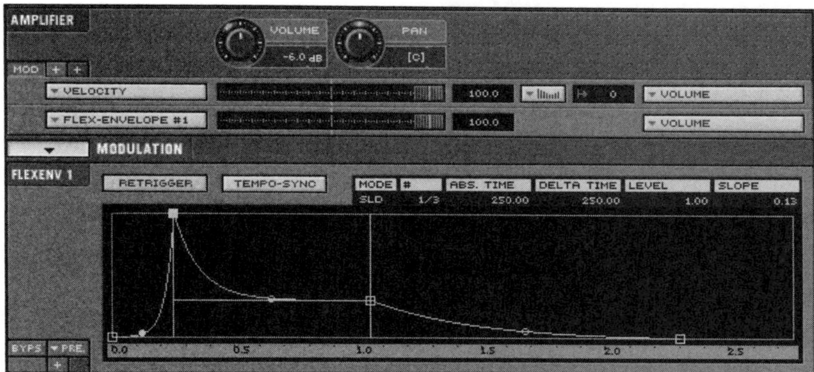

Figure 4.21

An envelope can alter the dynamics of a sample, or in this case, it can be used to modulate the Amplifier parameter.

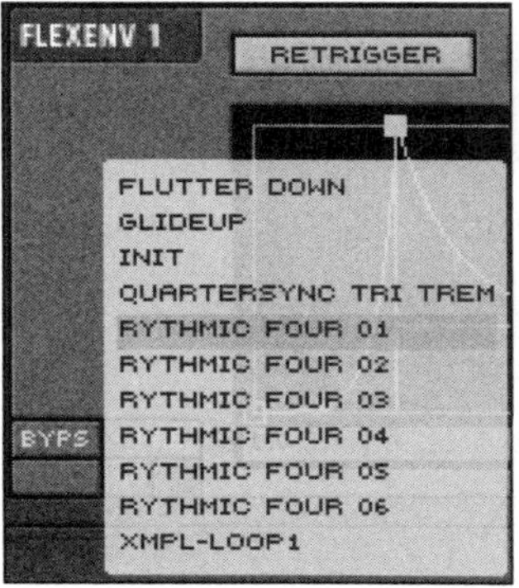

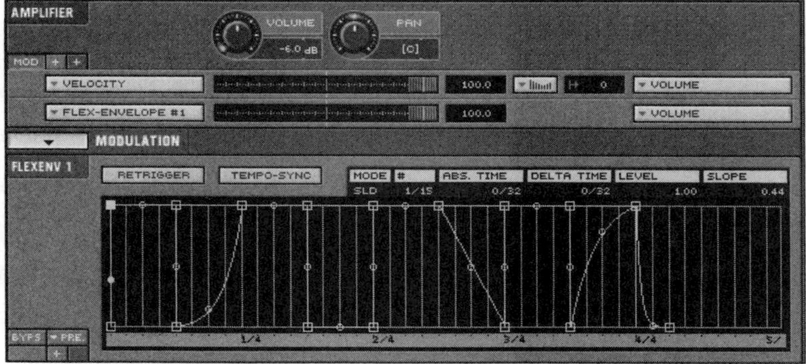

Figure 4.22

The Rhythmic Four 01 preset will cause the amplitude to jump up and down in volume.

Using Envelopes with GigaStudio

For this tutorial, we are going to use QuickEdit again to demonstrate the creative potential of the envelopes in GigaStudio. Before we begin, load a Giga instrument that includes a long sustained sample (such as a drum loop) into an available slot and press the Q button to open the interface. Looking at Figure 4.23, you can see that there are three envelope generators. In this example, we will just use the first envelope generator, since it shares a parameter set identical to that of the second envelope generator.

Figure 4.23
The QuickEdit window includes three envelope generators.

Assuming you have loaded your Giga instrument, set the first envelope generator to the following values:

- **Pre Attack**—Set to 0.
- **Attack**—Set this to 3 to create a gradual fade-in of the instrument.
- **Decay 1**—Set to 10 to create a slow decay.
- **Sustain**—Set to 21, which will intensify the Decay 1 value.
- **Decay 2**—Set to 21 to add some length to the envelope.
- **Release**—Set to 0 to have the instrument stop immediately after releasing the related MIDI note.

Once you are finished, you should see an envelope in the waveform display of QuickEdit that looks similar to the display in Figure 4.24.

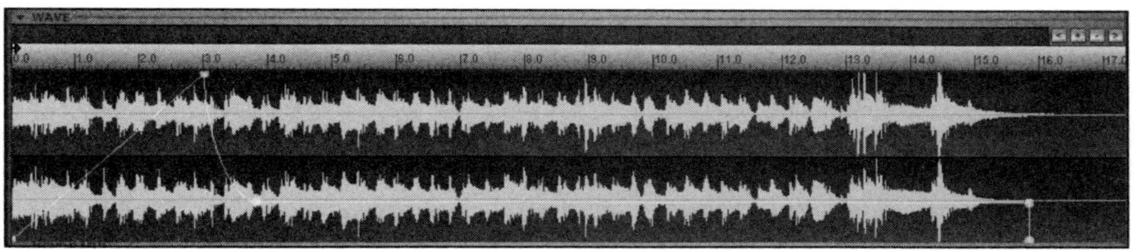

Figure 4.24

Now we have introduced an envelope with a slow attack to our instrument.

THE PITCH ENVELOPE

The third envelope generator introduces a pitch envelope to the loaded Giga instrument. This means that you can have the pitch of your instrument "ramp up" or bend up in pitch gradually as well as ramp down in pitch gradually. It includes the following parameters:

- **Attack**—This knob determines how fast or slow the pitch envelope effect will occur.
- **Depth**—This knob determines if the pitch envelope will ramp down when assigned a positive value or ramp up when assigned a negative value.

5 Audio Editors—Close Up

The audio editor is one of the most important components of a good sampling setup. Though today's software samplers house an impressive assortment of editing capabilities, those capabilities can be somewhat limited when compared to the editing capabilities of a robust, dedicated audio editing application. In this chapter, we'll tour the features of two of today's top audio editing applications: Sound Forge and Peak.

What Is an Audio Editing Program?

These days, an audio editing program is used to perform a number of different tasks such as mastering/burning CDs, building audio databases, and batch processing digital audio files. But an audio editor's main purpose is to provide a unique, non-linear platform in which to edit individual digital audio files precisely. This includes a basic edit such as deleting empty space from an audio file or a more complicated edit such as converting a stereo file into a mono file. Audio editing programs provide a number of unique tools and powerful features, which help make the process of editing audio less confusing.

From a sampling standpoint, an audio editor is essential for recording, manipulating, and vastly improving the audio quality of any samples or loops you want to use in your music. Not only do audio editors include many fine offline processes, but they also offer the ability to use real-time effects in order to create wild sound-designing possibilities.

> **THE WAVEFORM DISPLAY**
>
> The main interface of any audio editing program is the waveform display, which generates a graphical representation of a digital audio file. It provides a means by which to apply several edits to an audio file from a single viewpoint. As this is such a universal look shared by every audio editor available, it would be a good idea to get familiar with the basic layout before we get too deep into our editing programs for this chapter. Use Figure 5.1 as a reference while reading the following points of interest.
>
> - **Timeline**—Located at the top, a timeline provides a time-measured ruler that's read from left to right. This is used to determine the length of an audio file. As you play back an audio file, you'll see the cursor move from left to right.
> - **Amplitude Ruler**—Always located at the far left in any audio editor, this ruler is used to measure the amplitude content of a loaded audio file. It's typically displayed in decibel measurements and is read up and down.
> - **Playback Meters**—These display a graphical representation of the playback amplitude of a loaded audio file. In Figure 5.1, these are located on the far right, but in the case of the Mac program Peak, which we'll look at later, these meters are located at the bottom of the interface.

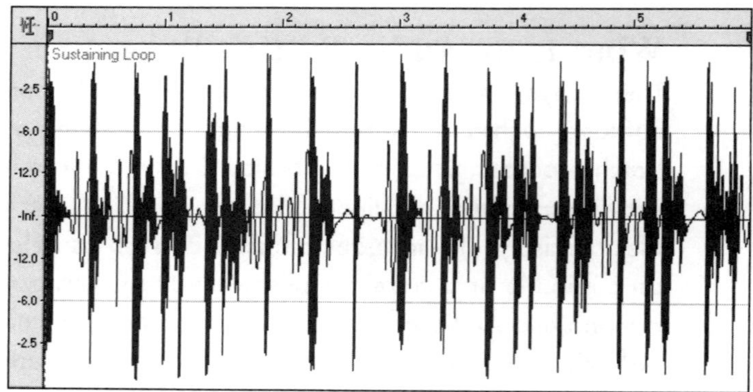

Figure 5.1
The waveform display is a universal look found in every audio editing program.

Meet Our Audio Editors—Sound Forge and Peak

Let's take a look at the audio editors we'll be using throughout this chapter, Sound Forge 7.0 and Peak 4.0.

Sony Sound Forge 7.0

Sound Forge 7.0 by Sony is one of those meat and potato audio editing applications that offers the basic necessities of a good audio editor and also includes some of the best real-time effects ever conceived, such as the

Acoustic Mirror and the Gapper/Snipper (see Figure 5.2). Sound Forge also has the capability to perform a number of unique tasks, such as synthesizing sounds, analyzing audio, and playing back video files.

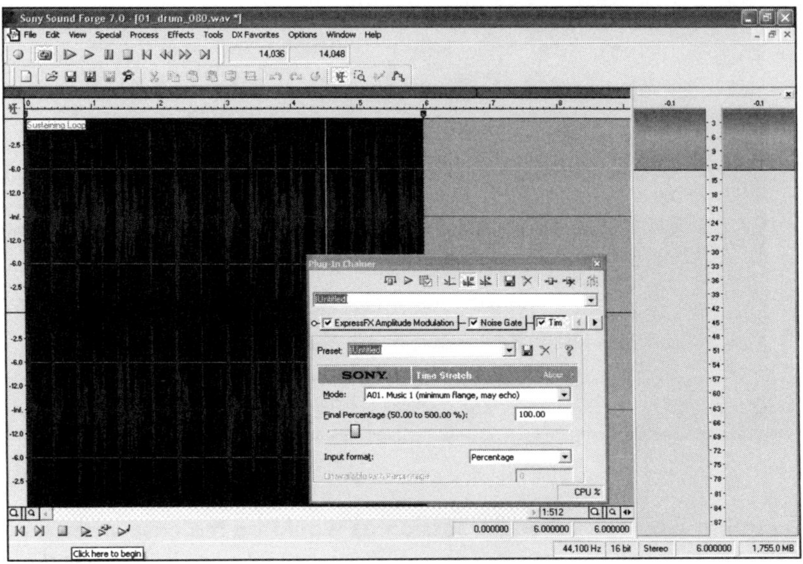

Figure 5.2

Sony's Sound Forge is a standard in digital audio editing for the Windows platform.

Bias Peak 4.1

Over the years, Mac-based audio editors have come and gone. I vividly remember using Sound Designer 2 by Digidesign many years ago in studios and thinking that it couldn't get any better than that. Boy, was I wrong; Peak by Bias showed me a way to edit audio quickly and use several real-time effects in the process (see Figure 5.3). Due to its reputation as a dependable, trouble-free audio application, Peak is now pretty much the only game in town for editing audio on the Mac.

Using Audio Editors for Recording

When running a sample recording session as we did in the previous chapter, using an audio editor to record the performances is a good plan, as it possesses some key advantages over using a DAW application such as Cubase or Pro Tools. For starters, the procedure for recording into an audio editor is drop-dead easy and efficient, which saves precious time for you and the talent you're recording. In addition, there's no need to go through the steps of

Figure 5.3

If you are a Mac user and are in need of audio editing, Bias Peak is your app.

creating and maintaining a session as would be the case when using a DAW application. In other words, the audio editor should be your right-hand man when recording samples.

In this section, we'll cover the steps of setting up, recording, splitting, and editing your samples with Sound Forge and Peak.

Setting Up to Record

Setting up either Sound Forge or Peak to record audio is simply a matter of selecting the appropriate audio hardware, setting your record preferences, getting levels, and finally pressing the Record button to begin recording. Let's examine each step of this process.

Let's begin by selecting the audio hardware for our recording session using Sound Forge. Select Preferences from the Options pull-down menu to launch the Preferences window. Looking at Figure 5.4, you can see that there are many different tabs to choose from here, but for this tutorial let's select the Wave tab. Once it is open, you should immediately see the upper and lower dialogs that allow you to select your playback and recording devices, respectively. When you click on either of these dialogs, Sound Forge will list any available audio hardware installed on your system. Looking at Figure 5.5, you can see that Sound Forge has listed the built-in audio card on my laptop, as well as the OmniStudio USB by M-Audio, which will be my audio hardware for the remainder of this chapter. Once this is selected, click on the Apply button below and then the OK button to close the Preferences window.

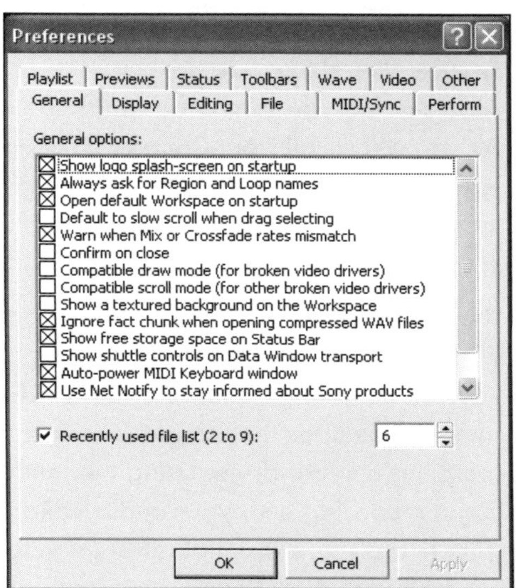

Figure 5.4

The Preferences window of Sound Forge is used to customize its impressive feature set to fit your needs.

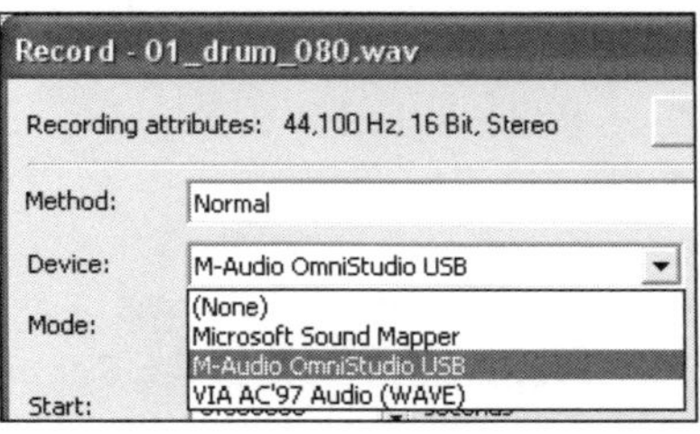

Figure 5.5

The Wave Preferences tab is used to select and set up your preferred audio hardware device for recording and playback. In this case, Sound Forge has listed the internal audio card from my laptop and the M-Audio OmniStudio USB, which is my preferred device.

In the case of Peak, setting up your audio hardware is a little different because there isn't a Preferences page. Click on the Audio pull-down menu and select Hardware Settings. This will launch the CoreAudio Settings window (see Figure 5.6).

Figure 5.6

The CoreAudio Settings window is used to select and set up your audio hardware.

Looking at this figure, you can see that Peak has listed the Built-In Audio Controller, which is the internal audio card of the Macintosh, and the M-Audio OmniStudio USB, which will be my audio interface controller for the remainder of this chapter. When this is selected, click the OK button to close the window.

Make the Recording

At this point, you should be ready to begin recording with your audio editor. As you will recall from Chapter 3, "Recording Your Samples," we discussed various mic placement techniques at great length. We won't be reviewing those here; the purpose of this section is to introduce you to the Record functions of both Peak and Sound Forge.

The key to recording audio efficiently is to make the process as streamlined as possible. When recording samples, this is best accomplished by recording your audio in large chunks of data, which are then split up into individual sample files after the session is over. For example, let's assume that you're sampling a snare drum. Using the method mentioned above, you would begin recording with your audio editor and let it continue recording as you sample the snare drum at different velocities and snare patterns. Once you've finished recording, you would then press the Stop button and end up with a single large audio file to split up and edit later, which goes incredibly fast, once you've become familiar with the basic splitting and editing functions. Keep this method in mind when you make your first recordings with Sound Forge and Peak.

Recording with Sound Forge

While you could simply press the Record button to begin recording, Sound Forge offers some additional record features that I would like to bring to your attention in this section. Assuming that you have selected the correct audio hardware as your recording input, click the Record button in the upper-left corner of the interface, use Special, Transport, Record, or simply use the Ctrl+R key command. This will activate and display the Record window (see Figure 5.7).

SET YOUR LEVELS

Before you begin recording, take a minute to make sure that you have a strong input signal. If it appears a little weak or quiet, increase the amount of input at the signal's source, which is done with your mixer. This will ensure that your signal will be recorded at the best amplitude possible. However, while setting your levels, make sure that your signal is not distorting or clipping.

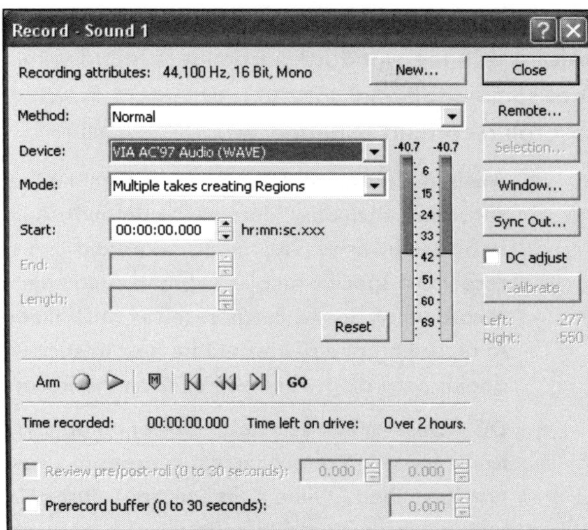

Figure 5.7

The Record window is used to begin the recording process within Sound Forge.

Once this window is open, you can begin recording by clicking the Record button in the lower-left corner of this window or by pressing the R key. Once you are finished recording, click the Stop button or just press R again, and the new recording will appear within the Sound Forge interface behind the Record window. At this point, you can now close this window and begin to edit your recording.

Standard Recording Parameters

Below are the standard parameters of the Record window.

- **Recording Attributes**—This displays the default recording attributes of the Record window. Looking back at Figure 5.6, you can see that this section is set to record a mono 16-bit/44.1kHz audio file. Click the New button just to the right of this display to adjust the attributes.
- **Device**—This pull-down menu is used to select the audio hardware to use as a recording device. As we already set this up a couple of sections ago, you should see that chosen device displayed here. If you don't, just click on the menu and select the preferred device.
- **Transport**—The lower portion of the Record window is used to activate the various transport controls of the recording process. Included here are Record, Play, Drop Marker, Go to Start, Go to Start of Last Take, Go to End, and the Go button.
- **Input Meters**—To the upper-right of the transport controls are the input monitoring meters, which are used to display any incoming signal during the recording process. To the lower-left of the meters is a Reset button.

Special Record Parameters

Along with the standard parameters found within the Record window, there are some additional special parameters, which can be used to optimize your overall recording experience.

- **Method**—This menu offers four different methods by which to begin your recording, including Normal (by default), Automatic: Time (starts to record at a specific time), Automatic: Threshold (starts to record when Sound Forge receives a specific amplitude), and Automatic: MIDI Timecode (starts to record when Sound Forge receives MIDI timecode). As this is an introduction to recording audio, it would be best to stick with the Normal setting, which begins recording when you click on the Record button.
- **DC Adjust**—When selected, this option adjusts the recorded signal according to the incoming direct current in order to avoid a DC offset (we'll discuss this further in the "Offline Edits" section). Just below the DC Adjust is a Calibrate button, which is used to calibrate the sensitivity of the DC Adjust option.

Recording with Peak

Recording audio with Peak is pretty straightforward, but it's not without a few bells and whistles here and there. Let's begin by performing a basic recording with Peak by clicking the Record button in the upper-right section of the graphic interface, which will activate and display the Record window (see Figure 5.8). You can also use the Apple+R key command.

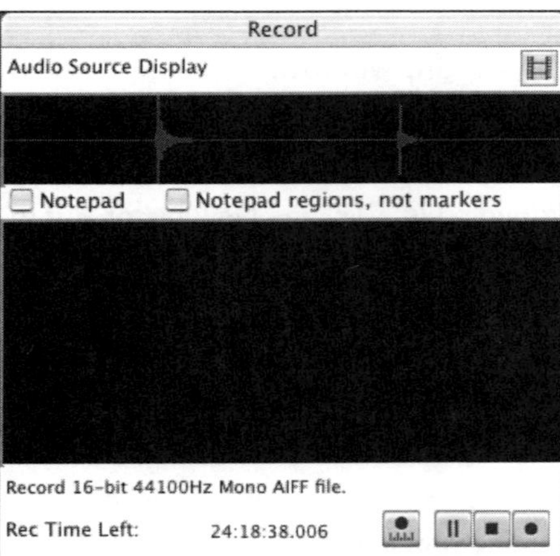

Figure 5.8
Peak's Record window is used to monitor and record your samples.

Once this is activated, you can begin the recording process by clicking on the Record button within the Record window. When the recording has begun, you can monitor your incoming signal in the upper half of the Record window, as you can see in Figure 5.8. Once the recording process is complete, you can click the Stop button, at which time the Record window will close and a new window will pop up, asking you to assign a location and name to your new recording (see Figure 5.9). After completing this task, click the OK button, and the new recording will automatically open.

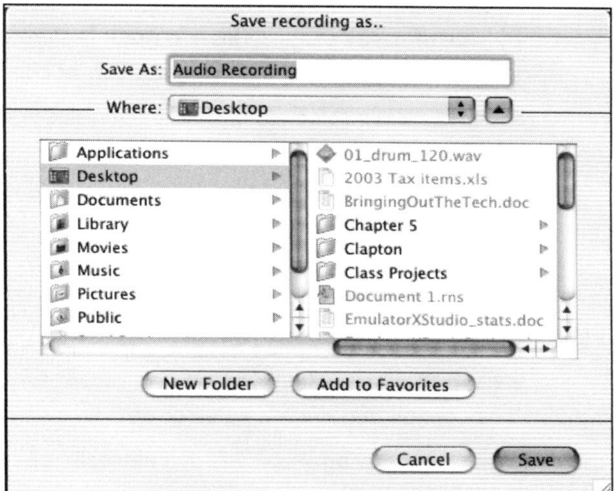

Figure 5.9

Once you stop recording, the window displayed here will ask you to assign a name and location for your recording.

Special Recording Parameters

In order to view the special recording parameters of Peak, you must first click on the Record Settings button, which is located in the lower-right corner of the Record window. If the Record window is closed, you can view the Record Settings window by selecting it from the Audio pull-down menu or using the Option+R key command (see Figure 5.10).

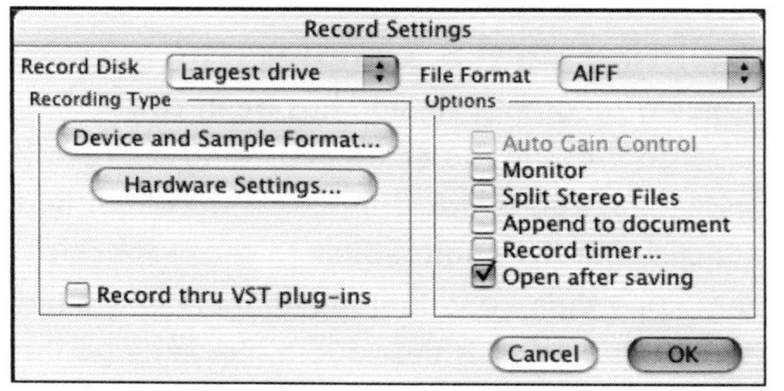

Figure 5.10

The Record Settings window is used to customize the Peak recording environment.

Let's review the various parameters of this window.

- **Record Disk**—This option allows you to select the hard drive to use when recording.
- **File Format**—This option allows you to select a preferred file format.
- **Device and Sample Format**—This button will activate a window to specify which audio engine Peak will use (OSX HAL, CoreAudio, or FireWire DV).
- **Record Thru VST Plug-Ins**—Checking this option allows you to record audio by way of a VST plug-in. This is a great feature if you want to pre-process your audio signal with a noise gate, EQ, or compressor.
- **Monitor**—When selected, this option enables you to monitor your recording while recording.
- **Split Stereo Files**—This option will split a stereo recording into two separate audio files (left file, right file).
- **Append to Document**—This option allows you to record new audio data to an existing audio file.
- **Record Timer**—This option assigns a specific amount of time to the recording process. For example, if you want to record for 10 minutes, select the Record Timer option and enter a value of 600 seconds.
- **Open After Saving**—Peak will automatically open a newly recorded audio file after saving it.

SAVE YOUR WORK

Once you've completed your recording, be sure to save your work immediately by selecting Save from the File pull-down menu or using the Ctrl+S key command on the PC or Apple+S on the Mac. Furthermore, once you have finished your recording session, you should immediately back it up to a CD, a DVD, or some kind of removable media.

Splitting Up the Samples

Once a recording session has been concluded and backed up, the next step is to go through the entire recording, extract the samples, and save them as individual audio files. This task is accomplished by using the Copy and Paste functions of the audio editor to select specific portions of the master recording, copy them, and then paste them into a new blank document, which can then be saved as a new audio file. Let's go through the steps of doing this.

Copying and Pasting Audio Files

Extracting samples and placing them into new separate audio files is a matter of five repetitive steps:

1. Select
2. Copy
3. New
4. Paste
5. Save

Keep in mind that while you want to be careful when performing any of these functions, your familiarity with the key commands and shortcuts will enable you to go through this rather tedious process quickly. Throughout this section of the chapter, I will take you through these steps and list their corresponding key commands to help speed up the process.

Selecting a Region

Selecting a region of an audio file is done by clicking and dragging along the length of the waveform display with your mouse. Looking at Figure 5.11, you can see that I have opened a stereo file in Peak that displays no selected regions. The next step is to click and drag to the right until enough audio data has been selected and release the mouse. This will create a selected region (see Figure 5.12).

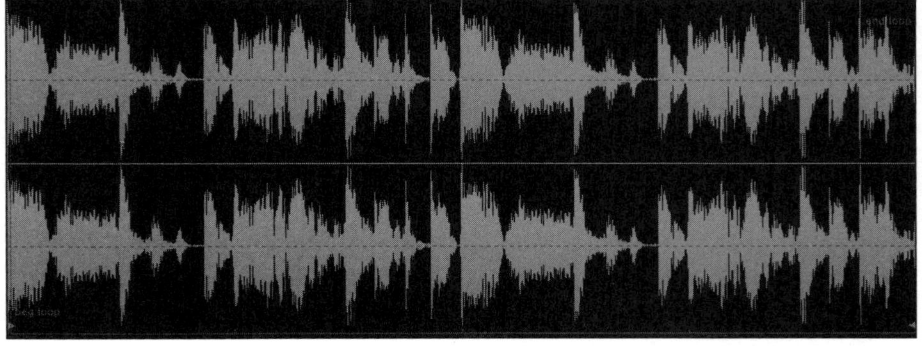

Figure 5.11

Here we have a stereo file that has been opened in Peak. No regions have been selected.

> **SELECTING STEREO REGIONS**
>
> When selecting regions from stereo audio files in Sound Forge or Peak, click and drag directly along the center divider between the two channels of the audio file (see Figure 5.13). This will ensure that you select a stereo region, rather than the left or right mono channel.

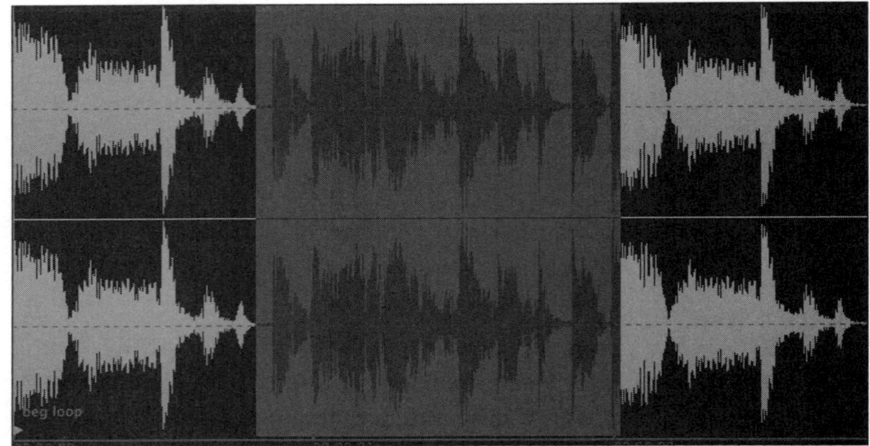

Figure 5.12
Clicking and dragging the mouse along the length of the waveform display will select a region.

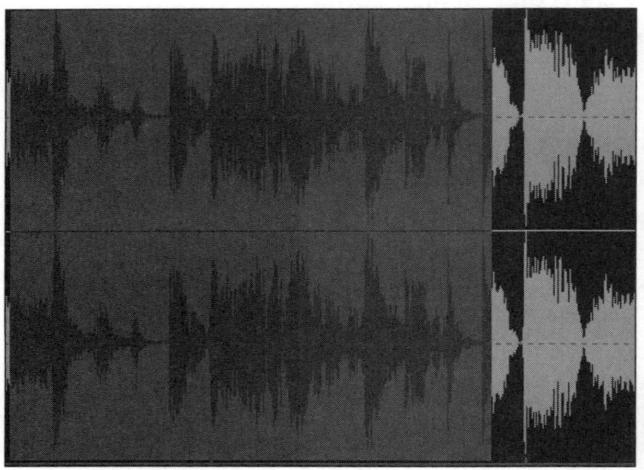

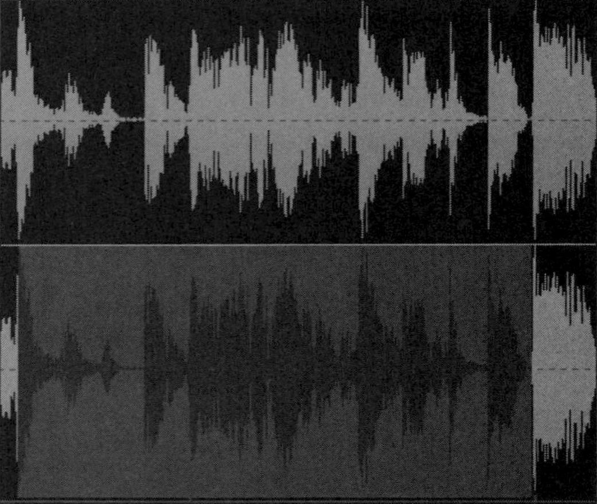

Figure 5.13
Clicking and dragging directly along the center divider of a stereo file will select a stereo region of an audio file, as you can see from the figure on the left, while clicking and dragging above and below this divider will select a mono region, as you can see from the figure on the right.

Copying the File

After a region has been selected, the next step is to copy that region to the virtual clipboard. This is done by using the Copy function, which is located under the Edit pull-down menu in both Sound Forge and Peak. Also note that the key command for performing this is Crtl+C on the PC or Apple+C on the Mac.

Pasting the File

Now that the region has been copied to the clipboard, you can place this region into a new blank audio file. This process is handled differently in Sound Forge and Peak. I'll begin this section by demonstrating with Sound Forge.

1 Select New from the File pull-down menu. This will launch the New File window (see Figure 5.14). Note that you can also use the Ctrl+N key command.

2 Use this window to specify the sampling rate, bit depth, and mono/stereo preferences. These preferences should match the settings of the copied region (for instance, 16-bit/44.1kHz). Click the OK button, and a new blank audio file will be created.

3 Select Paste from the Edit pull-down menu; this will paste the region into the new blank audio file. Note that you can also use the Ctrl+V key command.

Figure 5.14
The New File window is used to set the bit depth, sampling rate, and mono/stereo preferences.

Now let's see how this is done using Peak.

1 Click on the File pull-down menu and select either New Mono Document (key command Apple+N) or New Stereo Document (key command Shift+Apple+N). This will create a new blank audio file.

2 Select Paste from the Edit pull-down menu. This will paste the region into the new blank audio file. Note that you can also use the Apple+V key command.

Note that Peak has a cool little function that will help save you time when performing this task. Select a new region from an audio file and then select New, Document from Selection (key command Ctrl+N). This will automatically create a new audio file and place the selected region within it.

CONVERTING STEREO TO MONO

Both Peak and Sound Forge have the ability to convert a stereo file into a mono file. This comes in handy when you want to convert a stereo region of a single instrument, such as a snare drum sample, into a mono document, since snare drums are not typically handled as stereo files by most drum machines. This is done by selecting the stereo region, copying it, and then creating a new mono document. Upon attempting to paste the stereo region into the new mono document, Peak will launch the Mono to Stereo Conversion window, which will ask you to specify how much of the left or right channel of the audio file should be favored when converting the file to mono (see Figure 5.15). After the settings are made, click OK, and Peak will sum both channels of the stereo file and convert them to a single mono file. Note that Sound Forge converts and sums the stereo file automatically when pasting the stereo region into a new blank mono file.

Figure 5.15
The Stereo to Mono Conversion window is used to specify which channel to favor when pasting a stereo region into a mono file.

Saving the New File

The last step when creating new audio files is naming and saving them to a specific location on your hard drive. The quick and easy way to do this in either Peak or Sound Forge is to click on the File pull-down menu and select Save. This will bring up the Save window, where you can choose a name and location for your audio file, after which you can just click on the Save button, and that's that.

While saving is relatively easy, you should take into consideration the importance of organizing your new audio files so that you can locate and use them quickly. The last thing you want to worry about is searching your entire hard drive for that single kick drum sample that would work perfectly in your new song. On that note, I offer the following tricks of the trade to help you with your organization.

* **Numbering**—Proper numbering of your files will help immensely when compiling several samples that have similar content. Avoid using single-digit numeric values in your file names (snare_1.aiff). Instead, place a 0 in front of any single-digit numeric value (snare_01.aiff) to ensure that the file names will appear in their proper numeric order.
* **No Spaces Between Words**—Avoid using spaces between words in a file name, since this can lead to unforeseen complications when using your samples with different computers and platforms. Instead, use a _ (underscore) character between words to avoid these complications. For example, drum loop 80BPM.aiff would be written as drum_loop_80BPM.aiff.
* **Create/Use Folders**—When dealing with several samples of the same or similar content, creating and using folders will help you quickly locate these samples again for future uses. See Figure 5.16 for an example of this concept.

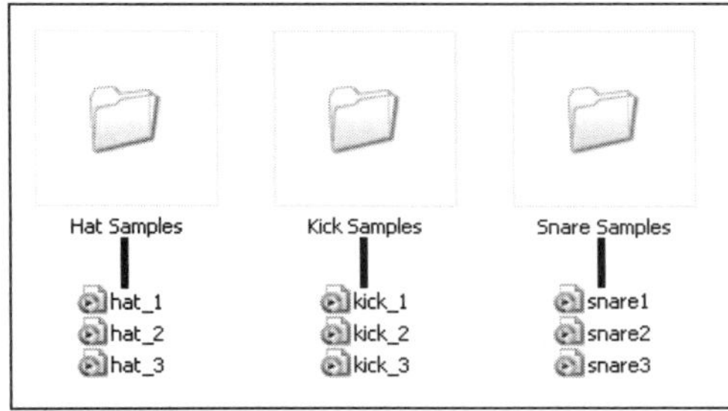

Figure 5.16
This diagram demonstrates the proper creation and use of folders when organizing drum samples.

Editing Your Samples

Programs such as Sound Forge and Peak are great solutions for editing audio samples. They offer simple, efficient ways to perform a number of editing tasks. In addition, audio editors offer numerous sampling-specific functions to make the process of assembling your samples into applications such as Kontakt and GigaStudio seamless. In this section, we'll discuss and demonstrate these various editing functions.

Creating Loops

Perhaps the most important editing tool an audio editor can offer an aspiring sampling artist such as you is the ability to locate and create loop points within a sample. As you will recall from Chapter 1, "An Introduction to Sampling," we discussed looping and the importance of loop points. We also reviewed how to do this in GigaStudio and Kontakt in Chapter 4, "Advanced Sampler Techniques." This section will show you how to put that knowledge to the test by creating loop points in both Sound Forge and Peak.

DESTRUCTIVE VERSUS NON-DESTRUCTIVE EDITS

When using any digital audio application such as Sound Forge or Peak, you'll commonly see the terms "destructive" and "non-destructive" editing. Let's define and discuss the differences between these two types of edits.

Non-destructive edits are those that do not overwrite the original data of an audio file. For example, let's assume you have a drum loop that you want to hear played backward. You can highlight the entire drum loop and then select the Reverse function from either Sound Forge or Peak, at which point the audio editor will perform the reverse process. Then you can play back the drum loop to monitor the results of the edit. Although this sounds like a permanent edit, this is not necessarily the case, as programs such as Sound Forge and Peak both contain an undo function that allows you to recover the original audio data by performing single or multiple steps back in your edits.

Destructive edits are those in which the original data of an audio file has been permanently overwritten. For example, let's assume you have a bass sample that contains empty space at the beginning and end of the audio data. Selecting the empty regions with your mouse and deleting them with the backspace key would technically be considered a non-destructive edit, as it would not permanently overwrite the original data within the audio file. But this changes when you save the audio file with the edits, as this will now make the edits permanent, hence a destructive edit.

EMBEDDED LOOPS

Once a pair of loop points has been established within a sample, they are embedded within the sample itself after the file is saved within the audio editor. Upon loading the sample into a sampler such as Kontakt or GigaStudio, those loop points will still be active and available to use.

Creating Loops with Sound Forge

In this section, I will show you how to create a "sustaining loop" in Sound Forge using an organ sample (see Figure 5.17). Like the sustain pedal on a piano, a sustain loop is a type of loop that will constantly recycle until its corresponding MIDI note is released, at which point the sample will play to its end. This type of loop is typically used to mimic the sustaining characteristics of wind and brass instruments, stringed instruments, and vocals.

Let's begin by creating a region that will be used to create our sustained loop. Locate an area of the sample where the amplitude is visually constant or sustained, which can be found toward the end of the sample. When this is located, click and drag a region of 1–2 seconds in length around that area (see Figure 5.18).

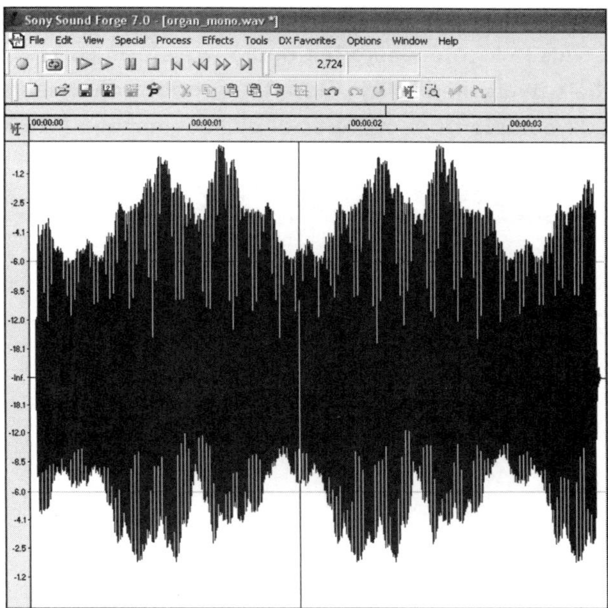

Figure 5.17
Here is our test organ sample, pre-looped.

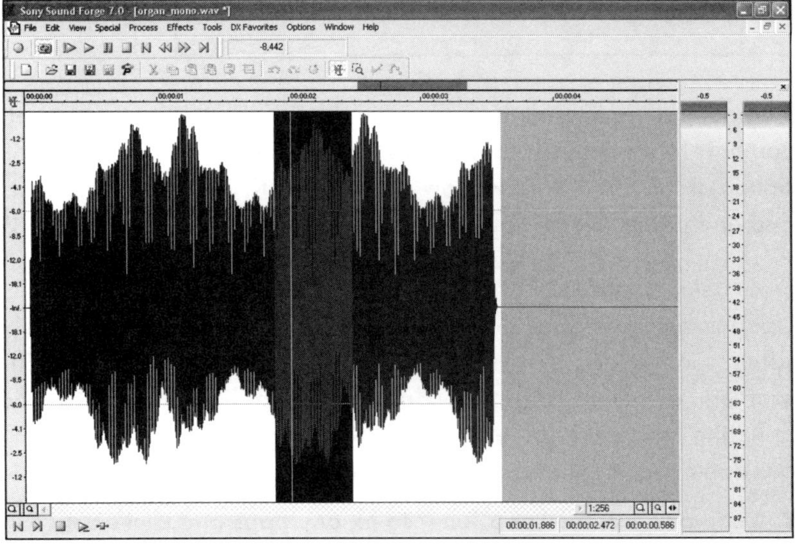

Figure 5.18
Our prime loop point of this sample can be found near the end of the sample. Look for a place where the amplitude is sustained and constant, as this will help to avoid pops and clicks.

After the region has been selected, click the Loop Playback button in the upper-left corner, or just use the Q key command. Press Play and listen for pops and clicks between the beginning and end of the selected region. If you hear any, you can adjust the region start and end points by navigating your mouse to the beginning or end of the region, at which time your cursor icon will change to a double-arrow icon that can be used to adjust the region points to locate where the audio waveform crosses over the zero axis line of the waveform display. Once the proper adjustments have been made, select Edit Sample from the Special pull-down menu (see Figure 5.19).

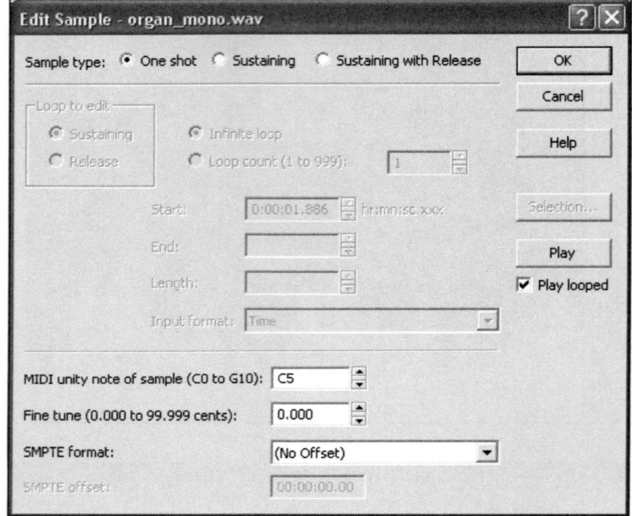

Figure 5.19

The Edit Sample window is used to create and embed loops within your samples.

Without getting into all the nitty-gritty details about this window, let me show you how to create your loop points quickly. Select the Sustaining with Release option at the top of this window and press OK. This will create loop start and end points, which you can hear upon playback (see Figure 5.20).

Fine-Tuning Loops

Upon listening back to the loop later on, you might notice an audible inconsistency in the loop that you missed when first creating the loop. This is not a problem, as Sound Forge provides a handy tool called the Crossfade Loop to fix the loop start and end points. Selecting Crossfade Loop from the Tools pull-down menu enables this function (see Figure 5.21).

You can also use the Loop Tuner to fix any pops and clicks between loop points (see Figure 5.22). Just select it from the View pull-down menu or use the Ctrl+L key command.

When you're finished cleaning up the loop, just save the audio file with the loop points and then import it into your sampler. Looking at Figure 5.23, you can see that the loop points we just created can be viewed from the Loop Editor of Kontakt.

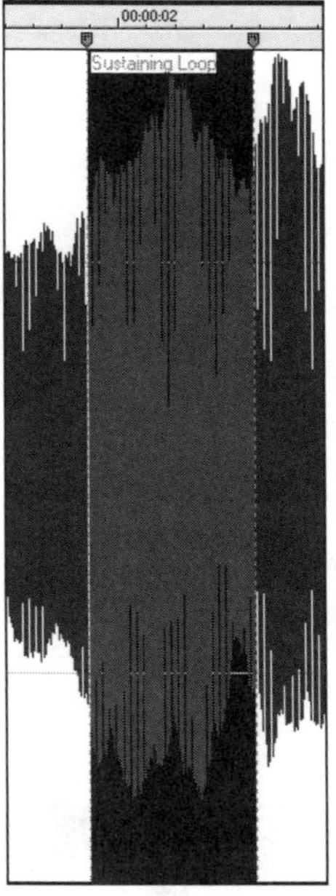

Figure 5.20

Now we have created a pair of loop points.

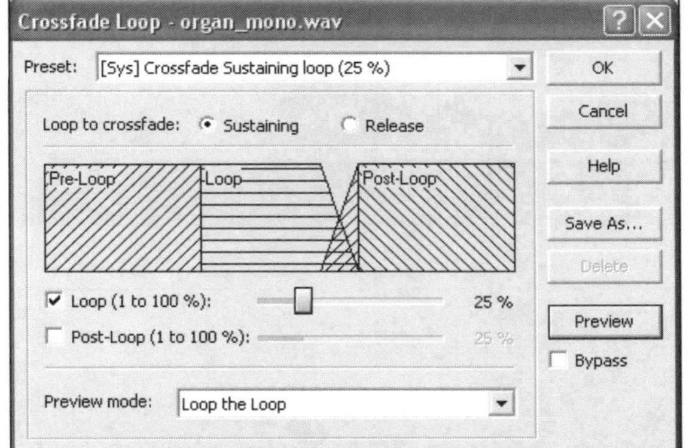

Figure 5.21

The Crossfade Loop tool is used to clean up any looping inconsistencies by adjusting the loop fades.

Creating Loops with Peak

In this section, I will show you how to create a sustaining loop in Peak using the same organ sample from the previous section (see Figure 5.24).

Let's begin by creating a region that will be used to create our sustained loop. Locate an area of the sample where the amplitude is visually constant, which can generally be found toward the end of the sample. Click and drag a region around that area (see Figure 5.25).

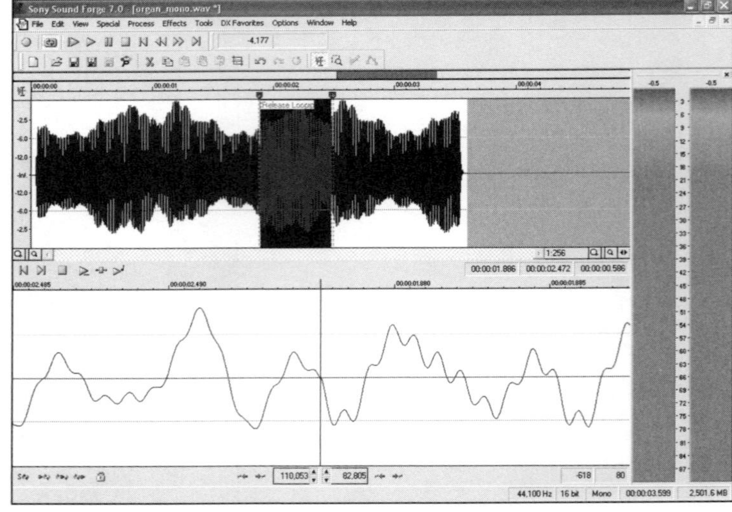

Figure 5.22
The Loop Tuner is used to correct any pops and clicks between loop points.

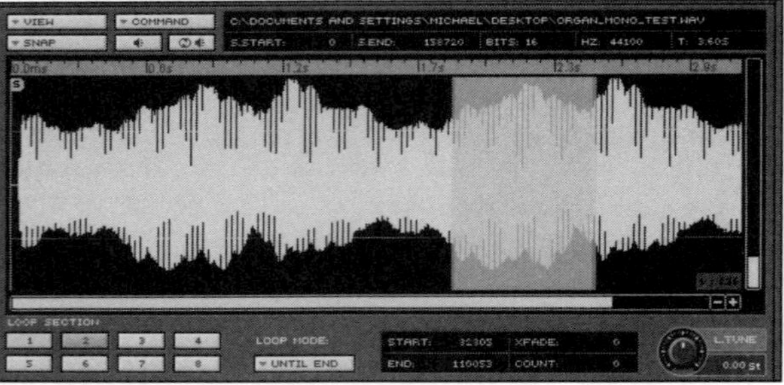

Figure 5.23
Once the audio file has been saved with the loop points, it can be imported into a sampler such as Kontakt and viewed from its Loop Editor.

Figure 5.24
Here's the same organ sample loaded into Peak, pre-looped.

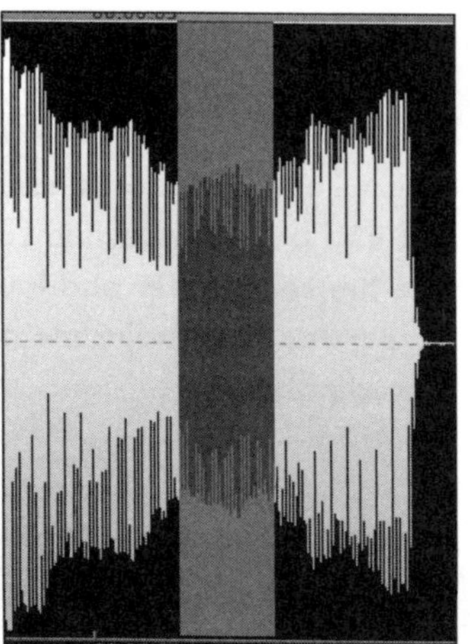

Figure 5.25

Our prime loop point of this sample can be found near the end of the sample. Look for a place where the amplitude is constant, as this will help to avoid pops and clicks.

After the region has been selected, you can drop in loop points by selecting the Loop This Section option under the Action pull-down menu. You will then see Beg Loop and End Loop markers in the waveform display (see Figure 5.26). Press Play and listen for pops and clicks between the beginning and end of the loop points. If you hear any, you can adjust the loop start and end points by navigating your mouse to the beginning or end of the loop and clicking and dragging the loop points left or right to locate zero crossings, where there is no audible activity.

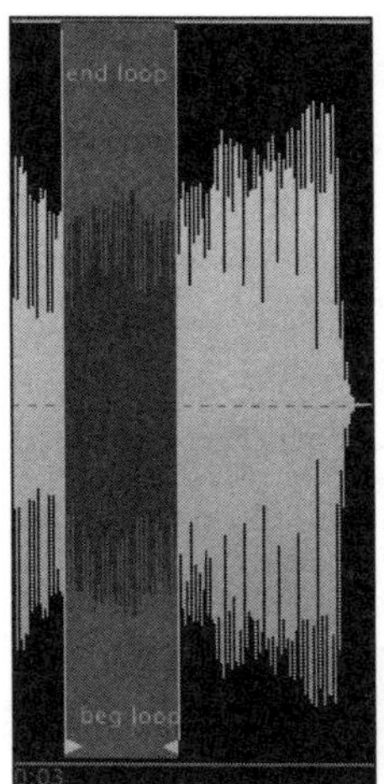

Figure 5.26

A loop has been established in the sample.

Fine-Tuning Loops

Upon listening to the loop, you might notice an audible inconsistency in the loop that you missed the first time around. This is not a problem. Like Sound Forge, Peak provides a handy tool called the Loop Tuner to fix the loop start and end points. Selecting Loop Tuner from the DSP pull-down menu will activate the Loop Tuner and launch its interface (see Figure 5.27). Once you have made your adjustments, just click OK, and the loop points will adjust accordingly.

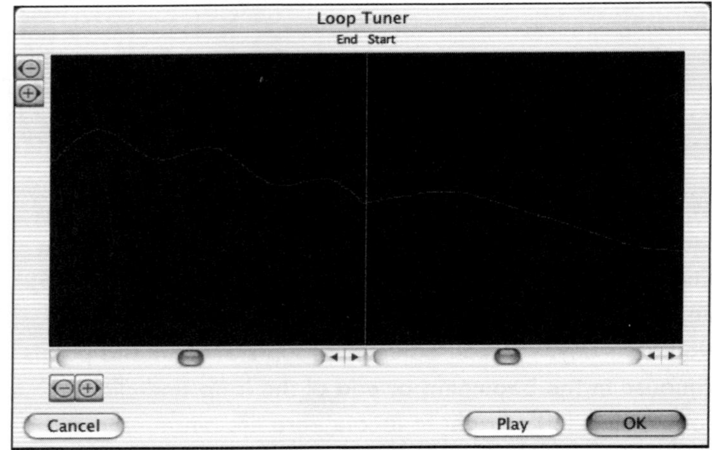

Figure 5.27

The Loop Tuner is used to fine-tune the loop points of your samples.

You can also use the Crossfade Loop and Envelope tool to fix any pops and clicks between loop points (see Figure 5.28). Just select the Crossfade Loop option from the DSP pull-down menu.

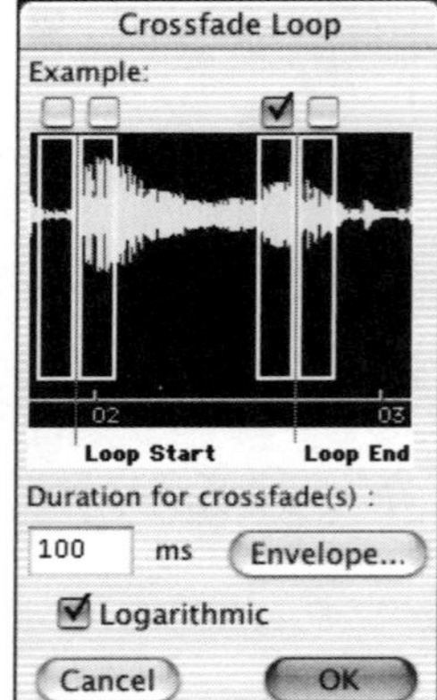

Figure 5.28

The Crossfade Loop tool is used to correct any pops and clicks between loop points.

Once you are done editing your loop points, you can save your audio file and load it into your sampler, and the loop points will still be viewed and active.

Offline Edits

An offline edit is a type of edit that is not performed in real time. This can include the simplest of edits, including deleting regions, normalizing, and creating fades. This can also include edits that require a little more comprehension and practice in performing, such as time stretching, pitch shifting, and panning adjustments. Throughout this section, I'll introduce you to a number of these offline edits, starting with deleting regions.

Deleting Regions

Deleting regions is simply selecting an undesired portion of an audio file with your mouse and then deleting it with the backspace key on your keyboard or using the Cut key command (Ctrl+X, Apple+X). This kind of edit is used primarily on audio files that contain unwanted empty space at the beginning or end of the file. To see this function, take a look at Figure 5.29 and read the caption below.

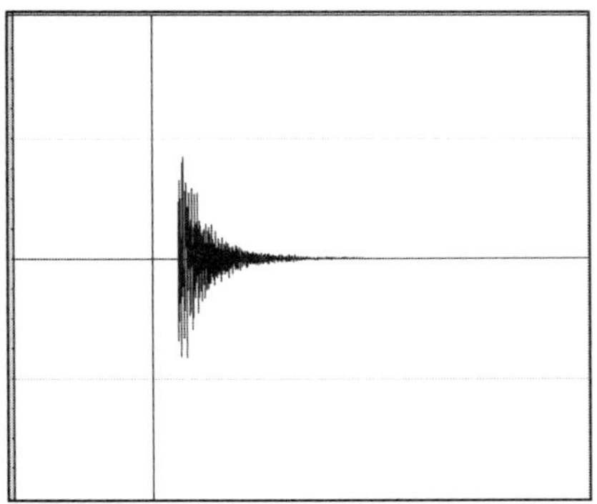

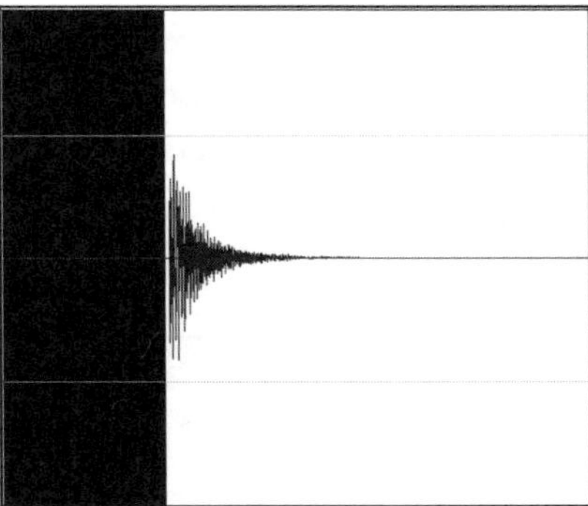

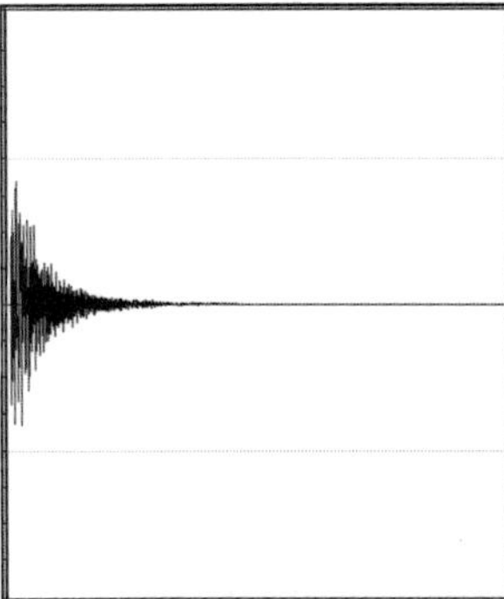

Figure 5.29

Looking at the left side of this figure, you can see that our drum sample contains a lot of empty space at the beginning of the file. I'll delete this space by selecting the empty region with my mouse (center) and then using the Cut key command Ctrl+X or Apple+X. Looking at the right side of this figure, you can see that the empty space has been deleted from the file. At this point, it would be a good idea to save your work by selecting Save from the File pull-down menu or using the Ctrl+S or Apple+S key command.

Normalization

Normalization is a function that finds the peak amplitude within an audio file, boosts it to an assigned amplitude level, and boosts the amplitude of the remaining audio data proportionately. This ensures that a sample can take advantage of its full dynamic range without clipping or digitally distorting. See Figure 5.30 below and read the caption for more information.

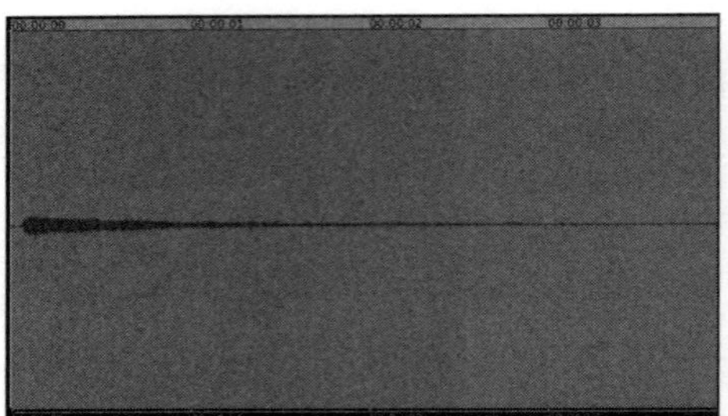
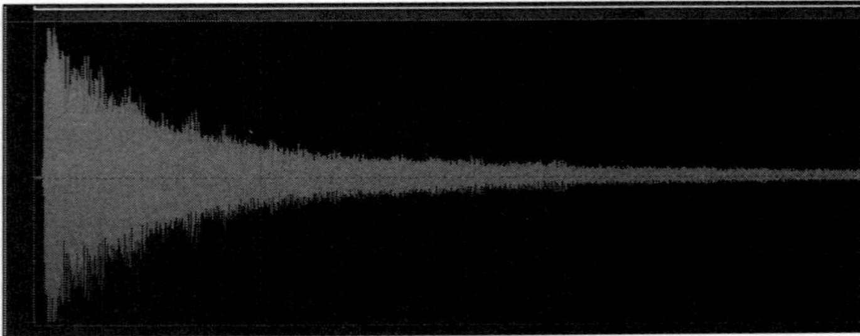

Figure 5.30

For this example, I have sampled a piano in Peak with minimal amplitude levels (as shown on the left) and applied a normalization process to the sample, which locates the peak amplitude and increases it to 0dB while increasing the rest of the sample's amplitude proportionately (as shown on the right). This results in a sample that plays back at its maximum amplitude potential while retaining its dynamic qualities.

This process can be applied to an audio file in Sound Forge by first selecting the entire audio file (Ctrl+A) and then selecting Normalize from the Process pull-down menu. This will launch the Normalize window, which offers many different normalization options, including a Preview function that allows you to monitor the process before applying it to your audio file (see Figure 5.31).

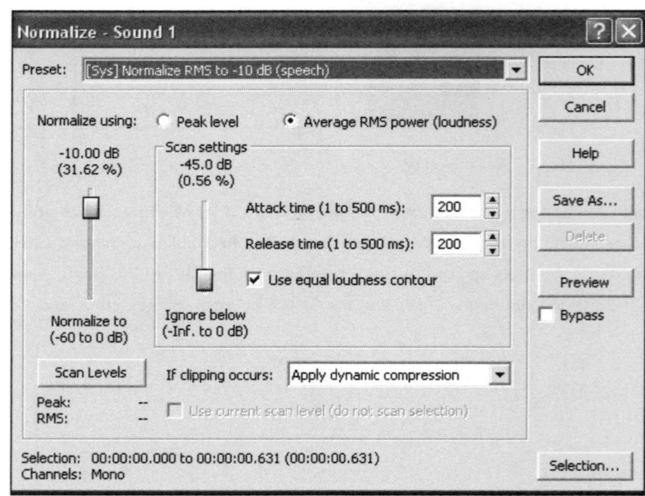

Figure 5.31

The Normalization window of Sound Forge offers many additional preferences and functions to shape the normalization before processing your audio file.

In Peak, normalization can be applied to an audio file by first selecting the entire audio file (Apple+A) and then selecting Normalize from the DSP pull-down menu. This will launch the Normalize window, which provides a slider to increase or decrease the amount of normalization to apply to your audio file (see Figure 5.32). Once you have set the slider, click the OK button and you're in business.

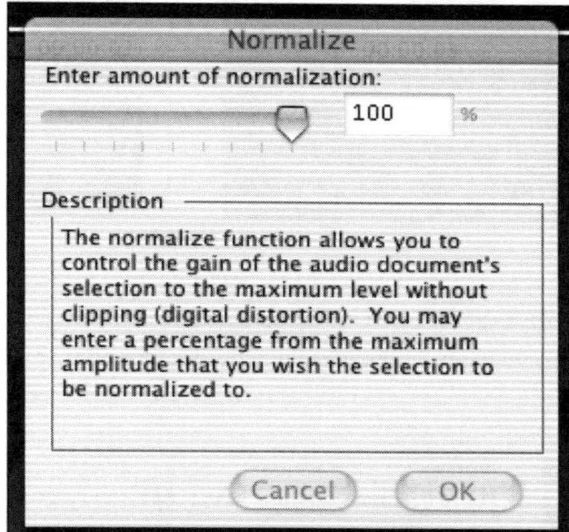

Figure 5.32

The Normalize window of Peak provides a handy definition of the Process and Amount slider.

KEEP IT CLEAN

When normalizing samples, it's imperative to remember that while you're increasing the overall volume of the sample, you're also increasing the volume of any noise embedded within the sample. So record your samples as cleanly as possible.

Reverse

The Reverse function is an offline process that creates a mirror instance of a selected region or entire audio file so that it can be played backward. It's very effective on drum loops and percussion samples in general (see Figure 5.33). To apply the reverse function to an audio file in Sound Forge, select a region or the entire audio file and then select Reverse from the Process pull-down menu. In Peak, select a region or the entire audio file and then select Reverse from the DSP pull-down menu.

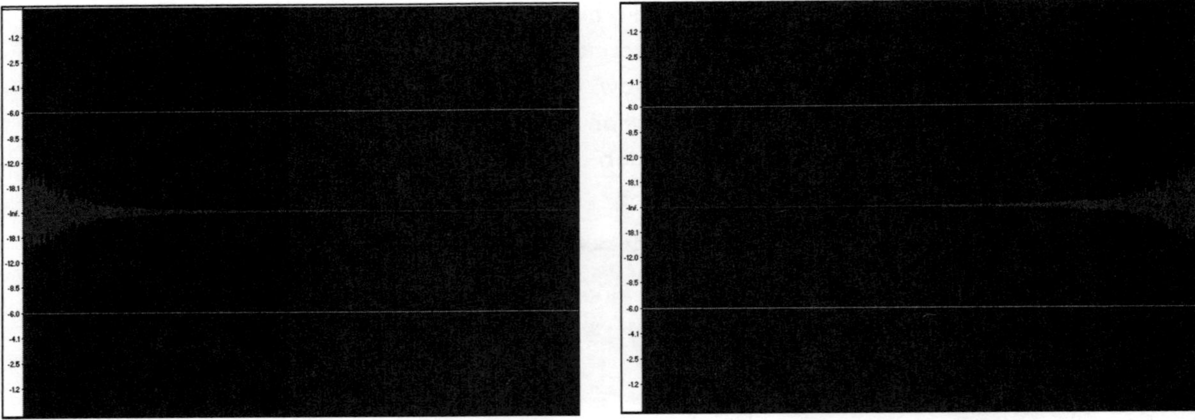

Figure 5.33

In the figure on the left, we have a crash cymbal, which is a perfect candidate for using with the reverse function as it can emulate the crescendo of a cymbal roll. The figure on the right displays the crash cymbal after being reversed.

> **CREATIVE REVERSING TIP**
>
> Here's a cool idea I sometimes use when working with drum loops to avoid the blandness of repetition. In Figure 5.34 I have selected the kick drum region of a loop, as I intend to reverse this region. After selecting the region, I apply the Reverse function, which results in a loop that sounds a little more interesting than it did before (see Figure 5.35).

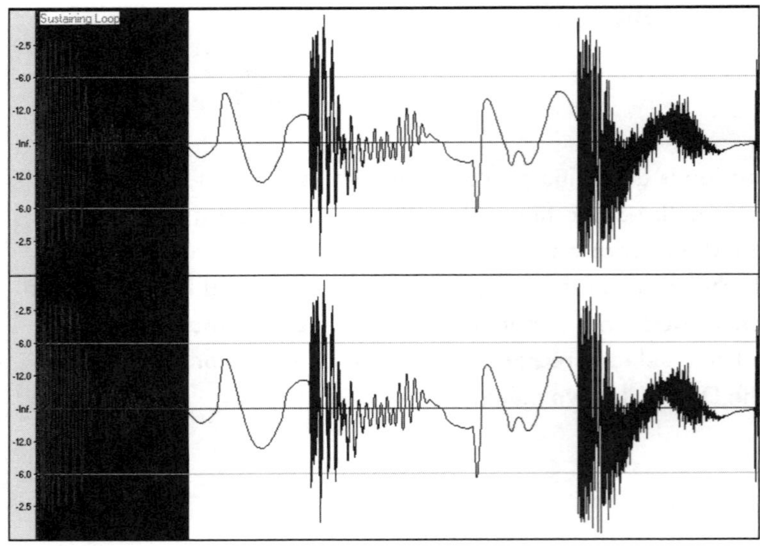

Figure 5.34

In this figure, I have opened a drum loop and selected a region on which I intend to apply a Reverse function.

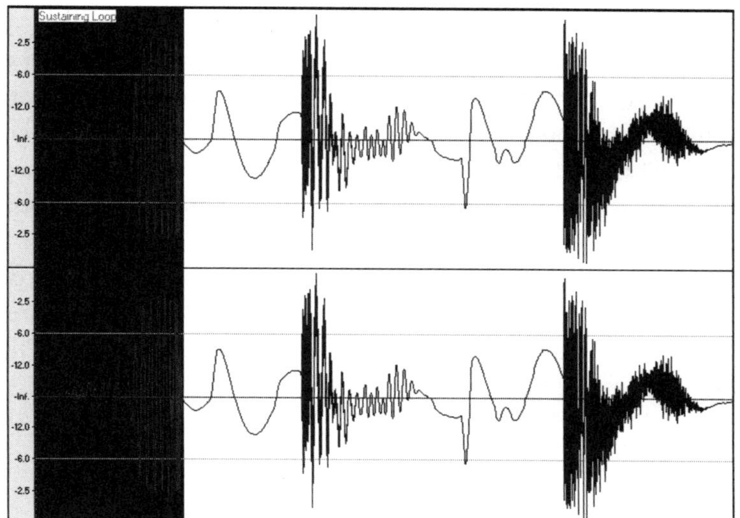

Figure 5.35

Here is the result.

Fades

Fades are used to alter the beginning or end of a sample by selecting the start or end region of a sample and then using the Fade function of either Sound Forge or Peak. They come in handy when you need to smooth the attack or decay of a sample, as you can see in Figure 5.36. To apply a fade-in/ -out using Sound Forge, first select the region and then select Process, Fade, In/Out. In Peak, select the appropriate region and then select DSP, Fade In/Fade Out.

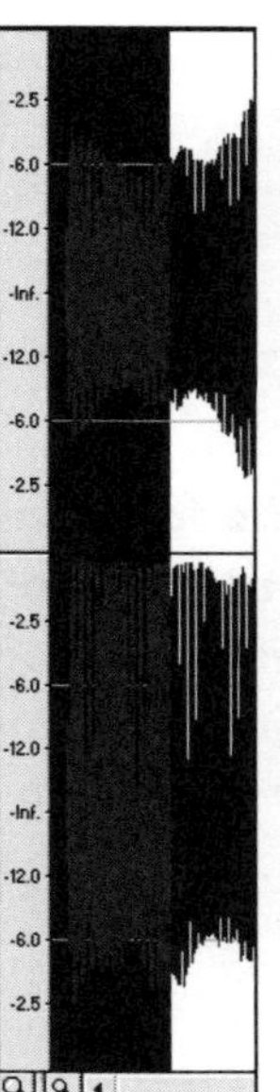

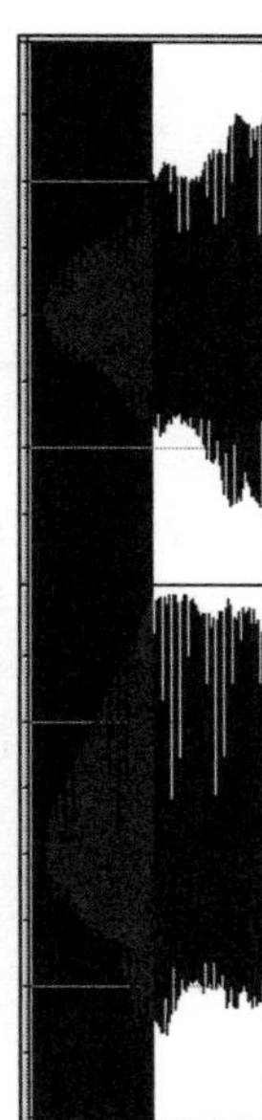

Figure 5.36

In the left figure I have selected a small region at the beginning of a sample and applied a fade-in to smooth out the attack of the sample, as you can see in the right figure.

DC Offset

When making analog to digital transfers, an anomaly known as a *DC offset* can occur, in which electric mismatches between your audio card and analog source create audible glitches and inconsistencies when applying different processes. While this is not a commonly encountered problem, it can be seen by zooming in on a problematic waveform and viewing its position along the zero level axis (see Figure 5.37). The DC Offset processor of Sound Forge and Peak corrects this anomaly by adjusting the waveform's position along the zero level axis of the waveform display. To correct this problem in Sound Forge, select the region, and then select Process, DC Offset. In Peak, select the region, and then select DSP, DC Offset.

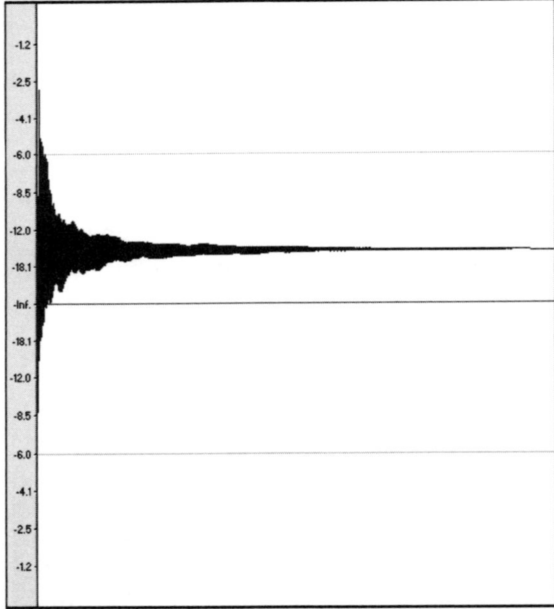

Figure 5.37
Looking at this waveform, you can see that it is a victim of DC offset by its off-center position along the zero level axis.

Creative Edits for Peak

Throughout the last section, I introduced you to the most commonly used offline edits that can be easily found in both Peak and Sound Forge. In this section, I will introduce you to a couple of additional offline edits that are exclusive to Peak and are great for creative sound design purposes.

Reverse Boomerang

The Reverse Boomerang is a process that mixes the original sample with a reversed copy, producing some very interesting results. In Figure 5.38 I have loaded a drum loop, selected the entire region, and applied the Reverse Boomerang process from the DSP pull-down menu.

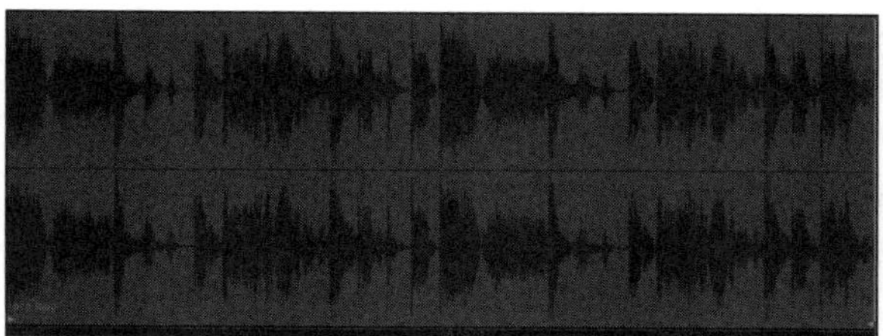

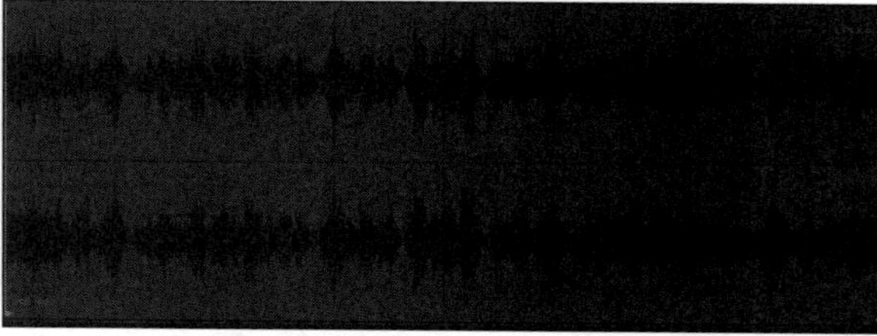

Figure 5.38

In the figure on the left, I have loaded a drum loop, selected the entire region, and processed it with the Reverse Boomerang. The result of this process can be seen in the figure on the right.

Rappify

Rappify is one of Peak's more eclectic offline processors (see Figure 5.39). It is a dynamic filter that can be applied to a drum loop or bass line to create a lo-fi effect. To use it, select a region of a sample and then select Rappify from the DSP pull-down menu. Set the adjustable slider to the desired amount of rappification and click the OK button to process.

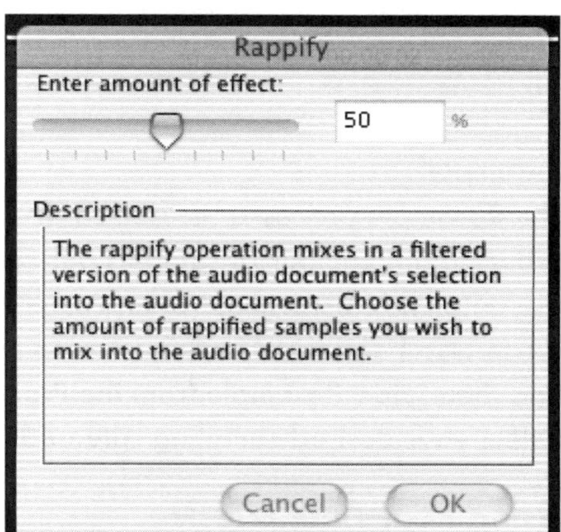

Figure 5.39

The Rappify processor is a dynamic filter that turns your hi-fi loops to lo-fi grunge.

Creative Edits for Sound Forge

Now let's have a look at a couple of Sound Forge offline processors, starting with the Gapper/Snipper.

Gapper/Snipper

The Gapper/Snipper processor is used to create a tremolo/warbling effect by chopping up a signal and cutting sections from it or inserting silence at determined frequencies. Select the entire region of an audio file in Sound Forge and select the Gapper/Snipper processor from the Effects pull-down menu to launch its interface (see Figure 5.40). If this is your first time using an effect like this, I suggest trying the presets until you get the hang of it. When you are satisfied with the effect, click the OK button to apply the process to the audio file.

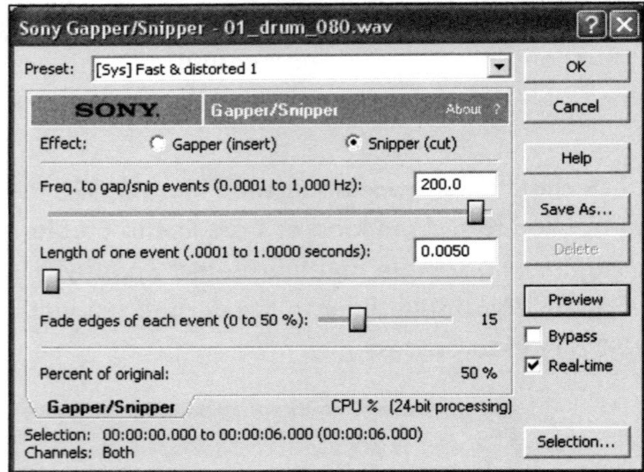

Figure 5.40
The Gapper/Snapper processor creates a tremolo effect by chopping up a signal. Try it with a drum loop and use the Fast & Distorted preset for fun.

Resample

The Resample processor is used to grunge down your ultra-clean samples by reducing the number of samples per second. It is a wonderful processor to use on a wide assortment of instruments to attain an old time sort of sound. It can also be used to increase the sample rate. To use it, select the region and then select Resample from the Process pull-down menu (see Figure 5.41). Select your desired sampling rate and click the OK button to process it.

Using Real-Time Effects

Aside from offline edits, both Peak and Sound Forge excel at making use of real-time effects to create wild and imaginative combinations of sounds and

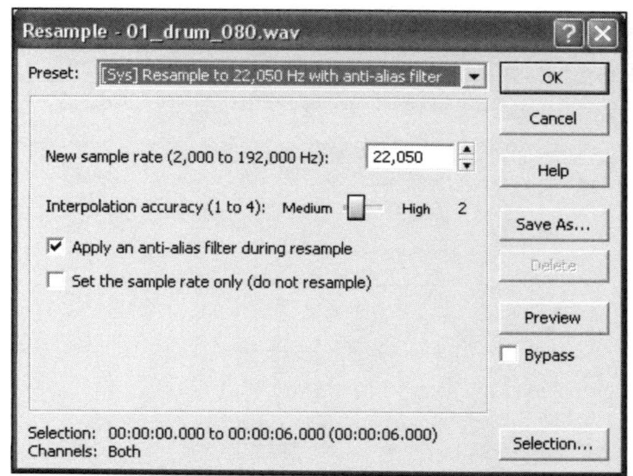

Figure 5.41

The Resample processor can be used to alter your crystal-clear drum loops and guitar samples to muddy lo-fi heaven.

textures. If you're unfamiliar with real-time effects, they are software emulations of outboard processors such as reverbs, distortions, and flangers that can be used within audio applications such as Sound Forge and Peak as plug-ins, which are sub-applications that run within a host program.

In this section, we'll look at using real-time effects within Sound Forge and Peak.

Using Effects with Sound Forge

As you probably already know, Sound Forge supports the DirectX plug-in format and includes many real-time effects such as delays, reverbs, and the excellent Acoustic Modeler. While we won't be able to cover all the included effects, I will take you through the steps of using them in Sound Forge by way of the Plug-In Chainer.

The Plug-In Chainer is a means by which several (up to 32) real-time effects can be compiled and used simultaneously within a single interface. It is a really cool feature, enabling you to create wild effect combinations that can be saved to be used again in the future. To activate the Plug-In Chainer, select View, Plug-In Chainer (see Figure 5.42). You can also use the Alt+9 key command.

Once you have the Plug-In Chainer open, we can load in some real-time effects. Click on the Add Plug-Ins to Chain button, located in the upper-right corner of the Chainer. This will launch the Plug-In Chooser window (see Figure 5.43).

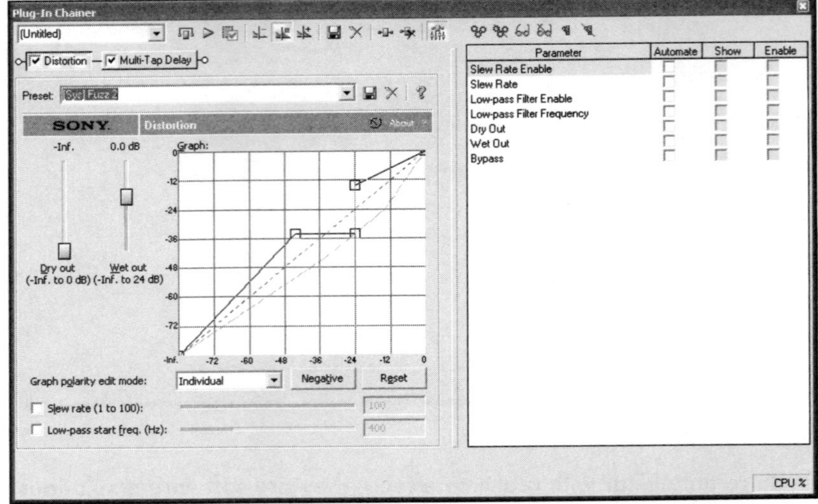

Figure 5.42
The Plug-In Chainer is used to compile several combinations of real-time effects at one time.

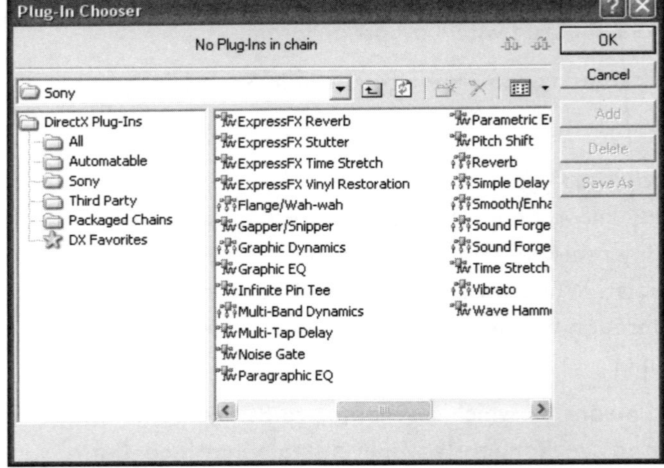

Figure 5.43
The Plug-In Chooser window is used to locate and activate real-time effects to be used in the Chainer.

For this example, I will choose a couple of the real-time effects that come with Sound Forge. First, I'll click on the Express FX Chorus to select it and click on the Add button to add it to our real-time effects chain. Next, I'll scroll to the right, select Reverb, and click the Add button to add it to our real-time effects chain. When I'm finished, I'll press OK, and both FX will be loaded into the Plug-In Chainer and be ready to use (see Figure 5.44).

After they're loaded into the Plug-In Chainer, the loaded effects can be previewed in real time by clicking on the Preview button in the upper portion of

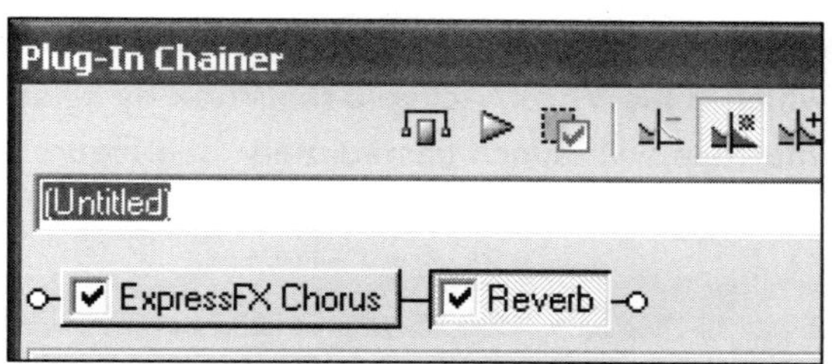

Figure 5.44
After clicking OK in the Plug-In Chooser window, my selected real-time effects are loaded into the Plug-In Chainer.

the Chainer interface. You should then be able to hear your sample processed by the real-time effects, which you can enhance even further by modifying the individual effects' parameters. Once you are happy with the overall mix of effects, you can process the sample with the effects by clicking the Process Selection button, located in the upper portion of the Chainer interface.

> **LEARNING MORE ABOUT SOUND FORGE**
> For those of you who want to learn more about Sound Forge, Course Technology provides a couple of ideal solutions, including the book *Sound Forge 6.0 Power!* by Scott Garrigus and the Sound Forge CSi Starter interactive CD-ROM by Robert Guérin. For more information, visit the Course Technology Web site at **www.courseptr.com**.

Using Effects with Peak

Peak supports the AudioUnit and VST plug-in formats, and it includes many fine real-time effects, such as the Freq4 Equalizer and Sqweez1.0 Compressor. Using real-time effects in Peak is a bit different from using them in Sound Forge, as there are a couple of different ways to do it. Clicking on the Plug-Ins pull-down menu, you can see seven options:

- **Insert 1**—This is used to load a real-time effect as an insert, which means that the sample is completely processed by the effect.
- **Insert 2**—This is used to load a real-time effect as an insert.
- **Insert 3**—This is used to load a real-time effect as an insert.
- **Insert 4**—This is used to load a real-time effect as an insert.
- **Insert 5**—This is used to load a real-time effect as an insert.
- **Vbox**—Similar to the Plug-In Chainer of Sound Forge, this is a means to load and configure a chain of real-time effects to be used to process a sample.
- **Bounce**—This function processes the sample with any active real-time effects.

Let's skip over the five inserts and get right to the best of the bunch here, which is the Vbox. Activate the Vbox by selecting Plug-Ins, Vbox, and the interface will launch immediately (see Figure 5.45).

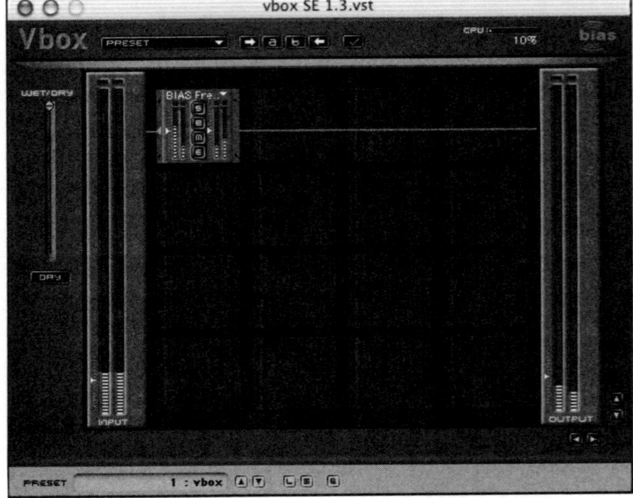

Figure 5.45
The Vbox is an intuitive interface to load chains of real-time effects.

Now that Vbox is open, let's load a couple of effects to use within the interface. I'll click on the first blank inactive box in the upper-left corner of Vbox and load an instance of the Freq4 (see Figure 5.46).

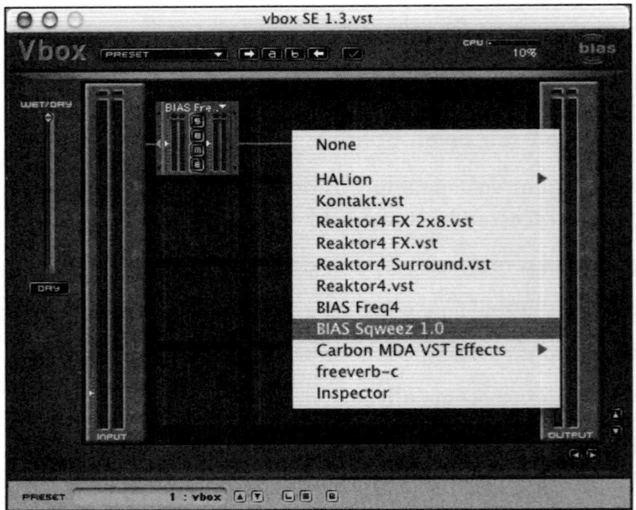

Figure 5.46
Click on any of the empty boxes to load a real-time effect into Vbox.

Looking back at Figure 5.45, you can see an LED meter on each side of the module to indicate that the effect is processing data, and you can also see four buttons:

- **Solo**—This will isolate the effect from any other active effects in Vbox.
- **Bypass**—This will bypass the effect.
- **Mute**—This will mute the effect.
- **Edit**—This will launch the graphic interface for the effect.

Now I will load another effect to show you how cool this feature really is. I'll click in the second empty box along the second row of the Vbox matrix and select an effect that's a bit more eclectic, such as the Dub Delay. Once it's activated, look at Figure 5.47, and you'll see that rather than feed the output of Freq4 into the input of the Dub Delay, it has split the signal at the source, which means that each effect is processing the sample separately, which produces an interesting overall mix.

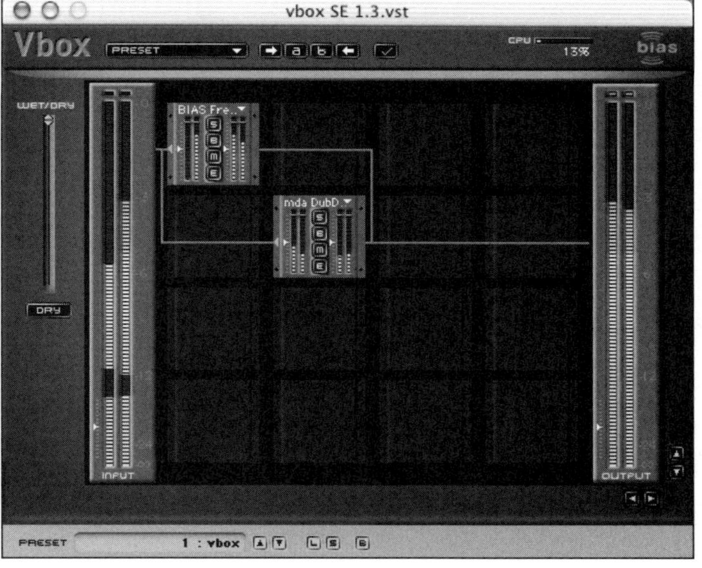

Figure 5.47
Once another effect is activated in another row of the Vbox matrix, Vbox splits the signal and sends it to each effect to be processed separately.

After you've found a mixture of effects you like, just select Plug-Ins, Bounce to process the sample with the loaded effects.

TOO MUCH FOR WORDS

As you can guess, there's much more than meets the eye when using real-time effects with Sound Forge and Peak. Since we don't have enough time to go through every nook and cranny of using effects with these applications, be sure to consult the manuals for some in-depth information on their particular features and procedures.

6 GigaStudio 3

When it comes to sampling in the virtual studio, GigaStudio 3 is the software sampler most used by both music professionals and hobbyists alike. When you see a movie or watch TV, I'd bet the money in my pocket that GigaStudio was used in some way to create its virtual orchestral soundtrack. With its simple, insightful graphic interface, GigaStudio 3 is considered by many to be a platform rather than just a sampler. In a nutshell, get ready to be wowed over the next several pages.

In this chapter, we'll cover the following topics:

- Configuration
- First look at GigaStudio 3
- Basic and intermediate/advanced Giga features
- Creating your first Giga instrument

A GIGA TO MATCH EVERY BUDGET

Tascam has three versions of GigaStudio 3 available, with prices to meet every budget. The only differences between each version are the number of simultaneous voices that can be played back (polyphony), the amount of included sample content, and the GigaPulse reverb effect. However, keep in mind that your processor speed, RAM, and hard drive determine the number of playable voices.

- **GigaStudio 3 Orchestra**—Has an unlimited number of voices and includes 17GB of content and GigaPulse.
- **GigaStudio 3 Ensemble**—Can play back 160 voices and includes 10GB of content.
- **GigaStudio 3 Solo**—Can play back 96 voices and includes 3GB of content. Also note that this version does not include the Distributed Wave Editor.

Configuring GigaStudio 3

Before launching GigaStudio 3 for the first time, you should configure your audio and MIDI hardware to ensure the maximum performance and potential from the Giga interface. To accomplish this, Tascam has provided utility software called the Configuration Manager, which is launched by selecting Start, Programs, Tascam, GigaStudio Configuration Manager. The interface should show up on your desktop in a flash (see Figure 6.1).

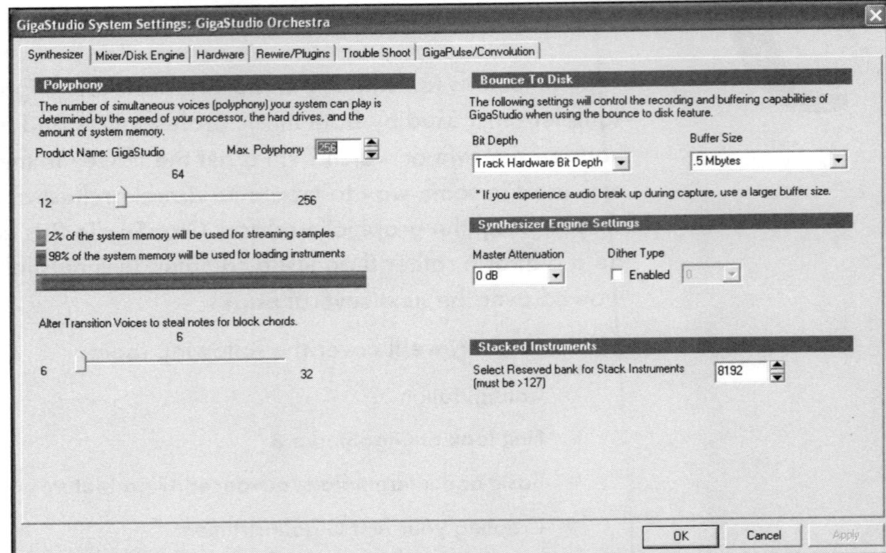

Figure 6.1

The GigaStudio Configuration Manager sets up your audio and MIDI hardware for use in GigaStudio 3.

Setting Up Your Audio Hardware

In this section, we'll set up your audio hardware to work with GigaStudio by way of the Configuration Manager. Please note that in order to use GigaStudio 3, you need to have an audio card that supports the Tascam GSIF driver standard. Read the following Note for more information about this driver. If your audio hardware doesn't have GSIF drivers available, you can also use GigaStudio via ReWire, which is a cool alternative way to go. I'll cover setting up ReWire later in this chapter. For now though, we'll assume that your audio hardware does support the GSIF standard and you're ready to go through the steps to set it up.

GSIF DRIVERS

Instead of adapting GigaStudio to work with the standard WDM and ASIO driver specifications, Tascam decided it was best to develop its own driver format to ensure the best performance possible with GigaStudio. GSIF 2 (GigaSampler Interface) drivers offer extremely tight, latency-free response from GigaStudio when used in real time.

What sets the GSIF 2 standard apart from ASIO or WDM? Tascam Marketing Manager Pete Snell explains: "ASIO and WDM are both 'user level' initiated drivers which force us to run audio through the kernel (the core of the operating system) and up to the user level before we have access to it. With GSIF 2 we are capable of real time FX processing on incoming audio as well as incoming MIDI."

Pete adds: "I am now seeing a 2–4ms increase from MIDI input to audio output with the new GSIF 2 drivers. I think we have finally reached and perhaps surpassed hardware samplers with latency response."

For more information about GSIF and to find out which audio cards support it, visit the Tascam Hardware Compatibility Web page at **www.tascamgiga.com/support/hardware.php**.

MY AUDIO CARD

My audio card is an Audiophile 2496 by M-Audio. This is a great, compact solution that includes two analog inputs/outputs, a S/PDIF digital I/O, and a MIDI I/O. For $149 MSRP, it's an affordable and versatile audio interface.

Let's begin by clicking on the Hardware tab of the Configuration interface. This tab configures your audio and MIDI setup (see Figure 6.2). The upper half of this tab, called the Hardware Adapter, is used to select your audio card, set the bit depth/sampling rate, and enable its available inputs and outputs. The lower half of this tab, called the MIDI Port Configuration, is used to select and arrange your MIDI inputs and outputs.

To select an audio interface, simply click in the upper-left pull-down menu of the Hardware tab, which will display a list of available GSIF and Direct Sound drivers. The type of driver selected should be displayed right next to the pull-down menu. Looking at Figure 6.3, you can see that I have selected my Audiophile 2496 card, which supports the GSIF standard.

Once the audio card has been selected, you can set its bit depth and sampling rate by using the corresponding pull-down menus below the audio card selector. If this is your first time setting up GigaStudio 3, I would use a bit depth of 24 bits and a sampling rate of 44100Hz (or 44.1kHz).

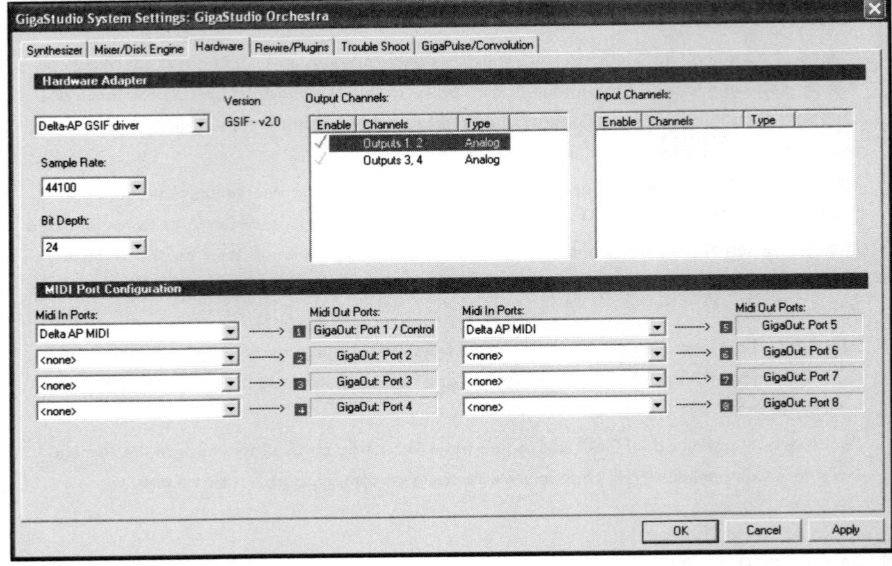

Figure 6.2
The Hardware tab selects and arranges your audio and MIDI setup.

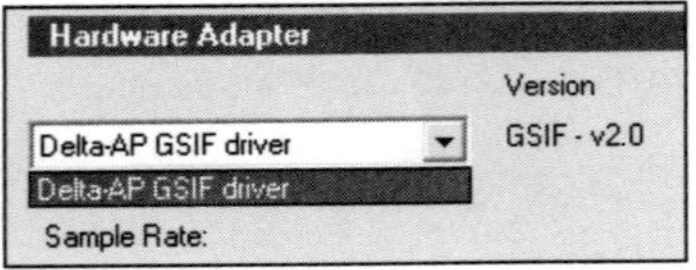

Figure 6.3
The Audiophile 2496 is my preferred audio card for GigaStudio, as it includes a GSIF driver.

The right side of the Hardware Adapter enables or disables your available audio inputs and outputs. Although I am using an audio card that has two analog inputs/outputs and a stereo digital I/O, the audio inputs are not yet supported in the current version of M-Audio's GSIF driver, so they are not listed in the inputs dialog (see Figure 6.4).

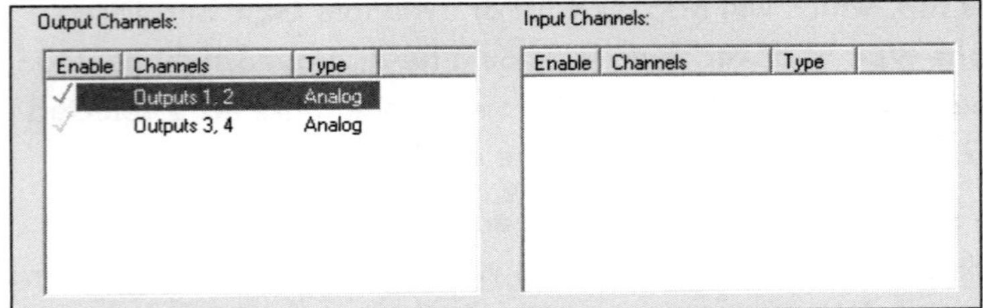

Figure 6.4
Place a check mark next to the appropriate audio outputs of your audio card.

At this point, my audio hardware has been selected and configured. Next we'll configure the MIDI hardware.

Setting Up Your MIDI Hardware

As previously mentioned, the lower half of the Hardware tab is dedicated to selecting and configuring your MIDI interface for GigaStudio. Although I will be using the MIDI interface included with the Audiophile card and a keyboard to trigger the samples, it should be noted that you could also use the virtual keyboard of GigaStudio to trigger samples without the need for a MIDI interface or keyboard. This makes for a very portable laptop solution.

Figure 6.5 shows the MIDI Port Configuration interface. As you can see, GigaStudio is capable of receiving up to eight physical MIDI inputs. Since this is an introduction to GigaStudio, let's keep it simple and use the first pull-down menu in the upper-left corner of this interface to select the Audiophile MIDI In as our input device.

Click the Apply button and then OK to close the window. We're now ready to begin using GigaStudio 3.

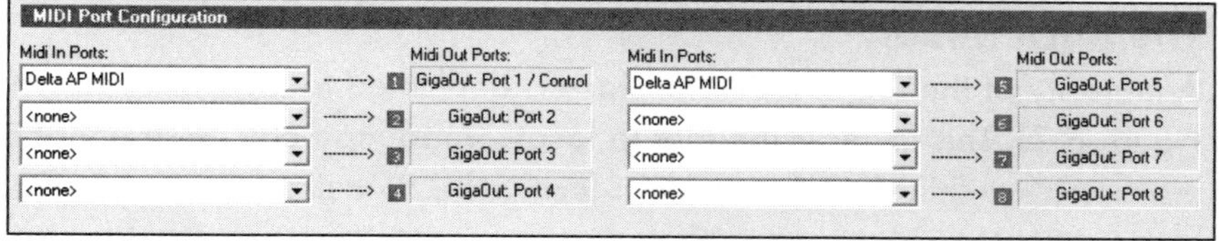

Figure 6.5
The MIDI Port Configuration interface assigns your MIDI inputs to GigaStudio.

The Giga Interface—A First Look

Launch GigaStudio 3 and take a look at its graphic interface (see Figure 6.6). To launch GigaStudio, select Start, Programs, Tascam, GigaStudio3. Throughout this section of the chapter, we'll cover the following topics.

- The MIDI Mixer
- The QuickSound Loader
- The DSP Station
- The Virtual Keyboard

Figure 6.6
The GigaStudio 3 graphic interface.

The MIDI Mixer

A majority of the GigaStudio interface is dedicated to the MIDI Mixer (see Figure 6.7). This mixer is the tool to locate, load, and edit a variety of Giga instruments within a *performance*, which is the default name of a GigaStudio session. It's like using the word *document* for a Microsoft Word file.

Figure 6.7
The MIDI Mixer loads and edits Giga instruments.

Looking at Figure 6.7, you can see that the MIDI Mixer is split into two sections.

- **Instrument Slots**—These are the individual spaces reserved for each loaded Giga instrument. From here, you can load up to 16 individual instruments (one for every MIDI channel) and then edit them using the supplied parameters to the right.
- **Tabs**—These are used to select the available MIDI ports, each of which contains 16 instrument slots. When you do the math, this gives you up to 128 individual Giga instruments that can be loaded into a single performance. However, keep in mind that each instrument will use up RAM, CPU, and hard drive resources, so at some point your computer will run out of juice. Also note that each version of GigaStudio offers a different number of tabs. The Orchestra version (shown in Figure 6.7) offers 8 tabs, the Ensemble version offers 4 tabs, and the Solo version offers 2 tabs.

> **SUPER SIZE IT**
>
> A majority of the graphic interface of GigaStudio can be resized to your liking by simply clicking and dragging any of its resize bars. For example, I can resize the MIDI Mixer by clicking and dragging the resize bar up and down (see Figure 6.8). The same can also be done with the DSP Station and the QuickSound Loader.

Figure 6.8
Click and drag any of the resize bars to adjust and customize the GigaStudio interface.

We'll discuss how to load and edit instruments later in this chapter. For now, let's discuss the QuickSound Loader.

The QuickSound Loader

The QuickSound Loader occupies the lower half of the GigaStudio interface (see Figure 6.9). While its primary use is to quickly load instruments into the MIDI Mixer, there's a lot more here than meets the eye. The QuickSound Loader can be used as a preview tool to audition instruments before loading them, and it has an intuitive search function that can locate Giga instrument files and individual digital audio files to load into the MIDI Mixer. In short, the QuickSound Loader is a "locate, lock, and load" audio database monster!

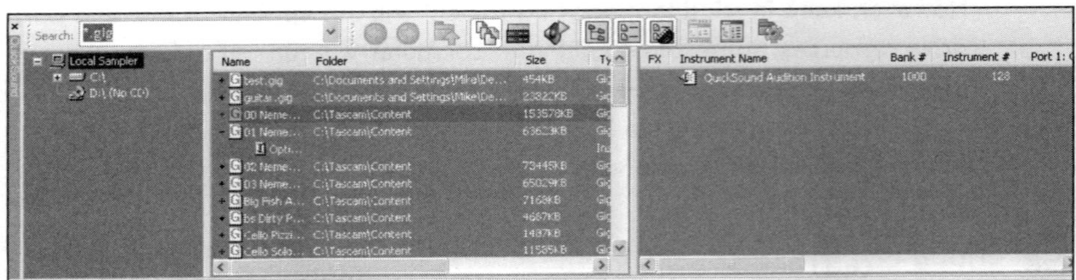

Figure 6.9
The QuickSound Loader searches, locates, auditions, and loads Giga instruments into your performance.

The interface of the QuickSound Loader is split into four sections:

- The Toolbar
- The Folder Tree
- The Instrument List view
- The Loaded Instrument view

The Toolbar customizes the layout of the QuickSound Loader and includes the following parameters:

- **Search**—This pull-down menu specifies the file format you wish to have the QuickSound Loader look for. Included are .gig, .gsi, .gsp, and .wav.
- **Previous/Next Folder/Up**—These buttons navigate through the folders of your computer, just like Windows Explorer.
- **Audition Mode**—When activated, the Audition mode enables you to load several Giga instruments into a selected slot one at a time in order to audition their sounds. For example, you can load a piano into instrument slot #1, but if you are not happy with it, you can double-click another instrument to load it into the same slot. The previous instrument will be detached but can be reloaded at any time.

- **Stack Instruments on One MIDI Channel**—When activated, this allows you to load multiple Giga instruments into the MIDI Mixer, which will respond to a single MIDI channel. This is a very cool idea for musicians who want to thicken up their sound by loading a piano Giga instrument and then stack a harp Giga instrument on top of that.
- **Audition Sample**—This button auditions samples within an instrument. Simply click on a Giga instrument from the Instrument List view and click the Audition button to hear a sample. You can also click this button again to stop the sample from playing while being auditioned.
- **Show/Hide**—These buttons are used to show or hide the Folder Tree, Instrument list, or Loaded Instrument list.
- **Dock/Maximize QuickSound Browser**—These buttons resize the QuickSound Loader. Click the Maximize button to max out the browser and the Dock button to restore it to the standard view.
- **QuickSound Settings**—This button will launch the GigaStudio Settings window and display the QuickSound Settings page (see Figure 6.10).

The Folder Tree is used like Windows Explorer. It browses through your entire computer in order to locate folders or drives that contain Giga instruments. It is also used to browse, convert, and import Akai formatted samples by way of your CD drive.

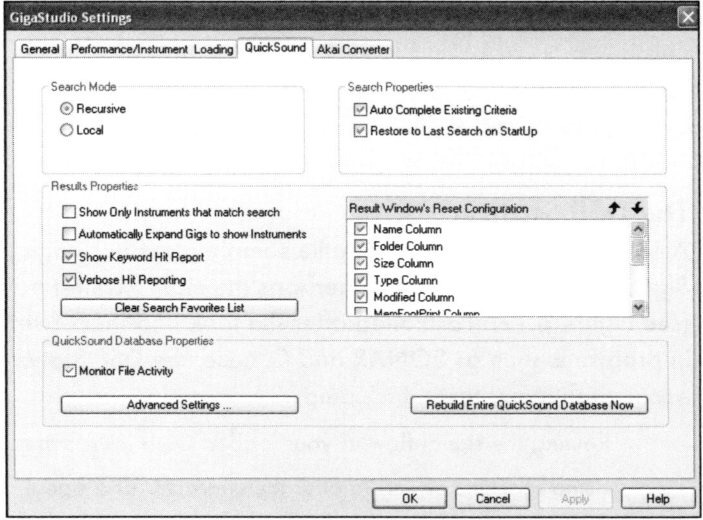

Figure 6.10

The GigaStudio Settings window customizes your GigaStudio interface. Currently, you are viewing this window with the QuickSound settings page.

IMPORTING AKAI SAMPLES

An important feature of GigaStudio is its ability to import Akai formatted samples, since there are a lot of GigaStudio users (like me) who own an extensive library of Akai samples. I'll take you through the steps of importing Akai samples later in this chapter.

The Instrument list displays the contents of an Instrument Search. Once located and displayed in this list, an instrument can be auditioned by clicking on it once and then clicking the Audition Sample button from the Toolbar. Additionally, instruments can be loaded into the MIDI Mixer by simply double-clicking on the instrument file or clicking and dragging it into the MIDI Mixer.

The Loaded Instrument list is used to list the entire loaded instrument contents within a GigaStudio performance. It is also used to unload single or multiple instruments from the GigaStudio interface and apply a special intelligent MIDI function called iMIDI.

You can close the QuickSound Loader by clicking on its Close Window button in the upper-left corner of the QuickSound interface or by clicking on the Toggle Loader Pane button in the master toolbar at the top of the Giga interface (see Figure 6.11).

Figure 6.11
Using its Close Window button can close the QuickSound Loader.

The DSP Station

Aside from an extremely versatile sample playback engine, the DSP (Digital Signal Processing) Station is perhaps the most exciting part of GigaStudio 3 (see Figure 6.12). Fashioned after the look and feel of virtual mixers found in programs such as SONAR and Cubase, the DSP Station is meant to accomplish many tasks, including:

- Routing the signal flow of your loaded Giga instruments.
- Using real-time effects to alter the character of a signal.
- Routing audio into the Giga interface to be recorded and used.

Figure 6.12

The DSP Station is a highlight of GigaStudio 3. It emulates the look and feel of a pro audio mixing board and includes some outrageous real-time effects, including the brand-new GigaPulse.

To activate the DSP Station, click on the Display DSP Station button in the master toolbar of the Giga interface. The MIDI Mixer will be closed, but it can always be seen again by clicking the Display MIDI Mixer button.

Looking at the bottom of the DSP Station, you can see that it is split into four tabs:

- **Inputs**—This is the default view of the DSP Station, and it alters the levels, pans, and mutes of the loaded Giga instruments within a performance. In addition, this tab adds insert effects, send effects, dynamics, and equalization to each individual mixer channel.
- **Groups**—This view controls the group channels of the DSP Station, which allow global control over multiple Giga instruments.
- **Aux Returns**—This view selects, activates, and edits any of GigaStudio's real-time effects.
- **Output Masters**—This view mixes the master outputs of GigaStudio as well as inputting a live audio signal for recording.

There are many features shared by these tabs. Let's take a closer look at each tab.

The Inputs Tab

As mentioned earlier, the Inputs tab alters the level and panning of each loaded Giga instrument within a performance. However, the Inputs tab is also used to introduce real-time effects, dynamics, and equalization by way of an extremely easy to use interface.

One Input—Two Views

Each input channel has a narrow and a wide view, which can be toggled between by clicking on the arrow pointing to the right at the upper region of the input channel (see Figure 6.13). The narrow view accesses commonly used parameters such as volume, pan, mute, and solo, while the wide view accesses the real-time effects, dynamics, and equalization.

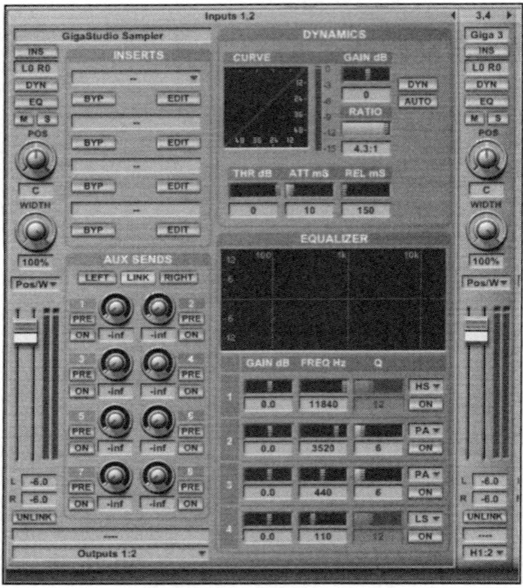

Figure 6.13
Each input channel can be viewed in either a narrow or a wide view.

Let's discuss the various basic parameters of the narrow view and then move on to the wide view. Read the list below and use Figure 6.14 as a reference image.

- **Input Source**—Select a source of signal input, which can be either a Giga instrument loaded into the MIDI Mixer or an input from your audio card.
- **Activation Buttons**—These buttons activate and bypass the insert effects, dynamic effects, and equalizer.
- **Mute/Solo**—These buttons activate and deactivate the mute and solo functions.
- **POS**—This knob adjusts the panning position of a stereo Giga instrument.
- **Width**—This knob enhances the panning position of a stereo Giga instrument.

- **Pan Mode Select**—This pop-up menu selects the function of the POS and Width knobs. The Position/Width mode is selected by default. When Mono Mode is selected, the POS and Width knobs become Pan Left/Pan Right knobs, which function independently of each other. When set to Reverse Mode, the POS and Width knobs become Pan Left/Pan Right knobs that are linked together.
- **Fader**—This adjusts the amplitude of the input channel. This fader can be used in stereo when linked or split into two independent faders when unlinked.
- **Fader Mode (Link Status)**—These buttons link and unlink the stereo input channel. When the input channel is unlinked, the stereo channel fader is split into two mono faders, and the left/right pan knobs function independently.
- **Outputs**—This dialog assigns an output to the input channel. By default, this is set to the master outputs of your audio card, but you can assign it to a group channel as well, which provides some interesting benefits that we'll discuss later.

Figure 6.14
This is the rundown of the narrow view of an input channel strip.

Into the Great Wide View

Now let's expand the view of the input channel and discuss its various parameters. Read the list and use Figure 6.15 as a reference image.

Figure 6.15
This is the rundown of the wide view of an input channel strip.

Let's begin with the Insert section of the wide view. As you read earlier in this chapter, an insert effect processes the entire signal of a Giga instrument, and each input channel supports up to four individual insert effects. This differs greatly from Aux Send effects, which process a mix of unprocessed and processed signals. That said, there are certain effects that work well as inserts, such as a compressor or equalizer, as they don't produce a noticeable amount of latency. However, there are other effects, such as reverb and delay, that don't work so well as insert effects because they can produce a great amount of latency. In either case, let's discuss the various insert parameters.

- **Insert Assign Slots**—These call up an insert effect to be used on a channel input. If you click and hold in this dialog, a pop-up window will list all the available insert effects to choose from. It should be noted that along with the included Giga effects, GigaStudio also supports the VST Plug-In format, which will appear in this list. After an effect is loaded, you can remove it by clicking on the assign slot and selecting Remove.
- **Bypass**—This button bypasses the loaded effect. This is a great way to A/B a Giga instrument with and without the loaded effect.
- **Edit**—This button launches the graphic interface of the loaded insert effect.

Just below the Insert section is the Aux Send section, which sends your dry Giga instrument to one or several (up to 8) real-time effects, such as a delay or reverb. That signal is then processed in the Aux Return tab (we'll talk about that later) and then returned to the overall mix. This gives you a mixed ratio of dry and wet or unprocessed and processed signal.

Using Aux Send conserves CPU power. Using a reverb as an Aux Send enables you to send multiple input channels to that single effect to be processed, rather than creating individual reverb effects for each channel, which would eat your precious CPU for lunch.

So we can agree that Aux Sends are a good thing, yes? Let's review the parameters of the Aux Send section.

- **Left/Right/Link**—These buttons are used to specify which channel will be used to send a signal to an effect. When Link is activated, both the left and right channels are sent to an effect. When it is inactive, you will need to select either the Left or Right button to specify which channel will be sent to a real-time effect.

- **On**—This activates the Aux Send.
- **Pre**—When activated, this puts the Aux Send into pre-fader mode, which means that the signal is sent to the effect before the input channel fader. Try activating this, sending some signal to an effect and then pulling the input channel fader back. You should hear the ghost reflections of the effect, as the fader in pre-fader mode no longer controls them.
- **Send Knob**—This knob sends a portion of your dry signal off to the real-time effect.

We'll be sure to revisit this section later in the chapter when I introduce you to the Aux Returns tab.

The Dynamics section enhances your Giga instruments by introducing a real-time compressor/limiter effect. The Dynamics section can be thought of as a supplementary insert effect, as it processes the entire signal just as an insert effect would. The Dynamics section includes the following parameters:

- **Graphic Display**—This produces a graphic representation of the gain response of a signal that is fed through the Dynamics section. You'll see this display change as the Dynamic parameters are changed.
- **DYN**—This button activates or bypasses the Dynamics section. Note that this button is also available on the input channel when in the narrow view.
- **Auto**—This button pre-calculates the make-up gain for a signal after being compressed. This ensures that the overall signal will sound balanced, even though it is being compressed.
- **Gain Slider**—This slider controls the overall output of the compressed signal.
- **Ratio**—This slider sets the compression/limiting ratio. It has a range of 1:1 (no compression) to INF:1 (limiting only).
- **Threshold**—This slider sets the threshold or "ceiling" to your compression effect.
- **Attack**—This slider determines when the compression effect will occur after the threshold has been reached. It has a range of 0 to 100ms.
- **Release**—This slider determines the amount of time before the compression effect is no longer used. It has a range of 5 to 5000ms.

ASSIGNABLE PARAMETERS

Just about any parameter in GigaStudio can be controlled via MIDI. Right-click on the parameter. A new window will pop open, prompting you to assign a MIDI controller to that particular parameter by turning a knob/pushing a slider of a MIDI controller device (see Figure 6.16). The controller you use can be anything from a Phat Boy by Keyfax to an EZBus by Event Electronics. Once finished, click OK and you're set.

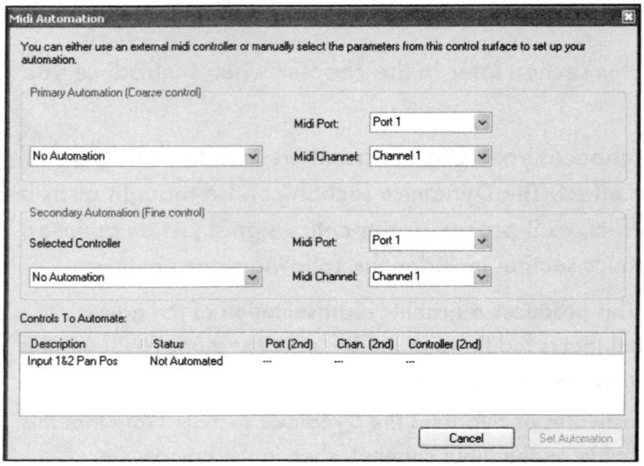

Figure 6.16

You can assign just about any Giga parameter to a MIDI controller of your choice by simply right-clicking and then turning a knob/pushing a slider on the MIDI controller of your choice.

Lastly, the Equalizer section introduces an equalizer (EQ for short) into your signal. Equalization enhances an overall signal by cutting and/or boosting the amplitude of specific frequency ranges called *bands* within the entire frequency spectrum. It is a very necessary effect when mixing your music through programs such as GigaStudio or DAW applications like Cubase or Pro Tools. Let's review the available parameters:

- **On**—Each of the four bands has an On button to activate that band. There are three values to this parameter: On (bright green), Off (gray), and Bypassed (dim green).
- **EQ Type**—This pop-up menu selects the type of EQ to apply to a specific band. You can choose between Off, Parametric, Notch, Low Pass, High Pass, Low Shelf, and High Shelf.
- **Gain**—This slider boosts or cuts the overall amplitude of an activated EQ band.
- **Frequency**—This slider is used to assign the center frequency of an activated EQ band. It has a range of 16Hz to 21kHz (or 21,000Hz).

- **Q**—This slider adjusts the width of the activated EQ band. It has a range of 1 to 36.

The Groups Tab

The Groups tab compiles a collection of signals from the Inputs tab in order to establish a global control over the entire collection from a single interface. This is very similar to the function of a buss fader that you would find on a hardware mixer.

How does a group fader work? Let's assume that you have a recording session that contains multiple audio drum tracks (channel one, kick; channel two, snare; and so on). While playing back your song, you decide that you would like to mute the drums from the mix, which means that you would have to mute every single drum track one at a time. Doing this several times over the course of a recording session can be tedious and frustrating. Grouping fixes all of this, as it enables you to route or "buss" every drum track to a single stereo pair fader, which includes its own assortment of parameters, including solo, mute, pan, and effects (both insert and Aux Send). Once all of your drum tracks have been routed to a single group fader, you can then control your entire drum ensemble from one interface (see Figure 6.17).

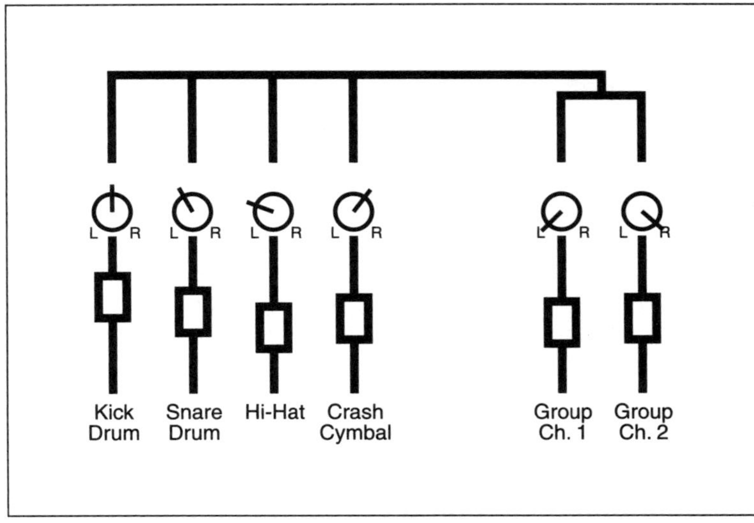

Figure 6.17
This diagram represents the concept of using a group channel to control multiple audio signals globally.

Creating and Using Groups

Figure 6.17 shows the purpose and intended use for the Groups tab. It globally controls the dynamics of multiple Giga instruments from a single control. Looking at Figure 6.18, you can see that a majority of the Groups tab parameters mirror those found on the Inputs tab. Each channel can be displayed in either a narrow or wide view and use insert and aux effects, dynamics, and equalization. That being said, there is really no reason to go over the individual parameter of the Groups tab, so I'll cut to the chase and show you how to set up a Group channel.

1. Let's begin by assuming that you have a song playing from a sequencer that triggers multiple Giga instruments loaded into the Inputs tab by way of the MIDI Mixer. Click at the bottom of channel one of the Inputs tab and select Group 1,2 to route the output of channel one to the first group channel of the Groups tab (see Figure 6.19).
2. Repeat the previous step with each additional input channel that has an active Giga instrument.
3. Switch to the Groups tab and play your song. You should now see the routed signals of the Inputs tab routed to the first channel of the Groups tab.
4. While the song plays back, activate the Mute and Solo buttons to hear the audible results.

Figure 6.18

The Groups tab is a set of 16 stereo faders that work in combination with the channels of the Inputs tab.

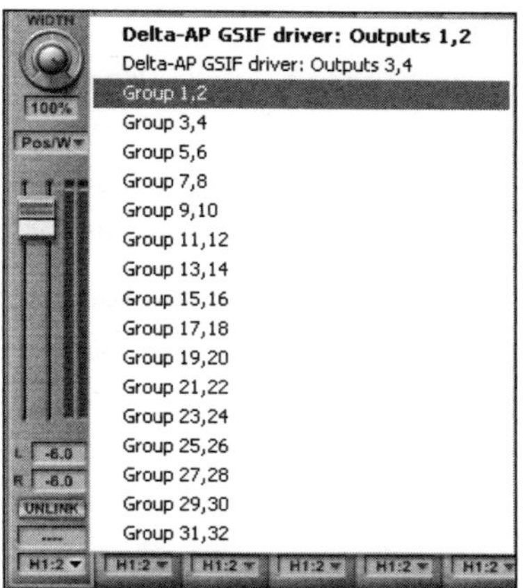

Figure 6.19

The audio output of channel one has been routed to the first group fader.

The Aux Returns Tab

The Aux Returns tab sets up your real-time effects to use with the Aux Send knobs of the Inputs and Groups tabs (see Figure 6.20). It is not all that hard to understand, since it's laid out clearly.

Figure 6.20

The Aux Returns tab activates the real-time effects you wish to use as Aux Sends. Note that each channel of this tab has four insert slots, which means that you can stack multiple effects onto a single Aux Return. Very cool indeed.

Setting Up Your Aux Sends

In this section, I will introduce you to the individual parameters of the Aux Returns tab and show you how to set it up to be used with the Inputs and Groups tabs. First, let's discuss the main parameters. Use Figure 6.20 as a reference and read the list below.

- **Insert Activation**—Located at the top of the channel strip, this button activates/deactivates/bypasses any loaded effects.
- **Insert Assign Slots**—These are used to load real-time effects as inserts. There are four slots per channel, and they can use either the provided native effects of GigaStudio or VST plug-ins.
- **Bypass**—Located below each insert slot, this button bypasses the insert effect.
- **Edit**—Located below each insert slot, this button launches the graphic interface of the active insert effect.
- **Fader**—This alters the amount of return level, which is responsible for returning an effect to the overall mix of GigaStudio.
- **Link/Unlink**—This button links or unlinks the stereo returns. When a return channel is unlinked, the fader is split into two separately controlled faders.
- **Return Name Field**—This assigns a name to your return channel. Just double-click in the field and type your chosen name. For example, if return channel one has a reverb loaded in it, you would want to name it Reverb in the field.
- **Channel Output**—Located at the very bottom, this pop-up menu allows you to assign your return channel to a specific audio card output.

Now that you understand the Aux Returns tab a little better, let's set it up with a reverb and apply that to a Giga instrument loaded into input channel one.

1. Navigate your mouse to the first insert slot of the first Aux Return channel, and then click and hold to display a list of available effects.
2. From the list, select NFX1 Reverb Multi from the Native FX subdirectory. This will launch the graphic interface of the effect and place it in insert slot one of the first Aux Return channel.
3. At this point, you can close the graphic interface of the effect, since we will just use the default settings for this tutorial.
4. Navigate back to the Inputs tab, select input channel one, and place it in its wide view.

5 Activate Aux Send one and use the Send knob to send a portion of the dry signal off to the NFX1 Reverb.

Now, play a few notes of the loaded Giga instrument, and you should hear the ghost reflections of the NFX reverb.

Let's go ahead and take it a step further by dropping a delay effect on the same Aux Return channel in order to create an FX chain.

1. Navigate back to the Aux Returns tab, select Aux Return channel one, and then click and hold in the second insert slot to display a list of available effects.
2. From the list, select NFX Tap Delay from the Native FX subdirectory. Just as before, the graphic interface will launch, at which point you can select the preset of your choice.
3. As Aux Send one is already sending a signal to this Aux Return channel, you can now play the Giga instrument to hear the reverb and delay effects simultaneously.

> **GIVE IT 100 PERCENT**
>
> When using the faders of the Aux Returns tab, I recommend leaving them at a value of 100% (or –6dB), so the returned processed audio signal will sound even within the overall mix. Remember, if you want to hear less of an effect on a Giga instrument, simply locate that channel on the Inputs tab and reduce the amount of signal being sent to the Aux Returns tab.

The Output Masters Tab

The final tab of the DSP Station is the Output Masters tab, which is primarily used to output the overall mix of Giga instruments within a session. Looking at Figure 6.21, you can see that there's not much to be had in this view because there is only a single stereo output. This is because my audio card includes a single stereo output, whereas audio cards with multiple outputs have many more outputs.

However, the Output Masters tab is also responsible for routing an audio signal into GigaStudio with the implied intention of recording it and creating a customized Giga instrument with that recording.

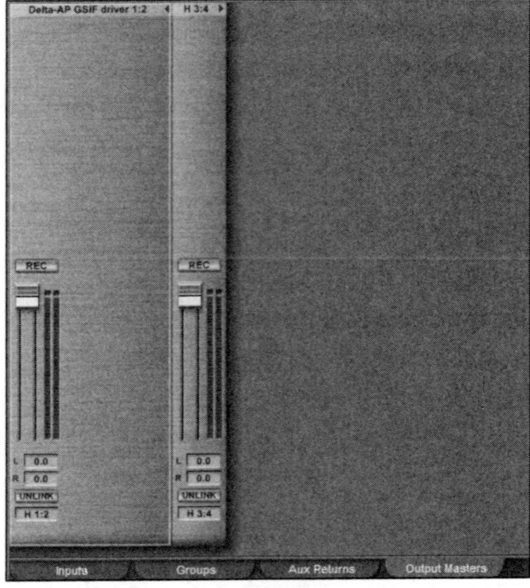

Figure 6.21
Although light on features, the Output Masters tab is used to output the overall mix of Giga instruments.

Using the Output Masters Tab to Record

In this section, I will introduce you to using the Output Masters tab to record an audio signal. Note that in order for this to work, you must have an audio card that supports the GSIF 2 standard and has an active input, which is done using the Hardware tab of the Configuration Manager (we looked at this earlier in the chapter).

1 Begin by navigating to the Inputs tab, select a channel, and set its input to the input of your audio card.
2 Next, set the channel's output to the output of your audio card.
3 Switch to the Output Masters tab and click on the REC button to record-enable the audio input (see Figure 6.22).

Figure 6.22
Click on the REC button on the output channel in the Output Masters tab to record-enable the audio input.

4 Begin recording by clicking on the Start Audio Capture button in the upper toolbar of the Giga interface. This will bring up a browser window asking you to assign a location to save your audio file when it is recorded. If this is your first time, I would suggest you navigate to the desktop, create a folder, and call it Giga Records or something similar. Additionally, make sure that, to avoid confusion later, you name your audio recording after the instrument you are capturing rather than just calling it something generic like "audio recording" or "my first recording." When you are finished, click Save, and you are recording (see Figure 6.23).

5 When you are finished recording, click on the Stop button.

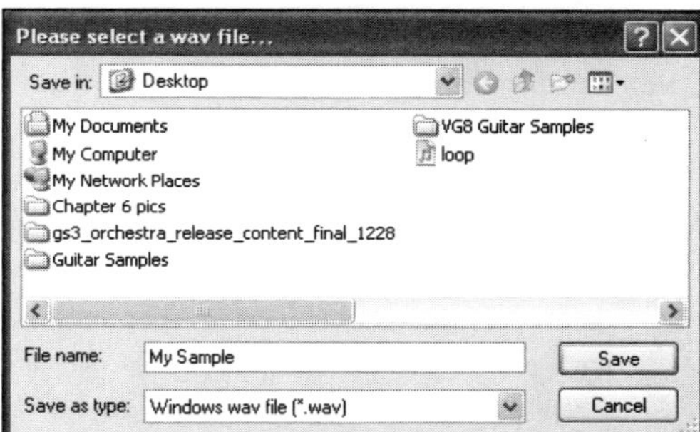

Figure 6.23
Before you can record, you must specify a location and name for your audio recording.

Once you have made enough recordings with the Audio Capture tool of GigaStudio, you can begin to create your first Giga instrument, but we'll hold off on that until the end of the chapter.

> **NO AUDIO CAPTURE WHILE USING REWIRE**
> Be aware that if you are using GigaStudio in ReWire mode (which we will discuss later in this chapter), the Audio Capture feature will not work. To use it again, you must quit GigaStudio, quit the DAW application, and then relaunch GigaStudio.

The Virtual Keyboard

The Virtual Keyboard plays and auditions Giga instruments after they have been loaded into an instrument slot (see Figure 6.24). Unlike the virtual keyboards of other soft synths and samplers, this keyboard has a few tricks up its sleeve, as you will learn in this section.

Figure 6.24
The Virtual Keyboard plays any loaded instrument in the GigaStudio interface. Just click on the appropriate instrument slot in the MIDI Mixer, and the corresponding samples will be displayed in the Virtual Keyboard.

To view the Virtual Keyboard, click on the Toggle Keyboard Pane button in the upper toolbar of the GigaStudio interface. Once activated, it will appear at the far bottom of the Giga window and display the keys that have no samples loaded in dark gray and keys that have samples loaded in standard black and white.

> **FLOATING KEYBOARD**
>
> The Virtual Keyboard can be detached from the interface and be used as a floatable mechanism, which is great for users like me who have two monitors. To detach the keyboard, simply click and drag it up to a stationary position above the QuickSound Loader (see Figure 6.25). Release the mouse, and voila!

Figure 6.25
Floating the keyboard is a handy way of customizing your Giga interface, especially if you have a dual monitor setup.

The Virtual Keyboard has the following parameters:

- **Zoom In/Out**—These buttons are used to increase/decrease the size of the Virtual Keyboard.
- **Scroll Left/Right**—These buttons are used to shift the viewable position of the Virtual Keyboard one key at a time.
- **Input Velocity**—These controls are used to alter the dynamic potential of the Virtual Keyboard. The input slider alters the amount of input velocity, which means that if you set it to a value of 50, the Virtual Keyboard will not play any velocity above 50. However, if you are using a Giga instrument with multiple velocity zones, you can click the Auto button to the left of the Input

slider and the Virtual Keyboard will become velocity sensitive, which means when a note is played at the top of a key, the sample will play the corresponding sample at its lowest velocity. But when the same note is played at the bottom of the key, the corresponding sample will play back at its highest velocity (see Figure 6.26).

Figure 6.26

When set to Auto, the Virtual Keyboard becomes velocity sensitive.

CUSTOMIZE YOUR WORKSPACE

Aside from floating the Virtual Keyboard, you can customize the look of GigaStudio to extremes by clicking and dragging either the QuickSound Loader or the Virtual Keyboard to just about any position on the Giga interface. For example, let's say you want to place the QuickSound Loader at the top of the Giga interface, followed by the MIDI Mixer in the middle and the Virtual Keyboard at the bottom. This is easily done by clicking and dragging the QuickSound Loader upward by its blue tab on the left and releasing the mouse once you have reached the top of the interface. The QuickSound Loader will then appear at the top of the Giga interface (see Figure 6.27).

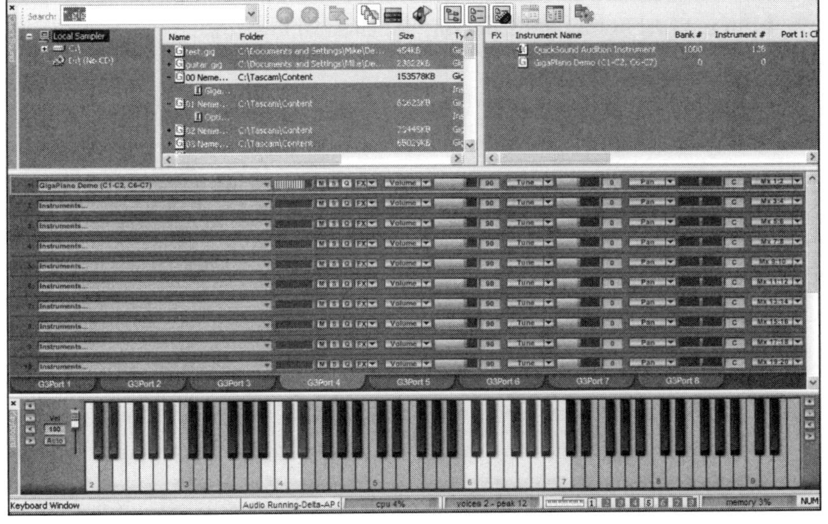

Figure 6.27

Clicking and dragging the QuickSound Loader or the Virtual Keyboard by its blue tab allows you to reposition them just about anywhere in the Giga interface.

Basic Giga Operations

Now that you're thoroughly familiar with the GigaStudio interface, it's time to take you through the steps of performing some basic operations such as loading and unloading instruments, editing instruments, and so forth. You can use this section as a "quick start" of sorts, as I'll be concentrating on the more advanced features of GigaStudio a little later.

WHERE TO INSTALL THE INSTRUMENTS

Unless you have a second hard drive installed in your computer, I recommend installing the provided Giga instruments in the same program folder as the application itself. Just open up the Tascam folder, create a new folder and name it Content, and then copy all the Giga instruments to that folder. That way, you keep the system nice and organized.

Loading Instruments

Assuming that you have installed all of your Giga instruments onto your computer's hard drive, let's now begin loading them into the MIDI Mixer. There are two ways to load instruments into any of the available 16 MIDI channels:

- From the instrument slots of the MIDI Mixer
- From the QuickSound Loader

Let's see how this is done, starting with the instrument slots.

1 In the first instrument's slot dialog, click on the down arrow.

2 A pull-down menu will appear, offering a few active choices. Select Load Instrument (see Figure 6.28).

Figure 6.28

The Instrument Slot pull-down menu loads and detaches Giga instruments from the MIDI Mixer.

3 An instrument browser window will appear, which you can use to locate and load Giga instruments (file extension .gig) into an empty instrument slot (see Figure 6.29).

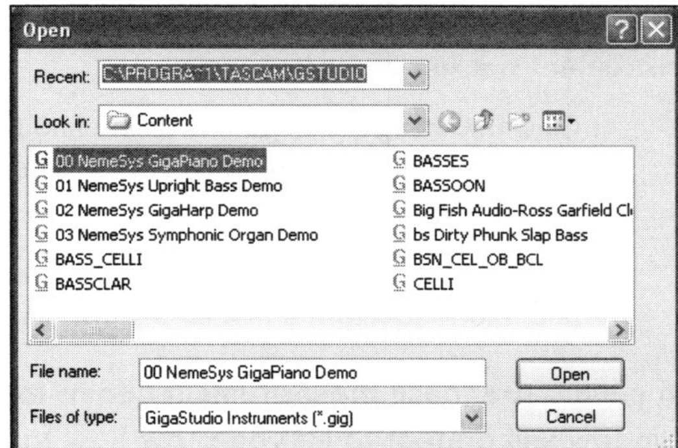

Figure 6.29
The browser window is used to locate and load Giga instrument files into an empty instrument slot.

> **WIPE IT CLEAN**
> Before proceeding, take a minute to reset the GigaStudio interface by clicking on the Reset button located in the upper-right corner of the GigaStudio interface.

Now let's use the QuickSound Loader to load a Giga instrument into an instrument slot. Make sure you have activated the interface by clicking on its icon in the Toolbar. Once activated, you should see the available instruments listed in the center window of the QuickSound Loader. If not, you may need to have GigaStudio rebuild your QuickSound database, which is done by right-clicking on the hard drive icon, located in the Instrument Tree window on the left side of the interface. Select Rebuild Entire QuickSound Database (see Figure 6.30).

Figure 6.30
If your installed Giga instruments are not listed in the QuickSound Loader, you should have GigaStudio rebuild your entire QuickSound database.

At this point, the Update QuickSound Database window will appear and prompt you to either scan your hard drive(s) for newly installed Giga instruments or cancel the operation entirely. To make the search even more specific, you can use the Advanced button to specify which hard drives to search. Once you have made your adjustments, click on Update QuickSound Database, and in a matter of seconds or minutes your computer will be scanned and a new QuickSound database will be created, which will appear in the center window of the QuickSound Loader.

Once this operation is complete, you can load a Giga instrument into an instrument slot in one of two ways:

- Click and drag the Giga instrument into the appropriate empty instrument slot. Release the mouse button, and the instrument should begin to load immediately.
- Double-click on the Giga instrument, at which point the instrument should begin to load into the first empty instrument slot immediately.

In either case, once the instrument begins to load into a slot, a progress window will appear to let you know how far along the loading process has gone (see Figure 6.31).

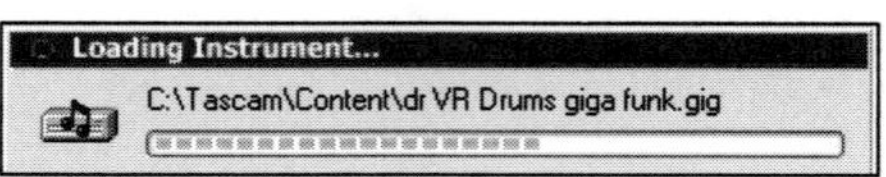

Figure 6.31
The progress window displays the amount of progress when loading Giga instruments into a slot on the MIDI Mixer.

Detaching/Unloading Instruments

Instruments can be removed from the MIDI Mixer in one of two ways:

- Detaching them from the instrument slot
- Unloading them completely from the QuickSound Loader

Although detaching and unloading might seem very similar, they're actually very different in purpose. *Detaching* an instrument means that you are simply removing it from the MIDI Mixer, but the samples that make up the instrument are still loaded in your computer's memory (RAM and hard drive). This is a great "go back" feature of sorts. For example, let's say you are working on a cue of film music and have loaded a woodwind section Giga instrument into an instrument slot, but later you decide that you would rather use a different Giga instrument. By detaching the instrument, you can reload it quickly back into an instrument slot should you change your mind.

Here's how to detach a loaded Giga instrument:

1. Navigate your mouse to an instrument slot with a loaded Giga instrument.
2. Click on its corresponding pull-down menu and select Detach Instrument. GigaStudio will do the rest (see Figure 6.32).

Figure 6.32

Detaching an instrument removes it from the MIDI Mixer, but the samples will remain loaded in the computer's memory.

Unloading an instrument is quite different, as it's used to detach the instrument from the MIDI Mixer and unload the samples from your computer's memory. Additionally, you can unload a single or multiple instruments from the MIDI Mixer, all by using the QuickSound Loader.

Here's how to unload an instrument:

1. Assuming that you have an instrument loaded into the MIDI Mixer, navigate to the Loaded Instrument view of the QuickSound Loader and right-click on the instrument you wish to unload.
2. A pop-up menu will appear asking you to either Unload Selected or Unload All (see Figure 6.33). If your intention is to unload a single instrument, then select the first option. Otherwise, select the second.

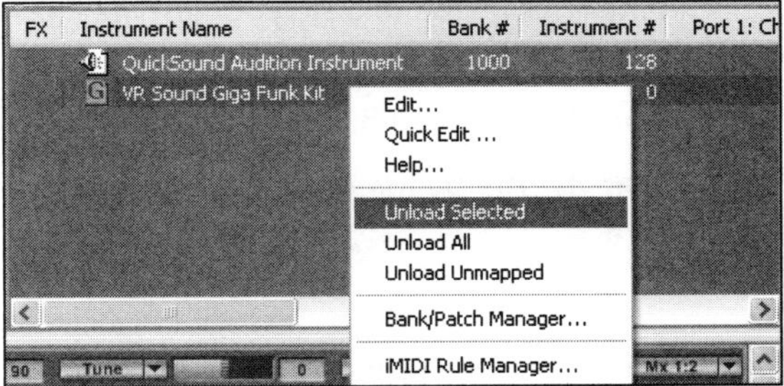

Figure 6.33

The Instrument list is used to list any active instrument in a GigaStudio session. Right-click on an instrument in this list to either unload it from the session or unload all of the instruments.

Editing Instruments

The best part about using samples (or any soft synth for that matter) is the capability to shape and mold your sounds by using the supplied editing functions. In GigaStudio 3, this is one of the application's strong points. GigaStudio offers three ways to edit instruments:

- MIDI Mixer
- QuickEdit
- GigaEdit

The MIDI Mixer is an easy and effective method of editing your loaded Giga instruments. From this interface, you can assign your instruments to different positions within the stereo field, add real-time effects, and alter the tuning of the loaded instrument. Look at Figure 6.34 and read the following list in order to get better acquainted with this editor.

Figure 6.34
The MIDI Mixer makes it possible to detune, pan, and affect your loaded Giga instruments.

- **Mute/Solo/QuickEdit/FX**—These buttons are used to perform specific mixing and editing functions. The Mute and Solo buttons are used to silence or isolate an instrument from the overall mix, respectively. The QuickEdit button launches the QuickEdit feature, which will be discussed later. The FX button edits the real-time effects.
- **Volume**—This button and slider adjust the volume of the instrument by way of MIDI messages.
- **Tune**—This button and slider adjust the master tuning of the instrument by way of MIDI.
- **Pan**—This button and slider assign the instrument to the stereo field.
- **Outputs**—This button assigns the instrument to a specific output of your audio card.

ADJUSTING DIFFERENT MIDI PARAMETERS

Aside from adjusting the volume, tune, and panning assignments of an instrument via MIDI, you can also use these buttons to manipulate other MIDI parameters. Looking at Figure 6.35, you can see that I have clicked on the Volume button, at which time a large pop-up menu appears, listing all of the available MIDI parameters to choose from. Once selected, that parameter will be displayed in the MIDI Mixer and can be manipulated by using the corresponding slider to the right.

Select Controller
0 Bank Select
1 Mod Wheel
2 Breath Controller
3 Undefined
4 Foot Controller
5 Portamento time
6 Data Entry MSB
✔ 7 Channel Volume
8 Balance
9 Undefined
10 Pan
11 Expression Control
12 Effect Control 1
13 Effect Control 2
14 Undefined
15 Undefined
16 GPC 1
17 GPC 2
18 GPC 3
19 GPC 4
20 Undefined
21 Undefined
22 Undefined
23 Undefined
24 Undefined
25 Undefined
26 Undefined
27 Undefined
28 Undefined
29 Undefined
30 Undefined
31 Undefined
32 LSB for Values 0
33 LSB for Values 1
34 LSB for Values 2
35 LSB for Values 3
36 LSB for Values 4
37 LSB for Values 5
38 LSB for Values 6
39 LSB for Values 7
40 LSB for Values 8
41 LSB for Values 9
42 LSB for Values 10
43 LSB for Values 11
44 LSB for Values 12
45 LSB for Values 13
46 LSB for Values 14
47 LSB for Values 15
48 LSB for Values 16
49 LSB for Values 17
50 LSB for Values 18
51 LSB for Values 19
52 LSB for Values 20
53 LSB for Values 21
54 LSB for Values 22
55 LSB for Values 23
56 LSB for Values 24
57 LSB for Values 25
58 LSB for Values 26
59 LSB for Values 27
60 LSB for Values 28
61 LSB for Values 29
62 LSB for Values 30
63 LSB for Values 31
64 Sustain Pedal
65 Partamento On/Off
66 Sostenuto
67 SoftPedal
68 Legato Foot Switch
69 Hold 2
70 Sound Controller 1
71 Sound Controller 2
72 Sound Controller 3
73 Sound Controller 4
74 Sound Controller 5
75 Sound Controller 6
76 Sound Controller 7
77 Sound Controller 8
78 Sound Controller 9
79 Sound Controller 10
80 GPC 5
81 GPC 6
82 GPC 7
83 GPC 8
84 Portamento Control
85 Undefined
86 Undefined
87 Undefined
88 Undefined
89 Undefined
90 Undefined
91 Effects 1 Depth
92 Effects 2 Depth
93 Effects 3 Depth
94 Effects 4 Depth
95 Effects 5 Depth
96 Data Increment
97 Data Decrement
98 Non Registered Parameter LSB
99 Non Registered Parameter MSB
100 Registered Parameter Number LSB
101 Registered Parameter Number MSB
102 Undefined
103 Undefined
104 Undefined
105 Undefined
106 Undefined
107 Undefined
108 Undefined
109 Undefined
110 Undefined
111 Undefined
112 Undefined
113 Undefined
114 Undefined
115 Undefined
116 Undefined
117 Undefined
118 Undefined
119 Undefined
Program Change
Fine Tune (Cents)
Coarse Tune (Semitones)

Figure 6.35

The Volume, Tune, and Pan buttons can also be used to select and alter any MIDI parameter, such as portamento and modulation.

While they both serve the same purpose, which is to edit the instrument, *QuickEdit* and *GigaEdit* work quite differently. QuickEdit is a real-time editor embedded in the GigaStudio interface, while the GigaEdit is an offline editor that makes edits of a more permanent nature.

I'll introduce these editors to you one at a time, starting with QuickEdit. Assuming you have a Giga instrument loaded into the MIDI Mixer, click on the Q button of the corresponding instrument slot to launch the QuickEdit interface (see Figure 6.36).

Figure 6.36
Once an instrument has been loaded into an instrument slot of the MIDI Mixer, click on the Q button to launch the QuickEdit interface.

As you can see, QuickEdit offers many of the standard real-time parameters that you would find on most hardware/software synths. The interface is split into four sections:

- **Articulation**—This includes all the standard synth parameters, such as LFOs, filters, and envelopes.
- **Dimension**—This section displays and edits any active dimensional parameters embedded within the Giga instrument, such as Key Down Velocity and Stereo. Note that you cannot add more dimensions from this editor. You must do this from GigaEdit.
- **Wave**—This section displays the waveform of a selected sample, and it is also where changes in envelope parameters are viewed.
- **Keyboard**—This acts similarly to the Virtual Keyboard on the main GigaStudio interface.

THESE EDITS ARE NON-DESTRUCTIVE

Any edits made within QuickEdit are non-destructive, which means that they do not overwrite the sample data of the loaded instrument.

When you are ready to close QuickEdit, just click on the Close Window button in the upper-left corner.

The next method for editing instruments is GigaEdit, which is an offline editor used to make permanent changes to the various parameters of a Giga instrument. Furthermore, GigaEdit can be used effectively to edit individual velocity layers and mapping assignments of samples included within an instrument. To launch GigaEdit, simply select Launch GigaEdit from the pop-up menu of an instrument slot. GigaEdit will immediately launch and load the selected instrument into its interface (see Figure 6.37).

Figure 6.37

Select Launch GigaEdit from the instrument slot in the MIDI Mixer to launch the GigaEdit interface.

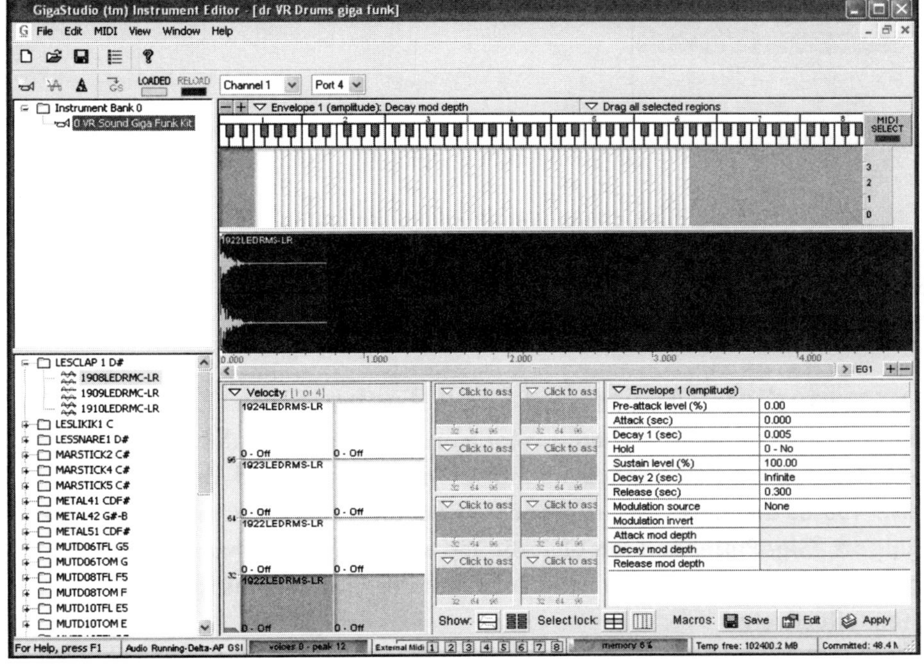

The GigaEdit interface is split into several sections, including the following:

- **Instrument Name**—This displays the name of the loaded Giga instrument.
- **Instrument Parameters**—This displays all the active parameters of the loaded Giga instrument.
- **Keyboard Mapping**—This maps out your samples along the Virtual Keyboard.
- **Velocity Zones**—This section edits the individual velocities of a loaded Giga instrument.
- **Additional Parameters**—This section assigns additional parameters such as LFO, envelopes, and velocity to a loaded Giga instrument.

Once you have made your edits to a Giga instrument, you can load it back into the GigaStudio interface by clicking the Load button in the upper-left corner. If you haven't saved your changes to the instrument, a pop-up window will prompt you to Save, Save As, or Cancel (see Figure 6.38). My advice would be to select Save As; this will leave the original instrument unaltered.

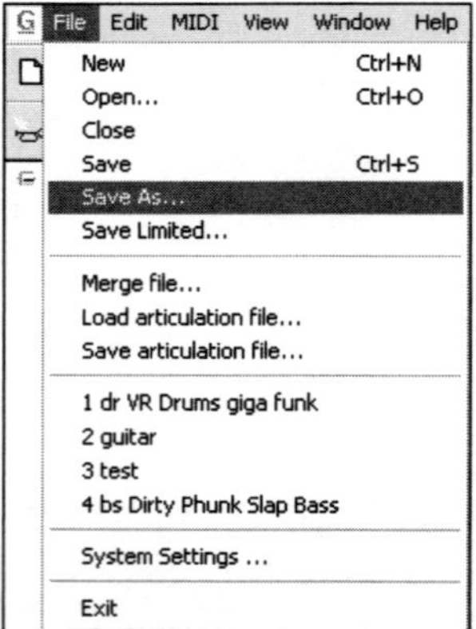

Figure 6.38
Before loading the instrument back into GigaStudio, you will need to save the changes by selecting either Save or Save As.

Intermediate/Advanced Giga Techniques

By now you can see that there's a lot more to GigaStudio than meets the eye. Not only is it an application that's easy to understand and use, but it also houses an impressive assortment of advanced features such as ReWire support, GigaPulse, and the QuickSound search engine. This section of the chapter will familiarize you with these features and demonstrate how to use them effectively.

GigaPulse

As you have read throughout the last several pages, there are a lot of cool features embedded within GigaStudio 3. One of GigaStudio's best new features is GigaPulse (see Figure 6.39).

Figure 6.39
GigaPulse is a unique reverb that uses convolution to emulate different rooms and environments to shape its sound. Note that it is available only with the GigaStudio Orchestral Edition.

Based on *convolution* (density), GigaPulse is a real-time reverb that shapes its sound by emulating mic placement and instrument resonance within a specific environment. Simply put, if you like the sound of a room, hall, or auditorium, and you would like to place your samples within these acoustic environments virtually, GigaPulse makes it possible. Furthermore, GigaPulse can work in a stereo or surround environment, making for an endless array of creative mixing possibilities.

As some of you know, this kind of technology is not all that new to the virtual studio; other programs, such as Sound Forge and Nuendo, have their own room emulators called the Acoustic Mirror and Acoustic Stamp, respectively. However, GigaPulse is much more efficient and versatile because it offers detailed control over the various elements that shape the effect to your liking, such as various mic placements within an environment and the emulation of an assortment of vintage and contemporary microphones.

GIGAPULSE VST

Although GigaPulse comes included with GigaStudio 3 Orchestral Edition, you can purchase GigaPulse separately as a VST plug-in for use with your favorite DAW application that supports the VST standard. Visit the Tascam Web site for more information at **www.tascamgiga.com**.

Before we begin our tour of the GigaPulse interface, let's take a moment to load it onto an input channel of the DSP Station. Assuming that you have a Giga instrument loaded and ready to go, follow these steps to set it up as an insert effect.

1. Begin by switching to the DSP Station; select input channel one and display its wide view.
2. In the first insert slot of input channel one, select GigaPulse Pro NFX from the Native FX subdirectory. This will activate GigaPulse and display its graphic interface.
3. Play your loaded Giga instrument, and you should now hear it processed entirely by GigaPulse.

The GigaPulse Parameters

Let's begin our tour of the GigaPulse interface starting at the top left corner, which is the Acoustic Space. Refer back to Figure 6.39 as we look at this incredible effect one section at a time.

Acoustic Space

The Acoustic Space displays a graphic representation of the current active space in a preset. It is also used to specify the various parameters that govern that active space. This is a good starting point for you to explore the feature set of GigaPulse.

The Acoustic Space contains the following parameters:

- **Bank**—This pop-up menu selects a specific bank file and has an .fxb file extension.
- **Impulse**—This dialog displays the impulse embedded within the selected bank file.
- **Preset**—This pop-up menu is used to select a preset variation on the bank.
- **Instrument**—This dialog lists the Giga instrument that's being processed by GigaPulse. In this case, since we have activated an instance of it on input channel one, it should list the currently active Giga instrument on that channel.

- **File**—This menu contains a list of options for opening, saving, and creating banks. There are many options here; refer to the GigaPulse manual for more information.
- **Cascade**—When activated, the Cascade function will loop the impulse of one signal and then feed it to the impulse of GigaPulse.

TURBO MODE, PURE MODE

Although we didn't discuss all of the options listed under the File menu, one option in particular needs some explanation: Turbo Mode > Pure Mode (not recommended). Whenever an instance of GigaPulse is activated, it is placed into Turbo mode by default, which means that it relies on the parameters of the Tail Model section (we'll look at this later) to determine the tail end of the reverb trail (such as ghost reflection). This allows GigaPulse to run in an optimized fashion, which basically means it is less taxing on your CPU.

Pure mode is much different. It is a purely computational process that determines the character of the tail end of the reverb tail without the need of the Tail Model section. While in some cases this might sound better than the Turbo mode, it is an extremely CPU-intensive function, so use it wisely.

Placement Selection

Placement Selection displays a diagram of microphone placements within a selected space. These microphone placements are closely related to the actual impulse reflections that were initially captured during the original recording session. Looking at Figure 6.40, we can see that there are seven microphone placements in this diagram, which are symbolized with round icons. Each of these microphones has been assigned a label to indicate its exact position within the diagram, including:

- **L**—Left Channel
- **C**—Center Channel
- **R**—Right Channel
- **Lw**—Left Wide
- **Rw**—Right Wide
- **Ls**—Left Surround
- **Rs**—Right Surround

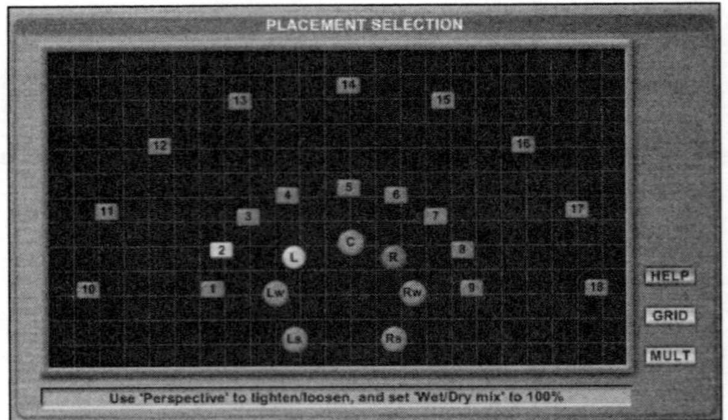

Figure 6.40
Placement Selection displays the microphone placements within a room environment.

Outside of these microphones are the locations at which each reflection was captured within the space. Looking back at Figure 6.40, you can see nine reflections captured in close proximity to the actual microphone placements, followed by an additional nine outer reflections. Furthermore, if you click on any of these reflection points, that location will be graphically displayed in the Acoustic Space section of the GigaPulse interface.

Input Levels

This section sets the input levels for the left and right channels of the GigaPulse interface and contains the following parameters:

- **Bypass**—When activated, this will bypass the GigaPulse effect entirely.
- **Master**—This knob alters the amount of input for the left and right channels simultaneously.
- **Left/Right**—These knobs alter the amount of input for the left and right channels independently.

Tail Model

As you read earlier in our discussion about Turbo mode of GigaPulse, the Tail Model determines the character of the end tail or ghost reflection of the reverb effect after three seconds have passed. The Tail Model has the following parameters:

- **Enable**—This turns the Tail Model on.
- **Overlap**—This basically works as a crossfade of sorts and enhances the transition between the original impulse of the early reflection to the Tail Model.
- **Level**—This knob adjusts the Tail Model to match the level of the initial reflection.
- **Cutoff**—This knob is used as a low pass filter.

The GigaPulse Microphones

Perhaps one of the coolest features of GigaPulse is its ability to further enhance and shape the overall reverb effect by emulating the audible behaviors of vintage and popular microphones. Over the next section, we'll take a look at some of these features, but the real fun of this is best found by sitting down with GigaPulse, feeding a signal through it, and experimenting with it.

Mic Masters

The Mic Masters section governs all of the emulated microphones within a GigaPulse preset. While adjustments to the individual microphones can be made with the Mic Groups, it's the job of the Mic Masters to control and maintain the relative values between each Mic Group.

The Mic Masters section includes the following parameters:

- **Mute**—This parameter mutes all of the microphones.
- **Mic Level**—This slider adjusts the overall amplitude of all active microphones.
- **Perspective**—This slider adjusts the perspective or positioning of each impulse response within a loaded bank.
- **Wet/Dry Mix**—This slider adjusts the mix of unprocessed or "dry" signal against the processed or "wet" signal.
- **Pre-Delay**—This slider adjusts the amount of pre-delay in a signal, which is the delay between the source and the starting point of the reverb.

Original/Replacement Mic

In the right corner of each Mic Group is the Replacement Mic section. This is used in combination with the Original Mic section to model a different microphone onto the one originally used to capture the sample. For example, let's say you sampled a piano using the popular Shure SM57 dynamic microphone. Upon listening to the samples when loaded into GigaStudio, you find that there exist certain audible characteristics inherent to the SM57 that you would like to alter, and this is where the Replacement Mic section comes into play.

1. First, you would select the SM57 from the Original Mic section's pop-up menu (see Figure 6.41).
2. After the original mic is selected, you would then use the Replacement Mic section's pop-up menu to select an alternate microphone model, such as the Neumann U87, which is a popular vintage mic.

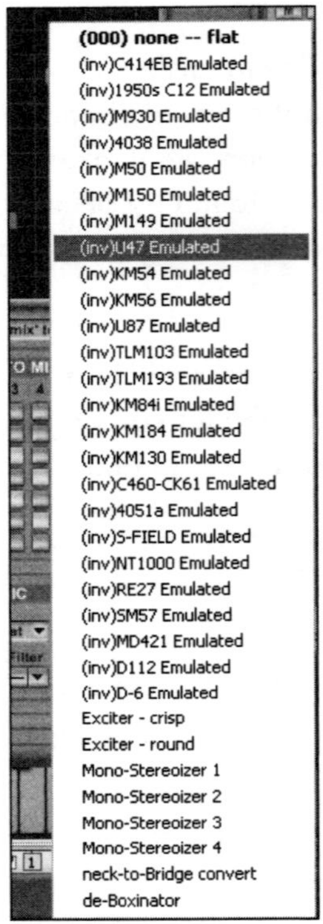

Figure 6.41
GigaPulse provides a wide variety of popular and vintage microphone models to use with the Original and Replacement Mic sections.

The Original/Replacement Mic section contains the following additional parameters.

- **Pattern**—The Pattern section specifies the shape of the capture direction of a microphone (cardiod, omnidirectional). Note that this is available only on specific microphones within the supplied list of models, such as the C12 and the U87.
- **Filter**—This section determines the roll-off point of the emulated microphone. As before, this is available only with specific mic models.

Using GigaStudio via ReWire

Another big development jump for GigaStudio 3 is its incorporation of ReWire technology, which gives you the ability to route the audio outputs of GigaStudio into the virtual mixer of a supported host application, such as Pro Tools and Cubase. This makes it possible to then mix the two programs together within one mixing environment.

In order for ReWire to work, you must have a ReWire Master program, such as SONAR or Logic and a ReWire slave program, which in this case is GigaStudio 3. When used together, the audio outputs of each loaded Giga instrument is routed internally to the ReWire inputs of the master application, at which point they can be further enhanced by virtual effects and EQs, and rendered internally as audio tracks.

A key benefit to using GigaStudio in ReWire mode is the ability to internally render (or mix down) your Giga instrument performances by way of the host application. This is a vast improvement from earlier versions of GigaStudio, which required users to route the hardware audio outputs of GigaStudio to the hardware audio inputs of the host application, thus leading to additional analog noise problems.

REWIRE MASTER PROGRAMS

At the time of this writing, the following PC audio applications are tested and supported ReWire Master applications:

- **Steinberg Cubase SX 2.0**
- **Steinberg Nuendo 1.52/2.0**
- **Cakewalk SONAR 2.0/3.0**
- **Ableton LIVE 2/3**
- **Sony Acid Pro 4.0**
- **Digidesign Pro Tools 6.1**

As you can see, there are many applications that function well as ReWire Master applications, and the procedures to set them up with GigaStudio can be found within the included GigaStudio 3 user's manual. However, to give you a general idea of how easy this is, I will take you through the steps of setting up GigaStudio with SONAR 3 by Cakewalk.

HYPERTHREADING

Hyperthreading is a relatively new technology used in today's Pentium 4 processor/motherboard combinations. If your computer was built within the last two years, there's a good chance that hyperthreading is activated. When attempting to use GigaStudio 3 as a ReWire instrument, you may encounter crashing problems, which are a result of a conflict with hyperthreading technology. To remedy this problem, restart your computer, access the BIOS settings, and deactivate hyperthreading. Then save your changes, allow the computer to reboot, and it should be smooth sailing from there.

1. Before launching GigaStudio, launch the Configuration Manager by selecting Start > Programs > Tascam > Configuration Manager.
2. Once launched, select the ReWire tab and activate ReWire by deselecting Disable ReWire Functionality (see Figure 6.42). Click Apply and then OK to close the Configuration Manager.
3. Next, launch SONAR, click on the DXi Synth Rack button to launch the synth rack, and select Giga 3 from the Insert button (see Figure 6.43). This will create a ReWire instance of GigaStudio 3 and create an audio and MIDI track on the SONAR Project window.
4. Double-click on the Giga 3 device in the DXi Synth Rack to launch GigaStudio 3.

At this point, the audio outputs of GigaStudio 3 have been routed to the SONAR mixer. Look at Figure 6.44 and you'll see that GigaStudio has indicated that it is in ReWire slave mode along the bottom toolbar of the interface, just to the left of the CPU meter.

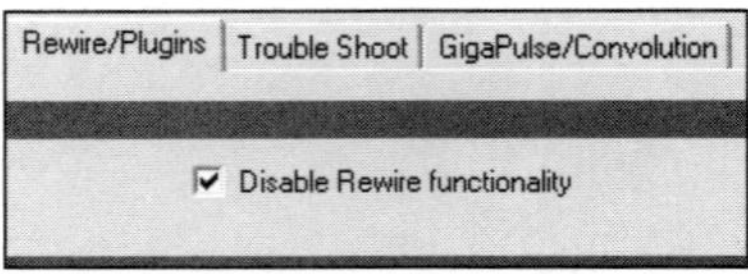

Figure 6.42
Disable ReWire Functionality must be turned off before using GigaStudio 3 in ReWire mode.

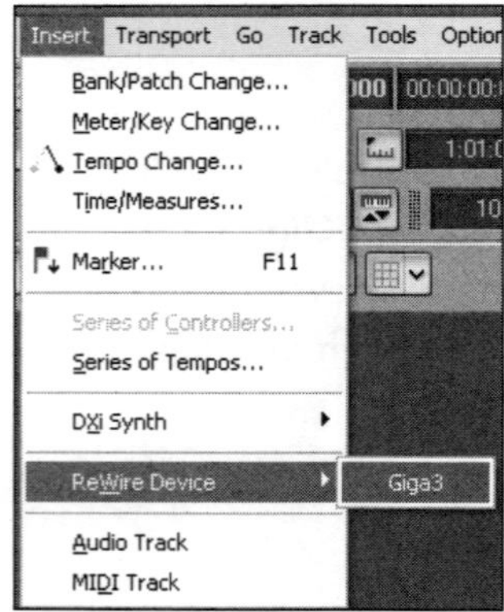

Figure 6.43
Select Giga 3 from the ReWire Devices subdirectory of the Insert dialog within the DXi Synth Rack.

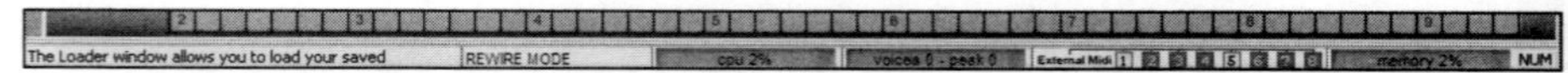

Figure 6.44
GigaStudio 3 is now in ReWire slave mode, as indicated by the bottom toolbar.

Searching for Samples

Another of GigaStudio 3's helpful new features is its integrated search engine, which is made possible by way of QuickSound. A search engine is used to seek out specific sounds and other file types that relate to any keyword you type into the search engine dialog. For musicians with extensive sample libraries, a search engine is a fundamental tool, as it makes it possible for musicians to quickly locate and load samples in order to get down to the business of making music quickly. And believe me, when you're working on a project where you're only being paid X amount of dollars for Y amount of work, you'll yearn for any tool that will help you get from point X to Y as efficiently as possible.

In the case of GigaStudio, the QuickSound search engine is capable of searching for the following file types:

- **gig**—GigaStudio Instrument File
- **gsp**—GigaStudio Session Performance File
- **gsi**—GigaStudio Instrument Performance File
- **prf**—GigaSampler Performance File
- **art**—Articulation File
- **wav**—Standard Windows Digital Audio File

The QuickSound Database

The GigaStudio search engine is based on the QuickSound database, which takes a virtual inventory of the relevant sounds and files from your computer. The search engine uses this inventory as a reference point to locate queried sounds and files. There's a good chance you've already had a little experience with the QuickSound database, as it comes into play the first time you launch GigaStudio (see Figure 6.45).

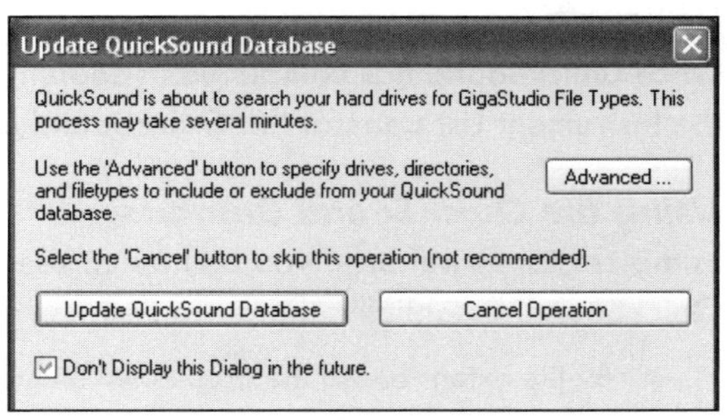

Figure 6.45
The QuickSound database takes a virtual inventory of the relevant sounds and files on your computer.

Building a QuickSound Database

At this point, you're ready to build your first QuickSound database, so you can either click Update QuickSound Database to begin the process or a better option would be to click on the Advanced button to make a few adjustments to your search (see Figure 6.46).

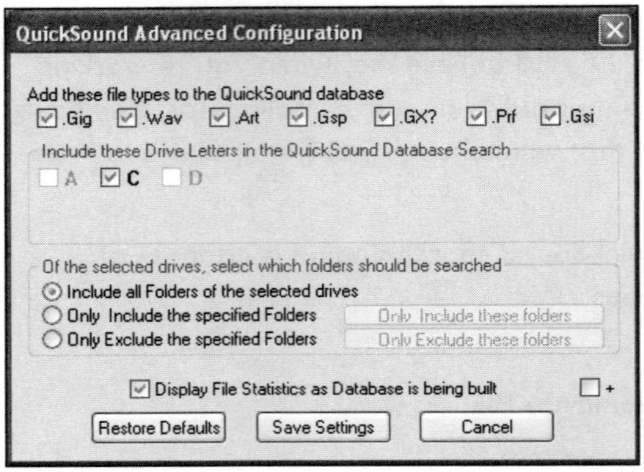

Figure 6.46
The QuickSound Advanced Configurations window makes adjustments to the QuickSound search parameters.

In this window, you have the following options:

- **File Types**—Use this check list to select or deselect the types of audio files you want QuickSound to search for.
- **Included Drives**—Use this check list to select or deselect the hard drives you want QuickSound to search.
- **Included Folders**—Use this section to specify exactly which folders or directories you want QuickSound to search.

Once your parameters have been set, click Save Settings and then click Update QuickSound Database to begin your search, which can take up to 1 minute, depending on how much data QuickSound has to search (see Figure 6.47).

Once QuickSound has completed its search, the contents will be displayed in the Instrument List pane of the QuickSound interface.

Using the QuickSound Database

In this section, I will brief you on how to use the database, once built by QuickSound. Essentially, there are two ways to use the database.

- By file extension via the drop-down menu.
- By keyword search.

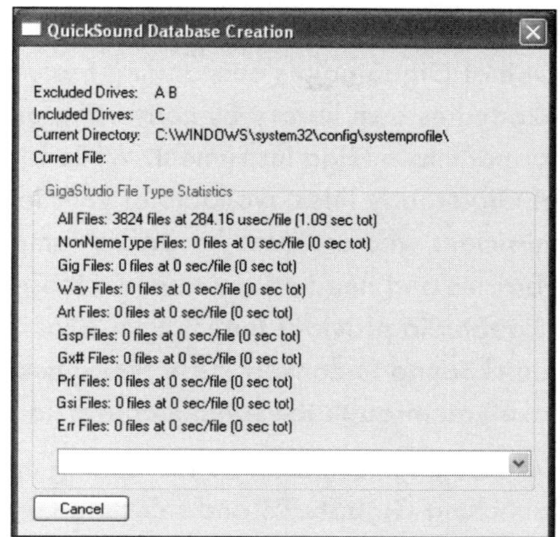

Figure 6.47

This is a detailed view of the QuickSound search as it begins. You can opt to view this window by selecting Display File Statistics as Database Is Being Built from the Advanced Configuration window.

Using the drop-down menu is the easiest way to begin. Currently, this menu should display the .gig file extension, which as you know is the GigaStudio instrument file format. However, clicking on this drop-down menu, you should see a list of all the available file extensions that I listed earlier in this section. Let's suppose you're looking for all of the .wav files on your computer, and you want the QuickSound database to locate and display them for you. Select .wav from the drop-down menu and in an instant, QuickSound will locate them and list them in the Instrument List pane to the right (see Figure 6.48).

The other way to search for Giga instruments and sounds is by using *keywords*, which consist of one- or two-word descriptions. For example, if you wanted to locate a piano sound or Giga instrument, you could type "Piano" into the drop-down dialog and press Enter on your keyboard, and QuickSound will locate and list all of the candidates in the Instrument List pane.

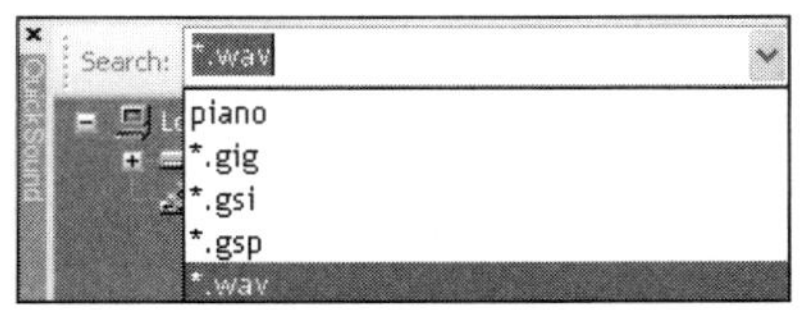

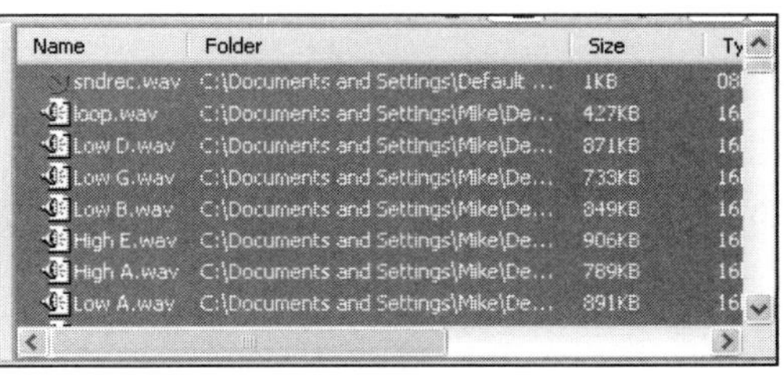

Figure 6.48

The QuickSound database can quickly list any file format by simply selecting the file format from the supplied drop-down menu.

Expanding Your Giga Library

One of GigaStudio's outstanding features has always been the ability to expand its own library by converting and importing the popular Akai sample format into a Giga instrument. While it's true that there are literally hundreds of Giga-ready titles available at your local musical instrument store, many musicians who use Akai hardware samplers have their own extensive sample libraries and need a way to move those samples into the virtual environment. GigaStudio provides the intuitive Akai Convert application that runs within QuickSound to convert these files quickly and efficiently. In this section, I will take you through the sample conversion process.

Let's begin this tutorial by first setting up our conversion preferences by launching GigaStudio and selecting GigaStudio Settings from the File pull-down menu. The GigaStudio Settings window will pop up, at which point I will select the Akai Converter tab to display its contents (see Figure 6.49).

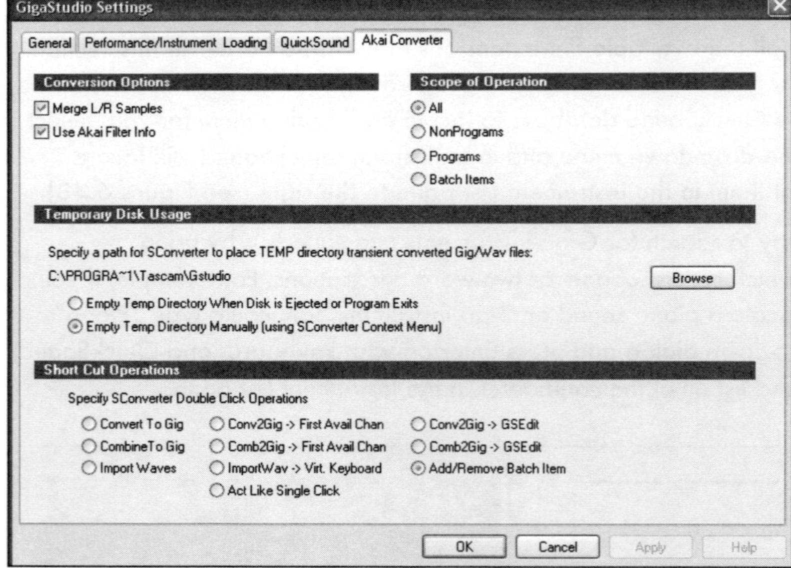

Figure 6.49

The Akai Converter tab of the GigaStudio Settings window sets the overall preferences for converting Akai formatted samples into Giga instruments.

The Akai Converter tab contains the following options:

- **Conversion Options**—This section specifies how an Akai formatted sample will be converted into a Giga instrument. You can select to merge the Left and Right channels into a single interleaved stereo file (very recommended), and you can select the option to include any filter data saved with the Akai sample preset (also recommended).
- **Scope of Operation**—This section specifies how involved the Akai converter will be in the conversion process, which means what kind of Akai samples and programs you wish to import and convert. You can choose All, NonPrograms, Programs, and Batch Items. If this is your first time using the Akai converter, I recommend sticking with the All option, as you can change this later.
- **Temporary Disk Usage**—This section specifies where and how GigaStudio will temporarily store any imported Akai samples and presets while being converted. Use the Browse button to specify a location to save any temporary files, and use the options below to specify how Giga will dump the temp files, once converted.
- **Short Cut Operations**—Selects a specific operation to take place if an Akai sample or file is double-clicked within the QuickSound interface. For example, if you double-click on an Akai file, you can have the Akai converter automatically begin the conversion process by selecting the Convert To Gig option within this section.

Once your preferences have been set, click the OK button to close the window. Now, let's convert an Akai-formatted CD-ROM into one or several Giga instruments. For this example, I will be using a sample collection called Retro Funk by Spectrasonics (**www.spectrasonics.net**).

1. Insert the CD. Once GigaStudio detects the CD, its contents will be displayed in the Folder Tree pane of the QuickSound Loader (see Figure 6.50).
2. The contents of an Akai CD are split up and viewed as partitions. Using the list of partitions in the Folder Tree, find the sample directory you wish to convert. Click on the directory to select it and display its contents in the Instrument List pane (see Figure 6.51).
3. Assuming you have located a sample or folder of samples you wish to convert, double-click on the file or folder to begin the conversion process. A new window will pop up asking you to select a directory to place the converted files. Once you have selected a directory, click OK to begin the conversion process (see Figure 6.52).
4. Once the files have been converted, they will be displayed as Giga instruments in the Instrument List pane (see Figure 6.53).

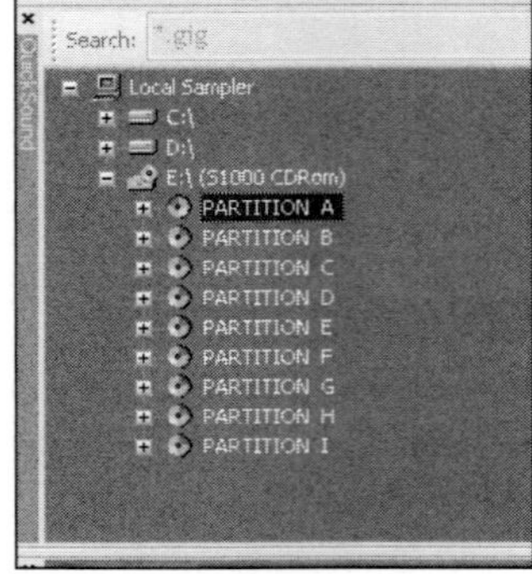

Figure 6.50
After inserting the CD, GigaStudio will display its contents in the Folder Tree pane of the QuickSound Loader.

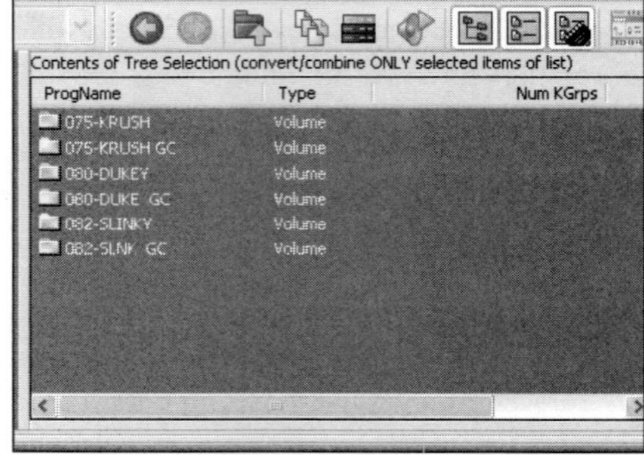

Figure 6.51
Once you locate the directory of samples you wish to convert, click on it once to select it and display its contents in the Instrument list.

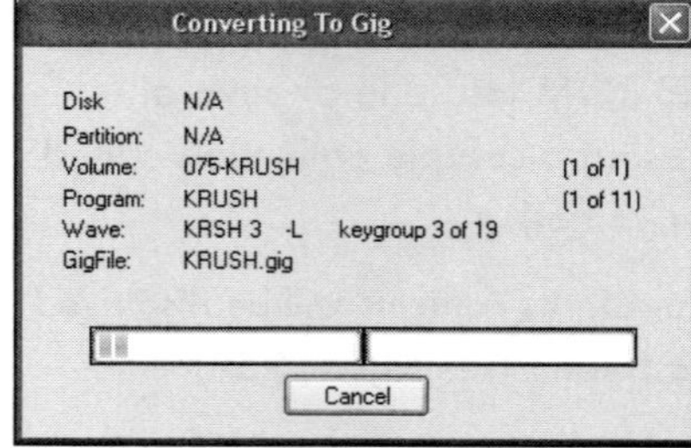

Figure 6.52
Once you have selected a directory to save your converted files, click OK and GigaStudio will proceed to convert your Akai samples into Giga instruments.

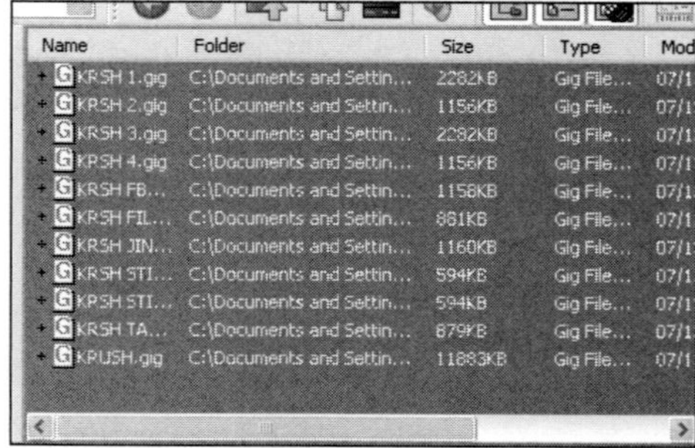

Figure 6.53
Our Akai files have been converted into Giga instruments.

CONVERTING MULTIPLE PARTITIONS

Converting Akai formatted samples one at a time tends to become more than just a little time consuming, so here's a quick way to convert multiple partitions at once.

1. Click once on the CD-ROM drive in the Folder Tree pane to display all of the partitions of an Akai CD in the Instrument List pane.
2. Click on the top partition in the Instrument list to select it and then hold down the Shift key and click the last partition at the bottom. This will select all the partitions at once.
3. Double-click on the bottom partition and the same pop-up window will appear, asking you to designate a location to place the converted Giga instruments.
4. Once a destination is selected, click OK, and GigaStudio will begin the conversion process, which will take a few minutes, depending on how much information needs to be converted.

Creating Your First Giga Instrument

When it comes to creating instruments with GigaStudio, there's the easy way and the hard way, literally. GigaStudio provides two different methods for importing, creating, and exporting Giga instruments, one being the Distributed Wave Editor (the easy way) and the other being the more coveted GigaStudio Editor (the hard way). And while not quite as intuitive as other competing software sampler construction kits, such as the one found in HALion, the EXS24, and Kontakt, it does offer some compelling advantages over the competition. In this last segment of our GigaStudio chapter, I will introduce you to these two editors and provide a few brief demonstrations to help you on your way to constructing your own Giga instruments.

The Distributed Wave Editor

The first sample editor we'll look at is the Distributed Wave Editor (DW Editor for short), which is a simple but effective way to import your samples and create your own customized instruments. The DW Editor is also linked to the audio capture feature of GigaStudio by providing a quick and seamless platform to import any audio samples directly into it.

After creating these new Giga instruments, you can improve upon them further by opening them in GigaStudio Editor, which we'll look at later.

Opening the Distributed Wave Editor

Opening the DW Editor is done from the GigaStudio MIDI Mixer. Select any MIDI channel slot and click on the down arrow. A pop-up menu will appear with the option Create/Edit Distributed Wave Instrument (see Figure 6.54). Select this option to open the DW Editor interface (see Figure 6.55).

Figure 6.54
Select any MIDI instrument slot and select Create/Edit Distributed Wave Instrument to launch the DW Editor.

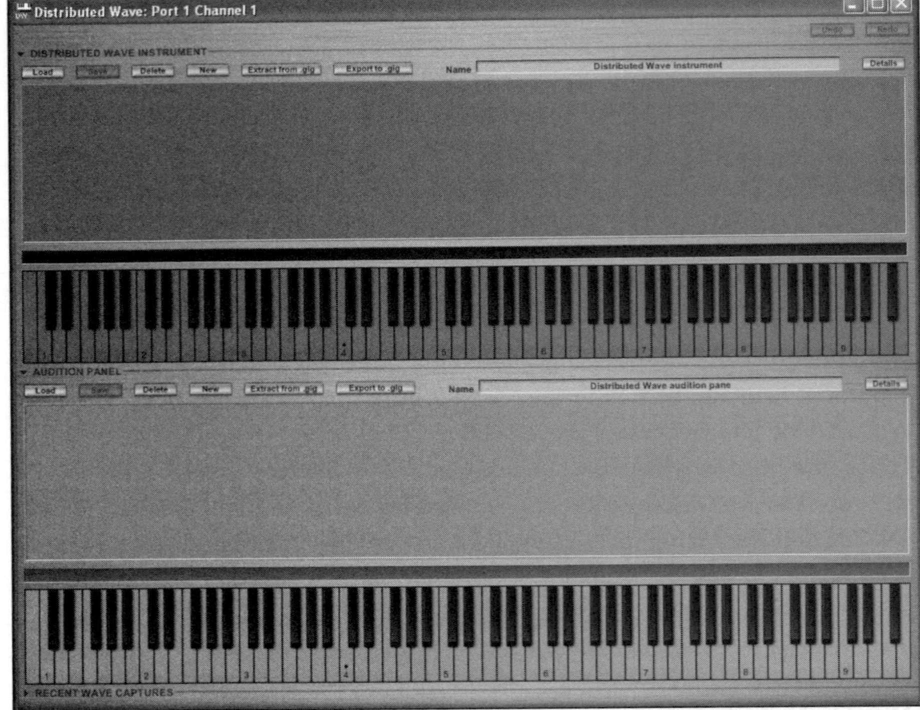

Figure 6.55
Here is the DW Editor, ready to import samples to create a Giga instrument.

Basic Layout of the Distributed Wave Editor

Looking back at Figure 6.55, you can see that the DW Editor is split into three different panels:

- **Distributed Wave Instrument Panel**—This is the top part of the graphic interface, which is responsible for configuring the global parameters of the Giga instrument to be built.
- **Audition Panel**—This panel auditions imported samples, which can then be saved or moved to the Distributed Wave Instrument panel.
- **Recent Wave Captures Panel**—This panel lists any recently recorded digital audio WAV files by way of the Audio Capture function of GigaStudio.

Using the Distributed Wave Editor

In this section, I will take you through the steps of quickly importing and exporting your samples as a Giga instrument via the Distributed Wave Editor. Note that if you are looking to create a multilayered Giga instrument, the DW Editor isn't really the best place to start, as it's not meant for that particular function. Therefore, I recommend skipping over this section and making your way down to the GigaStudio Editor tutorial that follows.

Importing Samples

Importing audio files into the DW Editor can be done by simply dragging and dropping the audio files into the Audition panel. Looking at Figure 6.56, you can see that I have a selection of prepared electric guitar samples listed in the Instrument List pane of the QuickSound Editor. I can click and drag these samples into the Audition panel of the DW Editor, at which point the samples will automatically be imported and mapped out chromatically.

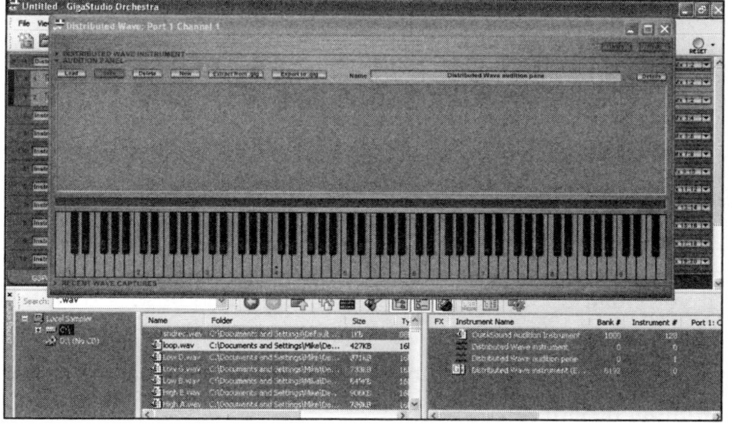

Figure 6.56
Samples can be dragged and dropped from a folder or from the QuickSound Loader to the DW Editor. Once a sample is dropped onto the DW Editor interface, you can quickly arrange the samples by clicking and dragging them up or down the Virtual Keyboard.

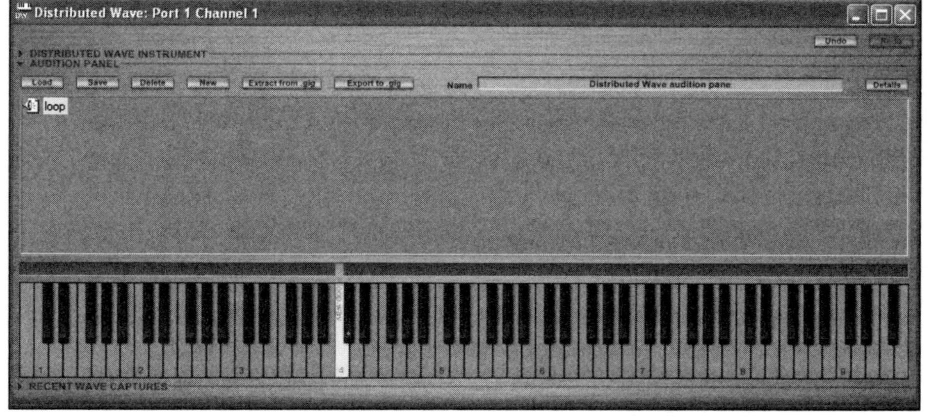

> **EXTRACTING GIGA INSTRUMENTS**
>
> The DW Editor also offers the ability to extract Giga instruments into the DW interface, with the intention of integrating your own samples in order to create a new, customized Giga instrument. However, as the DW Editor is a very basic editor, it is able to import only very simple Giga instruments, such as drum kits or loops. More specifically, the Giga instrument cannot contain any velocity data, mapping data, or other additional edit parameters such as filter or LFO data.

Exporting the Samples

Now that the samples have been imported and arranged, it's time to finish up by exporting the samples as a Giga instrument. Click on the Export to .gig button to begin the process. The Save Distributed Wave File window will pop up, asking you to specify a name and location to compile and export your Giga instrument to. Since this is probably your first time doing this, I would suggest that you keep it simple and export the new instrument to the computer desktop and give it a basic name so that you can find it again without much hassle (see Figure 6.57). Once you're finished, click Save, and the DW Editor will create a Giga instrument file.

The GigaStudio Editor

By comparison to the DW Editor, the GigaStudio Editor is by far a superior solution for creating and editing Giga instruments. It is an offline editor that runs independently of GigaStudio itself, but it has an interesting integration that allows for seamless porting between the two applications. For example, if you have a Giga instrument of string samples loaded into an instrument slot, you can import that instrument straight into the GigaStudio Editor with the click of your mouse, make your edits, and export it back to GigaStudio without hesitation.

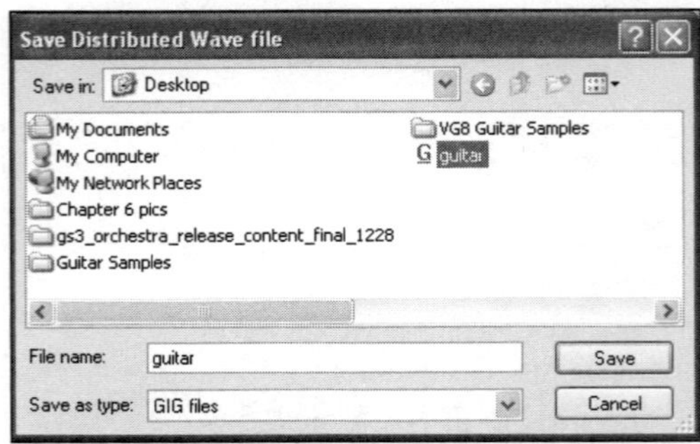

Figure 6.57

The Save Distributed Wave File window assigns a name and location to your new Giga instrument. As you can see here, I have named my instrument Guitar, and I am saving it to the desktop.

First Look at the GigaStudio Editor

As mentioned before, the GigaStudio Editor runs separately from the actual GigaStudio application, which differs from the DW Editor and QuickEdit, which run alongside the host application. To begin our tutorial, we need to launch the GigaStudio Editor by selecting Start, All Programs, Tascam, GigaStudio 3, GigaStudio Editor. As soon as the editor launches, you should see an empty interface similar to Figure 6.58.

Now that the GigaStudio Editor is open, the first thing to do is create a new instrument by selecting New from the File pull-down menu (key command Ctrl+N). A new blank Giga instrument should immediately pop up, which provides us with a good starting place to point out the main features of the interface. Use Figure 6.59 as a reference and read along with the following list.

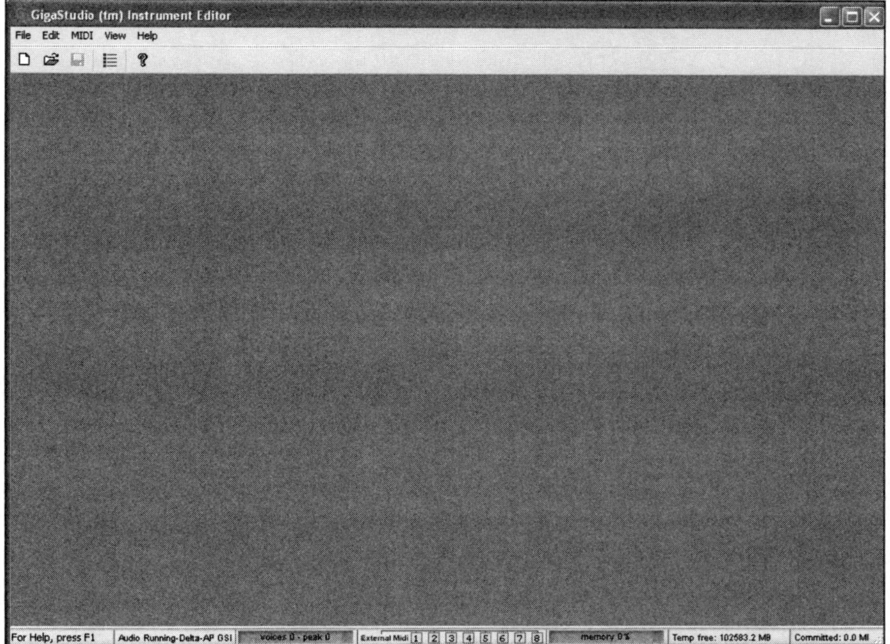

Figure 6.58
The GigaStudio Editor is a separate editor that runs independently of GigaStudio 3 and starts off with a blank interface when first launched.

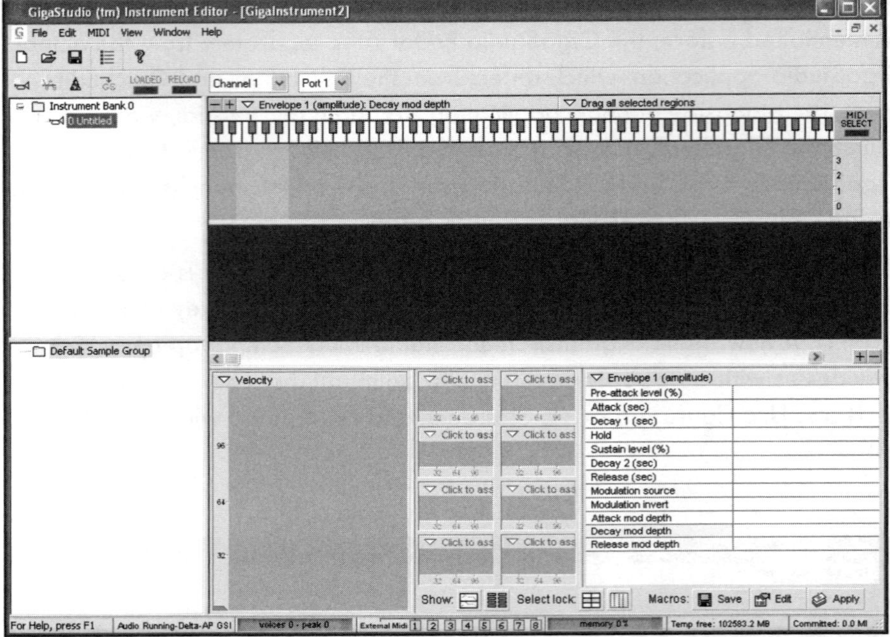

Figure 6.59

Select New from the File pull-down menu to start with a blank Giga instrument template.

- **Bank Tree**—Located in the upper-left corner, the Bank Tree lists all of the Giga instruments within a bank.
- **Group Tree**—Located just below the Bank Tree, the Group Tree lists all of the samples within a group. This is a helpful tool when you have samples that contain multiple velocities, such as guitars and pianos. You can create a group folder for the soft samples, another folder for the medium samples, and a third folder for the hard samples.
- **Mapping Editor**—Occupying the upper half of the GigaStudio Editor, the Mapping Editor arranges and maps your samples (called *regions*) out across the GigaStudio Virtual Keyboard.
- **Waveform Display**—Located just below the Mapping Editor, this section of the GigaStudio Editor graphically displays the waveform of a loaded sample.
- **Velocity Editor**—To the lower left of the Waveform Display, the Velocity Editor alters the amount of velocity assigned to an imported sample. It is also a great way to select a specific set of samples in order to apply an effect to just them and not the rest of the samples within an instrument.
- **Parameter Edit**—This section edits and introduces new parameters to a loaded sample or multiple samples, such as envelopes and LFOs.

Importing a Sample

Let's get down to business by importing our first sample and mapping it out with the GigaStudio Editor. For this demonstration, I'll take it easy and import a single drum loop, which is located on my desktop. But first, I have to set up a couple of preferences, which is done by selecting Preferences from the Edit pull-down menu (see Figure 6.60).

Set the following preferences:

1 First, set the Middle C setting to C3.
2 Next, make sure that the Unity Note for Imported WAV File dialog is set to Default to Middle C, which simply means that the root note of the imported drum loop will be middle C.
3 Last, make sure that there is only one velocity split, as we do not intend to create any this time around.
4 When finished, click OK to close the Preferences window.

Now we're ready to begin, so select Import Samples from the Edit pull-down menu. This will activate the New Sample window (see Figure 6.61).

I'll navigate to the desktop and locate the Loop.wav file, which I can preview by highlighting the file and then pressing Play in the upper-right portion of the browser. I'm ready to import the sample, so I'll click Open, and the sample will appear in the Group Tree. In order to import the sample onto the Mapping Editor, where it belongs, simply click and drag the file to the C3 position of the Mapping Editor and release the mouse. Now we have our first imported sample (see Figure 6.62).

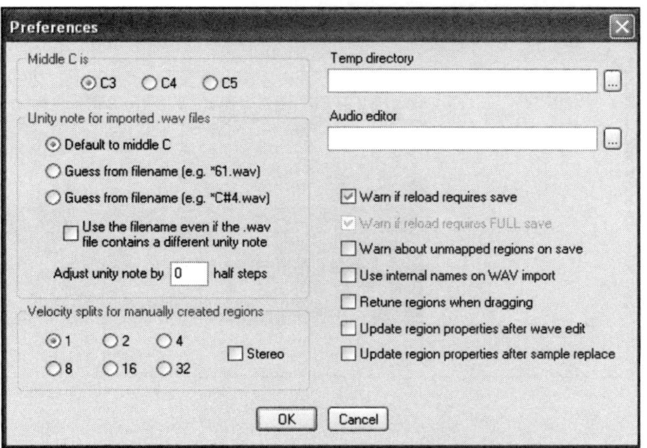

Figure 6.60

The Preferences window specifies how you want the GigaStudio Editor to handle any imported audio files.

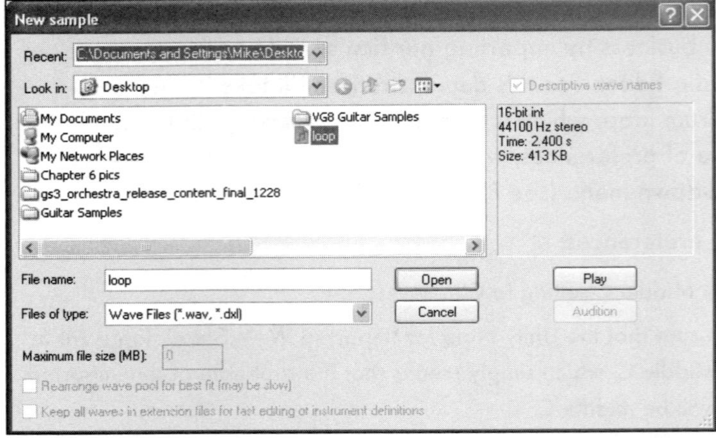

Figure 6.61

The New Sample window locates and loads samples into the GigaStudio Editor.

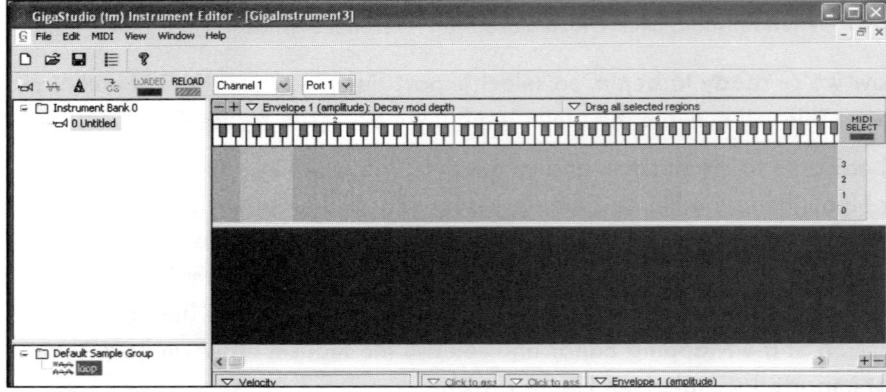

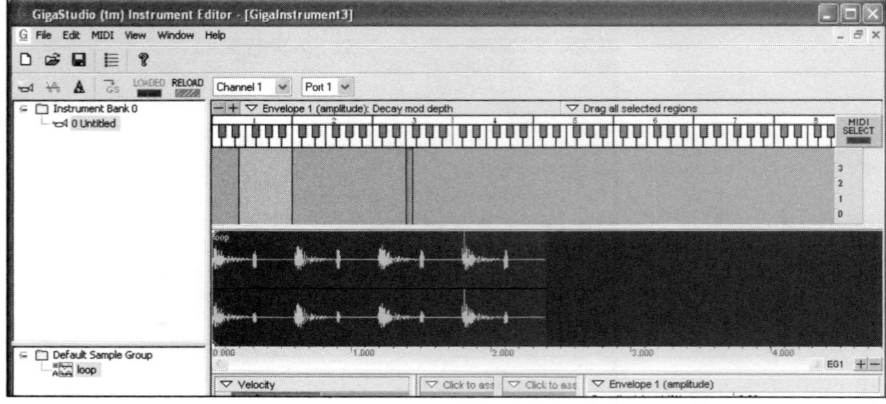

Figure 6.62

Click and drag the sample onto the Mapping Editor and release it just under the C3 note.

To finish this off, click and drag the right border of the sample to the right to extend the note range of the loaded sample by 3 or 4 notes.

Saving Your Giga Instrument

We're ready to finish off this tutorial, so let's save this sample as a Giga instrument by selecting Save As from the File pull-down menu. This will activate the Save As browser window. Assign your sample a name and location (the desktop would be a good idea) and press Save to export your sample as a Giga instrument (see Figure 6.63).

Let's put our new Giga instrument to the test by launching GigaStudio and opening our new instrument. Looking at Figure 6.64, you can see that the instrument is now loaded into the first instrument slot of the MIDI Mixer, and if you look at the Virtual Keyboard below, you'll also notice that the key range we set up in the GigaStudio Editor is reflected here as well.

Creating Your First Multisample Giga Instrument

By now, you should be acquainted with the GigaStudio Editor, so let's turn up the heat a little and construct a slightly more complicated Giga instrument using the Instrument Wizard, which is utility software embedded within the GigaStudio Editor to help you easily create multisample Giga instruments at the touch of a button.

To make this tutorial even more fun, I will be using 18 acoustic guitar samples, which are available for you to download from the Course Technology Web site (**www.courseptr.com**).

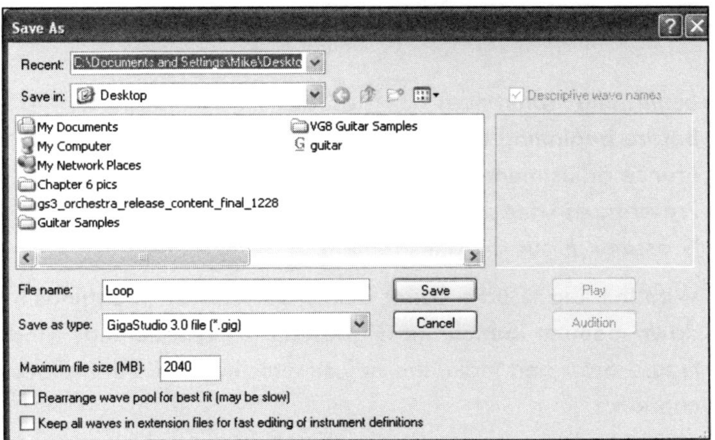

Figure 6.63

Our first Giga instrument is exported and ready to be used in GigaStudio.

Figure 6.64
Our new Giga instrument has been loaded into GigaStudio, and all is well.

> **THESE SAMPLES ARE COPYRIGHT SAFE**
> After going through the steps of this tutorial and creating your first Giga instrument, you might get the urge to use these samples in a song you're working on. This is perfectly fine to do because these samples are *copyright safe.* These samples were not taken from a sample collection. I created these samples sitting in front of my computer with a guitar over the course of an hour specifically for this tutorial. I encourage you to use these guitar samples freely in any songs you write with GigaStudio.

Setting the Preferences

Before beginning the tutorial, we should take a moment to make a few preference adjustments to the System Settings window and the GigaStudio Editor Preferences window. This is to ensure that the Instrument Wizard will correctly assemble our Giga instrument.

With the GigaStudio Editor active, select System Settings from the File pull-down menu to launch the GigaStudio System Settings window. Look at Figure 6.65 and make the adjustments indicated in the accompanying caption.

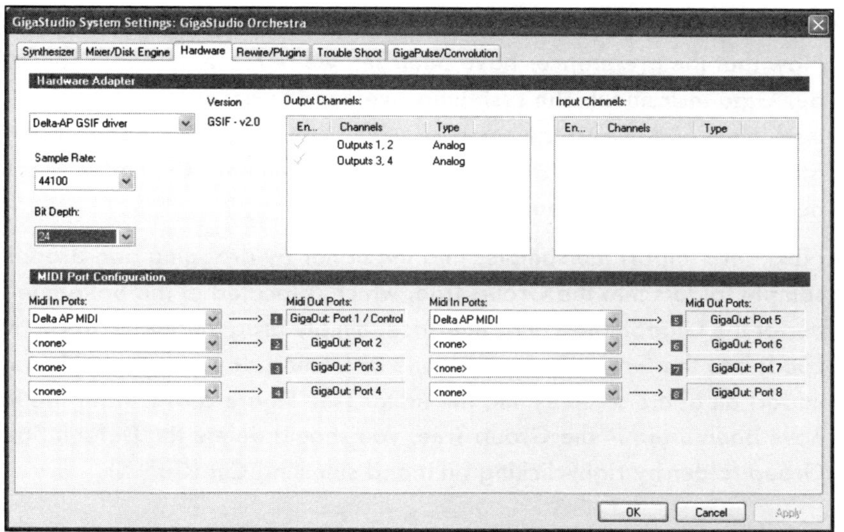

Figure 6.65

After opening the System Settings window, select the Hardware tab. Make sure that the correct GSIF driver is selected at the top left of this window and that Bit Depth is set to 24-bit, as the samples we will import are true 24-bit files. When you are finished, click Apply and then OK to close the window.

Next up, let's make a few adjustments to the editor preferences by selecting Preferences from the Edit pull-down menu. Look at Figure 6.66 and make the adjustments in the caption.

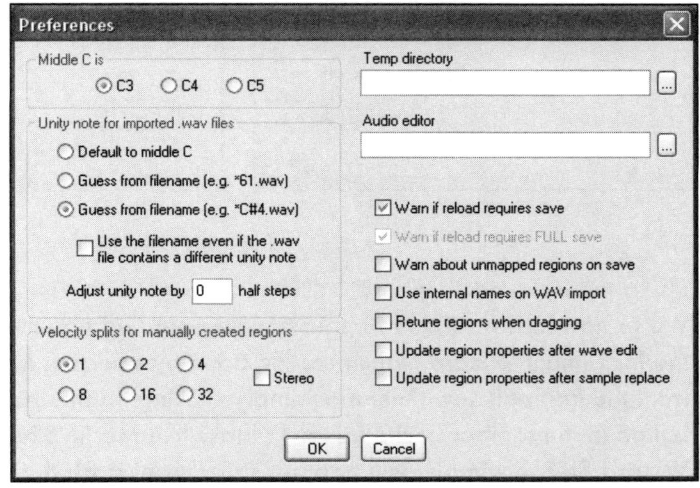

Figure 6.66

After opening the Preferences window, change the Middle C Is window to C3 to reset the central positioning for middle C on the GigaStudio Virtual Keyboard. Next, navigate to the Unity Note for Imported .WAV Files window and set this dialog to Guess from Filename (e.g. *C#4.wav), which tells the editor to determine the root note by using the file name as a reference. When you are finished, click the OK button to close the window.

Importing the Samples

Now that the preferences have been set, we're ready to begin constructing our Giga instrument. The first things we need to do are create a new blank instrument and import the samples, which can be done by drag and drop. Start by selecting New from the File pull-down menu (Ctrl+N) to create a new blank instrument template.

Next, let's import the samples into the editor by dragging and dropping the sample folders into the Group Tree, which is located at the bottom left corner of the GigaStudio Editor interface. Simply drag the folders (Soft, Medium, Loud) into the Group Tree either one at a time or all at once, which will import all of the samples into the editor (see Figure 6.67). After the folders have been listed in the Group Tree, you should delete the Default Sample Group folder by right-clicking on it and selecting Cut (Ctrl+X).

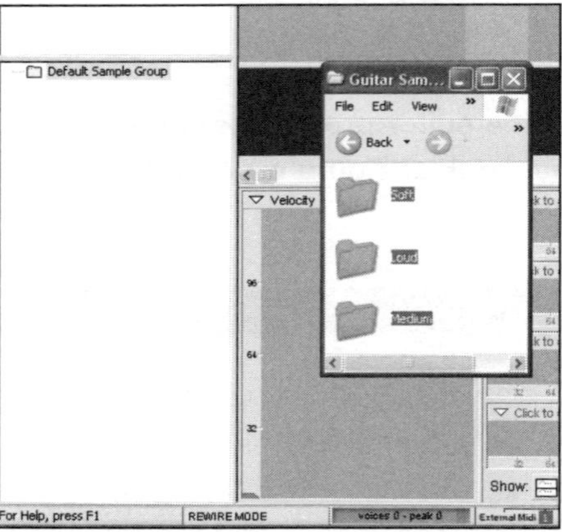

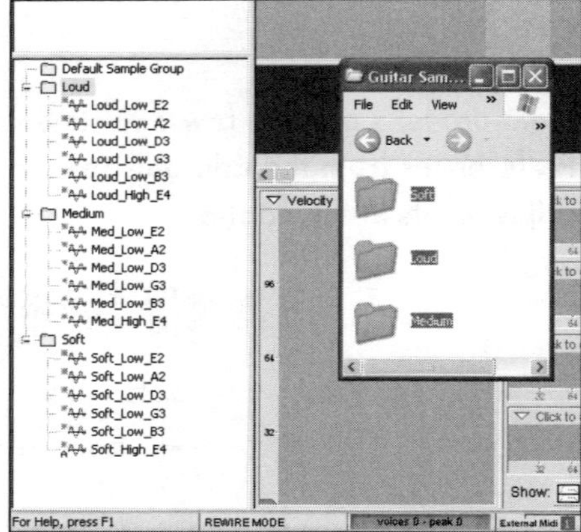

Figure 6.67
Importing samples into the Group Tree is simply a matter of drag and drop from the folder that contains the samples (left) to the Group Tree interface. Release the mouse and the folders and their corresponding samples will be listed in the Group Tree interface (right).

Using the Instrument Wizard

We're now in a position to begin building our Giga instrument by launching the Instrument Wizard, which can be done by selecting Instrument Wizard from the Edit pull-down menu or simply clicking on the Instrument Wizard button in the toolbar of the editor (it looks like Merlin's hat). The Instrument Wizard Step 1 window will pop up, so let's get started. Use Figure 6.68 and the following list to begin the building process.

1 Use the Name dialog to assign a name to your instrument. Try something simple such as Guitar.

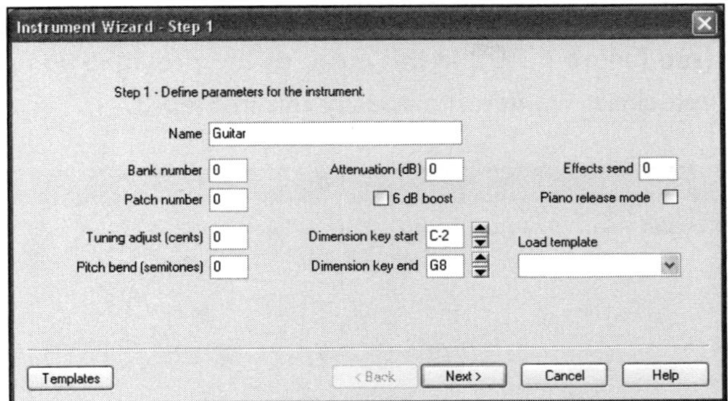

Figure 6.68

The Instrument Wizard Step 1 window begins the building process by assigning a name to our instrument and a desired note range.

2 Next, assign a note range to this instrument by using the Dimension Key Start/End dialog. Let's cover the entire Virtual Keyboard by setting the low note to C-2 and the high note to G8.

3 Click the Next button to proceed to the next step.

Let's push on and continue with the Step 2 window (see Figure 6.69).

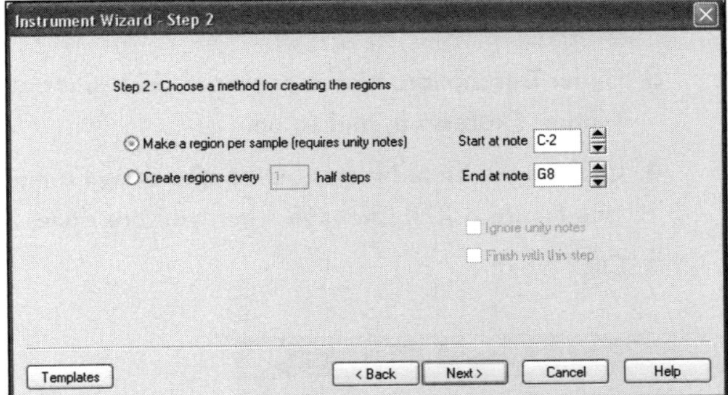

Figure 6.69

The Step 2 window specifies how the editor will create regions for each imported sample.

1 Select Make a Region per Sample (Requires Unity Notes). This simply means that the editor will create one discrete region per sample in the Group Tree.

2 Use the Start at Note and End at Note settings to set the key range to C-2 to G8.

3 Click the Next button.

Next up is Step 3, which deals with the overall dimensions of the instrument (see Figure 6.70). In this case, as the provided samples are set at different velocities, we need to specify this in Step 3.

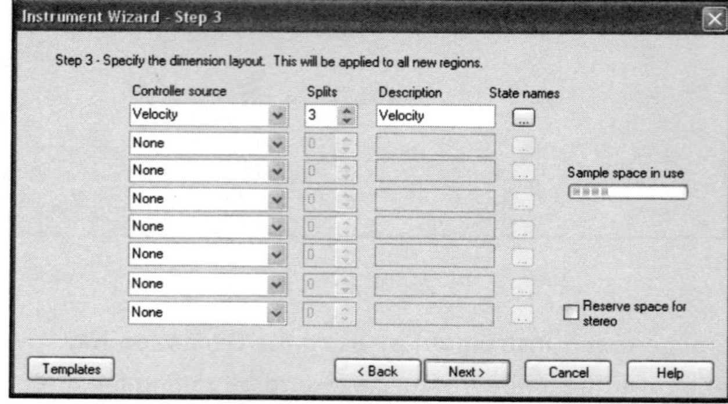

Figure 6.70
Step 3 involves specifying the dimensions of a Giga instrument.

1 Set Controller Source to Velocity by selecting it from the provided pop-up menu.

2 Set Splits to 3, which will produce three separate velocity splits (Soft, Medium, Loud).

3 Under Description, type a one-word description of the splits, such as Velocity, Timbre, Expression, and so on.

4 Click on the State Names button and assign a name to each velocity split (see Figure 6.71). Click OK when you are done.

5 Click Next.

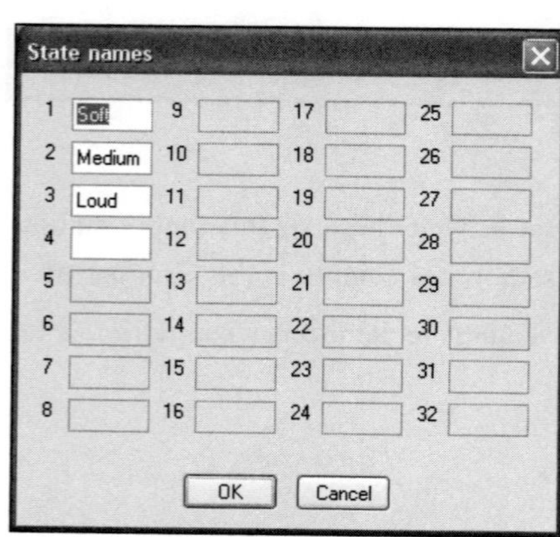

Figure 6.71
Use the State Names window to assign a name to each velocity split.

The Step 4 window assigns a group folder to a velocity group, which is done by clicking first on the group folder and then the appropriate velocity group (see Figure 6.72). As you can see in the figure, I have assigned the Soft group to the Soft Velocity group, the Medium group to the Medium Velocity group. When you are finished, click the Finish button, and the editor will build your Giga instrument (see Figure 6.73).

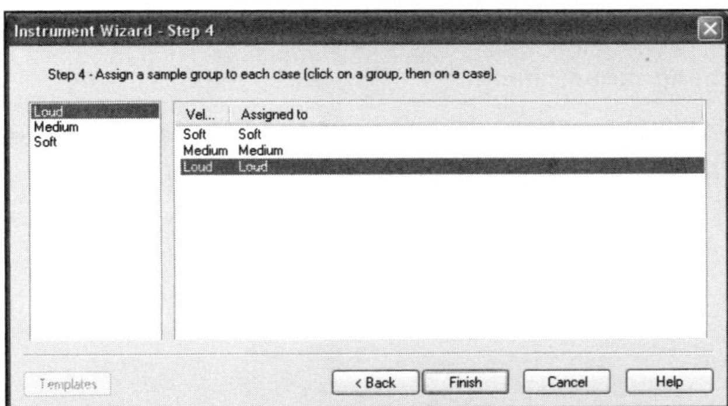

Figure 6.72
The Step 4 window assigns your group folders to the appropriate velocity groups.

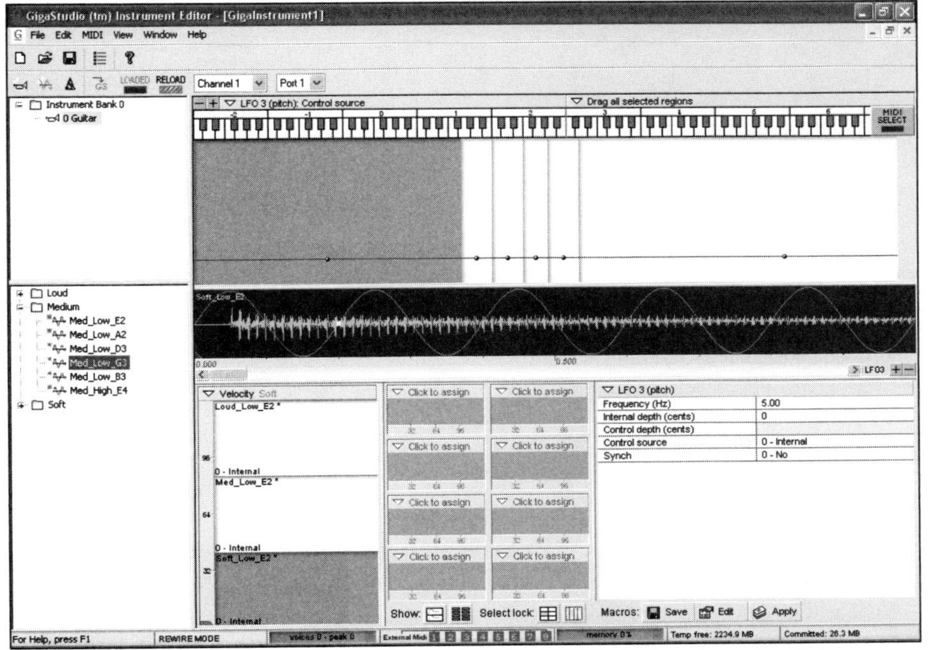

Figure 6.73
The Instrument Wizard has finished and has built our first multilayered, multisample guitar instrument.

SAVE YOUR WORK

Before moving any further, make sure you save your work by clicking the Save button in the editor toolbar and then assign a name and location to save your Giga instrument.

You can see why GigaStudio has become such a standard for software sampling over the years. With the new features such as audio capturing, GigaPulse, and ReWire support, it's sure to remain at the top of the sampling mountain.

Although we covered a lot of ground in this chapter, we have only just begun to unlock the creative potential of GigaStudio 3. Be sure to look in the included user's manual to catch up with some more advanced GigaStudio features.

Kontakt Tutorial

Since this book is intended for use by both Mac and PC users alike, it's only fair that I give the Mac users a good alternative to the Giga environment. Although there are a lot of Mac-based software samplers on the market, such as HALion, Mach5, and EXS24, Kontakt by Native Instruments is a good overall solution. There are a couple of reasons for this:

- **Supports All DAW Applications**—You name it, Kontakt supports it: VST, AU, DXi, RTAS, and standalone.
- **Dual Platform Ready**—Kontakt supports both the Mac and PC platforms, so even if you are a Windows user looking for an alternative to GigaStudio, this is a good choice.

Although we have taken a look at Kontakt once or twice already, we have not really taken the time to show you what this baby can do. In this chapter, we will take a walk-through of the Kontakt interface (see Figure 7.1).

Figure 7.1

Kontakt by Native Instruments is a fantastic software sampler that includes a large sample library and support for many other sampler formats.

WHAT VERSION SHOULD YOU USE?

Before we get knee deep in Kontakt jargon, take a minute to make sure that you are using the latest version, which in this case is version 1.5.3. You'll be glad you did because it fixes known graphical bugs and includes new features such as hard disk streaming.

If you don't have the latest version, download it from the Native Instruments Web site at **www.native-instruments.com**.

At First Sight

After completing the installation of Kontakt, you can choose to open it in its standalone mode, which means that no host application is required to use it. This is a cool feature because it enables you to use Kontakt in the same way as GigaStudio. This is the way we'll use it for most of this tutorial. Later on, I'll show you how to enable Kontakt in most popular host applications, such as SONAR, Logic, Digital Performer, and Cubase.

The Kontakt interface is split into two sections

- **The Browser**—Located on the left, the browser is used to locate, preview, and load both individual samples and instruments into the rack.
- **The Rack**—Located on the right, the rack is used to organize, play, and edit the loaded samples and instruments.

The Multi-Instrument Interface

Above the rack lays the multi-instrument interface (see Figure 7.2). This interface is used to manage the global parameters of Kontakt, including the loading and saving of instruments, the preferences, and the appearance.

Figure 7.2
The multi-instrument interface handles all the global parameters and settings for Kontakt.

KONTAKT'S STRUCTURE AND TERMS

Before we get too deep into the specifics of Kontakt, it would be a good idea to discuss the overall structure and terms that define the inner workings of Kontakt.

At the most basic level is the *sample,* which as you know by now is a small digital audio recording. Once imported, a sample is then placed in a *zone*. A zone is used to assign a playback position for the sample and stretch out the sample along the Virtual Keyboard of Kontakt. A zone can include sample data such as:

- **Hi-note/Low-note**—This assigns the highest and lowest notes that will trigger a sample via a MIDI keyboard.
- **Velocity**—This assigns the highest and lowest velocities that will trigger a sample via a MIDI keyboard.
- **Panning**—This assigns the sample to different positions within the stereo field.
- **Volume**—This assigns the overall volume to the sample itself.

As only one sample can be assigned to a zone, many additional zones can be created to import several different samples. Once imported and edited, these compilations of zones can be virtually linked together by creating a *group*. Doing this makes it possible to alter one zone and have the other linked zone follow accordingly. This is especially useful when it comes to using the internal effects of Kontakt, which we will be doing later in this chapter.

Once your zones and groups are set, you can then save them to a single file, known as an *instrument*. This could also be thought of as a *patch,* as it is sometimes referred to in the Kontakt manual. For example, when you load an acoustic guitar instrument into the Kontakt interface, you are actually loading a compilation of zones that contain multiple samples and are grouped together. Note that a Kontakt instrument file has the .nki extension in the file name.

Finally, Kontakt can save compilations of instruments into a single file known as a *multi-instrument.* This is extremely useful for composers who have a particular arrangement of instruments they like to use when composing. They can just save all of their favorite instruments (up to 16) into a single multi-instrument file that can then be loaded into Kontakt at will. Note that a multi-instrument file has the .nkm extension in the file name.

Let's cover these buttons one by one.

The Load/Save Menu

At the far left, the Load/Save menu is used to create, load, save, and edit a single instrument or multiple instruments.

- **New Instrument**—This option creates a new blank instrument, which will be displayed in the rack.
- **Load**—This option produces two choices: Load to New Instrument and Load Multi. When Load to New Instrument is selected, Kontakt will automatically create a new instrument in the rack and load the samples to that location. Load Multi is used to load multiple instruments at one time.

- **Save**—This option can save any changes made to a single instrument, or it can be used to compile multiple instruments into a single multi file.
- **Remove**—This option removes the loaded instrument.
- **Reset**—This option will reset or initialize the loaded instrument. This will unload all of the samples in an instrument and set every parameter back to its default value.

The Options Button

Clicking on the Options button will launch the Settings window, which can be used to edit the appearance and tuning, in addition to other useful functions. Looking at Figure 7.3, you can see that the Settings window has many different pages, which can be accessed by clicking on the Select button in the upper-left corner.

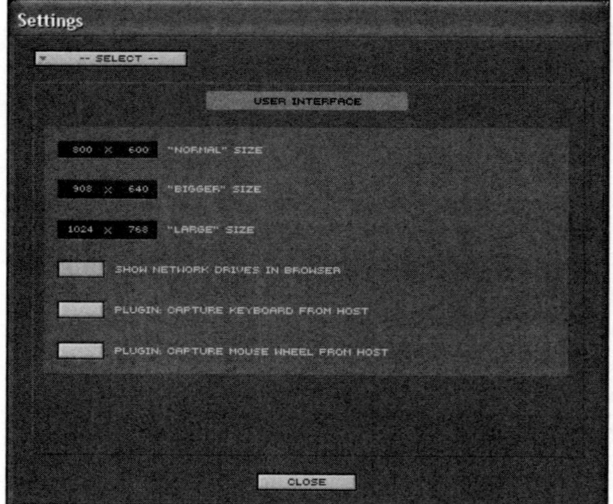

Figure 7.3
The Settings window is used to set up and optimize Kontakt for your virtual environment.

The first page to view is the User Interface page, which includes the following options:

- **Interface Size**—This allows you to allocate a specific pixel resolution to the Kontakt interface. Once any changes are made to the Normal, Bigger, or Large option, you can then toggle between each size in the View pop-up menu on the main Kontakt interface.
- **Show Network Drives in Browser**—When selected, this will cause Kontakt to display any hard drives connected via network.

- **Capture Keyboard from Host**—This option catches certain keyboard commands and routes them to Kontakt rather than to the host program. This is to solve a common problem of conflicting keyboard commands between the host application and Kontakt when it is being used as a plug-in.
- **Capture Mouse Wheel from Host**—This option catches the scroll wheel actions from the mouse for use in the plug-in.

The next page is the Engine page, which contains the following options:

- **Stereo Outputs**—This option assigns a number of stereo outputs to Kontakt. It has a range of 1 to 16 stereo pairs.
- **Mono Outputs**—This option assigns a number of mono outputs to Kontakt. It has a range of 1 to 32.
- **Lock Memory**—This option protects RAM-driven instruments from being swapped to disk when memory is getting low. This is to prevent computer crashes.
- **Use STD CC#7/CC#10 Master Volume & Pan**—This option links the standard MIDI controls of 7 and 10 to Kontakt's master volume and pan controls.
- **CPU Throttle**—This option is used to remove voices from Kontakt if and when a specific CPU use level is reached.
- **Sustain/Sustenuto Pedal Mode**—This pop-up menu is used to assign a function to the sustain pedal. There are four options, including Normal, Use as MIDI Controller, Use as MIDI Switch, Normal Plus MIDI Switch.
- **Solo Mode**—This pop-up menu is used to toggle between two solo modes.
- **Master Tune**—This parameter is used to change the master tuning of Kontakt. Note that holding down the Ctrl key on the PC or the Apple key on the Mac and then clicking with the mouse will set this parameter back to zero.

Next is the Handling page.

- **Double Clicking Sample Creates Instrument**—When selected, double-clicking on a sample in the browser will automatically create a new instrument in the rack. Also note that the sample will be loaded in and mapped out over the entire keyboard.
- **Use Sample's Icon for Auditioning**—When this option is selected, you can click once on a sample's icon to audition the sample without having to click on the Audition button in the browser.
- **Auto-Mute Newly Created Instrument**—When this is selected, a new instrument will be automatically muted once created.

- **Ask Before Removing Instruments/Zones**—This option activates a prompt to ask you before removing either a zone or an instrument.
- **Default Root Key**—This dialog is used to set a default root key whenever a sample is imported without an assigned root.
- **External Wave Editor**—This interface allows you to select a wave editing program to edit your samples. I'll show you how to use this feature later in this chapter.
- **Installation Base Path**—This interface allows you to designate the location of the Kontakt Program folder.

Next is the Load/Save/Import page.

- **Combine Akai/SF2 Samples to Stereo**—Converts dual mono samples in either Akai or Sound Font format into a single stereo file.
- **Bypass Filter when Importing Giga**—This option bypasses the input filter when a Giga instrument is converted and loaded into Kontakt.
- **Auto Convert Loaded Samples to 32-Bit**—This option converts samples to 32-bit files. Read the following Note for more information.
- **Save Patches in Kontakt 1.5.1 Format**—When this is selected, Kontakt will save any edits made in version 1.5.2 as version 1.5.1 format. This is to ensure downward compatibility.
- **Ignore Bypasses Modules when Importing Kompakt/Intakt**—When selected, this option will automatically delete bypassed modules from Kompakt and/or Intakt upon load.

MORE BITS = BETTER PERFORMANCE

As you now know from reading the preceding list, Kontakt supports a bit depth of 32, but that might seem a little confusing because digital audio in general has a maximum bit depth of 24. So what benefits can you expect to receive from converting samples to 32-bit? I posed this same question to Julian Ringel, who is the Kontakt Product Manager for Native Instruments:

"32-bit is the computer's native processor format. Upon loading of a non–32-bit sample, the sample gets transferred to the RAM and is stored there. When the sample needs to be processed by the CPU, it will be converted to 32 bits in run time, which is a real-time computation. This computation costs processing power.

"In the case that someone has enough RAM to store a 32-bit sample, they can convert the sample upon load to save CPU power, which otherwise would have been eaten by the conversion."

Julian also offers his short version of this lengthy process:

Converting to 32-bit upon load wastes RAM and saves CPU.

No conversion upon load saves RAM but requires more CPU.

Last up is the DFD page. This is used to apply different options to the Direct from Disc streaming options.

- **Active**—This option turns the DFD feature on/off.
- **Apply**—When any changes are made in this page, be sure to click on the Apply button to make them permanent.
- **Performance Menu**—This menu allows you to select different performance presets for Kontakt. The choices are Expert (selected by default), Normal, High Performance, Large Instruments, and Small Instruments.
- **Preload Buffer Size**—This slider assigns an amount of memory for preloading individual samples.
- **Voice Buffer Size**—This slider enables you to assign more RAM for each voice that will be streamed and less RAM for each sample that is loaded into RAM.
- **Reserved Voices**—This dialog sets the overall polyphony of Kontakt when using the DFD function. It has a range of 8–256 voices.
- **Autoload Patches in DFD Whenever Possible**—When this option is selected, Kontakt will import each sample format and use it in DFD mode, including Kontakt, Giga, EXS24, Akai, SF2, HALion, Battery, and LM4.

Once you have set your options, click on the Close button to return to the main Kontakt interface.

SUPPORTED SAMPLE FORMATS

Kontakt supports a wide variety of other sampler formats that can be easily imported into the interface. This makes it possible to expand your library greatly with all sorts of different sample collections. Formats include the following:

- Akai S1000/3000
- Emagic EXS24
- HALion and LM4
- GigaSampler
- Sample Cell
- SoundFont2

Kontakt also imports many digital audio file formats, including the standard AIFF/WAV files, REX files, and Sound Designer 2 files.

The View Menu

Moving on to the right, the View menu is used to set the viewable size of the Kontakt interface. As you will recall, the sizes are set within the Options window. To change the size of the Kontakt interface, select Normal, Bigger, or Large.

The last two buttons of the multi-instrument interface lend a hand to changing the appearance of Kontakt (see Figure 7.4).

- **Browser**—Clicking on this button will hide/unhide the browser section of Kontakt.
- **Rack**—Clicking on this button will hide/unhide the rack section of Kontakt.

Figure 7.4
You can hide and reveal parts of the Kontakt interface by using the Browser and Rack buttons.

The Rack

The Kontakt rack is where all of the action is (see Figure 7.5). This is where you can load instruments, edit them, apply effects to them, and either save them as new instruments or stack them up and save them as multi-instruments.

Figure 7.5
The Kontakt rack is where the action is.

In this section, I am going to take you through the inner workings of the rack step-by-step, as it can be a little confusing to understand. I would suggest that you read this section a few times, as the last part of this chapter concentrates on building your own Kontakt instrument, and this is where your knowledge will be put to the test.

Loading Instruments into the Rack

There are a few different ways to load instruments into the rack.

- Double-clicking on an instrument from the browser.
- Clicking and dragging the instrument from the browser to the rack.
- Using the Load/Save menu from the multi-instrument interface above the rack.

Let's go over each of these briefly.

Assuming that you have successfully installed the samples onto your hard drive and you can view the names of the instruments in the lower pane of the browser, double-click on the instrument you want to load into the rack. As soon as you do this, a progress pop-up window will appear, informing you that the samples are being loaded into the rack (see Figure 7.6).

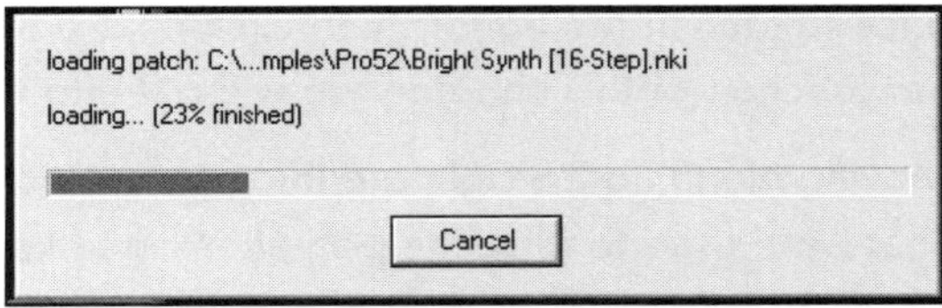

Figure 7.6
After double-clicking on the instrument, a progress pop-up window will appear.

The next way to load instruments is to simply click and drag them into the rack interface. As soon as you release the mouse, a progress pop-up window will appear, just as in Figure 7.6.

The last and somewhat tedious method of loading samples into the rack is to use the Load/Save menu from the multi-instrument interface. Navigate your mouse to this menu and select Load to New Instrument. This will bring up a file-browsing window where you can search for the Kontakt instrument file (see Figure 7.7).

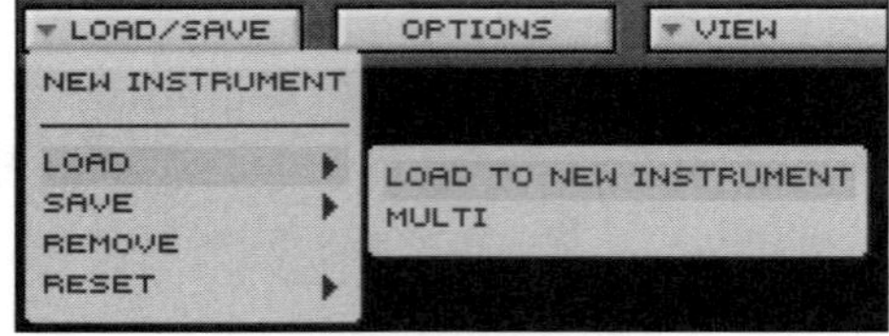

Figure 7.7
If you want to search high and low for your instruments, use the Load/Save menu.

The Instrument Header

Now that you have loaded an instrument into the rack (which is called the *instrument header*), let's discuss the main parameters of the instrument header (see Figure 7.8).

Figure 7.8
The instrument interface at its most basic is called the instrument header.

At the far left of the instrument header is the Edit button. This is used to launch the various editors associated with the loaded instrument. Click on it once to launch the editor, then click on it again to retract the editor. In the next section of this chapter, we will get into editing instruments.

Moving along, to the right are the global parameters of the instrument header. These are used to alter the polyphony and key range, and assign MIDI inputs.

- **Name Dialog**—This is used to change the name of the instrument. Just remember to save your changes should you make any.
- **Key Range**—This dialog is used to assign the highest and lowest keys that the instrument can be played in.
- **Velocity Range**—This dialog is used to assign an overall velocity to the instrument.
- **MIDI Channel/Indicator**—This is used to assign a MIDI input channel and to indicate when it receives MIDI data. Note that this dialog is set to OMNI by default, which simply means that the instrument will respond to any MIDI data it receives, regardless of the channel. If you wish to assign the instrument to a specific MIDI channel, just click on the dialog and select from channels 1–16 in the pop-up menu below. Also note that there is an additional option called GROUP, which I will cover later.

- **Polyphony**—This dialog assigns the amount of polyphony to the instrument. If you are not familiar with this term, it can be thought of as how many notes can be played at one time. On the left side of this dialog is the active amount of polyphony. You will see this value change as you play a note on your keyboard. On the right side of this dialog is the assigned amount of polyphony to the instrument. This has a range of 1 to 256 simultaneous notes. Just remember that the more polyphony you assign to your instrument, the more CPU needed, so if you are just playing a kick drum sample, you will not need more than a polyphony of two, so you can click and drag up or down in the dialog to change this value. You can also double-click on it and type in a new value.
- **File Size**—This is used to display how much memory is being used by the loaded instrument.
- **Output**—This assigns the instrument to a specific audio output. This relates back to the Mono/Stereo Outputs of the Options window.

GROUPED MIDI

Creating grouped MIDI channels is a great way to thicken up your overall sound by stacking up several Kontakt instruments and having them all respond to the same MIDI channel. For example, suppose you're writing a piece of music in which the woodwind and brass ensembles play the same notes. Ideally, you could create a Kontakt instrument of the brass ensemble, load the woodwind ensemble, and have them both listen to MIDI channel one from your sequencer. Let me show you how easy this is.

1. First load two Kontakt instruments.
2. Set the MIDI input channel on both instruments to Group.
3. Click on the Edit button for each instrument. In the source module of each instrument, you should now see a MIDI Group pull-down menu.
4. Set each instrument to the same MIDI group channel (1–16), and then play any key on your MIDI keyboard. You should hear both instruments responding to the same MIDI channel.

At the far right are the mixing parameters for the loaded instrument.

- **Solo/Mute**—These are used to isolate or silence the instrument, just like on a mixing board.
- **Tune**—This knob is used to alter the master tuning of the instrument.
- **Pan**—This knob alters the placement of the instrument in the stereo field.
- **Volume**—This knob is used to alter the overall amplitude of the instrument.

REMOVING INSTRUMENTS

Here's a quick and easy way to remove a loaded instrument from the rack. Click anywhere in the instrument header interface. This will highlight the instrument, at which time you can press the Delete or Backspace key on your keyboard to delete the instrument. Just remember that if you selected the Ask Before Removing Samples/Instruments option, you will get a pop-up menu to verify that you wish to delete the instrument.

Editing Instruments

Let's face it—the best part of creating synthesized music is to edit the sounds and textures by turning knobs and moving sliders. Kontakt gives you all of this and much more by providing various modules, such as envelopes and effects.

To begin, click on the Edit button of the instrument header (see Figure 7.9). This will display the basic editing parameters of the instrument.

Figure 7.9
Click once on the Edit button to begin editing your instrument. Click on it again to return the instrument to its compact view.

If this is your first time looking at the Edit view of a Kontakt instrument, it might seem a little confusing. This is probably due to the lack of familiarity you might find with other software samplers and synths, as a lot of them share similar design layouts such as filters, envelopes, and LFOs. In Kontakt, all of its editing potential is found within what are called *modules*. These are individual devices that are added onto a Kontakt instrument to enhance its overall sound. For example, if you wanted to introduce a filter to your instrument, you would need to create a *filter module*.

There are several different types of modules available, including:

- **The Instrument Header**—This houses the main editing parameters of the instrument (mute, solo, and so forth).
- **The Source**—This module specifies the sound source of the instrument. You'll see this the first time you click the Edit button.
- **The Amplifier**—This module is used to alter the amplitude of the instrument. You'll see this the first time you click the Edit button.

- **Group Insert Effects**—There can be up to six per group.
- **Insert Effects**—There can be up to six per instrument.
- **Send Effects**—There can be up to five per instrument.
- **Modulation Source**—This module specifies which modulation source (such as pitch bend or after touch) will alter one of several modulation destinations, including LFOs and envelopes.

Let's first discuss the roles that the Source and Amplifier modules play.

Getting to the Source

As stated earlier, the Source module is used to specify the sound source of an instrument using various types of synthesis algorithms. This is incredibly versatile, as it enables you to manipulate your samples and instruments in ways that just can't be done with other soft samplers.

Looking at the upper-right of the Source module, you will see the Source Algorithm pop-up menu, which currently reads Sampler. Clicking on this pop-up menu reveals many additional algorithms that can be selected (see Figure 7.10). Included here are the following:

- **Sampler**—This is the default setting, which treats the source as a standard sample playback module.
- **Tone Machine**—This setting activates Kontakt's granular synthesizer.
- **Time Machine**—This setting pairs granular synthesis with intuitive time-stretching features.
- **Beat Machine**—This setting slices up looped samples to be used at various tempos without altering the pitch.
- **Time Machine II**—Similar to Time Machine, this setting supports a much finer pitch shift and time-stretching algorithms.
- **Direct from Disc (DFD)**—This algorithm streams the sample from the computer's hard drive, much like GigaStudio.

Let's cover the basics of these algorithms.

The Sampler Algorithm

By default, the Sampler algorithm is selected whenever a new instrument is loaded or created. This encompasses all the standard audio functions of a RAM-based software sampler, in which the sample is loaded and played back from the installed RAM on your computer. In addition to this, the Sampler mode includes a loop editor for creating and editing loop points (more on this later).

Figure 7.10
The Source module includes many different algorithms for pushing your samples to new horizons.

Let's cover the basic parameters of the Source module when in the Sampler mode.

- **Tune**—This parameter adjusts the overall tuning of the Source in semitones.
- **Voice Groups**—This is used to assign a group to a special feature called a *voice group*. Read the Note below for more information
- **Tracking**—When activated, Tracking will cause a zone's pitch to change the higher or lower you play on your keyboard. Unless the instrument you are playing is a non-pitch specific instrument, such as a drum kit, this parameter will always be active.
- **Release Trigger**—When activated, the release trigger will play the loaded sample when the key is released.
- **Group Start Options**—This is a new feature to Kontakt 1.5 and is used to define multiple conditions when a group is to be played.
- **Reverse**—When active, Reverse will cause all of the loaded samples to play in reverse.

The Tone Machine

The next source algorithm is called the Tone Machine, which is essentially a granular synthesizer. Since we haven't covered granular synthesis yet, I'll provide the gist of it. Granular is a unique form of synthesis that involves the fusion of small periodic bursts of sound called *grains*. These grains can have durations of, on average, 10–50 milliseconds each and can originate from just about any sound source, such as samples or waveforms.

> **MORE FUN = MORE CPU**
>
> Although the Tone Machine is red hot in sound design potential, be aware that it is much more CPU intensive when compared to the Sampler algorithm.

In the Tone Machine, the mechanics of granular synthesis are applied to the loaded samples within an instrument. This gives you editing and sound design options like you've never heard. Let's cover the basic parameters of the Tone Machine. In the interest of time, we won't waste any reiterating common parameters found in the Sampler algorithm.

- **Smooth**—This parameter is used to remove unwanted digital artifacts from the sample. This alters the overall character of the sound.
- **Speed**—This parameter alters the speed of playback of the loaded sample. Note that this is independent of the pitch played on your keyboard.
- **Formant**—This parameter changes the placement of the formant or concentration of frequencies within the entire frequency spectrum.
- **DC Filter**—This parameter corrects any sonic imbalances caused by granular synthesis.
- **Legato**—When active, this parameter changes the playback position of different played samples. For example, if you play and hold a note and then press and hold another note, the starting position that the new sample begins to play back is the same as the first note.

The Time Machine

The next Source algorithm is the Time Machine. This is also another granular synthesizer, but the original sample pitch characteristic is preserved, no matter what speed is applied. The Time Machine shares many common parameters to the Tone Machine, but the overall effect that can be achieved is much different. Let's cover the main parameters.

- **Grain**—This parameter alters the size of grains used in the synthesis process. This is linked to the Hi-Quality button, located just to the right of the Grain knob.
- **Hi-Quality**—When activated, this parameter preserves the sonic characteristics of the loaded sample, regardless of how high or low a sample is played on the keyboard.

The Beat Machine

Continuing on, the next algorithm is the Beat Machine, which is another new feature to Kontakt (see Figure 7.11). This algorithm is used to slice up a sampled loop so that it can be used at the same tempo, regardless of pitch. Let me elaborate.

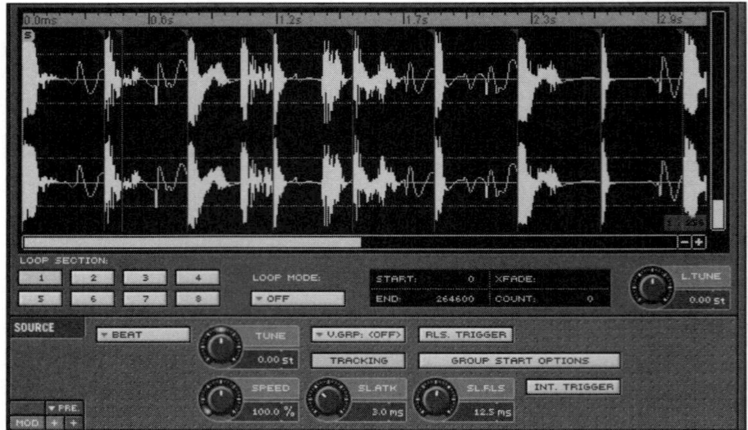

Figure 7.11

The Beat Machine will slice and dice your sampled loops.

When you load a sampled loop, such as a drum loop, into a sampler, that sample will play back its original pitch and tempo at its root note, which is typically C3, or middle C. If you play that loop again from any key other than the root, then the pitch and the tempo of the loop will be altered dramatically. When the sample is played in a lower key than the root, the loop will play back slower, and the pitch will be much lower. The exact opposite will happen when the sample is played back from a key higher than the root.

The Beat Machine cuts the loop into predetermined slices in order to preserve the playback rate. If you play the loop at a note higher than the root, the loop will play back at a higher pitch but at the same tempo as the root. Believe me, it's very chic.

The Beat Machine contains the following unique parameters:

- **Speed**—This alters the playback speed of the loop.
- **Slice Attack**—This parameter alters the attack of each slice in a loop.
- **Slice Release**—This parameter alters the release of each slice in a loop.
- **Internal Trigger**—When this is active, each slice can be individually altered.

The Time Machine II

Next up is the sequel to the original Time Machine, called the Time Machine II. However, the two should not be confused, as each serves a different purpose. The Time Machine II is used to perform much higher time-stretching and pitch-shifting possibilities.

A particular point of interest in the Time Machine II is the use of *transients,* which are high-energy spikes in the audio signal. These make up an important part of the sound (especially with acoustic instruments), so it's important to preserve them when making timing and pitch adjustments.

Let's cover its parameters.

- **Transient Size**—This knob adjusts the size of the transients that stay intact.
- **Transient Copy**—This activates a sort of transient protection. It's best to use this with samples that have many transients, such as drums.
- **Grain Size**—This knob adjusts the size of the transient grains.

Direct from Disk

The final Source algorithm is Direct from Disk. This is an especially exciting new feature in Kontakt, as it enables you to stream samples from your hard drive instead of loading them into the computer's RAM. The immediate benefit to streaming samples is having the ability to load several large, sustained samples into Kontakt without the worry of running out of RAM. This is not to say that RAM doesn't have its place in the process of streaming samples, as the instrument information and first few seconds of the sample are still loaded into RAM. Once Kontakt begins to play those first few seconds of the sample, the hard drive then picks up where the RAM left off, and the sample will play back in its entirety (see Figure 7.12).

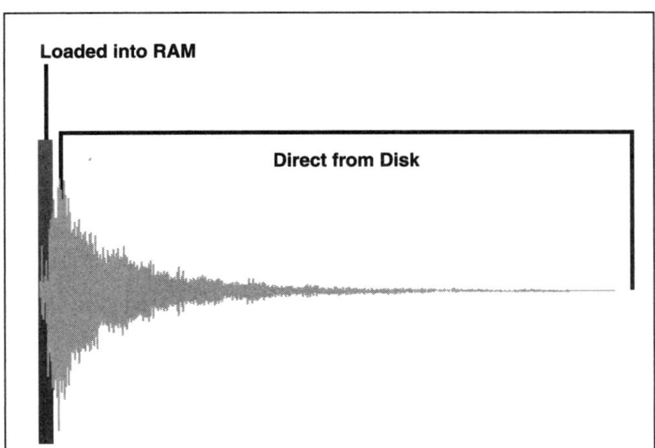

Figure 7.12
This screenshot of an audio file is to give you a better idea of how much RAM is actually used when streaming long sustained samples.

> **INSTALL THIS**
>
> Note that before Direct from Disk can be used with Kontakt, you must download and install the Direct from Disk (DFD) extension, which can be found on the Native Instruments Web site. Once this has been installed, you'll find an additional page in the Settings window (see Figure 7.13).

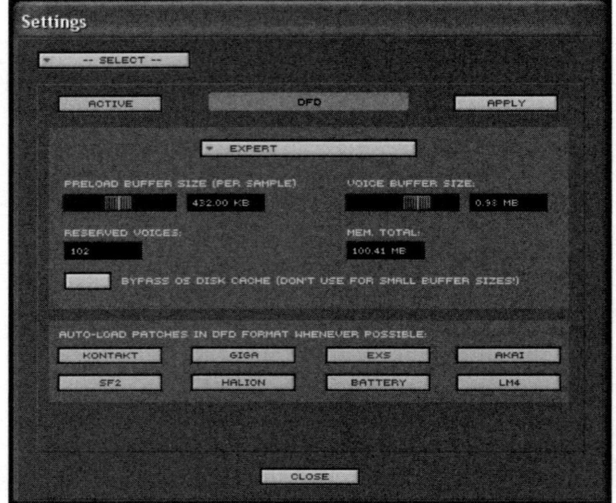

Figure 7.13
Once the DFD extension is downloaded and installed, an additional page will become available in the Settings window of Kontakt. It can be found by clicking on the Options button.

Looking at the available parameters of the Direct from Disk algorithm, you can see that they share those found in the Sampler algorithm. Keep in mind that the DFD page in the Settings window is the key to unlocking the potential of the streaming feature.

The Amplifier

The Amplifier is simply the module that is used to adjust the overall amplitude and panning assignment for an instrument (see Figure 7.14). Its parameters include:

- **Volume**—This parameter cuts or boosts the overall gain of the instrument.
- **Pan**—This parameter places the instrument in different parts of the stereo field.

An additional function of the Amplifier module is to activate and use real-time effects in Kontakt. This is done by clicking on the right-hand plus symbol (+) located in the far left corner of the module (see Figure 7.15).

Figure 7.14
The Amplifier module adjusts the amplitude and panning of an instrument.

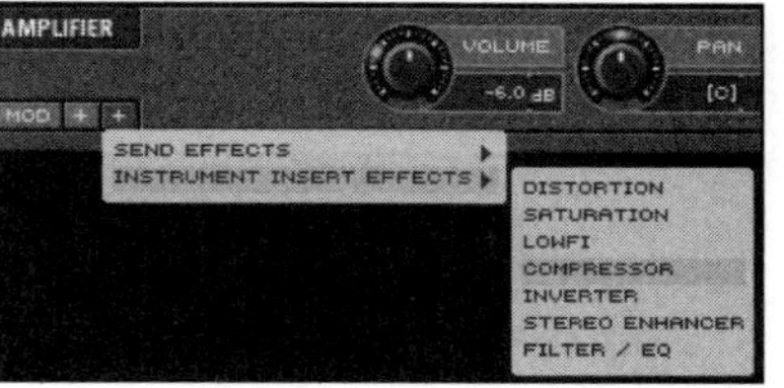

Figure 7.15
The lower-left corner of the Amplifier module is used for real-time effects and modulation.

Using Effects

While selecting different algorithms and reefing the volume of an instrument is fun, the real power of editing Kontakt instruments comes from the creative use of the embedded real-time effects. There are several to choose from in Kontakt, and they can be used in two different ways:

- As inserts
- As sends

An insert is a real-time effect that is used to process a signal entirely by routing the output of a dry, unprocessed signal to an effect, having that effect process the signal, and then routing the output of the effect to the overall mix. This results in a signal that is completely processed, or as we like to call it, *wet*. Looking at Figure 7.16, you can see a basic flowchart of an effect processor being used as an insert.

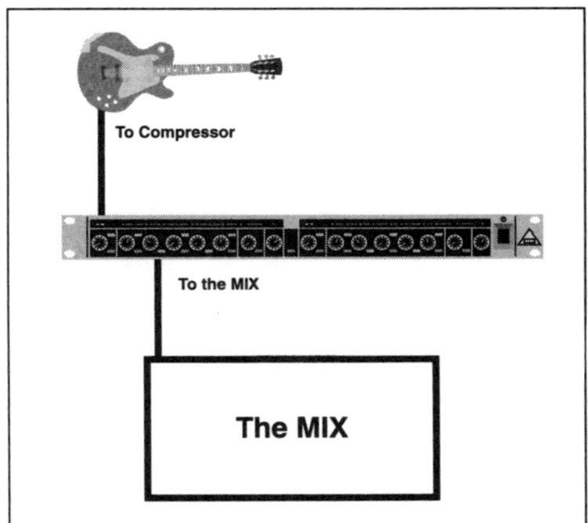

Figure 7.16
This flowchart describes the signal path of a basic insert effect. The output of the guitar is being fed to the inputs of a compressor effect, and the output of the compressor is then fed to the mix.

WHAT MAKES A GOOD INSERT EFFECT

Which effects should be used as inserts? My best advice is to avoid using any effect that creates a great amount of latency or delay. For example, distortions, compressors, and choruses are good insert effects, since the effects they create occur simultaneously (or nearly so) with the primary signal. In contrast, reverbs and delays make bad insert effects, since they produce an aftereffect, known as a tail end.

For a better understanding of the difference, have a look at the following figures.

In Figure 7.17, I have copied a drum loop onto two separate audio tracks. Looking closely at these tracks, you can see that they both occur at the same time and are in perfect sync.

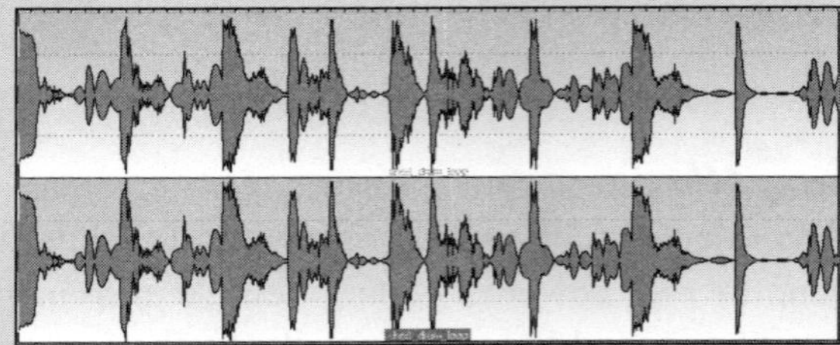

Figure 7.17
Our two audio tracks are dry and are in perfect sync.

Now I will introduce a distortion effect to the second audio track. Looking at Figure 7.18, you can see that even with the effected second track, the two tracks are in perfect sync. Hence, no latency.

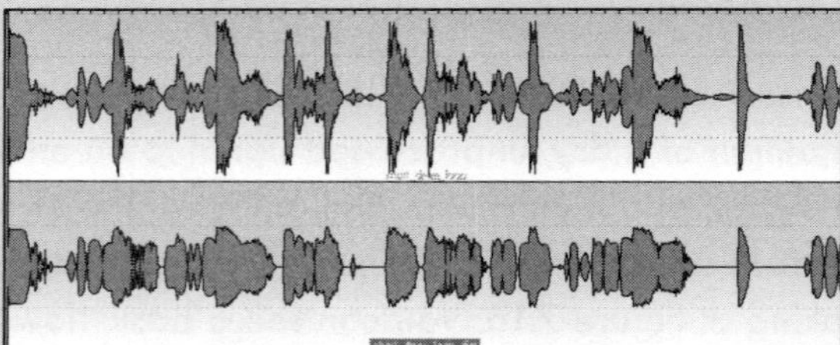

Figure 7.18
Although the second track is processed with distortion, they are still in sync.

Now, I will process the second track with a reverb, which produces an end tail. Looking at Figure 7.19, you can see that the two tracks are now well out of sync, which would suggest that a reverb is not a very good effect to use as an insert. Rather, a reverb would make a good Send effect, which is discussed below.

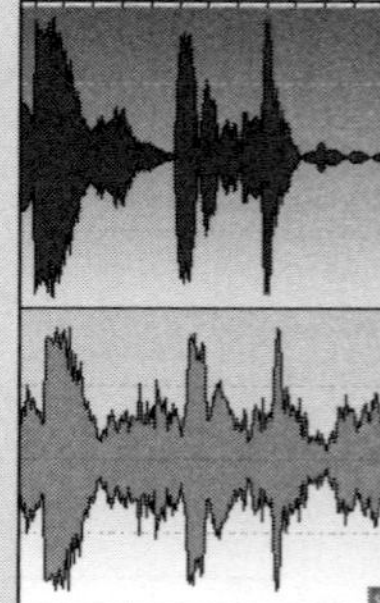

Figure 7.19
Now the second track is processed with a reverb, and as you can see, the two tracks are well out of sync with each other.

A *send* is a real-time effect that is a ratio of dry and wet, or unprocessed and processed, signals. To get an idea of how a Send effect works, check out Figure 7.20 while reading along with the following list.

1 The outputs of our signal (in this case, a keyboard) are fed to the input of a mixer.
2 The mixer splits the signal by way of the Send knob.
3 Increasing the amount of the knob sends a portion of dry signal to the inputs of our effect processor, which is a reverb. Meanwhile, the rest of the unprocessed signal is sent down to the fader.
4 The reverb effect processes the signal and sends that signal back to a part of the mixer known as the *return*.
5 The return is fed back into the main mix, which produces a blend of unprocessed and processed signal.

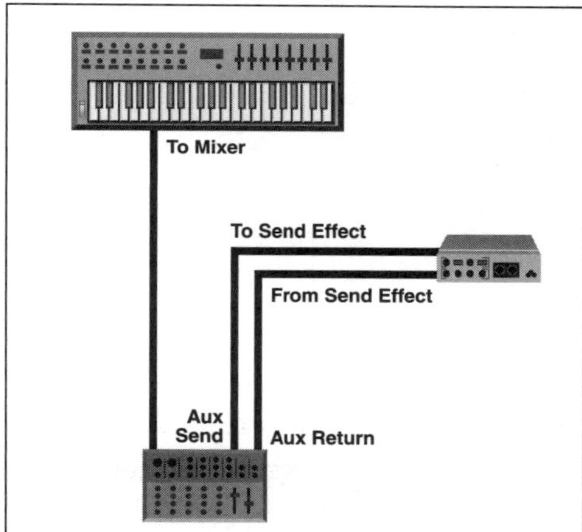

Figure 7.20
This is a standard flowchart for using Send effects. The output of the keyboard is routed to a mixer, which splits the signal by *sending* some of it to a reverb effect, while the rest of the dry signal is routed to the fader below. Meanwhile, the reverb's outputs are returned to the mix, which gives us a mix of dry and wet signals.

By now you should have a better idea as to the inner workings of using effects. Let's push forward and put that knowledge to the test by applying it to Kontakt.

Using Insert Effects with Kontakt

Loading and using insert effects in the Kontakt interface is easy to do. There are several to choose from, such as filters, EQs, compressors, and distortions.

There are also a few avant-garde effects to choose from as well, such as the Stereo Enhancer and Lowfi. In this section, I will show you how to use insert effects in two ways:

- **As Instrument Inserts**—This kind of insert is applied to the entire instrument.
- **As Group Inserts**—This kind of insert is applied to groups within an instrument.

Let's begin by setting up an instrument insert effect.

1. Click on the right-hand plus (+) button in the lower-left corner of the Amplifier module.
2. Select the Instruments Insert Effects subdirectory.
3. Choose from one of seven different insert effects, including Distortion, Compressor, or the Stereo Enhancer.

Once the insert effect is selected, it will appear in a new module just below the Amplifier module (see Figure 7.21).

Figure 7.21
Once an instrument insert effect is created, its interface will be placed just under the Amplifier module.

Creating a group insert effect is pretty similar, but is done by using the Source module. A group insert effect is an effect module that is applied to a specific sample or groups of samples within an instrument. Although we haven't discussed creating or editing groups yet, follow along with this quick example.

1. Click on the right-hand plus (+) button in the lower-left corner of the Source module. Select one of the listed group insert effects (Distortion, Saturation, Lowfi, Compressor, Inverter, or Stereo Enhancer). This will place the effect just below the Source module.
2. Once an insert effect has been selected, you can select a preset for that effect by clicking on the Pre button in the lower-left corner of the Effect module (see Figure 7.22).

Using Send Effects with Kontakt

In this section, I'll show you how to set up a Send effect with an instrument. As you will recall, a Send effect involves bussing a selected portion of dry,

Figure 7.22
As you can see, I have selected a compressor as my group insert effect module. Clicking on the Pre button of the compressor brings up a list of seven compression presets.

unprocessed signal to an effect, where it is then processed and sent back into the mix. The resulting effect is that of a ratio of dry/wet signals. For this example, I will select a reverb to be our Send effect.

1. Navigate to the bottom left corner of the Amplifier module and click on the right hand plus (+) button.
2. Select Reverb from the Send Effects subcategory. This will place two new modules below the Amp module: the Send Levels module and the Reverb module (see Figure 7.23).
3. Increase the Send Levels knob to assign more signals to the reverb.

Figure 7.23
A reverb effect has been created and placed below the Amplifier module.

At this point, you can now take it a step further and edit the parameters of the reverb to shape the overall effect. You can also create four additional effects to be used alongside the reverb. Just remember that each real-time effect requires more CPU performance from your computer, so keep an eye on the CPU meter at the top of the rack.

The Kontakt Editors

Looking back at Figure 7.8, you can see three new buttons located below the instrument header:

- **Mapping Editor**—This button will launch/hide the Mapping Editor.
- **Loop Editor**—This button will launch/hide the Loop Editor.
- **Group Editor**—This button will launch/hide the Group Editor.

In the next three sections, we will take a closer look at these editors.

The Mapping Editor

The Mapping Editor is used to import and place samples along the Kontakt Virtual Keyboard, which is also called the *zone field* (see Figure 7.24). In addition, the Mapping Editor is also used to layer these samples in zones, which can be used to create velocity layers (read below).

Figure 7.24
This is the Kontakt zone field. Once a sample or batch of samples is imported and mapped, clicking at the top of each key will play the sample at its lowest velocity. Clicking downward will play back the sample at greater velocities.

> **VELOCITY-SENSITIVE KEYS**
>
> A particular feature of the Mapping Editor I really dig is the velocity-sensitive keys on the Virtual Keyboard. Click at the top of any key, and you will hear the corresponding sample play back at its lowest velocity. As you work your way down the key, you'll hear the sample play back with greater and greater velocity.
>
> Additionally, you'll see a small red dash in the velocity map itself whenever you press a key. This is to indicate exactly how hard a velocity the sample is receiving.
>
> This is a cool feature, as I often find myself programming sequences without a MIDI keyboard around. I can then use this feature to get a better idea of what the samples will sound like at different velocities.

Importing Samples

Importing samples into Kontakt via the Mapping Editor is simply a matter of drag and drop. Once imported, the sample is then mapped along the Virtual Keyboard of the soft synth and is referred to as a *zone*. A zone is an assignable portion of the Virtual Keyboard (which is also known as the zone field) that contains a defined range of notes and velocities. For example, a zone can have a specified low note of D1 and a specified high note of G#1, giving you a seven-note range. This zone can also have a specific velocity from 1 to 127 assigned to it. Let's look at an example of loading a sample into the zone field.

In Figure 7.25, I have created a new instrument and activated the Mapping Editor to view the zone field. Looking at the browser in the left side of this figure, I have also located a drum loop, which will serve as our sample for this example. Now I will click and drag this sample into the zone field, but as I do, dragging the sample toward the top or bottom of the zone field can customize the key range of the created zone (see Figure 7.26). Once I have selected a specific location for the zone, I will release the mouse, and I will have imported the sample and placed it in a zone (see Figure 7.27).

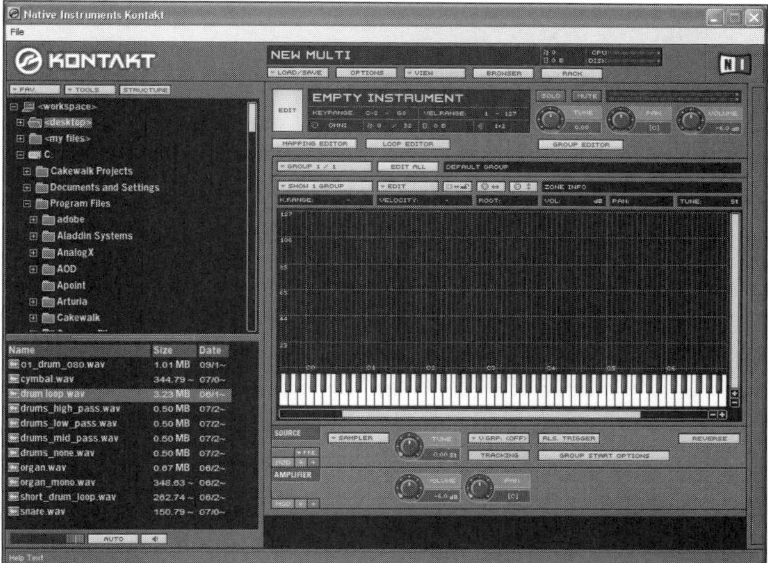

Figure 7.25

Our blank instrument has been created, and a drum loop waits in the browser to be imported.

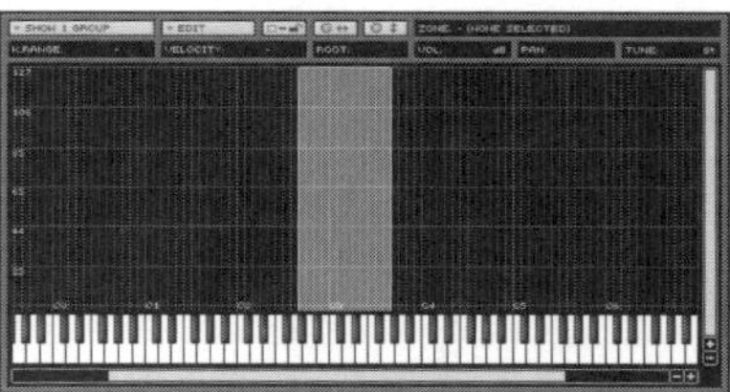

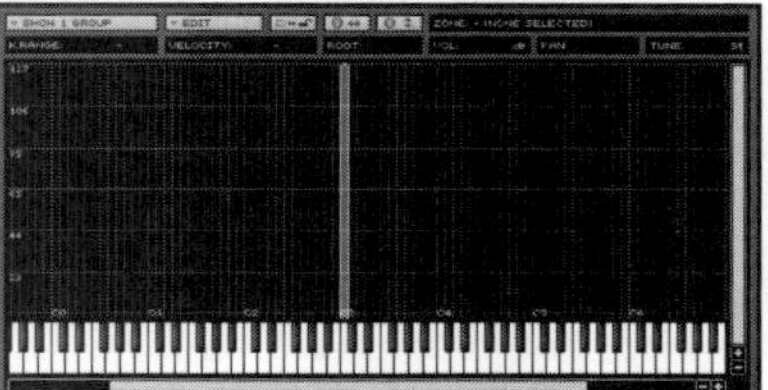

Figure 7.26

After clicking and dragging the sample into the zone field, you can customize the size of the new zone by dragging the sample up or down the zone field.

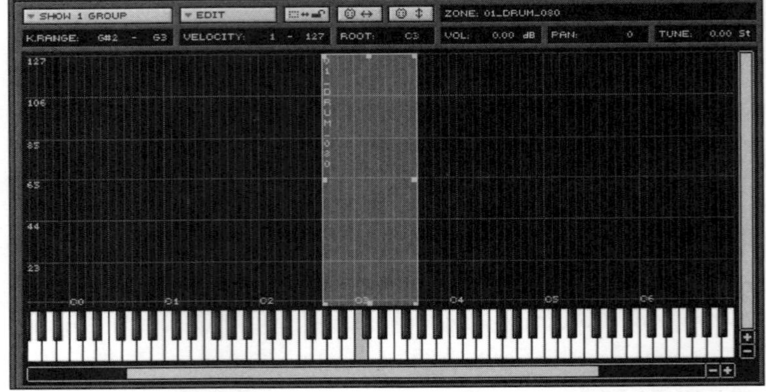

Figure 7.27

The sample has now been imported and placed in a zone.

> **BUILDING INSTRUMENTS**
>
> At the end of this chapter, I will take you through the steps of creating a multilayered Kontakt instrument of acoustic guitar samples.

After a zone has been created, you can perform some initial edits to it, such as changing the key or velocity range. Altering either the key range or velocity will specify which keys and velocities will trigger the zone. This is done by first navigating your mouse to the zone borders, at which point the mouse icon will become an icon that points in two directions (see Figure 7.28). Then it is simply a matter of clicking and dragging to the left or right to alter the key range or up and down to alter the velocity range (see Figure 7.29).

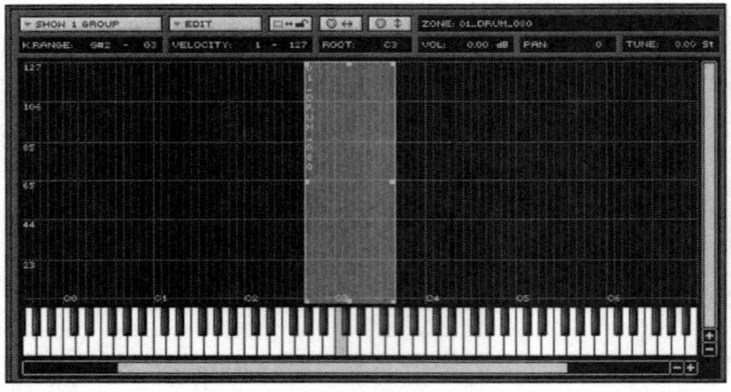

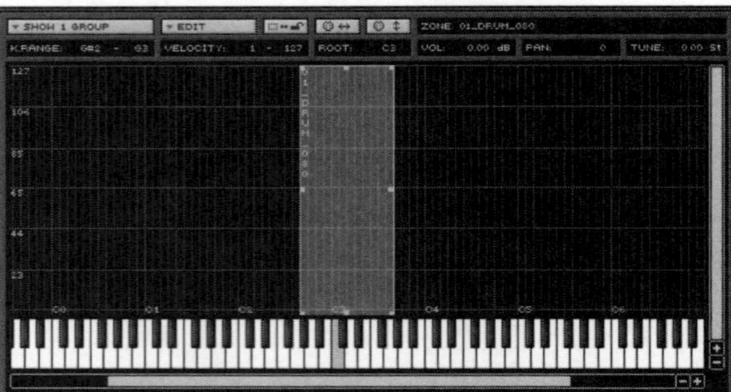

Figure 7.28

Navigating your mouse to the zone borders (left) changes your mouse icon into a dual-direction arrow icon (right).

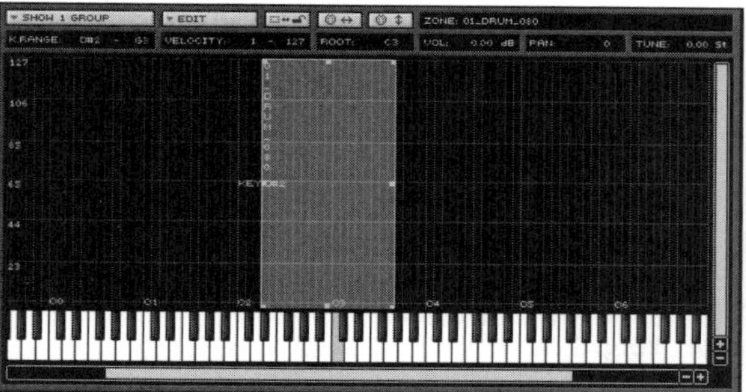

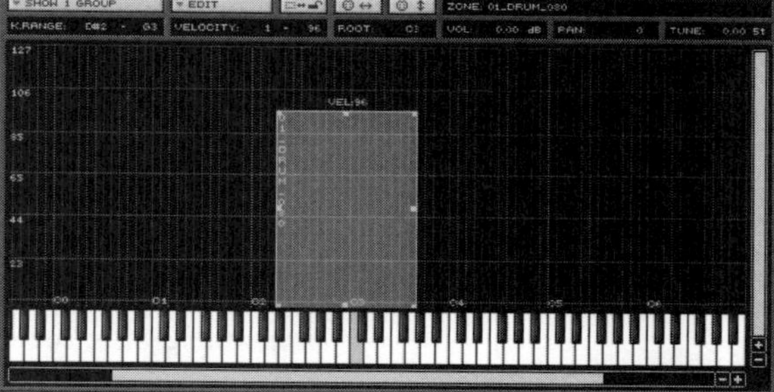

Figure 7.29

Now, just click and drag to the left or right to change the key range (left) or up and down to alter the velocity range (right).

Creating Groups

When one or several zones have been created within the zone field, it is a good time to move those zones into groups. A group is a sampler function that merges several zones to be edited as one. For example, let's say you have three kick drums velocity-mapped to one key of the zone field. Grouping these zones together enables you to apply any edits to these three zones simultaneously, such as applying a compressor, reversing the samples to play backward, and so on.

From a performance perspective, grouping samples is a powerful function because it facilitates the use of different playback algorithms for various samples. For example, let's say you're using an instrument of drum samples. You could group specific samples, such as kicks and snares, to be stored and played back via the computer's RAM, as they do not have long sustained sounds. At the same time, you could group other samples, such as cymbals and toms, to be stored and played back via the computer's hard drive, as they inherently contain long sustained sounds.

Creating groups is very easy to do. In fact, when a new instrument is created, there is already an empty available group called Default Group waiting for you to import samples to. Let's use the drum loop sample from the previous section and go through the steps of reimporting it and then placing it into a group.

1. Click in the Group Name dialog to rename it (see Figure 7.30).
2. Now, reimport the sample into the zone field.
3. Next, import another instance of the sample into the zone field so that you have two samples loaded into the instrument (see Figure 7.31).

At this point, both samples are now in a group together, but we want to place one of the samples into its own group, which is done as follows:

1. Click on one of the zones to select it.
2. Now click on the Edit button in the Mapping Editor and select Move to New Blank Group. This will place the zone in its own group (see Figure 7.32).
3. Click in the Group Name dialog box and rename it from Default Group to something else, such as Drum Loop 2.

Figure 7.30
Begin with a new blank instrument and then rename the group.

Figure 7.31
Now, import two instances of the sample so you have two samples in your instrument.

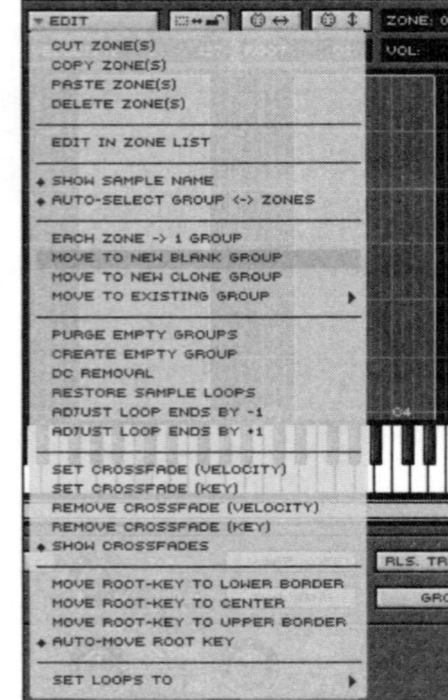

Figure 7.32
Select Move to New Blank Group from the Edit pull-down menu on the Mapping Editor. This will place a selected zone into its own blank group.

Editing Zones/Groups

Once you have imported, organized, and mapped your zones and groups, you can further enhance the instrument by using the Edit button functions. Since this list of Edit functions is fairly long and a bit over the top for Kontakt beginners, let's just touch on a couple of its key features.

The Edit menu provides several options for cutting, copying, and pasting single or multiple zones at one time. For example, let's say you have a Kontakt instrument loaded with several zones that you don't need. You can simply click and drag a box around the unwanted zones to select them and then select Delete Zones. A pop-up window will appear, asking you to verify the deletion. Click OK and you're finished.

Another key feature of the Edit menu is its ability to easily place a newly created zone into its own group. This is an especially cool feature for instruments that contain several zones that need to be placed into separate groups. Click and drag a box around all of the zones and then select Each Zone, 1 Group from the Edit menu.

Additional Editing Tools

Just to the right of the Edit menu are a few additional tools:

- **Lock Zones**—When this is selected, you will no longer be able to move or alter a zone in any way, grouped or ungrouped.
- **Set Key Range**—When this is selected, you can play two notes on your MIDI keyboard to automatically set the key range of a zone.
- **Set Velocity Range**—When this is selected, you can play two notes on your MIDI keyboard at different velocities to automatically set the velocity range of a zone.

Setting Up Crossfades

Setting up crossfades is a very straightforward procedure. A *crossfade* is a process that involves creating a seamless transition or *morph* from one sample to another. For example, if you have two samples that share an overlapping key range or velocity value, you can set up a crossfade to smoothly morph between the overlapping values. To demonstrate this function, I will use two zones that share the same key range and have overlapping velocities.

1. First, select one of the two zones.
2. Next, hold down the Shift key on your keyboard and click on the other zone. This will select both zones, and you will see the overlap between the two zones.

3 Select Set Crossfade (Velocity) from the Edit menu. This will place a crossfade in the overlapping area between the two zones (see Figure 7.33).

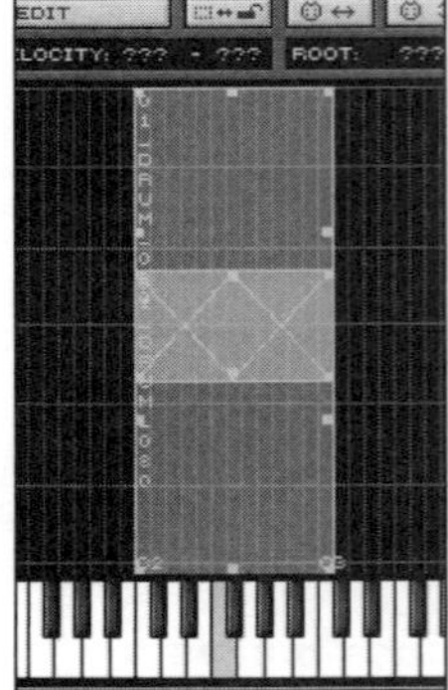

Figure 7.33
Setting up a crossfade between two zones is easy to do in Kontakt.

To remove the crossfade, just select both zones again and select Remove Crossfade (Velocity) from the Edit menu.

The Loop Editor

The Loop Editor is used to set up loop points for any samples loaded into the Kontakt interface (see Figure 7.34). As you may recall from earlier chapters, looping a function is used to conserve a sampler's memory by infinitely repeating a selected section of a sample to produce the illusion of a sustained sound. Kontakt's Loop Editor does this and much more, as you will come to find over the course of this section. Select a zone, then click on the Loop Editor button to activate it.

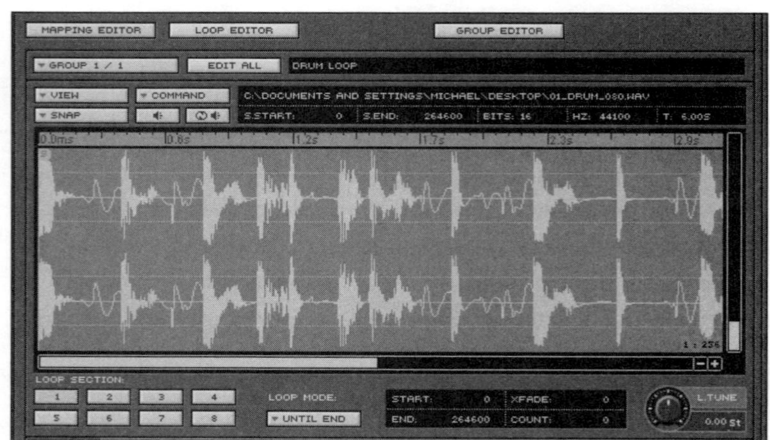

Figure 7.34
The Kontakt Loop Editor is where you can set up to eight loop points throughout a sample.

Let's begin in the upper-right corner of the editor with Sample Info.

Sample Info

Located in the upper-right half of the Loop Editor, Sample Info displays the looping and overall information about the loaded samples, including:

- **Sample Start**—Displays and sets where the sample begins.
- **Sample End**—Displays and sets where the sample ends.
- **Bits**—Displays the sample's bit depth.
- **Hz**—Displays the sample's sampling rate.
- **T**—Displays the total time of the sample.

View Menu

The View menu of the Loop Editor is used to jump to specific areas of the sample and loop. Its settings include these:

- **Go to Loop Start**—This will jump to the beginning of the loop.
- **Go to Loop End**—This will jump to the end of the loop.
- **Go to Sample Start**—This will jump to the beginning of the sample.
- **Go to Sample End**—This will jump to the end of the sample.
- **Show Both Channels**—When a stereo sample is loaded and selected, this will display both the left and right channels.

Also included in this menu is the Loop Edit mode, which when selected splits the waveform display of the Loop Editor into two sections. The section on the left shows the end of the loop, and the section on the right shows the start of the loop (see Figure 7.35). This is useful for judging and adjusting loop points to create a seamless stream from start to finish.

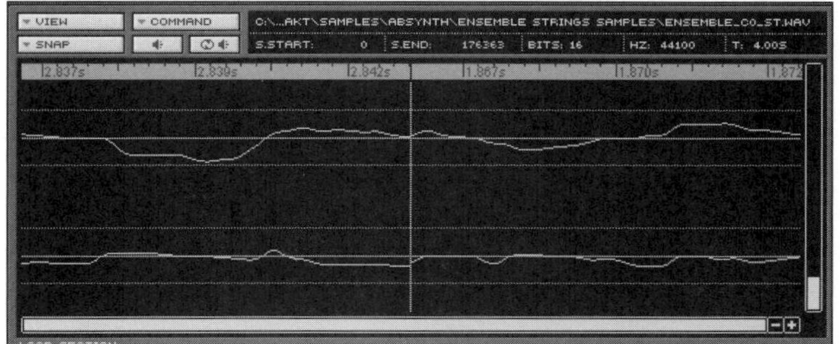

Figure 7.35
The Loop Edit mode is used to view and adjust the loop points of a sample.

Snap Menu

The Snap function is used to help prevent any pops and clicks in your loop points by nudging your loop start/end points to where the signal amplitude is zero. These points are also called *zero crossing*.

- **Zero-X**—This function snaps the loop start and end points to the nearest zero crossing.
- **Value**—This function snaps the loop start to the amplitude of the loop end and vice versa.

Command Menu

The Command menu is used to perform a series of tasks to help determine the loop point, in addition to others.

- **Restore Sample Loops**—This undoes any loop edits you have performed while in the Loop Editor.
- **Find Loop End > (Long)**—If you're unhappy with your current loop points, this function will search for a possible loop end point in your sample and will lengthen the overall loop if needed.
- **Find Loop End > (Short)**—This function will search for a possible loop end point in your sample, but it will stay within the confines of your original loop settings.
- **DC Removal**—This function removes any digital artifacts within your sample. Note that this is a destructive edit, which will permanently rewrite the sample data.
- **Open Sample in External Editor**—When selected, this function will launch your favorite digital audio editing application such as Wavelab, Sound Forge, Peak, or Spark.

Audition Buttons

Located just below the Command menu, these buttons are used to audition the sample and the looped portion.

- **Speaker Icon**—When selected, this button will play the sample from start to finish.
- **Speaker/Loop Icon**—When selected, this button will play the looped portion of a sample until it is clicked on again.

Loop Section

To the far left of the Loop Editor is the Loop Section, where you can store and recall up to eight discrete loop points for your sample. This is done by selecting one of the empty loop banks, setting the loop start and end points with the Start and End dialogs on the lower-right side of the Loop Editor, and then selecting the appropriate loop mode, which we will talk about now.

Loop Modes

There are six available loop modes in the Loop Editor:

- **Off**—Turns off the loop mode.
- **Until End**—Plays the loop until the note ends.
- **Until End...**—Plays the loop forward and then backward.
- **Until Release**—Plays the loop as long as the note is held down.
- **Until Release...**—Plays the loop forward and then backward.
- **One Shot**—Plays the sample from start to end without regard to any MIDI note off messages.

Editing Options

The last section of the Loop Editor is the Editing Options, which include:

- **Start**—Sets the loop start.
- **End**—Sets the loop end.
- **Tune**—Used to fine-tune each loop.
- **Xfade**—Determines the amount of crossfading between the loop start and end.
- **Count**—Determines how many times a loop will repeat before moving to the next looped section or the end of the sample.

Creating a Loop Using the Loop Editor

Now that you are familiar with the tools and menus of the Loop Editor, let's go through a step-by-step tutorial to show you how easy it is to create a loop. The loop we'll create will involve using a drum loop and then establish a loop start, loop end, and loop mode. As you can see in Figure 7.36, I have created a new blank instrument. I also created a new zone by importing a drum loop onto the Mapping Editor and placed it at the C3 note. Now I'll just click on the zone and activate the Loop Editor (see Figure 7.37).

Before beginning this tutorial, let's select a loop mode from the Loop Mode menu. Since this is probably your first time using the Loop Editor, I suggest using Until Release. This mode will cause Kontakt to loop the sample until the corresponding MIDI note is released. Note that once you do this, the entire sample will be highlighted.

Figure 7.36
A new blank instrument has been created, complete with a zone that contains a drum loop.

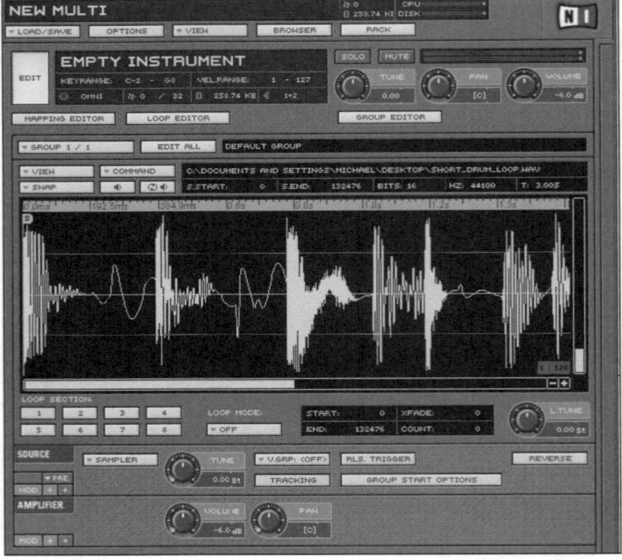

Figure 7.37
The loop is now viewable within the Loop Editor.

1 Navigate to the Loop End dialog of the Editing Options, then click and drag downward to shift the loop end point to the left. Place the end point anywhere along the waveform. It would be best if you placed it in front of a visually audible marker, like a hi-hat sound or kick drum sound (see Figure 7.38).

2 Click the Speaker/Loop icon to hear a preview of the loop. If it needs adjustments, click and drag the loop end point to the left or right.

3 Click on the View menu and select Loop Edit Mode (see Figure 7.39).

4 The Loop Edit mode is used to make fine adjustments to the loop start and end points in order to make a seamless transition. You can make the adjustments by clicking up or down in the Loop Start and End dialogs to shift the samples to the left or right. The trick here is to find a point where the loop end and start share common amplitudes, as you can see in Figure 7.39.

5 Once you are finished, exit the Loop Edit mode by selecting it from the View menu.

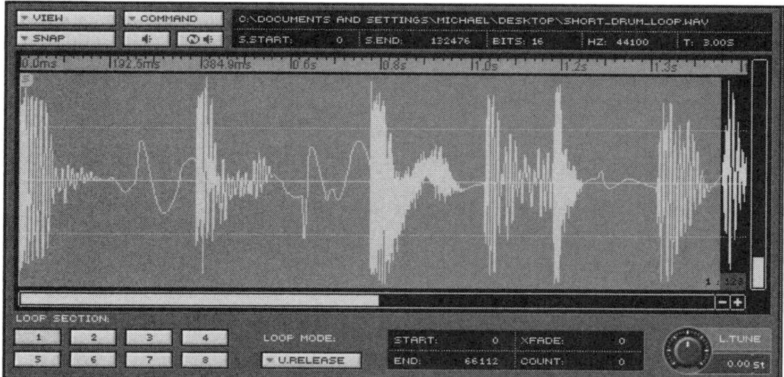

Figure 7.38

Click and drag the loop end point to the left and place it in front of a visually audible location within the waveform.

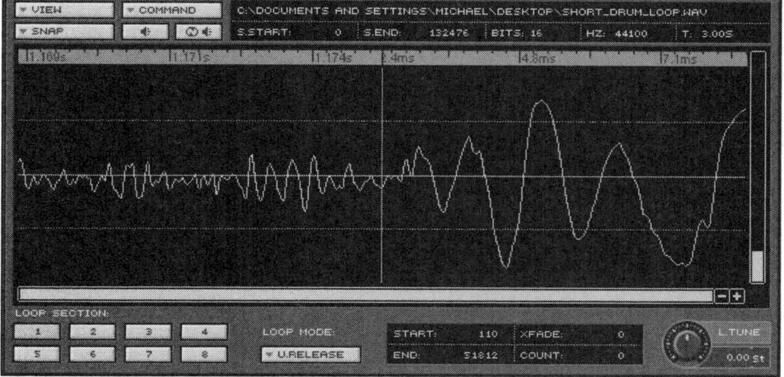

Figure 7.39

The Loop Edit mode is used to make fine adjustments to the loop start and end points.

Remember, creating loops takes a lot of time and patience, so don't be afraid to try different combinations of values. As a finishing note, try one of the other loop mode options such as the Until Release, which will make the loop play forward and backward.

The Group Editor

The Group Editor serves only two main purposes:

- Selects and edits the name of any active group with the Group Name menu.
- Specifies whether any edits made to the groups are individual or universal with the Edit All button.

The Edit All button must be deactivated in order to make any individual changes to any active groups within your instrument. For example, if you want to place a group insert effect on one group of effects and have the rest of the groups remain bone dry, Edit All needs to be turned off.

The Browser

The left side of the Kontakt interface, called the browser, is dedicated to the organization and location of samples and instruments that can be loaded into the rack (see Figure 7.40). Although it looks a little confusing at first, you'll be a browser master in no time.

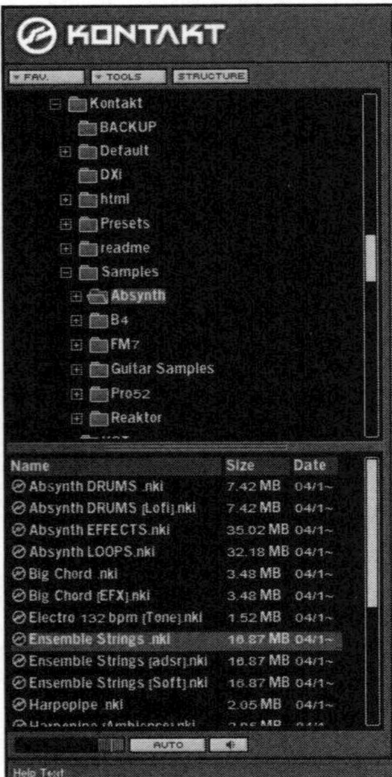

Figure 7.40
Kontakt's browser is used to organize and locate instruments and samples.

The browser is split into two panes. The upper pane is used to organize and display the different folders on your computer, much in the same way as

Windows Explorer or Panther. The lower pane is used to display the individual instruments and samples with its own dedicated audition utility.

The Upper Pane

The upper pane of the Kontakt browser is where you can navigate through your entire computer in just a matter of mouse clicks to locate samples and instruments on your computer's hard drives or on the CD-ROM drive. Because doing this repetitively can become tedious, the upper pane houses some supplementary features to help you locate your samples and instruments quickly. The upper pane can also be used to convert different sample formats into Kontakt instruments.

Basic Navigation of the Browser

In this section, I will take you through a quick tour of using the upper pane of the browser to navigate and locate your installed samples and instruments. Before we begin, I'll assume that you have located a proper space on your computer's hard drive to install the Kontakt samples provided in your package. If this is not the case, I suggest placing them in a new folder called Samples in the Kontakt Program folder on the PC or the Kontakt Applications folder on the Mac. Let's get started.

1. At the top of the upper pane is the Workspace icon, which is essentially the same thing as My Computer. Click on the plus icon next to it to expand and display its contents.
2. You should now see a list of icons underneath the Workspace icon that represent your computer's hard drive. Click on the plus icon next to it to expand and display its contents.
3. Once it is expanded, click on the plus icon next to the Applications folder on the Mac or the Program Files folder on the PC.
4. By now, if you are on the Mac, you should see the Kontakt folder with a plus icon next to it. If you are on the PC, you will find a Native Instruments folder. In either case, click on the plus icon next to the folder to expand and display its contents.
5. If you are on the PC, you should see the Kontakt folder now. Click on the plus icon to expand and display its contents.
6. At this point, you should see the Samples folder. Expand it and you should see a list of different sample folders. Expand the first folder, which should be the Absynth folder.

7 You'll see that the Absynth folder contains many different subfolders dedicated to different instruments. Click once on the Absynth folder, and all of the Absynth Kontakt instrument files should appear in the lower pane of the browser (see Figure 7.42).

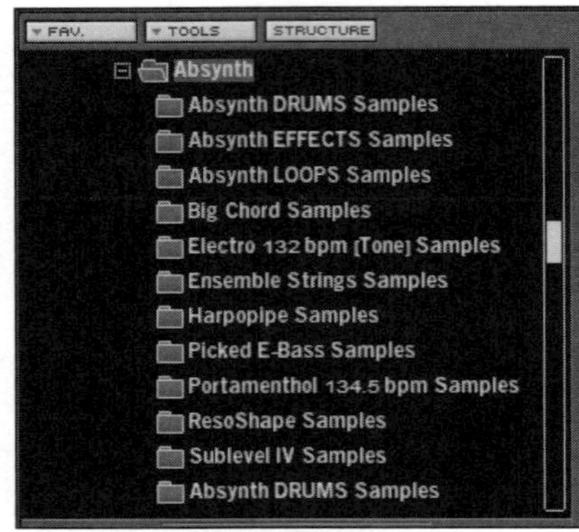

Figure 7.41
If you are not sure where to install your Kontakt samples, create a new folder in the Kontakt Program folder, name it Samples, and copy the samples to that location.

Figure 7.42
Once you locate your Absynth folder, click on it, and the Kontakt instrument files will be displayed in the lower pane.

Using Favorites for Quick Navigation

Once you have used the method I outlined in the previous section more than two times, it's a sure bet that you will be looking for a way to find samples and instruments more quickly. It just so happens that Kontakt has a handy solution called Favorites.

Favorites are files that reference specific locations on your hard drive where instruments and samples reside. They are very similar to Internet bookmarks, in that they remember these locations and can be organized in several different ways. They are very easy to configure, as you will see in this section.

Let's begin by looking at the FAV pop-up menu, which is located just above the upper pane of the browser (see Figure 7.43). If you click once on this menu and hold, you'll see a few choices:

- **Add to Favorites**—This option stores the current location in the master list of Favorites.
- **Configure Favorites**—This option launches a new window that provides a method of organizing Favorites. More on this later.
- **Samples**—This is a subdirectory to store sample Favorites.
- **Instruments**—This is a subdirectory to store Kontakt instruments as Favorites.
- **Multi**—This is a subdirectory to store Kontakt multi-instruments as Favorites.

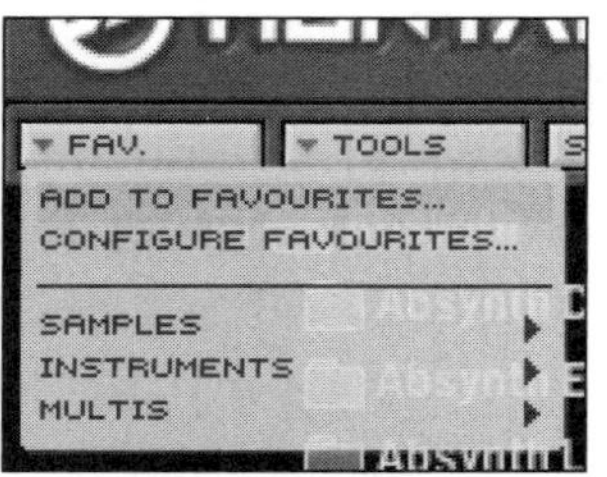

Figure 7.43
The FAV pop-up menu is used to select, add, and configure your Favorites.

The easiest way to do this is to locate a folder that contains samples, such as AIFF or WAV files, or a folder that contains Kontakt instrument or multi-instrument files. Once it is located, right-click with your mouse on the PC or hold the Ctrl key and click with your mouse on the Mac and you will be given the option to place the Favorite into the Samples, Instruments, or Multi folder. You will also see an Insert Here option to save the Favorite in a master list. Once this is done, click on the FAV pop-up menu and you should see the Favorite in the directory you saved it in.

Another way to accomplish this is to click once on the folder that contains the samples, instruments, or multi-instruments you want and then use the FAV pop-up menu.

Configuring Favorites

Once you have amassed a list of Favorites, you will probably want to organize your Favorites list by creating folders to place the Favorites in. Select Configure Favorites from the FAV pull-down menu; this will launch the Favorites window (see Figure 7.44).

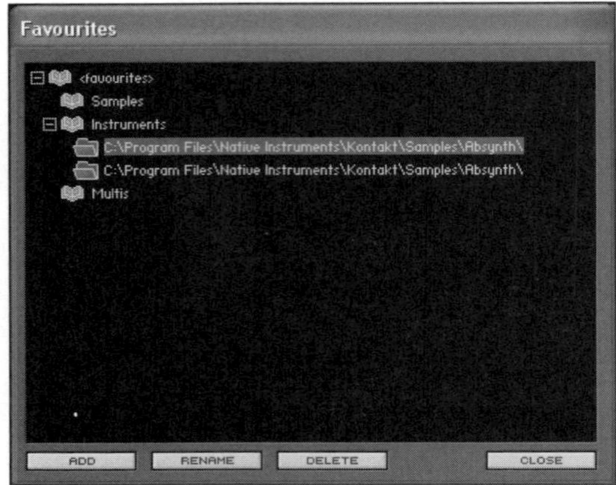

Figure 7.44

The Favorites window is used to organize your list of Favorites. Placing a Favorite into the proper subdirectory is simply drag and drop.

In Figure 7.44, you can see that there are a few different buttons to work with.

- **Add**—This button creates a new Favorites subdirectory. Use this button to create subdirectories for instrument categories, such as basses, guitars, pads, synths, and so on.
- **Rename**—This button allows you to rename any Favorite or subdirectory in the Favorites window.
- **Delete**—This button deletes any Favorite or subdirectory in the Favorites window.
- **Close**—This closes the Favorites window.

Working with Tools

Looking to the right of the FAV menu is the Tools menu, which serves a few purposes:

- Refreshes the browser list.
- Searches for instruments and samples.
- Converts Akai and GigaSampler files.
- Displays different sample/sampler formats.

The Structure

The last button at the top of the upper pane of the browser is Structure. This is used to display the contents of a loaded instrument or multiple instruments in the rack. To understand this button, you will need to first load an instrument or two into the rack.

Once an instrument is loaded, click on the Structure button, and the contents of your loaded instrument will be displayed in the upper pane (see Figure 7.45).

Figure 7.45

The Structure lists the contents of your loaded instruments.

At this point, you should be seeing just the instruments with their MIDI input channels listed next to them. Click to expand and view the contents of the first instrument, and you should see four subcategories called Groups, Zones, Modules, and Voice Groups (see Figure 7.46)

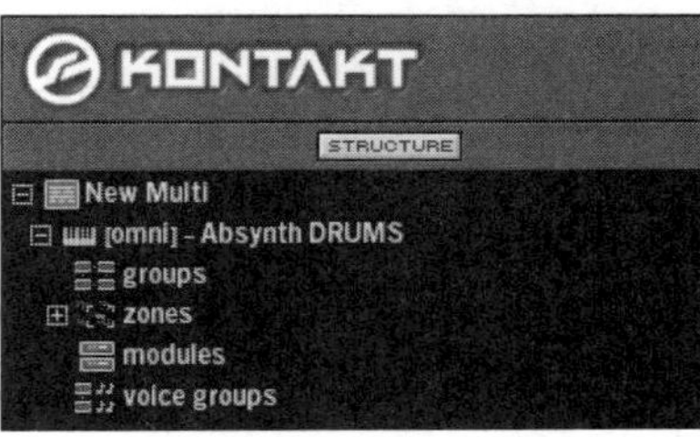

Figure 7.46

Here are the main contents of the instrument listed in the Structure view.

Clicking on any of these subcategories will list its corresponding contents in the lower pane of the browser (see Figure 7.47). From this point, you can perform specific edits to the contents of each subcategory, such as renaming groups or altering voice groups.

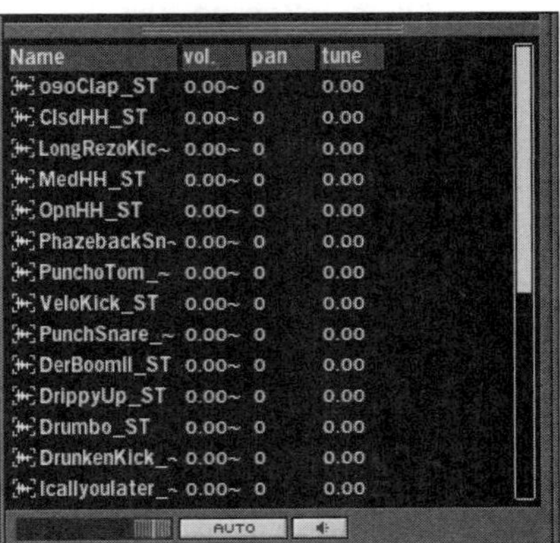

Figure 7.47

Once a subcategory is chosen, its contents will be displayed in the lower pane.

The Lower Pane

The lower pane is not nearly as complex, as that would not really make sense. In this case, the lower pane is used to list, audition, and load samples and instruments into the rack (see Figure 7.48).

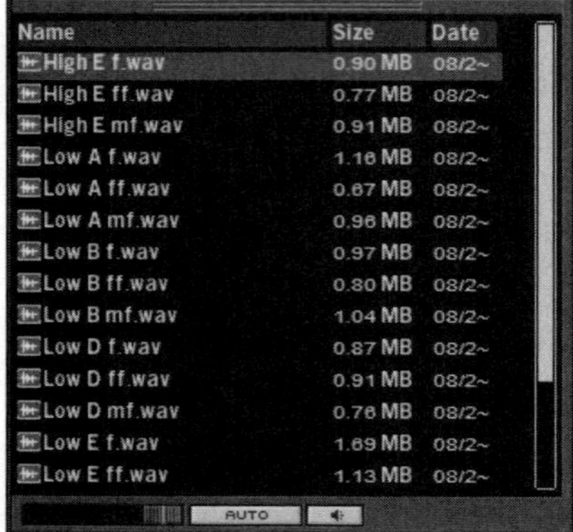

Figure 7.48

The lower pane of the browser is used to list, audition, and load samples and instruments.

We've already learned that we can drag or double-click instruments or samples into the rack from the lower pane.

At the far bottom of the lower pane is the Audition utility, which is used to audition samples before importing them into the rack. This is especially handy if you are creating your own customized Kontakt instrument, as it will allow you to "try before you buy," so to speak.

The Audition utility has three controls.

- **Audition Volume**—This slider adjusts the playback volume of the sample. Note that it does not affect the sample once it is loaded into the rack.
- **Auto**—When active, the Auto function enables you to play back samples by just clicking on them.
- **Audition**—This button is used to play and stop the auditioning of samples.

WORKS ONLY WITH SAMPLES

The Audition function works only with samples and not with instrument or multi-instrument files.

Using Kontakt with Your Sequencer

Once installed, Kontakt is a cinch to use with your sequencer. In this section of the chapter, I will walk you through the steps of setting it up with various popular sequencers.

HONORABLE MENTION

Although this section covers a fair number of sequencers, we can't cover them all. For more information about using Kontakt with your particular sequencer, check out the support section of the Native Instruments Web site at **www.native-instruments.com**.

Kontakt with Nuendo/Cubase SX

Nuendo and Cubase by Steinberg are very popular sequencers and DAW applications used in many Mac and PC virtual studios (see Figure 7.49). Although they look a bit different graphically, setting them up with Kontakt is exactly the same.

Figure 7.49

Nuendo (left) is one of the cutting-edge postproduction apps on the market, and Cubase SX (right) is a sure bet for music composition and production.

Before we begin, we'll assume that you are quite familiar with the layout and basic functionality of Nuendo and Cubase. Okay, let's get started.

1 Navigate to the Devices pull-down menu and select VST Instruments. This will bring up the virtual instruments rack.

2 Navigate to the first instrument space at the top of the rack where No VST Instrument is seen. Click here and you will see a pop-up menu displaying all of the available VST instruments. Select Kontakt.

3 Once selected, the Kontakt interface will open, and a new audio track will appear in the Nuendo/Cubase Project window.

4 Navigate to the Project pull-down menu and create a new MIDI track. This will place an empty MIDI track on the Project window. Look at the Output dialog of this track, and you will see that it is set to its default MIDI output.

5 Click on the MIDI Output dialog of the new MIDI track, and you should see Kontakt as an output option. Select it and arm the MIDI track so that it can receive MIDI data.

6 At this point, if you have an instrument loaded into the Kontakt interface, you should be able to play it in real time from your MIDI keyboard.

Kontakt with Pro Tools LE

Always known as the industry standard in music and audio production, Digidesign finally decided to take the plunge a few years ago in the consumer market by introducing the mBox 001 and 002 audio interfaces, along with a light version of its DAW application called Pro Tools LE (see Figure 7.50). Although skeptical of its lighter feature set, over the last couple of years, I have found Pro Tools LE to be a highly competent program that feeds the needs of the hobbyist and professional musician alike.

Figure 7.50
Pro Tools LE by Digidesign uses the RTAS plug-in format.

For best results, follow the steps in this tutorial with a blank Pro Tools project.

1 Launch Pro Tools.
2 Create a new Stereo Auxiliary Track by selecting File, New Track.
3 Create a MIDI track using the same method.
4 Toggle to view the mixer by selecting Windows, Show Mix.
5 Navigate to the upper portion of the Aux track, where insert effects are selected and used. Click on the first empty slot and select Kontakt from the pop-up menu. This will place an instance of Kontakt on the Aux track and launch the Kontakt interface.
6 Next, select the MIDI track and assign its output to Kontakt. Additionally, designate a MIDI channel for Kontakt and arm the track to trigger and monitor any loaded instruments in Kontakt.

Kontakt with Logic

Logic by Emagic is one of those sequencing programs that most tech junkies dream about (see Figure 7.51). It's an application that dives into the outer reaches of MIDI and digital audio unlike most others. Since Apple owns Emagic, it was the first sequencer/DAW application to support the Audio Unit plug-in format. Let's set it up with Kontakt.

Figure 7.51

Logic by Emagic is a sequencer/DAW application that pleases advanced computer musicians with its robust feature set.

1 Launch Logic and create an audio instrument track.
2 Double-click on the audio instrument track to launch the Logic mixing environment.
3 Locate the newly created audio instrument track, click and hold on its insert point, and select Kontakt. This will launch the Kontakt interface.
4 Arm the track to monitor through Kontakt.

Kontakt with Digital Performer

Digital Performer is another Mac-exclusive sequencer/DAW application (see Figure 7.52). Used by many film composers, Digital Performer is a complex but user-friendly complement to Kontakt. Note that you must have the latest version of DP 4.1 to use Kontakt as an audio unit.

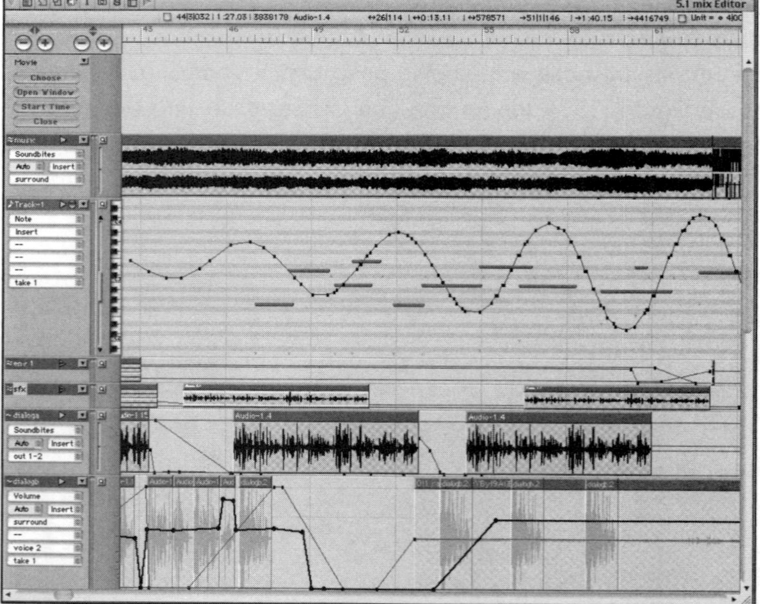

Figure 7.52
Digital Performer by Mark of the Unicorn is a Mac-only sequencer used by many popular composers, such as Don Davis (*The Matrix*) and Trevor Rabin (Yes).

1 Launch Digital Performer and create a new project.
2 Create a new instrument track by selecting Project, Add Track, Instrument Track, Kontakt.
3 Double-click on the Kontakt slot on the DP mixing board to launch its graphic interface.

4 Create a new MIDI track using the same method.
5 Select the MIDI track and set its output to Kontakt.
6 Arm the MIDI track to monitor from Kontakt.

> **GET THE LATEST VERSION**
>
> You will need the latest version of Digital Performer for this tutorial to work. Take a quick trip to the MOTU Web site (**www.motu.com**) and make sure that you download the latest Audio Unit Bundle file. This will enable you to use Kontakt and any other Native Instruments product.

Kontakt with SONAR

Of all the sequencing and DAW applications that have come and gone over the years, none has impressed me quite as much recently as SONAR (see Figure 7.53). It has got a great graphic layout and is easy to use.

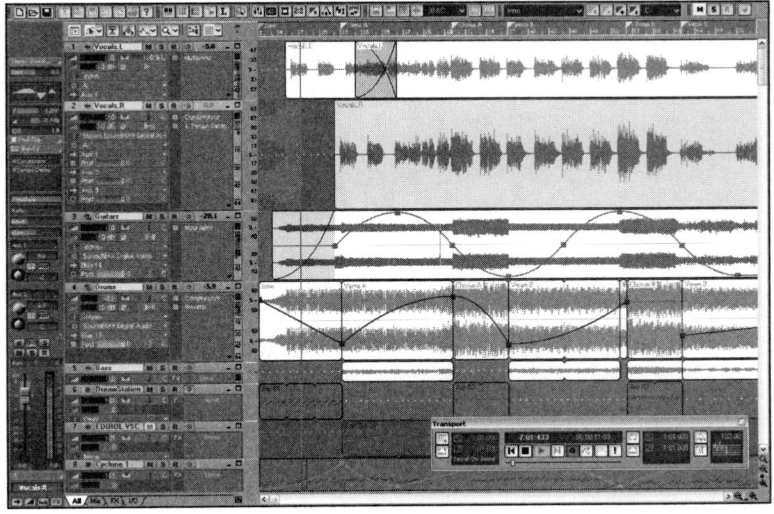

Figure 7.53
SONAR by Cakewalk is a fantastic DAW application that sports some impressive features.

1 Launch SONAR. Once a project is open, click on the DXi Synth Rack button.
2 From the DXi Synth rack, select Kontakt. This will load it into the synth and launch the graphic interface.
3 Create a MIDI track if needed and assign its output to Kontakt.
4 Arm the MIDI track to monitor through Kontakt.

Kontakt with Project5

Project5 is another music composition application by Cakewalk (see Figure 7.54). Unlike SONAR, Project5 is not a DAW. It is simply a sequencer application that uses soft synths and a sampler to create music with an easy to use interface.

Figure 7.54

Project5 is a synth workstation that includes support for DXis and VSTis and can also be used via ReWire.

1. Launch Project5 and start a new song.
2. Click on the Add button and select Kontakt from the list of DXi synths. This will create a sequencer track for Kontakt and launch the interface.
3. Select a Kontakt instrument.
4. Arm the sequencer track to monitor through Kontakt.

Creating a Kontakt Instrument

At long last, it's time to get "in Kontakt" with your sampling skills and build your first instrument. Since I'm a guitarist by trade, I have created a batch of acoustic guitar samples that we will use to import, structure, and build our first Kontakt instrument. Furthermore, the samples I have prepared were recorded at different velocities and have already been looped, so this will end up being a multilayered instrument.

After you have finished this tutorial, you can go back to the sampling guidelines we discussed in Chapter 3, "Recording Your Samples," and use them to record samples and build instruments on your own.

> **GET THE SAMPLES**
>
> Before proceeding, make sure to pop over to the Course Technology Web site at **www.courseptr.com** and locate the *Sampling and Soft Synth Power!* page to download the example material for Chapter 7. There you will find a compressed file that contains all the samples we'll be using. It's about 7MB, so if you are on a slow dial-up connection, go walk the dog around the block a couple of times or get a cup of coffee to kill some time while you wait.
>
> After downloading and decompressing the Samples folder, leave it on the desktop.

Getting Started

Navigate to and click on the Load/Save pop-up menu and select New Instrument. This will create a new empty instrument in the rack (see Figure 7.55).

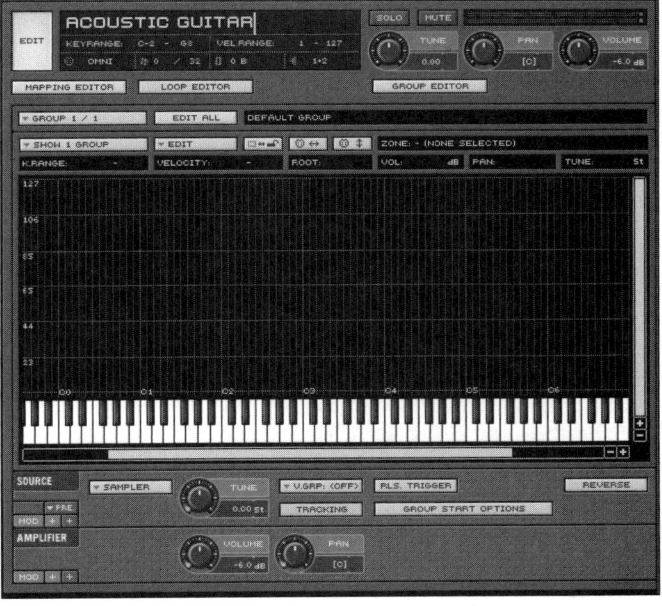

Figure 7.55
Our empty instrument is ready to go. Click once in the Name dialog and rename it Acoustic Guitar.

Now, click on the Edit button to expand the instrument and click on the zone field to display it in the rack.

Finding the Samples

The next hurdle in this process is to locate the samples you just downloaded. The folder containing the samples should be located on your computer's desktop so that you can just click and drag the folder into the Kontakt folder and be able to locate them easily later (see Figure 7.56).

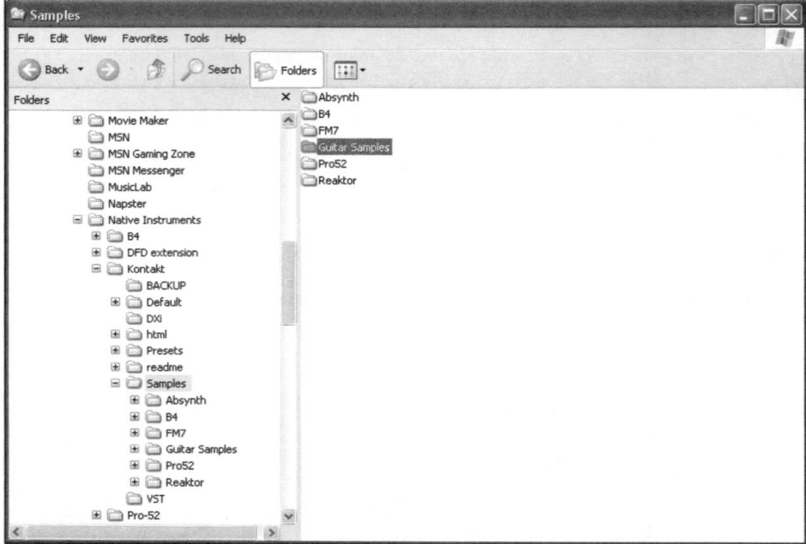

Figure 7.56

After downloading the Guitar Samples folder, make sure that you drag it into the Kontakt Program folder so that you can easily locate the samples again later.

At this point, you can import the samples into Kontakt by clicking and dragging them into the zone field from your computer's browser window, which is tedious. The easier way to locate and load the samples is to use the Kontakt browser. Using the upper pane of the browser, use the file tree to locate the Kontakt Program folder, and you should see the Guitar Samples folder within. Double-click on Guitar Samples to display its content, which will be the Single Notes folder. Click once on this folder and the individual samples should appear in the lower pane (see Figure 7.57).

Importing the Samples

Importing the samples into Kontakt is easy as pie, so I'm going to take you through the step-by-step process of importing each sample one string and dynamic at a time. Follow along as we import the low E *mezzoforte* sample.

1. Start by scrolling down to the bottom of the sample list in the lower pane of the browser and locate the Low E mf.wav file. Click on its sample icon to preview the sample.

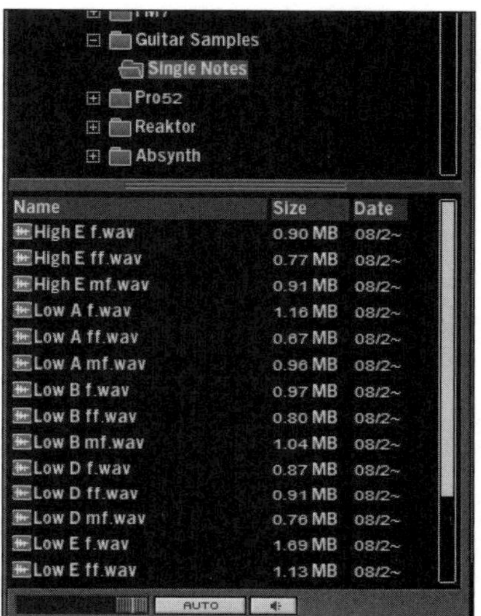

Figure 7.57

The guitar samples have been located using the browser and are ready to import into our new instrument.

2. Now, click and drag that sample onto the zone field of the Mapping Editor. Locate the C1 note on the keyboard and release the mouse in that area to finish importing the sample. The first sample is now imported into a newly created zone (see Figure 7.58).
3. Looking at the sample's information, you can see that the root of the sample is displayed as C1. This is incorrect because the intended root of this sample/zone should be E1. Click and drag the note to the right until the Root dialog shows E1.
4. Next, let's expand the note range of this sample by navigating to the middle nodes on the sides of the zone. Click and drag these nodes to the left and right until the note range of this zone is D1 and G#1 (see Figure 7.59).
5. Finally, navigate your mouse to the upper portion of the zone and then click and drag down to adjust the velocity range of the sample so it reads as 1–69 (see Figure 7.60).

Now, let's import the next low E sample, which has a *forte* dynamic.

1. Locate the Low E f.wav file.
2. Click and drag it into the zone field of the Mapping Editor. Make sure not to overlap the previously loaded sample (see Figure 7.61). Release the mouse, and the sample will import into a new zone.

Figure 7.58

Click and drag a sample into the virtual zone field of the Mapping Editor to import it and create your first zone.

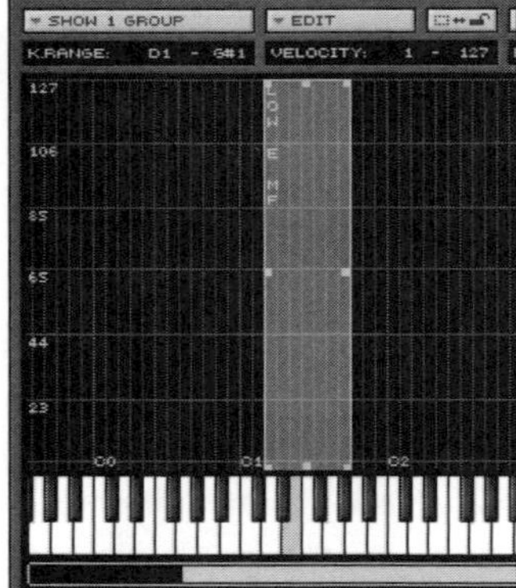

Figure 7.59

Use the nodes on the sides of the zone to adjust its key range to D1-G#1.

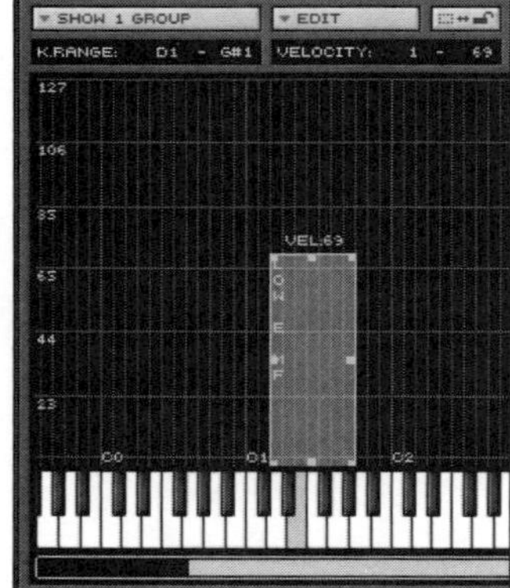

Figure 7.60

Now click and drag down on the top of the zone to adjust the velocity range to read 1-69 and you are finished.

3 Now, adjust the velocity range of the zone to read 70–99.

4 Next, click and drag the zone to the left or right (depending on where you imported it to on the keyboard area) until the Root dialog reads E1 (see Figure 7.62).

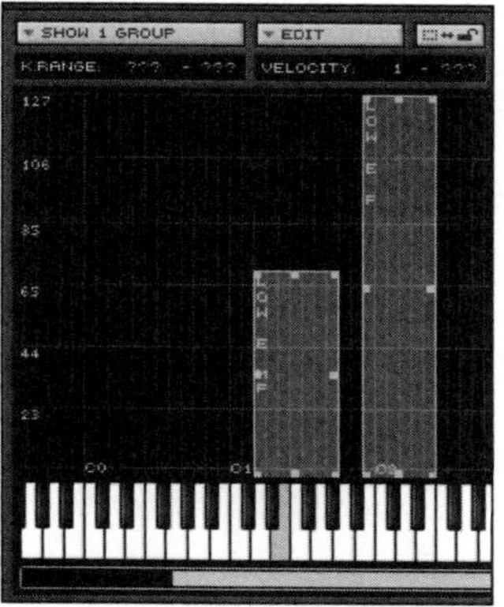

Figure 7.61
Click and drag the second sample into the keyboard area.

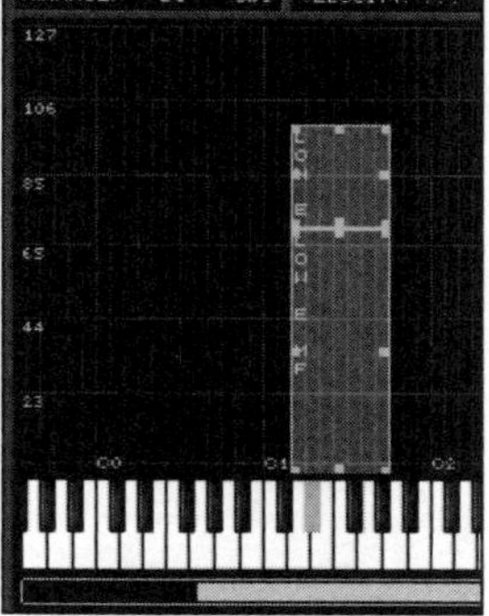

Figure 7.62
Now both samples have been mapped out.

Last up is the *double forte* Low E sample. Repeat the same steps as before, but make sure the velocity range of the zone is set to 100–127. When you are finished, the three imported samples should look like Figure 7.63.

Now, use the steps of these previous tutorials to build the rest of the Kontakt instrument. Here is a list of the appropriate roots, key ranges, and velocity ranges for each sample.

- **Low A mf.wav**—Root A1, Lo Key A1, Hi Key C#2, Lo Vel 1, Hi Vel 69
- **Low A f.wav**—Root A1, Lo Key A1, Hi Key C#2, Lo Vel 70, Hi Vel 99
- **Low A ff.wav**—Root A1, Lo Key A1, Hi Key C#2, Lo Vel 100, Hi Vel 127

- **Low D mf.wav**—Root D2, Lo Key D2, Hi Key F#2, Lo Vel 1, Hi Vel 69
- **Low D f.wav**—Root D2, Lo Key D2, Hi Key F#2, Lo Vel 70, Hi Vel 99
- **Low D ff.wav**—Root D2, Lo Key D2, Hi Key F#2, Lo Vel 100, Hi Vel 127
- **Low G mf.wav**—Root G2, Lo Key G2, Hi Key A#2, Lo Vel 1, Hi Vel 69
- **Low G f.wav**—Root G2, Lo Key G2, Hi Key A#2, Lo Vel 70, Hi Vel 99
- **Low G ff.wav**—Root G2, Lo Key G2, Hi Key A#2, Lo Vel 100, Hi Vel 127
- **Low B mf.wav**—Root B2, Lo Key B2, Hi Key D#3, Lo Vel 1, Hi Vel 69
- **Low B f.wav**—Root B2, Lo Key B2, Hi Key D#3, Lo Vel 70, Hi Vel 99
- **Low B ff.wav**—Root B2, Lo Key B2, Hi Key D#3, Lo Vel 100, Hi Vel 127
- **High E mf.wav**—Root E3, Lo Key E3, Hi Key A3, Lo Vel 1, Hi Vel 69
- **High E f.wav**—Root E3, Lo Key E3, Hi Key A3, Lo Vel 70, Hi Vel 99
- **High E ff.wav**—Root E3, Lo Key E3, Hi Key A3, Lo Vel 100, Hi Vel 127

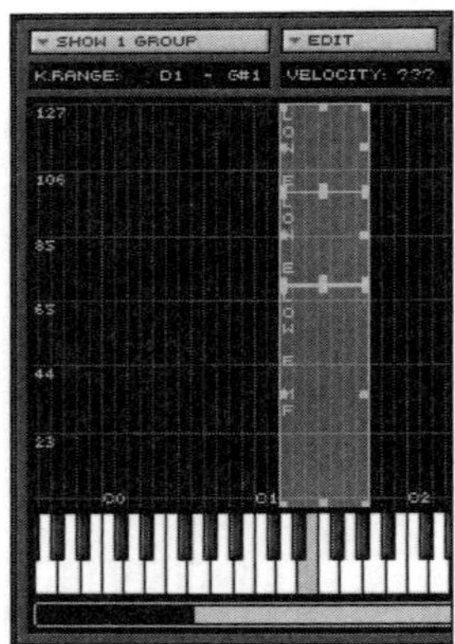

Figure 7.63
Now all of the samples for low E have been imported. You can trigger them with your MIDI keyboard or by clicking on the Virtual Keyboard in different areas to hear the different velocity layers.

Once you are finished importing the samples, you should get an instrument that looks like that in Figure 7.64.

> **SAVE YOUR WORK**
>
> Remember the golden rule of computing and save your work as you follow along with these tutorials. Just select Save Instrument from the Load/Save pop-up menu at the top of the Kontakt interface.
>
> Additionally, save the instrument file in the Guitar Samples folder. That way, when you click once on the Guitar Samples folder in the future, the browser will display the instrument in the lower pane of the browser.

Figure 7.64

Now the Kontakt instrument is Komplete.

Grouping the Samples

Now that the instrument has been created, this would be a good time to place each zone in a group. This will enable you to manipulate the attributes of each zone individually. For example, you could set up a filter on one group but not another. It's a neat feature of Kontakt, and it can be done very easily.

1. Click and drag a marquee around all the zones. Release the mouse to select them all.
2. Click on the Edit pop-up menu in the Mapping Editor and select Each Zone, 1 Group.
3. Now all of the zones are grouped and can be selected from the Group pop-up menu.

After the groups have been created, you can begin to assign different groups to different effects and even different playback algorithms. For example, let's select a group from the low E note and apply a compressor effect just to that sample.

1. Click on the Group Editor button to have it appear in the rack.
2. Click on the Edit All button to deactivate it.
3. With the Mapping Editor still open, click on the low E group with the highest velocity.

4 Click on the right plus (+) button on the Source module and select Compressor from the Group Insert Effects subdirectory. This will launch the Compressor interface and place it just below the source (see Figure 7.65).

5 Play the corresponding MIDI note to the Low E group, and you should now hear the compressor effect on just that group.

Figure 7.65
Select any of the group insert effects to apply to an individual group.

Here's another idea to share with you. Let's say you would like to change the playback algorithm on one sample from DFD mode to Tone Machine. Not a problem at all.

1 With the Mapping Editor still open and Edit All still inactive in the Group Editor, select the group you want to alter.

2 Using the Source module, select a different algorithm such as the Tone Machine or perhaps the Sample setting.

3 Make your settings to the sample and trigger it from a MIDI keyboard or the Virtual Keyboard to hear the effect.

In short, there's very little you can't do with Kontakt. While this chapter has provided a fairly comprehensive overview of the Kontakt interface, there are many other hidden secrets buried within the interface that are also explained in the Kontakt manual.

8 An Introduction to Software Synthesis

Welcome to the second part of this book, which covers software synthesis. In the next five chapters, we'll explain and explore all of the imaginative possibilities made possible by these synth wonders. In a nutshell, soft synths are software emulations of hardware-based synthesizers that can be used within sequencing applications as plug-ins. Soft synths offer affordable ways for musicians to integrate new sounds and textures into their music, as well as rediscover classic synths that are no longer available as hardware but are available as software. As you can imagine, over the last 4–5 years, software synthesis has caused quite a stir in the virtual studio community, as it offers keyboardists and synthesists the ability to realize their music potential at very little cost.

- **Better Sounds**—Soft synths give users the ability to not only try new forms of synthesis that were previously difficult to realize through hardware, but also to relive old memories of favorite hardware keyboards that were either discontinued or too expensive to purchase and maintain.
- **Better Timing**—As soft synths respond with sample-accurate precision, they have much better overall timing when compared to their hardware counterparts.
- **They Look Cool**—Okay, so maybe this isn't the biggest selling point of soft synths, but you have to admit I'm right here. They do look cool, and isn't that half the fun?

WHERE IT ALL BEGAN

Believe it or not, software-based synthesis has been around a lot longer than you might think. But back in those archaic times of the early 90s, soft synths such as Turbo Synth by Digidesign and Generator by Native Instruments had graphic interfaces that were awkward and confusing to not-quite-savvy computer musicians.

The modern era of the soft synth craze began with the program ReBirth by Propellerhead Software (see Figure 8.1). This was a self-contained synthesizer groove machine that could be used to create pattern-driven techno rhythms by employing the use of software-emulated classic synthesizers and drum machines.

More information on ReBirth can be found by visiting the Propellerhead Web site at **www.propellerheads.se**.

Figure 8.1

ReBirth by Propellerhead Software emulated the classic TB303 Bass Synth and the TR808/909 drum machines.

Some Sound Advice—Fundamentals

Before we begin talking about synthesis, let's go over some of the fundamentals of audio. Understanding audio terms and how they apply to synthesis will help you understand the inner working of the soft synths we'll be covering throughout the rest of this book.

Sound is typically described by two characteristics:

- **Frequency**—The pitch of sound.
- **Amplitude**—The volume of sound.

Frequency and Amplitude

A sound can simply be defined as a vibration that is capable of being detected by a human ear. When our eardrums vibrate, we are hearing a sound. The rate at which our eardrums (and the sound-producing object) vibrate is called the vibration's *frequency*.

Frequency is measured in units called Hertz (or Hz), named after the German scientist Heinrich R. Hertz. A Hertz is defined as the number of vibration cycles that a sound produces in one second. A single Hertz is equal to one cycle per second, which is far too low a frequency for the human ear to detect. The Hertz unit is usually combined with metric system prefixes to produce various subdivisions. These are commonly known as the kilohertz (kHz), the megahertz (MHz), and the gigahertz (GHz).

A finely tuned human ear is capable of detecting a broad frequency range, from 20Hz to 22.05kHz (22,050 Hz). The range narrows as we grow older and as our hearing is dulled thanks to the effects of listening to loud noises over long periods of time. It's important to treat your hearing like gold!

So how does the frequency spectrum translate into musical terms? Let's consider the cello, which has a pretty wide frequency range, as an example. When a low C note is bowed on the lowest string, the string vibrations are very slow, as the diameter of the string is quite thick in comparison to the highest string. This produces a very low frequency of 65.5Hz, which in turn means that the note is very low in pitch. On the other end of that spectrum, if your cello player were to then play a C note on the highest string, the vibrations would be much more rapid, creating a tone with a higher frequency of 523Hz.

Frequency also has a counterpart element, *amplitude*, which is simply the volume of the sound and is measured in units called *decibels*. Every sound has a frequency and amplitude. If we play one piano note softly, the frequency is constant and the amplitude is low. If we play the same note again but strike the key harder than before, the frequency will be the same, but the amplitude will be higher, giving us a louder sound.

Simple Waveforms

When it comes to synthesis in its most basic form, there are five simple waveforms that can be generated electronically. A visual representation of these waveforms can be plotted on a graph, and from this we can identify its harmonics (frequencies) and amplitudes. Each waveform has its own unique characteristics and intended uses.

- Sine Wave
- Square Wave
- Pulse Wave
- Saw Tooth Wave
- Triangle Wave

Sine Wave

The sine wave is the most basic and familiar wave shape; it produces a smooth waveform that is purely proportional and periodic (see Figure 8.2). Unlike the other waveforms that we will discuss in this section and in the rest of the chapter, a sine wave contains a single harmonic. The sine wave is the vital building block for constructing more complex waveforms, which you will see for yourself in Chapter 11, "Additive Synthesis: Sine of the Times," when we cover additive synthesis.

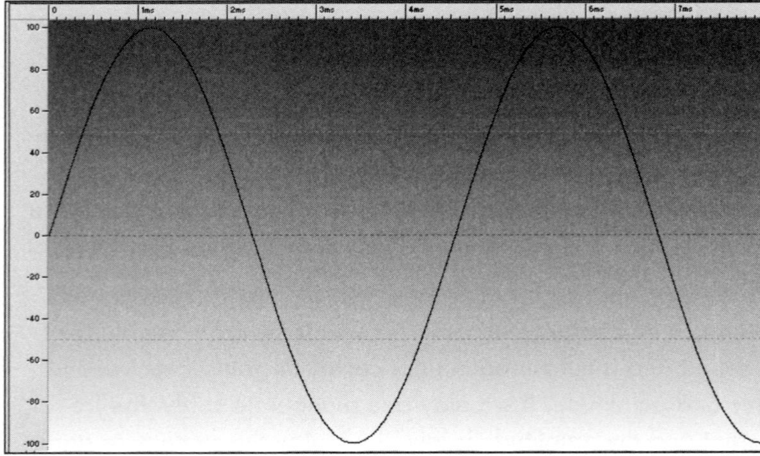

Figure 8.2
The sine wave is the most basic of all waveforms.

Square Wave

A square wave is also thought of as a simple waveform, except that it contains multiple odd-numbered harmonics (see Figure 8.3). This simply means that each harmonic of a square wave is calculated by multiplying the fundamental harmonic by an odd number. Additionally, the amplitude assigned to each harmonic is adjusted by odd-numbered fractions.

For example, let's suppose that you have a square wave that oscillates at a frequency of 220Hz, which is an A note. The first, or fundamental, harmonic would be 220Hz, the third harmonic would be 660Hz (220Hz×3), the fifth harmonic would be 1100Hz (220Hz×5), the seventh harmonic would be 1540Hz (220Hz×7), and so forth. As for the amplitudes of each harmonic, if the fundamental harmonic is set at 0dB (the peak level), the third harmonic would be one-third of that value, the fifth harmonic would be one-fifth of the fundamental, and the list goes on.

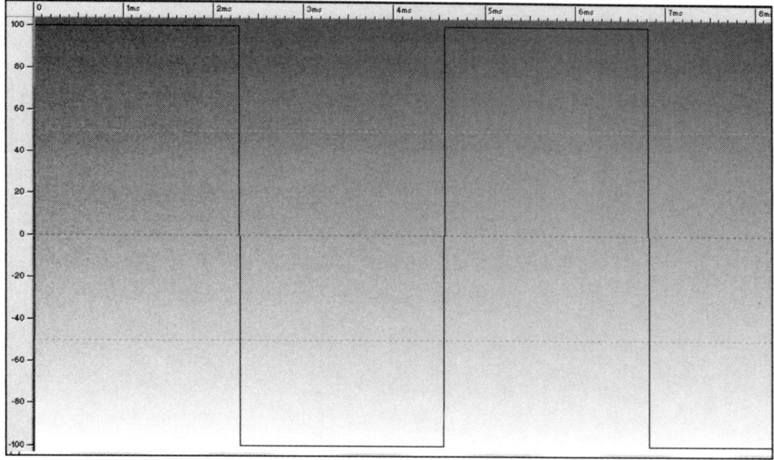

Figure 8.3

The square wave has a very hollow sound, resembling that of a clarinet.

Pulse Wave

The pulse wave can be thought of as a distant cousin to the square wave, as they both contain a similar yet different harmonic structure (see Figure 8.4). While a pulse wave does contain odd-numbered harmonics (fundamental, third, fifth, etc), it also contains the second, sixth, and tenth harmonics as well.

Saw Tooth Wave

The saw tooth wave quite possibly may be the most complete waveform of this bunch, as it contains all the harmonics in the natural harmonic series (see Figure 8.5). It produces a sharp, brassy sound perfect for building trumpet sounds.

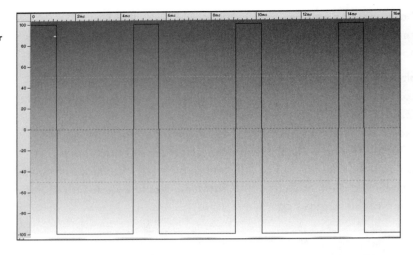

Figure 8.4
The pulse wave sounds similar to the square wave but brassier.

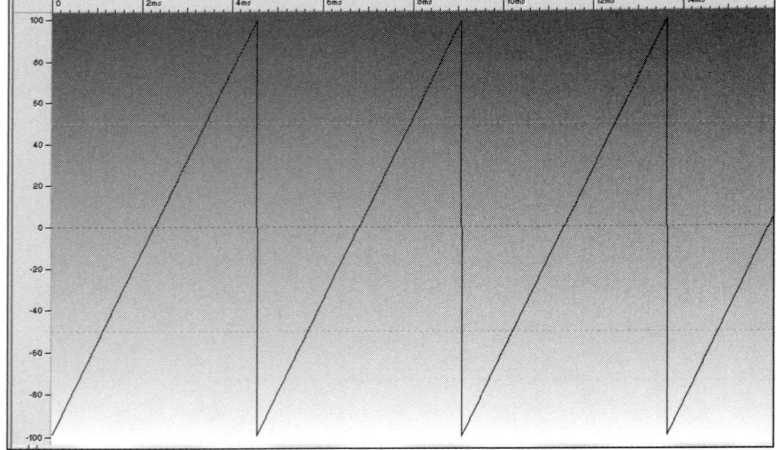

Figure 8.5
The saw tooth wave has a sharp, brass-like tone.

Triangle Wave

The triangle wave looks similar to the saw tooth in harmonic structure, but its amplitude characteristics are very different (see Figure 8.6). A triangle wave contains odd-numbered harmonics, like the square wave. In fact, if you were to play them side-by-side, they would sound similar. But while the triangle contains the same harmonic set, the amplitudes of each harmonic differ greatly in value. For example, if we have a fundamental harmonic of 220Hz with amplitude of 0dB (the peak level), the third harmonic would be 660Hz as it was with the square wave. But the amplitude of the third harmonic would be the squared value of one-third of the fundamental harmonic; that is, one-ninth instead of one-third. As a result, the third harmonic and on would be much quieter than it would were this a square wave instead of a triangle.

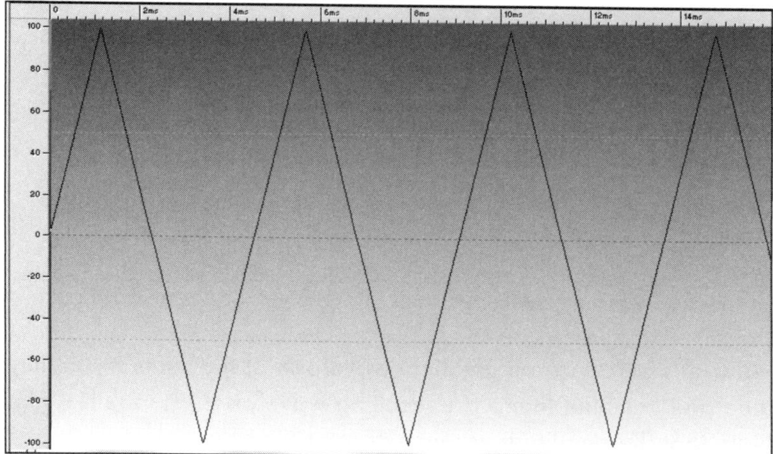

Figure 8.6

The triangle wave sounds similar to the square but softer.

Phase

So far we have been discussing waveforms as single entities. But as you can guess, if this was the limit of modern synthesis, it would sound pretty boring, as there is only so much one can do with a single waveform. So with that thought in mind, let's advance our thinking and move on up to combining waveforms and the resulting new dynamic, called *phase*.

Phase is a mathematical relationship between multiple signals of either the same or different waveforms in which the oscillation of the two waveforms occurs at the same or different times. Phase can be used to strengthen or cancel out a fundamental waveform by introducing an identical waveform at the same or different time, respectively. When used creatively, phase can create new synthetic textures between two different waveforms by shifting the position of one waveform against another. This creates a "chorus-like" effect that can be enhanced even further with tuning parameters. We'll be sure to dig into this topic in future chapters and tutorials. For now, let's look at some examples.

In Figure 8.7, you can see a basic sine wave oscillating at a frequency of 440Hz and at an amplitude of –6dB, which is a little on the soft side.

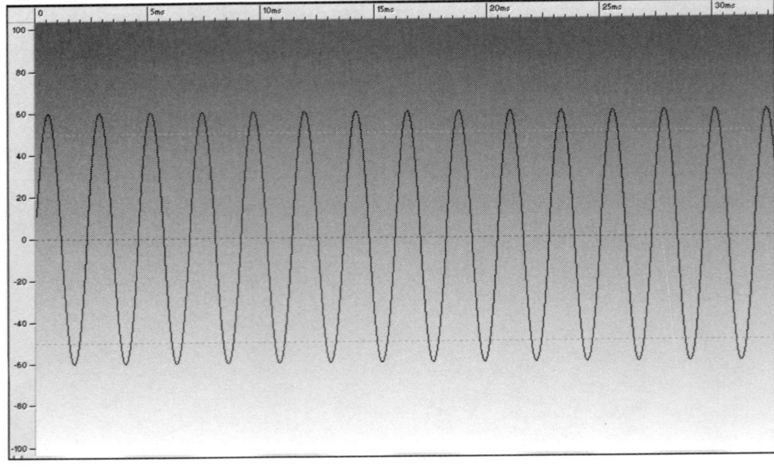

Figure 8.7
Our fundamental sine wave

Now let's introduce an identical waveform at the same frequency and amplitude and combine them. The resulting waveform will look like Figure 8.8. Note that the amplitude is much greater than before.

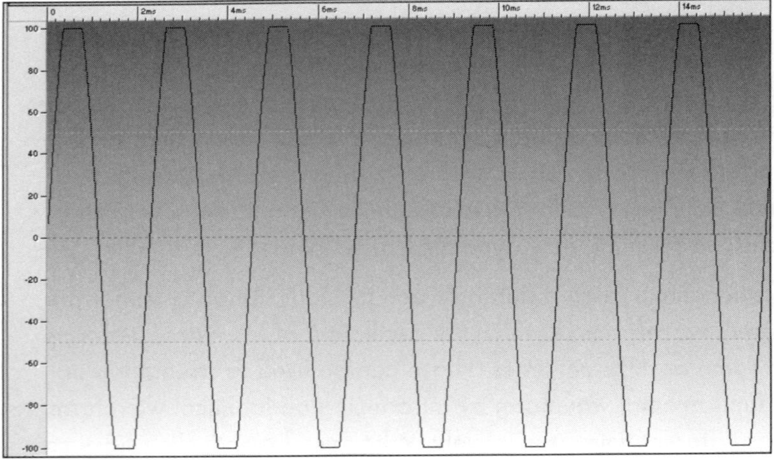

Figure 8.8
The two waveforms are merged.

Now let's take a step in the other direction and continue using our fundamental waveform, but this time we will introduce another waveform of the same frequency and amplitude that occurs at a slightly different time than the fundamental. The resulting waveform shown in Figure 8.9 has greater amplitude than before but not quite as much as in the previous example.

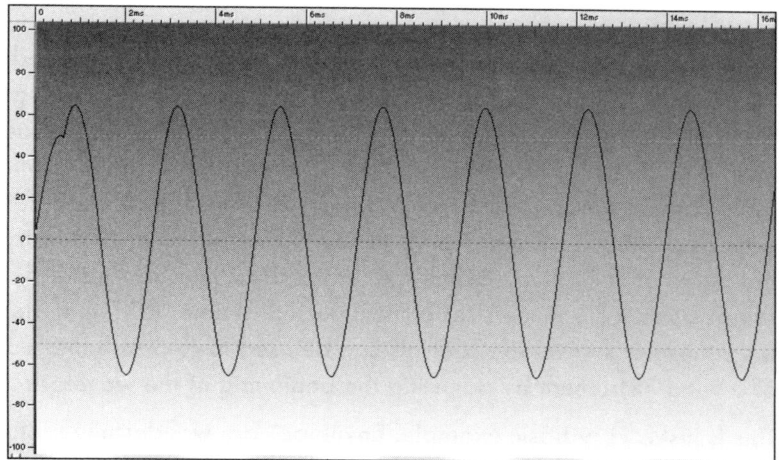

Figure 8.9

Now the waveforms are a little out of phase.

For the final example, I will start with the fundamental waveform, but this time the second identical waveform that I introduce will be much further in time from the fundamental. In simpler terms, when the fundamental's waveform is oscillating above the line of zero activity (*compressing*), the identical waveform will oscillate below the line of zero activity (*refracting*). As shown in Figure 8.10, the merging of these two waveforms results in a signal that is cancelled out or contains little to no amplitude.

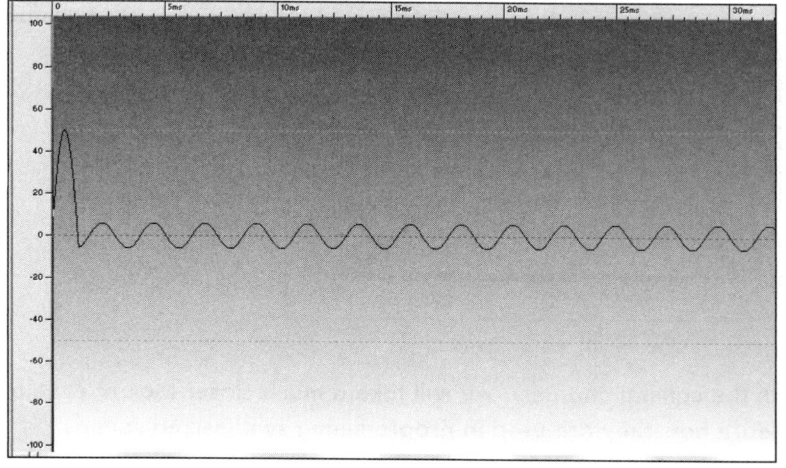

Figure 8.10

Now the waveforms are canceled out.

As you will come to find later in this book, phase can be used to create some very interesting sound textures with little difficulty.

Envelopes

An envelope governs how a sound evolves over a specific period of time. It also shapes the playing characteristics of a waveform by altering the attack and sustain. For example, let's suppose you would like to program a waveform similar to that of a flute or clarinet. We all know that wind instruments have a much slower attack than does an instrument that is plucked or struck, such as a guitar or drum. That is to say, the sound of a wind instrument does not begin at its highest volume the way a drum hit does—instead, it typically ramps up to full volume over a short period of time. With that idea in mind, a synthesizer's envelope controls can be used to re-create the realistic feel of a wind instrument by adjusting the beginning of the waveform.

This is just a very basic example. Envelopes are wonderfully useful tools that play a very important role in synthesis.

The four parameters of an envelope (see Figure 8.11) are these:

- **Attack**—This determines the amount of time needed for the amplitude of the waveform to reach its peak level.
- **Decay**—This determines the amount of time needed for the amplitude to descend to the level set by the Sustain parameter.
- **Sustain**—This stage of the envelope determines how long the amplitude will remain constant as long as a key of a MIDI keyboard is held.
- **Release**—This determines the amount of time before the amplitude of the waveform fades away completely after the key has been released.

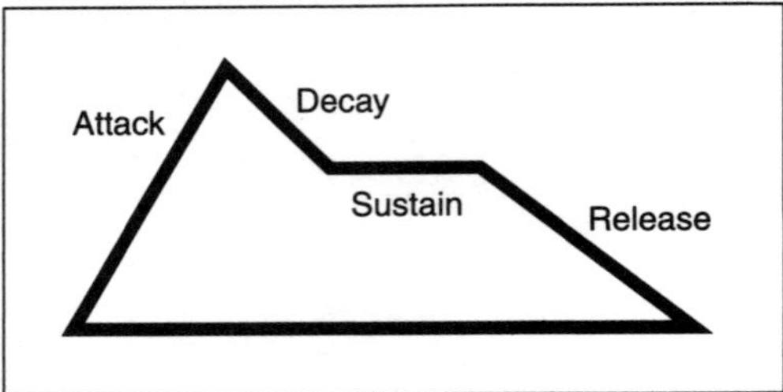

Figure 8.11
The basic diagram of an envelope

In the coming chapters, we will take a much closer look at envelopes and learn how they are used in programming synthesized sounds.

A Soft Synth for Every Mood

Make no mistake, there are soft synths to fit every musician's needs. Whether you just want some good basic sounds to create backing tracks for your songs or you're a real synth enthusiast who's anxious to explore every niche of synthesis and push the creative envelope, you can bet that there is a soft synth to meet your requirements.

In this section, I will introduce the five types of synthesis that we will cover throughout the rest of this book. They will include:

- **Subtractive**—Covered in Chapter 9, "Subtractive Synthesis—Close Up."
- **Frequency Modulation**—Covered in Chapter 10, "FM Synthesis—Super Freq."
- **Additive**—Covered in Chapter 11, "Additive Synthesis—Sine of the Times."
- **Sample-Based**—Covered in Chapter 12 "RAM Synthesis."

Subtractive Synthesis

Subtractive is the most basic form of synthesis in both the hardware and software environments. Casually referred to as analog synthesis, it uses three fundamental components to create sound.

- An oscillator
- A filter
- An amplifier

Understanding subtractive synthesis on a basic level is very easy. The first module, known as an oscillator, produces sound by generating waveforms. These waveforms have various shapes and frequencies (or rates of oscillation) and produce different textures and pitches, respectively.

After a sound has been generated, the next module, the filter, identifies and subtracts a range of frequencies from the overall sound, or frequency, spectrum. This modifies the timbre or texture of the waveform, making it possible to shape the sound to emulate different instruments (such as pianos, strings, or percussion). The filter itself can be further manipulated by introducing an envelope, which helps to define the shape of the filter effect over time.

The final module in subtractive synthesis is the amplifier, which increases the overall amplitude (or volume) of the signal created by the oscillator/filter combination. As is the case with the filter, the amplifier has its own envelope, which defines the shape of the sound's volume over time.

That's the basic story of subtractive synthesis. We'll dig deeper into the subject in Chapter 9.

Additive Synthesis

Additive synthesis is almost the exact opposite of subtractive synthesis. It is the method of creating sounds by combining simple sound waves. This type of synthesis is derived from the research of Jean Baptiste Fourier, who demonstrated that any complex sound could be broken down into a series of sine waves varying in frequency and amplitude. Additive synthesis is achieved by adding sine waves together to create new waveforms.

There are three fundamental components to additive synthesis:

- **Harmonics**—These are the frequencies themselves. Also known as *partials.*
- **Amplitudes**—These are the individual volumes that each frequency is assigned.
- **Envelopes**—These are needed to mold and influence the harmonics and frequencies.

Additive synthesis begins with breaking down a simple waveform into its component parts and analyzing the harmonics and amplitudes that make it up (see Figure 8.12).

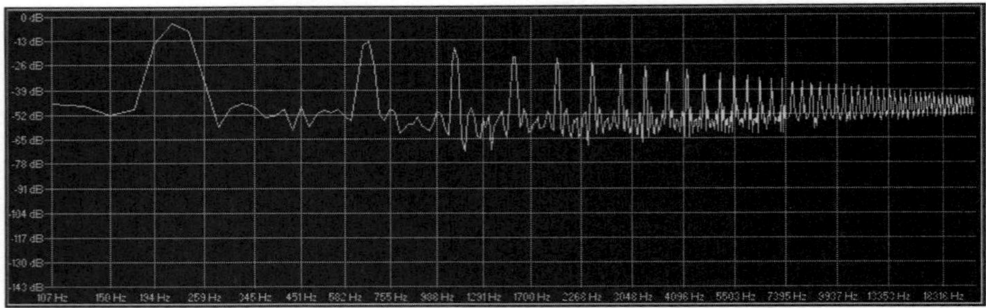

Figure 8.12
In this figure, you can see the frequencies and amplitudes that make up the basic elements of a square wave.

After these frequencies and amplitudes have been identified, the structure can be used as a model for re-creating the original sound through the combination and adjustment of sine waves of varying pitches and amplitudes. As a finishing touch, envelopes and noise generators can be used to further refine the sound. In the end, we find ourselves with a new waveform that sounds very similar to the original. But this is where the fun really begins, as additive synthesis also includes additional sound generators and a morphing timeline to further develop our new waveform in ways that just can't be done with other synthesizers.

I'm sure you're thinking that this is a bit on the complicated side, and you wouldn't be far from the truth there. However, as you will learn in Chapter 11, additive is not all that difficult to comprehend at all.

Frequency Modulation (FM) Synthesis

Frequency modulation, or FM, synthesis became popular in the 1980s with the introduction of the DX-7 by Yamaha. Frequency modulation was developed in 1973 by John Chowning, who discovered that complex sounds could be produced with the use of two oscillators.

The FM synthesis model requires two essential building blocks:

- The carrier
- The modulator

The carrier is the fundamental, or center, frequency, which has its own oscillator, amplifier, and envelope. The modulator is responsible for altering the carrier by using its own oscillator, amplifier, and envelope, thereby creating the modulating frequency. When combined, these two building blocks create and output what is known as the frequency deviation, or the difference between them. This deviation is the resulting sound that you hear (see Figure 8.13).

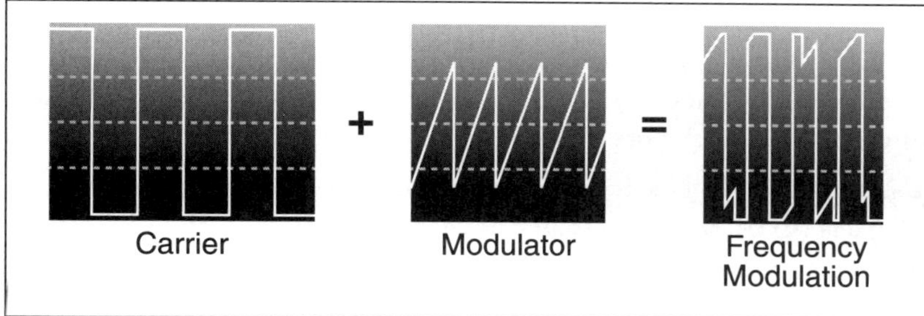

Figure 8.13

In this demonstration, we have the carrier, which is a square wave, oscillating at 220Hz, with an amplitude of 0dB and with little or no envelope parameters present. The next figure is the modulator, which is a saw tooth wave oscillating at 300Hz with an amplitude of -4dB and a slow attack. The last figure on the right is the resulting sound produced by the carrier and modulator, known as the frequency deviation.

Sample-Based Synthesis

Earlier in the book, we discussed digital sampling as a means of creating your own samples through programs such as GigaStudio and soft synths such as Kontakt. For some musicians, this is a good way to go, as it allows them to express their compositional ideas a little more clearly through their own means.

For others, digital sampling is seen as overkill because it takes a lot of time to master. This led to the need to create soft synths that were not only easy to use but also sounded great with little need for further editing. This is the void that sample-based synthesis fills.

A sample-based soft synth is one that compiles, stores, and plays back digital samples exclusively from the computer's RAM (random access memory). This differs greatly from the other forms of synthesis we've discussed so far, as sampled-based synthesis is not dependent on oscillators to generate waveforms.

Although sample-based synthesis is not dependent on oscillators to generate sound, developers of these soft synths have embedded additional synthesis properties and functions, such as envelopes and filters, in order to make them a creative outlet for playing and sequencing in your DAW applications. We'll take a closer look at sample-based synthesis in Chapter 12.

Soft Synth Formats

Soft synths work within your computer in one of three ways:

- **RAM-Based**—This form of soft synth uses a computer's installed RAM to play back digital audio samples. A good example of this kind of soft synth would be the Stylus by Spectrasonics (see Figure 8.14).
- **Hard Drive-Based**—This form of soft synth uses a combination of RAM and hard drive to play back samples. Soft samplers such as GigaStudio, HALion, Kontakt, and the Mach5 are prime examples (see Figure 8.15).
- **CPU-Based**—This type of soft synth primarily uses a computer's central processing unit (CPU) as its main source of generating signals, such as Reaktor by Native Instruments (see Figure 8.16).

Different Synth Formats

Once the coolness and originality of soft synths were realized, it was only a matter of time before every DAW developer wanted to tap into the growing interest within his user base and develop soft synths that would work within their host applications. Several new or updated application-specific formats were developed to allow users to integrate these soft synths into their virtual environments and access them as plug-ins. As these new formats were being developed and released, soft synth developers caught on quickly and began adapting their synths to work within each virtual environment.

Figure 8.14

The Stylus Groove Module is a loop-playing, booty-shaking groove machine like no other.

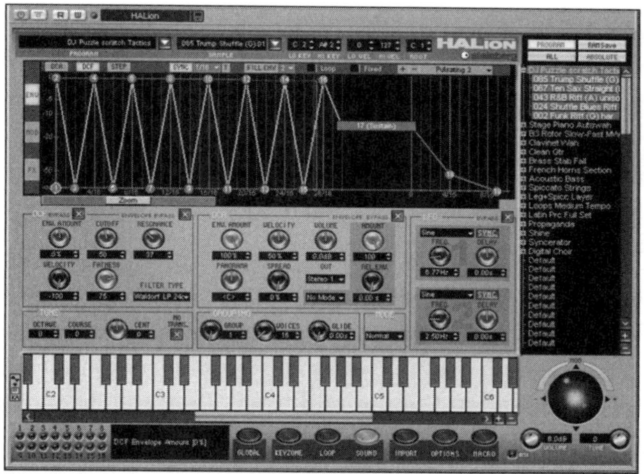

Figure 8.15

The HALion by Steinberg is a software-based sampler that plays a majority of each loaded sample from your computer's hard drive.

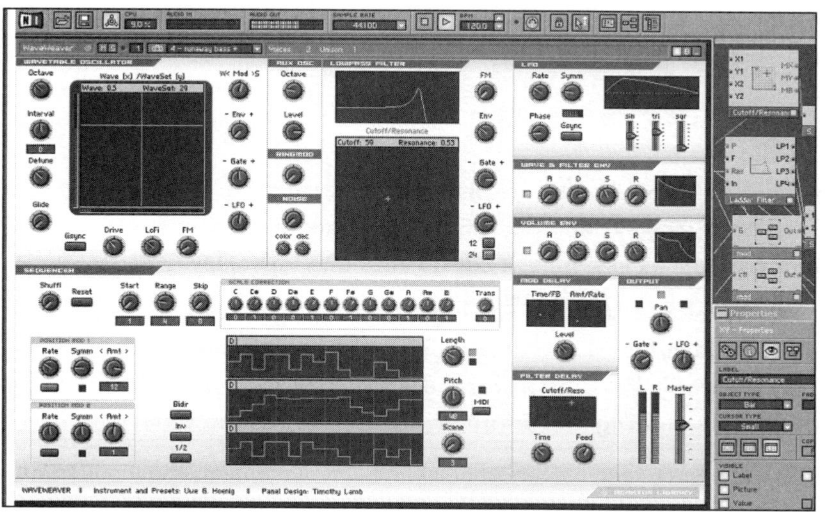

Figure 8.16

Native Instruments' Reaktor is a CPU-based soft synth that supports every type of synthesis that we will talk about throughout the rest of this book.

In this section of the chapter, we'll cover the major formats.

VST

Introduced in 1996, Steinberg's Virtual Studio Technology (VST) was a major turning point in digital recording. Up until that point, recording audio on a computer was an awkward and overly expensive venture because it required additional digital signal processing (DSP) hardware to process analog-to-digital signals. VST gave users the ability to bypass this expensive necessity and tap into the processing power of the computer's CPU. This eventually led to the introduction of software-emulated effect processors such as reverbs and delays to be used as plug-ins, which are sub-applications that run inside of host applications such as Cubase. Better yet, Steinberg freely distributed the development specifications to anyone who wanted to develop plug-ins for this format. As you can imagine, this technology caught on like wildfire, as hundreds of plug-ins began to surface within the software development community. Some plug-ins came from well-known and respected hardware companies such as TC Electronics and Lexicon, while others came from bedroom programmers.

In 1999, Steinberg announced a new improvement to its line of plug-ins by incorporating the ability to generate sound and receive MIDI data, called VST instruments. These VST instruments could work in any application that supported them, such as Cubase and Logic. They caught on quickly, and before long there were more VST instruments than you could shake a stick at.

Some of the more popular VST instruments include those manufactured by Steinberg, such as the HALion, D'Cota, and LM4. Native Instruments also makes some great VST instruments, including Reaktor, which is the synth's synth.

Audio Unit

Audio Unit is an Apple-exclusive plug-in format that is embedded within the OSX operating system. Like VST plug-ins and instruments, Audio Unit shares similar qualities in synthesis capabilities and versatility.

Since its release, Audio Unit plug-ins have grown considerably popular among the virtual studio communities that want to push their sparkling new G5s to new limits. Support for the Audio Unit format can be found in Logic 6 by Emagic and Digital Performer 4.1 by Mark of the Unicorn.

Some of the more popular Audio Units include those manufactured by Emagic, such as the EXS24 and EVP73. There are also many third-party Audio Units, such as the Cube by VirSyn or the Reaktor.

DXi

The DXi format was developed by Cakewalk and Microsoft and is derived from the popular DirectX plug-in format. The Windows-exclusive DirectX plug-in architecture was developed and released in competition with the VST format more than six years ago. While it was and still is a popular format, the major drawback to DirectX plug-ins was its inability to automate its parameters. Of course, this took a turn for the better with the release of Cakewalk's SONAR, at which time a new DirectX was released that finally made automation possible. After this breakthrough, Cakewalk introduced its own line of soft synths that supported the DXi format, such as the Dream Station and the synth bliss PSYN (pronounced "sine"). Consequently, many software companies stepped up and developed their own line of DXis, such as the Arturia Moog Modular and FXpansion's BFD.

RTAS

Not wanting to miss out on all the fun, Digidesign launched its own line of real-time plug-ins that could be used with its Pro Tools LE (Light Edition) systems, known as RTAS (Real Time Audio Suite). Like VST, Audio Units, and DXi, RTAS plug-ins and soft synths use the computer's CPU to process an audio signal. This differed greatly from Pro Tools' TDM format, which was costly and limiting due to its need for additional DSP hardware. Nevertheless, over the last year, the RTAS format has become quite popular, and you can easily find several plug-ins and soft synths that support it, such as the Native Instruments product line and IK Multimedia's SampleTank.

GETTIN' THE SKINNY ON SOFT SYNTHS

A good source of information about soft synths for every platform is the KvR Instrument Resource Web site at **www.kvr-vst.com**.

There you will find user forums on which you can ask for advice and support, an intuitive database that will help you find the right soft synth for you, and a news headlines page that will keep you up to date on all the happenings in the soft synth world.

ADAPTATION

One of the drawbacks to the variety of plug-in formats is that they can't be used in every DAW application. For example, if you use the latest version of Logic, VST instruments are not compatible, but they were before the whole Audio Unit development push began. Developers had to go back to the drawing board and rewrite their plug-ins and soft synths to meet the Audio Unit specification. Not every developer jumped on board to update his software, leaving some users unable to use their favorite synths with their favorite DAW.

Enter FXpansion, a company that has recently released a series of software utilities called *adapters* that allow VST plug-in and instrument users to use their soft synths and plug-ins in other applications.

There are three flavors of adapters available:

- **VST to Audio Unit Adapter**—This utility adapts any OSX VST instrument or plug-in for use in a program that supports Audio Units, such as Logic or Digital Performer.
- **VST to RTAS Adapter**—This utility adapts any Windows or OSX VST instrument or plug-in for use in a program that supports RTAS, such as Pro Tools LE.
- **VST to ReWire Adapter**—This utility adapts any Windows or OSX VST instrument or plug-in for use as a ReWire instrument.

These adapters are $99 each, making it a pretty good deal for users who have already dropped a lot of money on their initial investments. More information can be found by visiting the FXpansion Web site at **www.fxpansion.com**.

FIVE MINUTES WITH CHARLIE STEINBERG

I had the privilege of working for Steinberg as an associate for over four years. During my visits to the head office in Hamburg, I had the honor of meeting and striking up a friendship with the man himself, Charlie Steinberg (see Figure 8.17). Charlie is the chief developer of the VST platform, which was introduced in 1996. Since then, he has continued his development work on a large collection of Steinberg products, including Cubase SX, Nuendo, and VST plug-ins and soft synths.

Steinberg was not the first company to develop soft synths, but they were the first to integrate soft synths into DAW applications by presenting them as plug-ins. In my opinion (and I'm sure many others would agree), VST instruments were a remarkable step forward and launched an entirely new way to create music within the virtual studio.

Therefore, when I agreed to write this book, I felt that it would be a good idea to give you, the readers, a look at soft synths from a developer's perspective. Charlie seemed like the right guy for the job, so I jotted down a few questions and e-mailed them off, and now I present to you five minutes with Charlie Steinberg (he's a busy guy).

Figure 8.17
Mr. Cubase himself, Charlie Steinberg

MP: Charlie, thank you very much for taking the time to speak with us today. I'm sure the readers will get a kick out of this.

CS: As we say, "Man soll den Tag nicht vor dem Abend loben." (Don't count your chickens before they hatch. :-)

MP: By now, most computer musicians know about your VST technology, so I would like to get right to the soft synths. When did you first come up with the idea of integrating soft synths into the VST environment?

CS: Actually, not too late after the VST SDK (software development kit) was made public. The SDK was not originally designed for public release; we just felt it would be easier to encapsulate audio processors into modules. When we realized how fast this interface became established, it was sort of a natural step to also apply it to MIDI instruments. In fact, one of the driving forces was the vision of a much-improved MIDI, along with VST audio quality and sample accurate timing...a dream come true!

MP: As this was a new technology, how long did it take to develop the basic code for the VST 2.0 standard?

CS: Hmmm, the actual part of the interface is pretty lightweight, and it didn't take long to define it. It took much longer to develop a real instrument based on this, to create some sample code for third parties to hook in, and of course implement the other side of the fence (in Cubase).

MP: If you can recall, what was the general reaction when you announced the development of VST instruments?

CS: In the very beginning, there was not a significantly overwhelming reaction as far as I can recall, probably because VST plug-ins as such were still evolving. But it didn't take long until the users realized the potential of the combination of a MIDI instrument and a VST plug-in. It also took a while until the Cubase version was available everywhere...but yes, it did take off then almost immediately.

MP: When was the point that you knew that you had created something special?

CS: Before it was published :-) Seriously, to me it was obvious that this was the next step. It is a logical conclusion following the path of replacing studio gear by software modules, the mixer, FX, and then the instruments. We were not the first to create software synthesizers, but even though there was a lot to do, we packed it into VST plug-ins. And that was indeed the beginning of another revolution. As said, when the "VST instrument aware" Cubase version came out, it didn't take long until VST instruments took off, and it became obvious that this would be a long-term thing when so many vendors started to create their instruments.

MP: What are your favorite Steinberg and non-Steinberg VST instruments?

CS: It's tough if not impossible to pick a few; there are too many great instruments out there. Well, Hypersonic, HALion, Plex, The Grand, LM4 Mk II, Battery, B4, Atmosphere, Waldorf...but it's really impossible to make such a selection, too easy to forget some.

MP: As you know, there are at least a few hundred different soft synths available that cover just about every type of synthesis in the book. Is there anything else that you as a developer would like to see in the near future?

CS: Yes, but I wouldn't want to tell you. :-)

Subtractive Synthesis—Close Up

Subtractive is considered to be the granddaddy of all synthesis. It relies on non-digital means to generate sound, producing unique textures and ambiences perfect for soothing pads, big fat basses, or lead lines of monophonic bliss. Subtractive is also considered by most to be the tinkering synth of choice for musicians who love to turn knobs, push sliders, and generate sounds by patching different modules together.

In the soft synth world, subtractive is the most commonly emulated form of synthesis. At the time of this writing, there are close to 200 different soft synths available that emulate the characteristics of subtractive synthesis. While some are more complex than others, the fundamental principles of subtractive synthesis remain the same for most of the software emulations. In this chapter, we will take a close look at this form of synthesis and its origins. We'll wrap up by introducing you to two subtractive soft synths and providing tutorials on programming patches that will make your music come alive.

Bob Moog—Where It All Began

If subtractive synthesis could be summed up in one word, it would be *Moog*. Robert Moog was one of the founders of the modern day synthesizer with his groundbreaking contributions to subtractive synthesis. Originally a builder and distributor of transistor driven Theremins (the following Note), Moog and Theremin composer Herbert Deutsch shared a common interest in seeing new developments in electronic instruments. This led to the testing and development of the first subtractive synthesizer, the Moog Modular. This was pretty much the first commercially available subtractive synthesizer and was based on a series of hardware devices encased in a modular apparatus. The signal had to be physically "patched" or routed from one hardware device to another. For example:

1 You began with the oscillator by selecting a waveform.
2 That signal would then be routed to a filter to manipulate the frequencies of the oscillator.
3 The output of the manipulated signal could then be patched to an envelope that could adjust the attack, decay, sustain, and release of the filter.
4 The output of the envelope would then be routed to an amplifier with an envelope that would adjust the attack, decay, sustain, and release of the amplitude.
5 The resulting signal would then be routed to a hardware mixer or external amplifier.

There are many other devices and modifications that could be introduced along the signal flow, including a control voltage sequencer, which would make it possible to create programmed melodic lines of music, known as *sequences*. And this was well before the introduction of MIDI—nearly 20 years earlier, in fact.

THE THEREMIN—THE FIRST SYNTHESIZER

While the Moog Modular was the first subtractive synthesizer, the Theremin was the first synthesizer (see Figure 9.1). Looking like something out of a science fiction movie, the Theremin was an oscillator synthesizer with two long antennas, one protruding from the top (for pitch) and one from the side (for volume), and was encased in a wooden cabinet. It was played completely by hand movements—but the hands never touched the instrument! One hand controlled the pitch by moving closer or further away from the vertical antenna, while the other hand controlled the volume with the horizontal antenna. This made the Theremin a very interesting instrument to both see and hear in action.

The Theremin was invented in the 1920s by Soviet physicist Leon Theremin and was subsequently a hit among musicians because it had a very distinctive sound that would later go on to be used in science fiction film classics such as *The Day the Earth Stood Still* and songs like "Whole Lotta Love" by Led Zeppelin.

While the Theremin itself was and still is an extremely exciting instrument to hear and play, the story of Leon Theremin and his infamous abduction by the KGB is even more so. If you'd like more information on Theremin and his inventions (allegedly including the surveillance "bug"), you can rent the documentary entitled *Theremin: An Electronic Odyssey* at your local video store.

For you PC users, there is even an emulated soft synth Theremin called the Mysteron (see Figure 9.2), which can be downloaded free at the KvR Instruments Web site (**www.kvr-vst.com**).

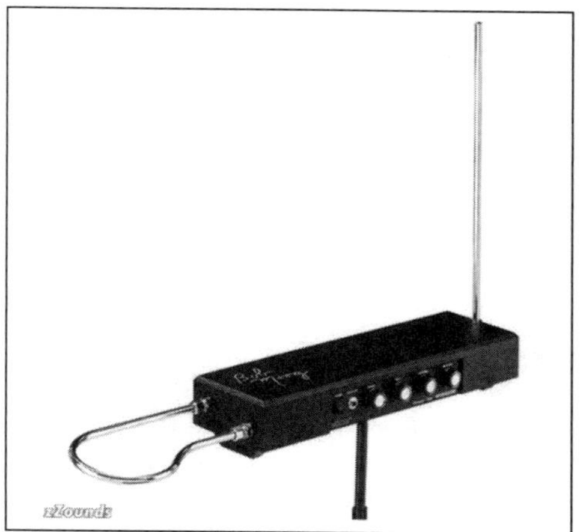

Figure 9.1
The Theremin is considered to be the first synthesizer and was used on many famous recordings, including "Whole Lotta Love" by Led Zeppelin.

Figure 9.2
The Mysteron by FXpansion is an emulation of the Theremin and is a free download at **www.kvr-vst.com**.

Upon its release, the Moog Modular was a huge success and went on to be used on several hit records of the 60s and 70s, including the famous *Switched On Bach* (see Note below). The only real problem with the Moog Modular was its lack of portability; it was very large and heavy. With that in mind, Moog developed and released the Mini Moog, which housed the synthetic excitement of the Moog Modular but was enclosed in a portable case. This led to several variations, such as the Multi Moog and the Poly Moog, all of which can be seen at **www.synthmuseum.com**.

Unfortunately, some bad business deals went down (as they do so often in the music business), and Moog Music eventually went out of business around 1977. Moog started another company called Big Briar and went back to designing and building Theremins. Eventually, in the mid-to-late 90s, Moog Music was back in business and better than ever with new synths and gadgets to appease the masses of Moog followers. You can learn more about Robert Moog by visiting his Web site at **www.moogmusic.com**.

SUGGESTED LISTENING—*SWITCHED ON BACH*

It would be impossible to discuss Robert Moog's synths without including a mention of Wendy Carlos. Her pioneering skills as a sound designer, musician, and film composer have been heard throughout the last four decades with such albums as *Beauty in the Beast* or the soundtracks to *Tron* and *The Shining*. But to truly appreciate her contributions to synthesis, we must go back to 1968, when analog was in its infancy—with modules, patch cables, and single note polyphonic keyboards.

Switched On Bach was a revelation in analog synthesis in the 60s. It was a record that paired subtractive synthesis with the musical genius of good old J.S. Bach. Thanks to Carlos' precision playing and programming skills, Bach's two-part inventions and fugues had never sounded more brilliant and energetic. The album has sold well over a million copies worldwide and has received three Grammy awards. Furthermore, it has spawned several "sequel" releases from Carlos, including two more albums of Bach's music in addition to many other electronic interpretations of classical pieces.

If you're looking for other Wendy Carlos albums to satisfy your craving for subtractive synthesis, I recommend picking up the soundtrack to *A Clockwork Orange*, which includes an additional 10-minute original piece of music that didn't make it into the film.

Subtractive Fundamentals

To begin our lesson on subtractive synthesis, you should first familiarize yourself with the basic components that make it possible. This will be useful later in this chapter when we begin to create customized patches for our chosen soft synths.

Subtractive synthesis makes use of five main modules or fundamental components:

- Oscillators
- Filters
- Envelopes
- LFOs
- Noise Generators

PHYS ED 101

When I was new to this whole game of virtual synths, I was quite confused by the use of the term *analog synthesis* within the confines of the digital realm. Think about it. How can anything "analog," which comprises physical parts and patches, such as a Moog or Oberheim synthesizer, exist in the digital world, which relies on just 0s and 1s? The answer is physical modeling.

Physical modeling is a form of programming that uses sets of equations to emulate the inner workings of an instrument. In the case of subtractive synthesis, physical modeling is used to emulate the oscillators, filters, and amplifiers. The benefit of physical modeling is that the performance characteristics of the modeled instrument can be accurately reproduced. A good example of this is a guitar string that's picked too hard, causing the produced tone to play sharp. Physical modeling is a simple enough concept to understand, but a lot of thought must go into formulating and creating the equations, and then they must be programmed.

If you want to learn more about the inner workings of physical modeling, you can read all about it at this Web site: **www.harmony-central.com/Synth/Articles/Physical_Modeling/**.

In Figure 9.3 you'll see a visual representation of the signal flow in a standard subtractive synthesizer. The oscillator generates a waveform (sine wave, square wave, and so on), which is then routed to a filter. The filter alters the timbre of the oscillator's waveform by filtering out, or *subtracting*, various frequencies from the waveform's frequency spectrum. After the filter, an envelope generator is introduced to manipulate the dynamic characteristics of the "filter effect." For example, this envelope can be used to create a slow attack on the filter, thus creating a bubbly filter effect. It could also be used to sustain the filter effect over a prolonged period of time. This is typically called a *filter envelope*.

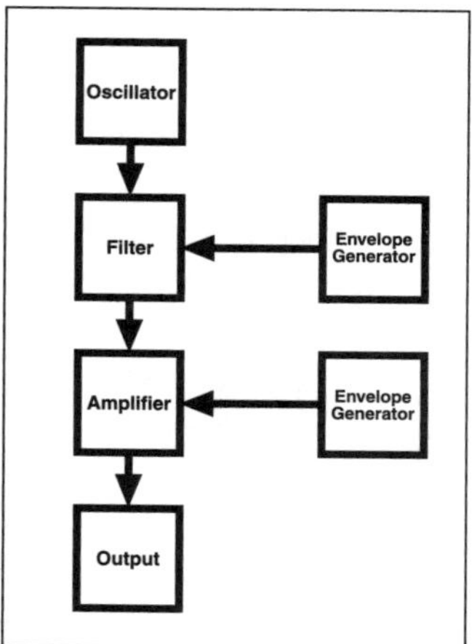

Figure 9.3

This diagram represents the signal flow in a standard subtractive synthesis model.

After an envelope generator has processed the filtered signal, its output is fed to the input of an amplifier, which determines the volume of the output. After that, another envelope generator, called the *amp envelope,* adjusts the dynamics of the output amplitude (volume). The resulting signal is then fed to your mixer for monitoring.

Now that you have a basic understanding of the subtractive signal flow, let's discuss each of these modules in more detail.

Oscillators

At the ground level of subtractive synthesis is the oscillator. It's used to generate periodic waveforms of different shapes and frequencies, which are then manipulated and modified by additional modules. As you'll recall from the previous chapter, I introduced you to the common waveforms of subtractive synthesis and their audible characteristics, such as:

- **Sine**—Contains a single harmonic and has a smooth, mellow tone.
- **Square**—Contains odd-numbered harmonics and has a hollow tone.
- **Pulse**—Like the square wave, except with additional even-numbered harmonics.
- **Triangle**—Like the square wave, except with different variations in the amplitude of each harmonic.
- **Saw Tooth**—The most complex waveform, which contains all harmonics in the natural harmonic series.

Through the magic of software synthesis, many subtractive soft synths, such as the Subtractor (included with Reason 2.5), include several waveform variations based on these standard waveforms in order to provide a greater variety.

KNOW YOUR WAVEFORMS

Becoming familiar with the audible characteristics of the various waveforms makes it much easier to design specific sounds. For example, if you were planning to create a bass synth sound, a good combination of waveforms would be the sine wave (for a good, solid bass tone) and a saw tooth to give it a sharp brassy punch.

We'll explore the different combinations later in this chapter, when I take you through the steps of creating various instruments via subtractive.

The pitch of these waveforms is determined by the rate of oscillation, which was also discussed in the previous chapter.

Filters

Filters play an important role in subtractive synthesis, as they are used to reject or "subtract" specific frequencies from a generated waveform, changing the character or timbre of the sound. When used effectively, a filter can make your synthesizers sound warm and fuzzy or thin and nasal at the turn of a knob. It can be used to create the popular synth sweeping effect that makes ears perk up with delight on the dance floor, or create deep, rich bass sounds that make your studio walls shake and shudder. In this section of the chapter, I will introduce you to common filter parameters and briefly discuss the various filter types found on most subtractive synthesizers.

A filter operates by two main parameters:

- **Cutoff Frequency**—This parameter is used to specify where a filter will function within the frequency spectrum of a waveform. When the cutoff is used to alter a filter, it opens and closes the filter within a specific frequency range. For example, if you are using a filter to reject mid-to-high frequencies (a *low pass* filter), the cutoff parameter determines the range of low frequencies that can pass through the filter.
- **Resonance**—This parameter works in combination with the cutoff frequency and is used to emphasize, or boost, the frequencies around the cutoff frequency.

In order to keep the filter effect interesting, most subtractive synthesizers offer several filter types or variations that produce very different results when used creatively. Let's take a look at the three most commonly used filter types. Use Figure 9.4, which depicts a drum loop with no filters applied to it, as a reference.

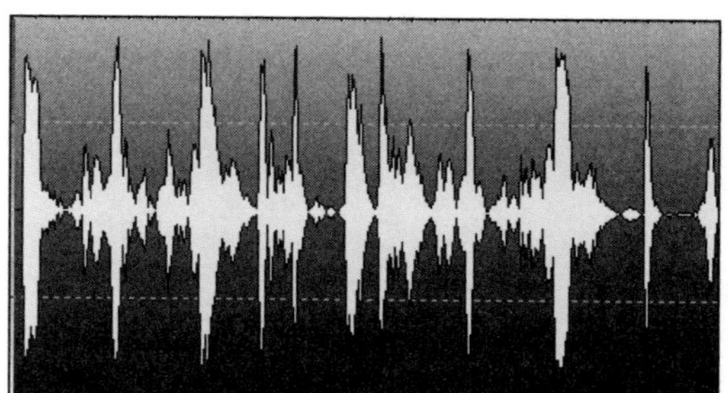

Figure 9.4

Here we have a drum loop with no filter applied to it. Compare this waveform with the three filter types that follow.

- **Low Pass**—This filter allows low frequencies to pass through without being altered (see Figure 9.5).
- **Band Pass**—This filter cuts both the high and low frequencies, leaving the mid frequencies alone (see Figure 9.6).
- **High Pass**—This filter allows high frequencies to pass through without being altered (see Figure 9.7).

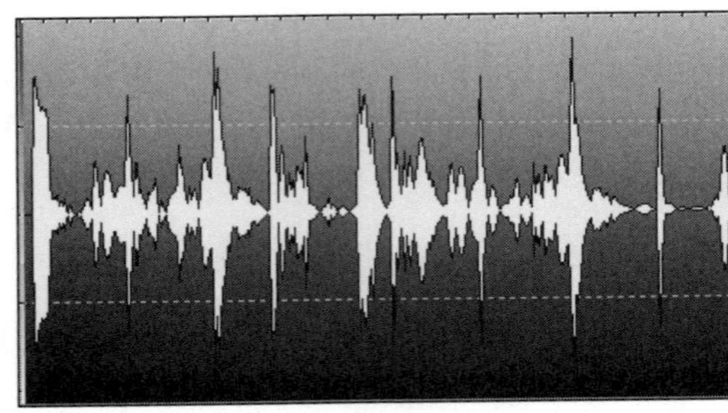

Figure 9.5
A low pass filter cuts high frequencies while allowing low frequencies to pass through.

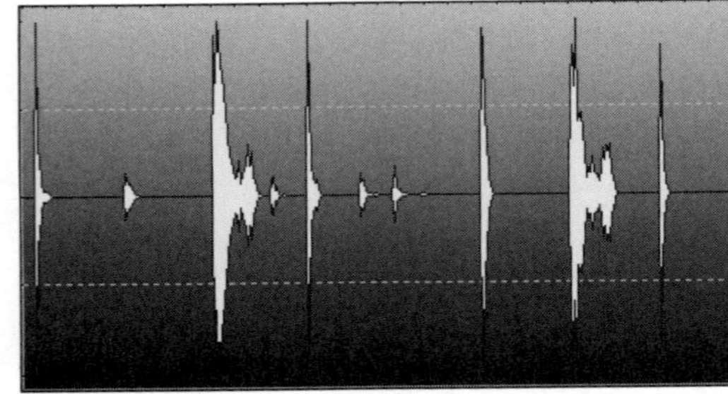

Figure 9.6
A band pass filter cuts both high and low frequencies.

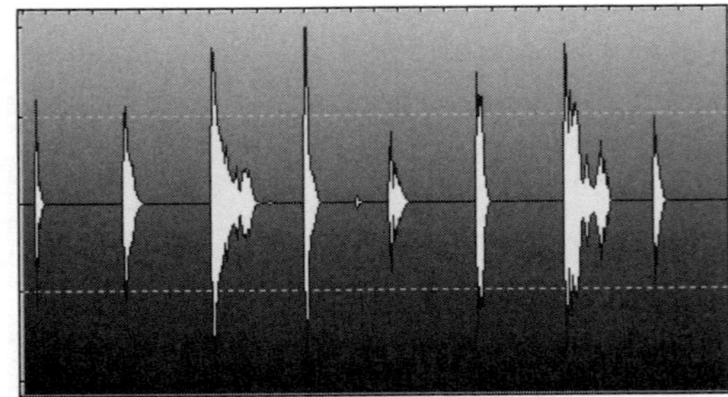

Figure 9.7
A high pass filter cuts low frequencies while allowing high frequencies to pass through.

Envelopes

An envelope governs how a sound evolves over a specific period of time. It also shapes the playing characteristics of a waveform by altering the attack and sustain. In subtractive synthesis, you'll typically find two types of envelopes:

- **Filter Envelope**—A filter envelope modifies the characteristics of a filter. It can be used to create long, sustained filter sweeps and percussive filter-powered stab sounds.
- **Amp Envelope**—An amp envelope shapes the volume characteristics of the synthesizer. This is useful for creating long, sustained patches (such as pads) or medium to short sustained patches (such as bass synths or percussion).

LFOs

An LFO, or low frequency oscillator, is a close relative to a standard subtractive synth oscillator. In some ways, an LFO can be thought of as a standard oscillator because it is capable of generating a waveform and frequency. However, the purpose of an LFO differs greatly from that of a standard oscillator in two ways:

- The LFO can generate only waveforms with low frequencies. Hence, they are audibly transparent or unheard. However, you can hear the effect that a LFO creates when it is routed to a standard oscillator.
- The purpose of an LFO is to modulate or alter a specific parameter of a patch, such as a filter or another oscillator. That means that the LFO itself is never actually heard, only its effect on other synth parameters.

Let's suppose that you have a subtractive synth playing a pad chord progression and you would like to spice it up by assigning a filter to it and have that filter open and close in time with the tempo of your song. After routing a filter to the active oscillators of the synth, an additional connection is made from the output of the LFO to the modulation input of the filter. Now all that is left is to assign a waveform and frequency or rate of oscillation to the LFO and you're in business.

Of course, this is just a simple description of the LFO, but you'll see it in action when we build a subtractive synth patch.

Noise Generators

A noise generator can be thought of as another oscillator, since it does generate sound. But this oscillator does not generate a pitched waveform. Rather, it generates noise that can be used for several sound design and instrumental possibilities, such as wind noises and percussion sounds.

There are two types of noise that can be generated by most subtractive synthesizers (including the Pro-53 and Moog Modular): white noise and pink noise.

White noise contains every frequency from 20Hz to 20kHz in equal amounts. It has a frequency characteristic in which the amplitude is raised by 3dB with each increasing octave (see Figure 9.8). It sounds very similar to television static noise and can easily damage your speakers, not to mention your hearing, if not used properly.

Pink noise is a close relative of white noise. Pink noise is essentially white noise that has been filtered to reduce its volume between each octave (see Figure 9.9). This is done to compensate for the increase in the number of frequencies per octave. Each octave is reduced by 6dB, resulting in a signal that has equal energy at every octave. Its signal is constant and less present than white noise. As it's less likely to damage your gear, pink noise is a perfect candidate for testing studio gear.

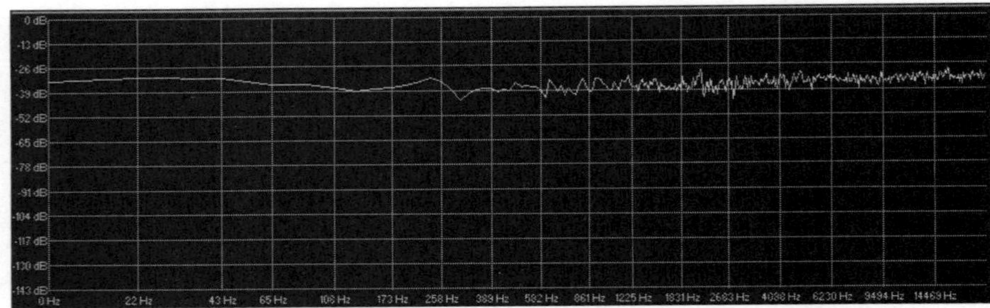

Figure 9.8

This FFT graph represents the frequency content of white noise.

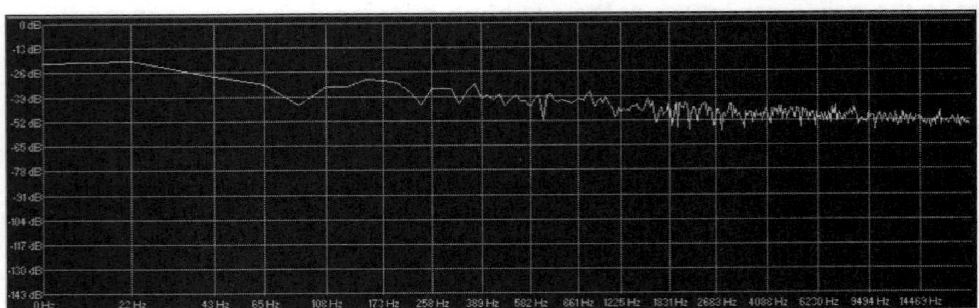

Figure 9.9

This FFT graph represents the frequency content of pink noise. Notice how it differs greatly in amplitude when compared to white noise.

Meet Our Synths—Pro-53 and the Moog Modular

Now it's time to get to know our subtractive soft synths for this chapter, which are the Native Instruments Pro-53 and the Arturia Moog Modular (see Figure 9.10). The Pro-53 is a software emulation of the classic Prophet 5 hardware synth by Sequential Circuits, while the Moog Modular emulates the vintage hardware synth of the same name.

Why are we looking at two synths? The main reason is to demonstrate two different takes on subtractive synthesis. On one side, we have the Pro-53, which is a self-contained soft synth that can be easily programmed once you understand the basic layout. The Moog Modular on the other hand is a soft synth that requires intimate knowledge of subtractive synth practices just to program your own sounds. I like to think of the Moog Modular as an empty canvas, waiting for your next masterpiece to be painted.

Figure 9.10

The Pro-53 by Native Instruments (left) is a subtractive soft synth that's affordable and easy to understand. The Moog Modular (right) is a much more complicated soft synth and emulates the functionality and sound of the original Moog Modular hardware counterpart.

> **HONORABLE MENTION—THE SUBTRACTOR**
>
> It would be a crime against synthetic nature not to mention one of my favorite subtractive soft synthesizers, the Subtractor. This soft synth is exclusive to Reason 2.5, a soft synth workstation by Propellerhead Software. Its usefulness is virtually boundless because it can be used for many different textures and elements in electronic music, including leads, pads, FX, and percussion. With its well-designed graphic interface, it's also a great synth to help you learn to create your own great-sounding patches.

The Pro-53—A Subtractive Prophet

The Pro-53 by Native Instruments is a software emulation of the classic Prophet 5 synthesizer designed by Dave Smith of Sequential Circuits (see Figure 9.11). Released in 1978, the original Prophet 5 was a great achievement in subtractive synthesis because it was the first fully programmable polyphonic synthesizer. Aside from the fact that it had five-note polyphony, the Prophet 5 was the first microprocessor-driven synthesizer of its kind, giving it the ability to store patches and programs. Over 7,000 of these beauties were made, making it one of the more popular synths of its day, and it was used by a long list of popular musicians, including Tony Banks (Genesis) and Richard Wright (Pink Floyd). Over the years, the Prophet 5 has remained a cult classic among electronic musicians and was feverishly sought after in many a pawnshop and used ad. Today, all of the inherent traits of the Prophet 5 have been integrated into the Pro-53, along with some additional key features, making it a great synth to demonstrate the potential of subtractive synthesis.

Figure 9.11
The Prophet 5 was the first subtractive synthesizer with the ability to play five notes simultaneously. Photo courtesy of Matt Bassett (http://users.adelphia.net/~cygnusx_1/// <http://users.adelphia.net/~cygnusx_1/>)

> **GET THE DEMO VERSION**
> You can download a demo version of the Pro-53 from the Native Instruments Web site at **www.native-instruments.com**.

Loading Pro-53 Programs

Programs are loaded in the Programmer section just above the Virtual Keyboard (see Figure 9.12).

Figure 9.12
The Programmer is used to navigate the programs of the Pro-53.

When the Pro-53 is first launched, there are approximately 888 different programs to choose from. However, in order to access these programs, you must understand the various program navigation parameters, which include:

- **Load**—This button launches the browser window, which is used to locate and load Pro-53 programs (.p5p), banks (.p5b), files (.p5f), or all (.p5a).
- **Save**—This button launches the browser window, which you can use to save a Pro-53 program, bank, file, or all to a specific location.
- **Record**—This button places a custom program in a specific location on the Program Select buttons. Once a patch has been created, click on it and then use any of the Program Select buttons to place the program in that location.
- **File**—This selects any of the eight available Pro-53 files. A file contains eight banks of programs. To select a specific file, click once on the File button and then click on any of the eight Program Select buttons.
- **Bank**—This button selects any of the available banks within a file. To select a bank, click once on the Bank button and then click on any of the eight Program Select buttons.
- **Program Display**—This is a numeric display of all the available programs within the Pro-53. You can change programs from this display by clicking and dragging up or down within the interface.
- **Program Select**—These buttons select any of eight programs within a bank.

PEEK-A-BOO

A neat eye candy trick is to hide the graphic keyboard from the Pro-53 interface. This is good for conserving space on the desktop. Just click on the Pro-53 logo to hide the keyboard, and then click on it again to show the keyboard (see Figure 9.13).

NO MIDI KEYBOARD? NO PROBLEM

A useful feature found throughout the Native Instruments product line is the ability to trigger its synths straight from your computer keyboard without the need for a MIDI keyboard. This is especially handy for us laptop jockeys who travel a lot. Use the lower rows of keys to trigger the low octaves of the Pro-53 and the upper rows to trigger the high octaves.

Figure 9.13
Click on the Pro-53 logo to show and hide the Keyboard section of the Pro-53 interface.

Let's begin our tour of the Pro-53, starting with the Oscillator section.

The Oscillator Section

At the top center of the Pro-53 is the Oscillator section, which is responsible for generating its sounds (see Figure 9.14). To the immediate left is the Mixer section, which governs the amplitude of each oscillator and includes a white noise generator.

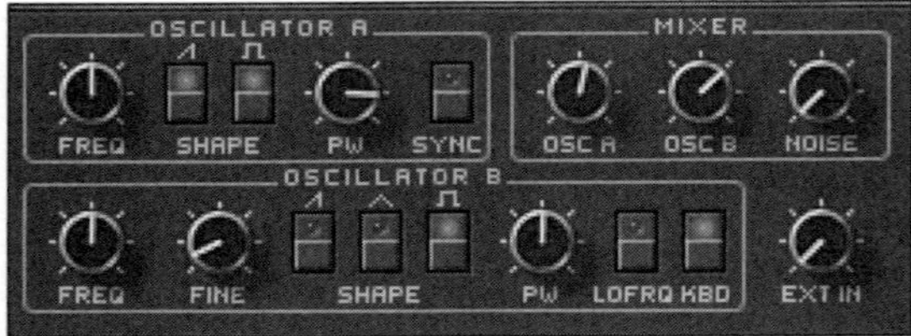

Figure 9.14
The Oscillator section of the Pro-53 is where its unique sound is generated.

Oscillator A

Oscillator A is the primary sound source of the Pro-53 and includes the following parameters:

- **Freq**—This parameter assigns a pitch to the oscillator. It has a four-octave range.
- **Shape**—This parameter sets the waveform to be generated by the oscillator. You can select the saw tooth, a pulse wave, or both.
- **Pulse Width**—This knob sets the amount of pulse width.
- **Sync**—When activated, this compels Osc A to restart its waveform in sync with the waveform of Osc B. Furthermore, when active, the Freq knob of Osc A affects the timbre (or character) of the two oscillators, while the Freq knob of Osc B controls the pitch of the two oscillators.

GETTING IN TUNE WITH THE PRO-53

A handy feature of the Pro-53 is the A-440 button in the lower-right corner of the Pro-53 interface. When this is activated, the Pro-53 emits a pitched A-440 tone, which can be used as a reference to fine-tune your oscillators.

Additionally, the Pro-53 can be retuned to non-Western pitch standards, to meet the needs of world music enthusiasts. For example, if you want to play a piece of music written for bagpipes, just click on the NI logo and select Load Microtuning. In the browser window that opens, you can locate and load different tuning schemes into the Pro-53.

Oscillator B

Located just below Oscillator A lies its counterpart, Oscillator B. While they share common functions, Oscillator B includes a few additional unique parameters:

- **Fine**—This parameter makes fine adjustments to the tuning of Osc B. It has a range of one semitone.
- **Lo Freq**—This parameter turns Osc B into a low frequency oscillator. When it is activated, the speed of the LFO can be adjusted with the Freq, Fine, and PW (pulse width) knobs.
- **Keyboard**—When activated, this parameter compels Osc B to be controlled by incoming MIDI messages.

The Mixer

The Mixer section of the Pro-53 is where you adjust the individual amplitudes of the oscillators and noise generator. Its parameters include:

- **Osc A**—This knob adjusts the volume of Oscillator A.
- **Osc B**—This knob adjusts the volume of Oscillator B. Note that when using Oscillator B as a modulation source, you will want to assign a value of 0.
- **Noise**—This knob introduces an audible white noise into the mix. White noise in limited doses can be used to create effective percussion sounds. In large doses, it can be used to create ambient noises such as rain or wind. Note that the Pro-53 can also generate pink noise by way of the Wheel-Mod (wheel modulation) section.

The Filter Section

The Filter section of the Pro-53 offers a standard set of controls to shape the timbre of your sound by subtracting frequencies from the frequency spectrum (see Figure 9.18). It also includes an envelope to adjust the dynamics of the filter effect.

USING THE PRO-53 AS AN AUDIO EFFECT

Unbeknownst to some, the Pro-53 includes a unique audio input feature called the Pro-53fx that allows it to be used as a virtual effect on your audio tracks. This makes it possible to put vocals, guitars, and other instruments through the Pro-53 filters and envelopes, which in turn spells inspiration. Try the following example:

1. Let's assume that I have an audio track of a guitar playing long, sustained chords. Begin by placing an instance of the Pro-53fx on the insert point of the audio track (see Figure 9.15). Once this is done, you should not hear the audio track any longer, as the Pro-53 must be triggered via MIDI.
2. Increase the value of the Ext In parameter, found in the upper-center portion of the Pro-53 interface. Also, make sure that the oscillators are turned off (see Figure 9.16).
3. Create a MIDI track and route its output to the Pro-53fx (see Figure 9.17). Also, write in a quick MIDI sequence on the track.
4. Press Play on the Transport panel of the sequencer, and you should hear the audio track play back through the envelopes and filters of the Pro-53, which is triggered by the MIDI sequence you just wrote in.

Figure 9.15

Using the mixer insert points of your DAW application, load an instance of the Pro-53fx.

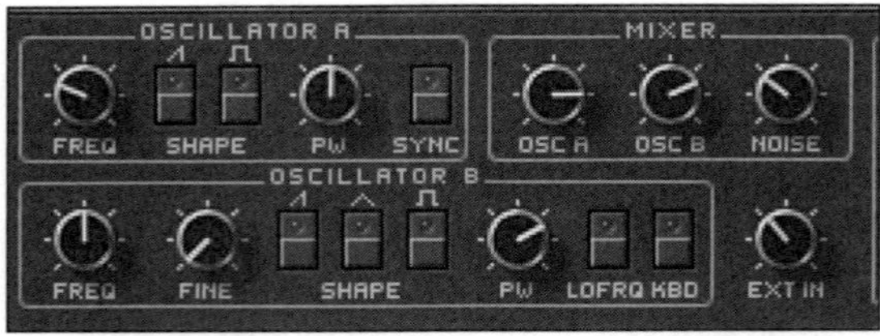

Figure 9.16

Next, turn off Oscillators A and B and assign a value to the Ext In parameter.

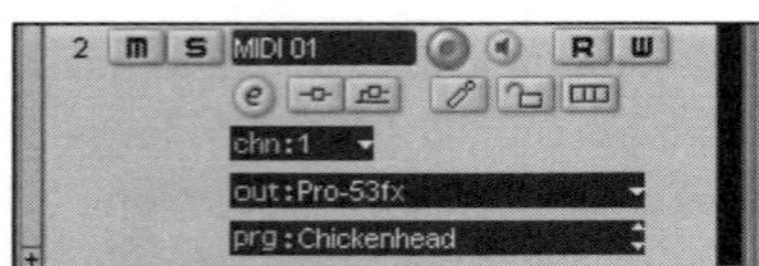

Figure 9.17

Create a MIDI track, assign its output to the Pro-53fx, and write in a MIDI sequence.

Figure 9.18
The Filter section of the Pro-53 operates in either Low Pass or High Pass mode and contains an additional Inversion parameter, which generates a mirror reflection of the filter envelope parameters.

The Filter section includes the following parameters:

- **Cutoff**—This knob specifies where the filter will function within the frequency spectrum.
- **Resonance**—This parameter emphasizes different frequencies around the set value of the cutoff parameter.
- **Envelope Amount**—This parameter determines how much the filter envelope will affect the cutoff parameter. Increasing its value and the attack parameter causes the filter to open up gradually, which creates a sweep sound.
- **Keyboard**—Also known as *key tracking*, this parameter alters the amount of cutoff effect according to different MIDI notes played on the keyboard. For example, when this parameter is set to it lowest value, the filter effect will sound the same regardless of which MIDI notes are triggered. When set to its highest value, the filter effect will intensify with the higher notes triggered.
- **High Pass Filter**—When activated, the high pass filter will obstruct the low end of the frequency spectrum while allowing the higher frequencies to pass.
- **Attack**—When the filter envelope is triggered, the attack parameter determines how much time passes before the envelope reaches its maximum value, which means the envelope is completely open.
- **Decay**—Once the maximum value is reached, the decay parameter determines the length of time until the value begins to drop.
- **Sustain**—After the value begins to drop, the sustain parameter determines at which value the envelope should remain.
- **Release**—Once the envelope has reached its rested value, the release parameter determines how long it will take until the envelope will fade out after releasing the note.
- **Invert**—When activated, this parameter inverts the effect of the filter envelope. Try activating it and increase the envelope amount and attack parameters of the Filter section. When the envelope is triggered, the cutoff will close instead of opening

The Amplifier

The Amplifier section of the Pro-53 assigns an envelope to the amplitude (see Figure 9.19). Since it shares the same envelope parameters as the Filter section, we won't repeat that here, but there is an additional amplifier parameter called *hold*.

Figure 9.19

The Amplifier section of the Pro-53 is used to enhance the amplitude.

When active, the hold parameter holds and sustains a note when it is triggered from either the Virtual Keyboard or by a standard hardware MIDI keyboard. This is useful when designing sounds; it makes it possible to adjust the parameters of the Pro-53 and hear the changes in real time without having to trigger the synth constantly or hold down a sustain pedal. Hold is also useful when using the Pro-53 as an audio effect, allowing you to preview the effect on your audio signal without having to trigger notes constantly.

Additional Play Parameters

Next up are the remaining play parameters of the Pro-53, which control its performance, sound, and tuning, including:

- **Glide**—This knob controls the amount of glissando between notes when the Pro-53 is in Unison mode. It's incredibly effective on monophonic programs in particular, as the one note will slide to another, resulting in slippery lead and bass lines.
- **Unison**—When activated, this makes the Pro-53 react like a monophonic synth, in which it can play only one note at a time. However, unlike a monophonic synth, Unison includes an additional feature that allocates more voices to the single note played in accordance with the value set by the polyphony dialog to the right of the Unison button. In other words, if you have a polyphony value of five and the unison parameter is active, the Pro-53 will assign all five notes of polyphony to play the same note simultaneously, just slightly detuned, to create a chorus effect. This thickens up the sound dramatically.
- **Voices**—This dialog allocates a specific number of voices to be played simultaneously by the Pro-53. This value can be increased and decreased by clicking and dragging the mouse up and down within this dialog.
- **Analog**—This parameter mimics the unpredictable behavior of an analog synthesizer and is an especially interesting addition to the Pro-53. The tiny deviations in analog circuitry are replicated and assigned to this parameter.

- **Velocity**—When activated, this makes the Pro-53 velocity sensitive, which means that its sound will differ greatly according to how hard a note is played on your MIDI keyboard. Furthermore, the Virtual Keyboard of the Pro-53 is also velocity sensitive and can be heard when any note is clicked or played from top to bottom. The original Prophet 5 was not velocity sensitive, so this feature really adds expression to the sounds of its soft synth counterpart.
- **Release**—When activated, this parameter allows the release parameter values of the amp and filter envelopes to be heard. When inactive, the release of the Pro-53 is set to its minimal settings.
- **Tune**—This knob alters the master tuning of the Pro-53. Unless you have a specific sound idea in mind, you should leave this at its default position.
- **A-440**—As mentioned earlier in this chapter, the A-440 button emits an A-440 tone, which can be used to fine-tune the oscillators of the Pro-53.
- **Volume**—This knob governs the amplitude of the Pro-53.

FEWER VOICES—LESS CPU

It's important to point out that the Voices dialog directly relates to the performance of the Pro-53. The more voices you assign to the Pro-53, the more CPU is eaten up in your system. With that in mind, you may want to pull back a little on the number of assigned voices, depending on what kind of sound you require from the Pro-53. For example, if you are going to use the Pro-53 to play long, sustained pad sounds, then you could probably do okay with 8 to 10 voices. But if you are going to have the Pro-53 play a kick drum or synth percussion of some kind, it is highly unlikely that you will need more than 1 assigned voice, which your CPU will thank you for.

Destination—Modulation

The modulation section of the Pro-53 makes it possible to create some wild variations in both frequency and tone to one or several parameters (see Figure 9.20). It's split into three modules:

- LFO
- Poly-Mod
- Wheel-Mod

The LFO Module

The LFO module generates a modulation signal for use with the wheel modulation controls located below. Here are the module's parameters.

Figure 9.20
The Modulation section of the Pro-53.

- **Envelope Trigger**—This parameter automatically triggers the LFO whenever a note is held down. If you don't have a MIDI keyboard handy to try this, activate the hold parameter in the Amplifier section and click on any key of the Virtual Keyboard to hear the envelope trigger in action.
- **MIDI**—When activated, this will lock the Freq parameter to the tempo of a host application, such as a Cubase or SONAR.
- **Freq**—This knob controls the rate of the LFO frequency. It has a range of .04Hz to 20Hz.
- **Shape**—This section assigns a waveshape to the output of the LFO. You can select one or all of the shapes, including the saw tooth, triangle, and pulse wave.

> **SAMPLE & HOLD MODE**
> When all three waveshapes have been selected in the LFO module, it goes into Sample and Hold mode. This mode randomly modifies the waveshape of the LFO effect after each cycle, resulting in a varied and unpredictable signal, perfect for creating a one-of-a-kind sound.

Poly-Mod

The Poly-Mod section accepts the input of either the filter envelope or Oscillator B or both and routes that as a modulation source to any or all of three destination parameters. For example, you could have the filter envelope modulate the timbre of Oscillator A, or have Oscillator B modulate the filter. Let's discuss the included parameters.

- **Filter Envelope**—This knob assigns the output of the filter envelope to any or all three destinations.
- **Oscillator B**—This knob assigns the output of Oscillator B to any or all three destinations.

- **Destination**—These parameters assign the values set by either the Filter Envelope knob, the Oscillator B knob, or both to the frequency parameter of Osc A, the pulse width parameter of Osc A, or the cutoff filter of the Filter section.

Wheel Modulation

The wheel modulation module introduces a performance and expression element into the sound of the Pro-53 by assigning single or multiple parameters to the modulation wheel of the Virtual Keyboard.

- **LFO/Noise**—This knob mixes between two sources of modulation that are then assigned to different destinations and heard when the modulation wheel is triggered. When the knob is turned counterclockwise, the LFO becomes the source of modulation. Turning this knob to the right introduces a pink noise generator as the modulation source.
- **Destination**—These parameters assign the modulation source to one or many different Pro-53 parameters. Included here are Frequency A/B, Pulse Width A/B, and the Cutoff Filter.

The Delay Effect

The Pro-53 has undergone several revisions in the years since its initial release in 1999 (back when it was the Pro-5). When the Pro-5 made the jump to the Pro-52, Native Instruments included an embedded delay effect that could be used in real time to alter the character of the Pro-52 (see Figure 9.21). Even better, there's more than one delay in action here—try four of them! Click on the Power button in the lower-left corner of the delay interface and let's have a look at the different parameters.

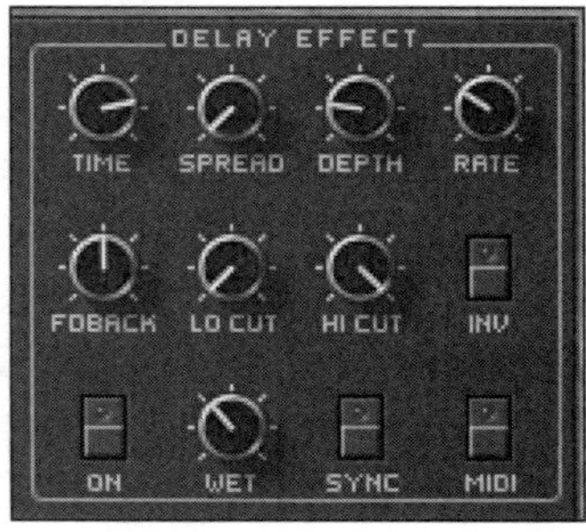

Figure 9.21

The delay effect of the Pro-53 may be just the ambience you need to spice your programs up a bit.

- **Time**—This knob adjusts the time between each reflection of the delay effect. It has a wide range of 1 millisecond to 1 second.

- **Spread**—This parameter adjusts the stereo positioning of the delay effect. As the delayed signal progresses, you'll hear each reflection of the delay move from left to right in the stereo field.
- **Depth**—The Depth knob activates and assigns a value of intensity to the LFO embedded within the delay effect. The purpose of this LFO is to modulate the delay time parameter, which results in a wavering pitch effect. It can very easily outshine the sound of the Pro-53, so easy does it.
- **Rate**—This parameter sets a rate of modulation to the depth parameter.
- **Feedback**—This knob routes the output of the delay effect back to its input, resulting in a delay effect that never ends or a tight flanging effect.
- **Low Cut**—This parameter is essentially a high pass filter, which can filter out the low frequencies of the delay reflections, leaving the higher ones to be toyed with.
- **Hi-Cut**—This parameter is a low pass filter, which performs exactly the opposite effect as the low cut.
- **Invert**—When activated, this parameter inverts the phase of the audio signal being fed through the effect. Essentially, it ever so slightly alters the quality of the affected signal by canceling out certain frequencies.
- **Wet**—This knob alters the mix between the dry, or unaffected, signal and the wet, or affected, signal.
- **Sync**—This button synchronizes the LFOs of each delay embedded within the effect.
- **MIDI**—This parameter synchronizes the delay effect to the tempo of a host application, such as Cubase or Logic.

Programming the Pro-53

In this section of the chapter, we're going to put the Pro-53 to work by programming a couple of custom sounds from start to finish. Over the course of the next few pages, you'll learn how to program a heavy-duty bass sound and an out-of-this-world pad sound.

Programming a Bass Sound

Programming a bass sound is typically an ideal starting point for beginners to synthesizer programming. Let's begin by initializing the Pro-53 to remove the currently loaded preset.

1. Click the Load Pro-53 button in the lower-left corner of the Pro-53 interface. This will launch a browser window.

2 Locate and open the Pro-53 Program folder, and then open the Presets folder.

3 Locate the empty presets (see Figure 9.22). Select one of four options: empty (1) to initialize the currently selected program, empty (8) to initialize eight Pro-53 programs, empty (64) to initialize an entire Pro-53 bank, or empty (512) to initialize the entire Pro-53.

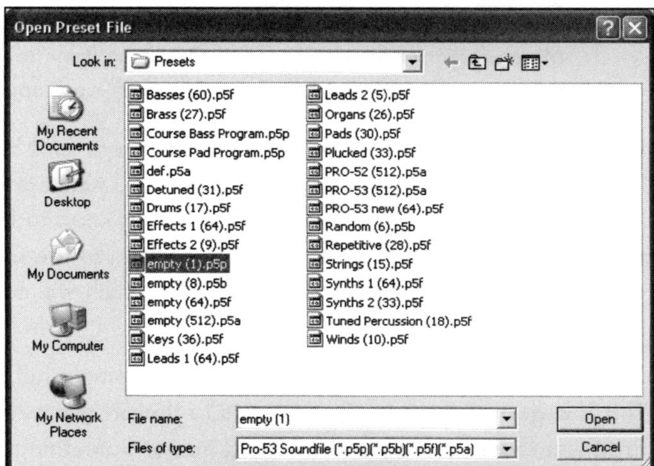

Figure 9.22

Select any of the empty presets to initialize the Pro-53.

Now you're ready to begin your first programming tutorial. Let's begin with setting up Oscillator A to the following values:

- **Waveforms**—Switch waveforms by first deactivating the saw tooth wave and then activating the square wave.
- **Mixer**—Increase the amplitude of Oscillator A by adjusting the Osc A knob in the Mixer window. Set this to the 2 o'clock position.

Since this is a bass patch, it should sound tight and punchy, which can be easily accomplished by using the amp envelope. Set its parameters to the following values:

- **Attack**—0.
- **Decay**—50, or the 12 o'clock position.
- **Sustain**—0.
- **Release**—0.

Once you have made these adjustments, trigger a couple of notes and you'll hear a punchy bass sound, with a hollow tone, courtesy of the square wave generated by Oscillator A. Let's introduce Oscillator B into the mix by using the following values:

- **Fine Tuning**—Adjust this to 9 o'clock to slightly detune Oscillator B against A.
- **Waveform**—Select both the saw tooth and square waves.
- **Keyboard Tracking**—Activate this parameter to keep Oscillator B in tune with Oscillator A.
- **Mixer**—Increase the amplitude of Oscillator B by adjusting the Osc B knob in the Mixer window. Set this to the 2 o'clock position.

Play the program now, and it should sound nice and boomy. Let's thicken it up even more by using the Unison function. Activate Unison and set the Voices dialog to 5. Also, increase the Analog knob to introduce some analog discrepancies into the program. You can also use the Glide knob to introduce a slight portamento effect to the program, which will cause the bass program to slide between notes.

At this point, the program should sound extremely full, loud, and bass heavy. This is a good time to assign a name to the program and save it. Click in the Program Name dialog and assign a name. Something simple like Course Bass Program will be fine for now (remember, you can always change it later). Save the program by clicking the Save button and selecting Save Edit Buffer (see Figure 9.23). A browser window will pop up, prompting you to assign a name and location to the program. Click Save and you're finished.

Figure 9.23
Select Save Editbuffer to save the parameter settings of an individual Pro-53 program. Note that you can accomplish this same task by selecting Save Single Program from the File pull-down menu.

At this point, you can take it a step further and use the Filter and Delay sections to enhance the ambience and character of the bass program, but let's save that for our next tutorial, which involves programming a pad sound.

Programming a Pad Sound

Aside from bass sounds, subtractive synthesizers excel at filling in the empty spaces in a mix with a good pad sound. The Pro-53 includes many good and, more importantly, usable pad programs, but there's nothing quite as fun as "rolling yer own," so to speak. Let's begin this tutorial by first initializing the edit buffer of the Pro-53 using the same method discussed in the previous tutorial. Once completed, increase the polyphony of the Pro-53 by assigning a value of 8 to the Voices dialog. Now we can begin to create our pad, starting with Oscillator A. Set the parameters of Oscillator A to the following values:

- **Waveform**—Activate the square wave so that we can hear both waveforms play at the same time.
- **Pulse Width**—Set this knob to 9 o'clock to create a flanging sound between the two waveforms.

Next, let's use the amp envelope to create a long, sustained sound. Activate the release parameter and plug in the following values:

- **Attack**—3 o'clock.
- **Decay**—1 o'clock.
- **Sustain**—3 o'clock.
- **Release**—1 o'clock.

If you play the programmed sound now, it won't sound too creative yet. In fact, it sounds downright boring. Let's remedy this by using the Filter section to create a sustained sweep that we'll manipulate even further by way of the Poly-Mod section. Set the filter parameters to the following values:

- **Cutoff**—12 o'clock.
- **Resonance**—12 o'clock.
- **Envelope Amount**—12 o'clock.
- **Keyboard Tracking**—3 o'clock. This will enable the filter to open up faster when high notes are played.
- **Filter Attack**—5 o'clock.
- **Filter Decay**—12 o'clock.
- **Filter Sustain**—3 o'clock.
- **Filter Release**—1 o'clock.

Play the pad sound now, and you should hear a long, sustained sound coupled with a filter that opens slowly. Now would be a good time to introduce Oscillator B into the mix. Begin by assigning a value of 9 o'clock to the Osc

B knob in the Mixer section to layer it under Oscillator A. Next, plug in the following values for Oscillator B:

* **Waveforms**—Activate the triangle and square waveforms.
* **Freq**—Set this parameter to its lowest potential.
* **Fine**—Set this to about 9 o'clock to fine-tune Oscillator B. Note that further adjustments may be required.
* **Keyboard Tracking**—Activate this parameter to keep Oscillators A and B in tune with each other.

Play the pad sound now, and you should hear a full mixture of both oscillators. Before proceeding, you might want to add a little noise to the mix by using the Noise knob in the Mixer section. Increase this parameter slightly and play the pad again to hear the results.

Next up is the Poly-Mod section, which we'll use to have Oscillator B modulate the pulse width of Oscillator A, which will create a heavy wavering effect as the filter opens up. Set the Osc B knob to the 12 o'clock position and select PWA (Pulse Width A) as your destination. Play the pad sound now, and it should sound much more interesting than when we began this tutorial.

The final step in this programming tutorial involves the Delay section. Activate this section by clicking the On button in the lower-left corner of the Delay section. Next, use the Wet knob to hear the delay effect (50%, or 12 o'clock, would be a good value) and use the following values for the delay parameters:

* **Time**—Set this parameter to the 3 o'clock position. This will create a long time between delays, so you might want to set this to a lower value later.
* **Spread**—Set this parameter to its highest value.
* **Depth**—Set this to 9 o'clock.
* **Feedback**—Set this to 3 o'clock.
* **Lo Cut**—Set this to its lowest value.
* **Hi Cut**—Set this to its highest value.

Before finishing, be sure to assign a name to this program and save it using the steps listed in the bass programming tutorial.

DOWNLOAD THE SOUNDS

Feel like comparing sounds? Navigate to the Course Technology Web site (**www.courseptr.com**) and click on the Downloads link.

The Arturia Moog Modular 2.0—Blast from the Past

The Moog Modular by Arturia is a soft synth that emulates the classic Moog Modular subtractive synthesizer of the 60s right down to the onboard control voltage sequencer (see Figure 9.24). It's the kind of synth that every musician suffering from a strong case of "tweakus maximus" should have. It generates synthetic sounds and moods so juicy that it bursts at the seams with original ideas to make your music come alive.

Figure 9.24

The Moog Modular is a subtractive soft synth that encourages extreme tweaking.

THERE'S MUCH, MUCH MORE

Although this part of the chapter is going to cover many of the Moog Modular key features, it is by no means a substitute for the Moog manual. I'll be sure to call attention to additional points of interest that you might want to explore in the manual, but this section of the chapter will get you hip to the creative potential of modular synthesis in no time.

TRUE ANALOG EMULATION EXPLAINED

While it's true that many subtractive soft synths come close to sounding like a Moog, the Moog Modular's "secret sauce" comes from the development and implementation of Arturia's exclusive True Analog Emulation (TAE) embedded within the synth.

True Analog Emulation is a technology geared to accurately reproduce the unpredictability and the sonic quality of analog circuitry through digital means. This is accomplished through four essentials:

- **Aliasing Free Oscillators**—*Aliasing* is an audio anomaly heard as distortion that occurs when all of the requirements of the Nyquist sampling theorem are not met. In the case of most other subtractive soft synths, aliasing is a commonly encountered problem when reproducing the higher frequencies of an oscillator through programming.
- **Better Waveform Generation**—Another common issue encountered when using subtractive soft synths is the all too perfect reproduction of generated waveforms. While the aural quality of these waveforms is perfect, they do not accurately reproduce the aural characteristics of a true analog oscillator, which can sometimes function with a certain degree of instability and quirkiness.
- **Better Filter Generation**—Through TAE, the Moog Modular's filters have been programmed to accurately reproduce the characteristics of the filters found within the likes of the Minimoog, which in turn results in a tighter roll-off curve than a filter found on other subtractive soft synths.
- **Soft Clipping**—This part of TAE introduces a limiting effect into the signal flow, which prevents the generated signal from being too loud.

Navigating the Interface and Loading Patches

The first time you launch the Moog Modular, in either standalone or plug-in mode, you will want to take a minute to familiarize yourself with the basic layout of this soft synth monster. It's easy to get lost in a mess of virtual cables and jacks. Additionally, you'll also want to select your preferred audio card and latency to ensure the best performance possible. Selecting Configuration from the File pull-down menu will launch the Configuration window (see Figure 9.25). This window includes the following parameters:

- **Audio Protocol**—This drop-down menu determines which audio driver format the Moog Modular will use.
- **Audio Driver**—Once an audio protocol is selected, this drop-down menu will list all of the available hardware that supports it.
- **Knob Control Type**—This drop-down menu is used to select one of three types for controlling the virtual knobs of the Moog Modular: linear, circular, or circular relative.

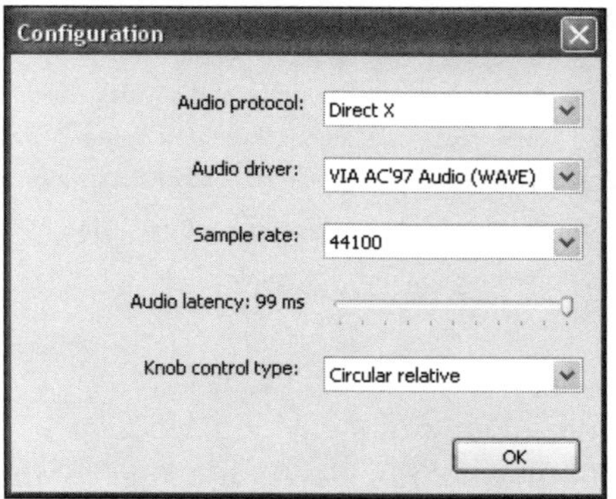

Figure 9.25

Before using the Moog Modular, be sure to set up your audio hardware to ensure the best performance possible. Note that this step is not necessary when using the Moog Modular as a plug-in within a DAW application such as Cubase or Pro Tools.

Next, you'll want to set up your MIDI hardware, which is done by using the MIDI drop-down menu, located in the upper-left corner of the Modular interface. Once selected, choose a MIDI input channel (1–16) and you should be good to go.

Loading Presets

The first thing you'll want to do with the Moog Modular is check out the included presets; there are many to choose from. This is all handled in the upper-left corner of the graphic interface just under the MIDI drop-down menu. In Figure 9.26 you will see that the presets are divided into three categories:

- **Bank**—This menu is a master list that displays all of the available banks.
- **Sub Bank**—This menu displays all of the available sub-banks, such as basses, guitars, and sequences.
- **Preset**—This menu lists all of the presets within a selected sub-bank. Use the drop-down menu to the left to select the preset from a list or the spin controls to the right to scroll through the list one preset at a time.

Figure 9.26

The preset section of the Moog Modular is split into three sections: Bank, Sub Bank, and Preset.

BLANK SYNTH TEMPLATE

Before beginning our tour of the Moog Modular interface, you will want to start with an empty template, which means that there are no active connections on the interface. That way, you can begin building a patch from scratch as we go through the motions.

This can be done by selecting Bank, User, Blank, Blank_Synth.

Now you're ready to begin.

Three Views of the Moog Modular

There are three views, or pages, of the Moog Modular that give you access to its various programming features via the Page Selector in the upper-right corner of the interface. The first page is the Sequencer/FX page, which is used to compose sequenced lines of synthetic delight and flavor the sound of the Moog Modular by incorporating a Filter, Delay, or Chorus effect (see Figure 9.27).

Figure 9.27
The Sequencer/FX page is used to compose sequences and enhance them with real-time effects.

Next up is the Synth page, which is where patches are conceived, routed, and manipulated beyond belief (see Figure 9.28).

Finally, the Keyboard page is used to display a more compact view of the Moog Modular interface (see Figure 9.29). It also includes many global parameters, which alter the overall sound and presence of the Moog Modular.

CLICK AND DRAG

A new feature to the Moog Modular 2.0 is the ability to scroll up and down the Moog interface. Just click and drag up and down anywhere along the wooden frame of the Moog interface.

Figure 9.28

The Synth page is where all of the virtual signal routing is done.

Figure 9.29

The Keyboard page offers a compact view that's not so overwhelming.

Modules—Lay of the Land

Since the Moog Modular is such a complex soft synth, the best way to understand its inner workings is to discuss each module one at a time. To conclude our discussion on each module, I will take you through the steps of connecting it to the next relevant module, which will bring us that much closer to generating a sound. By the time everything is said and done, we should be stylin'.

Let's begin with the Oscillator module.

Oscillator Module

The Moog Modular Synth page features nine oscillators grouped in threes; each group is governed by an additional controller module called the driver (see Figure 9.30).

Figure 9.30
There are nine oscillators grouped in threes on the Synth page of the Moog Modular.

The function of the driver is, as its name suggests, to drive the three oscillators assigned to it. It controls the master tuning of the three oscillators simultaneously in addition to adjusting the pulse width of each oscillator's active waveform. Its parameters include:

- **Frequency**—This knob sets the master tuning of all three oscillators. Note that each oscillator may also be individually tuned on its own.
- **State**—This switch sets the tuning unit of increment to be altered by the frequency knob. It can be semitones (for finer adjustments) or octaves.
- **Pulse Width**—This knob alters the pulse width of the waveforms generated by the oscillators.
- **FM Inputs**—These inputs generate frequency modulation between the oscillators and another source of audio, such as the noise generators.
- **PWM Inputs**—These inputs modulate the pulse width of the driver by connecting it to another module.
- **Keyboard Follow**—This dialog alters the pitch of the oscillator according to notes played on the Virtual Keyboard.
- **Sequencer Choice**—This dialog determines which sequencer line this oscillator will follow once the sequencer is triggered.

Located to the right of the driver are the three corresponding oscillators, which include the following parameters:

- **Frequency**—This knob alters the tuning of the individual oscillator. Once set, this tuning can be further manipulated by the frequency knob of the Driver module.

- **Range**—This knob sets the oscillator's octave range.
- **Synchronization**—This switch activates the sync feature of the oscillator.
- **Synchro Input**—This input is used to specify which oscillator to synchronize to.
- **FM Inputs**—These inputs are used to generate frequency modulation between the oscillators and another source of audio, such as the noise generators.
- **Waveform Outputs**—These are used to select and generate a specific waveform. Included here are sine, triangle, saw tooth, and square.

TOOL TIPS

Float your cursor over any parameter of the graphic interface; click on it, and a Tool Tip dialog window will appear, indicating the current value of that particular parameter. Additionally, the Tool Tip will display any specific editing information relevant to that particular parameter. For example, if you float over the Oscillator frequency parameter and click on it, the Tool Tip window will inform you that you can use the right mouse button to make tuning adjustments in semitone increments and the left mouse button to make fine-tuning adjustments in cent increments. Make your adjustments and then release either mouse button to hide the Tool Tip window.

These Tool Tips are extremely helpful when getting to know the Moog Modular.

Before we move on to the Filter module, let's make our first connection with Oscillator 1 to begin designing a simple patch.

1. Click and hold on the saw tooth waveform output jack to display the virtual cable that accompanies it. This serves as the connection needed to route the output of a module to the input of another module. Looking at Figure 9.31, you can see a series of yellow-framed boxes around all the various input destinations to which we can route the saw tooth of Oscillator 1.
2. Drag the mouse and virtual cable to the input of Filter 1 (located in the upper-left corner of the interface). Release the mouse, and you have now made your first connection (see Figure 9.32). Note that if you press a key on your keyboard, you won't hear a signal yet. This is because we haven't routed this signal to an amplifier, which is the final destination for any signal.

Filter Module

The Moog Modular includes three filters that can process many different signal sources. Additionally, each of these three filters includes four types of filters, making for some very interesting combinations. Looking at the top

Figure 9.31

Once you click and hold on outputs or inputs of any module, the Moog Modular displays all of the possible destinations by framing them in yellow. This helps to take a lot of the guesswork out of making connections.

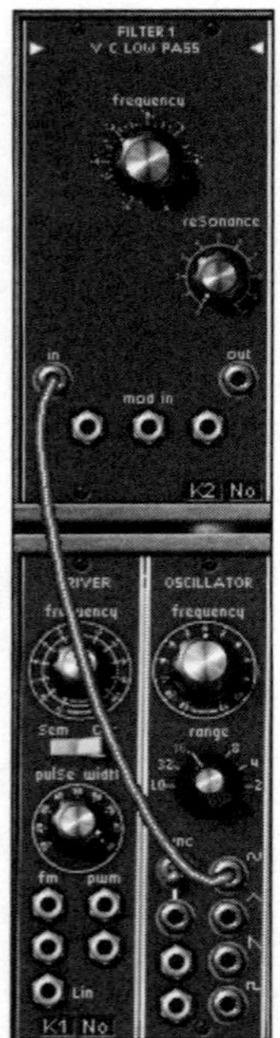

Figure 9.32

Our first connection is made to the input of Filter 1 in the upper-left corner of the interface.

of Filter 1, you can see that it's set to be used as a low pass filter, which is good for creating some deep bass sounds. However, if you click on the name of the filter, you can toggle between the four filter types, including:

- Low Pass Filter
- Hi Pass Filter
- Filter Coupler
- Multimode Filter

Let's look at the different uses and parameters for each filter mode.

As mentioned before, the low pass filter is used to reject the high frequencies of the spectrum while allowing the low frequencies to pass through. The low pass filter has a steep roll-off curve of 24dB per octave; its emphasis on the lower frequencies creates deep bass sounds, and the filter can be routed to an envelope to generate wide, sweeping filter effects. Since we have discussed some of the common parameters such as cutoff frequency and resonance earlier in this chapter, there's no need to redefine them here. Rather, its unique parameters include:

- **Input**—This input can receive signals from various sources on the synth interface, including oscillators and noise generators.
- **Output**—This output jack routes the output of the filter effect to many destinations.
- **Modulation Inputs**—These inputs accept a modulation signal from one of several different sources such as oscillators, LFOs, and noise generators. Once you've made a connection, you can click and drag on the ring of the jack to increase or decrease the modulation effect.
- **Keyboard Follow**—This dialog alters the pitch of the filter according to notes played on the Virtual Keyboard.
- **Sequencer Choice**—This dialog determines which sequencer line this filter will follow once the sequencer is triggered.

The high pass filter performs the opposite function of the low pass filter. Its job is to reject the low frequencies of the spectrum while allowing high frequencies to pass through. In the high pass interface, you can see that it shares all of the same parameters as the low pass, minus the Resonance knob.

The filter coupler is a band reject/band pass filter. A band reject filter rejects a set mid-range of frequencies within the spectrum, but without the need for resonance. A band pass filter performs the exact opposite task within the same frequency range. Looking at the interface, you can see that it includes a few exclusive parameters, such as these:

- **Width**—This knob assigns the bandwidth of the frequency spectrum to be altered by the band reject/band pass filters.
- **Mod Width Input**—This input enables the width parameter to be modulated by another signal. Try connecting it to the waveform output of an LFO.
- **FM Inputs**—These inputs enable the frequency parameter to be modulated by another signal.

Finally, the multi-mode filter is a Jack-of-all-trades filter that incorporates the common parameters of all the different filter modes and has a lighter roll-off curve of 12dB per octave, which makes it a strong effect but not too strong. The selector knob at the top of the filter specifies what kind of filter to use. The possibilities include:

- Low Pass
- Band Pass
- Notch
- High Pass
- Low Shelf
- High Shelf
- Bell

An additional parameter in the multi-mode filter is the Gain knob, which alters the amplitude of the filter effect when in the bell, high shelf, and low shelf filter modes.

Now it's that time you've been waiting for, our next connection. This time we are going to make a connection from the Filter module to the Amplifier module so that we can finally hear the patch we're going to design. Click and hold on Filter Output and drag a virtual cable to the VCA Input of the Amplifier module (see Figure 9.33). Release the mouse and you now have a complete connection, which you can preview by playing the Virtual Keyboard of the Moog Modular or by using your MIDI keyboard.

Figure 9.33
Click and drag a connection from the output of the Filter module to the VCA Input of the Amplifier module to make a complete connection.

THE SECRET FILTER

There is an additional high pass and low pass filter in the upper-right corner of the interface (see Figure 9.34). These filters don't offer as many bells and whistles as the filters we just looked at, but they are very easy to use. Just route a signal to the input of the desired filter and then route the output of the filter to another destination, such as the amplifier or an LFO.

Figure 9.34

Located in the upper-right corner, these additional low pass and high pass filters are great for further filter manipulation.

Bode Frequency Shifter

An exciting new feature of the Moog Modular 2.0 is the Bode frequency shifter, which was a seldom-seen but highly versatile add-on module to Moog synths in the 70s. A frequency shifter works much like an effect called a *ring modulator,* in which two merged signals produce additional tones called *side bands.* The major difference between these effects is the frequency shifter's ability to output its sidebands independently, in addition to its summed output.

The best way to hear the Bode frequency shifter in action is to select the Bode Shifter preset, which is included with the Moog Modular. Refer to Figure 9.35 and read the following list of connections.

1. Connect the saw tooth outputs of Oscillators 1 and 2 to mixer inputs 1 and 2. Press the Link button to route them to a single output.
2. Route the output of mixer channel 1 to the input of the Bode frequency shifter.
3. Route the Mix output of the Bode to the inputs of Filter 2.
4. Route the outputs of Filter 2 to the inputs of an Amplifier module.

Figure 9.35
The Bode frequency shifter can quickly transform your clean synth sounds into a digital distortion meltdown in no time.

Envelope Modules

There are four modulation envelopes in the upper-right portion of the Moog Modular interface. These can alter the character of several different destinations throughout the interface. Since we have talked about the individual envelope parameters a few times already, there's no need to repeat that here. Rather, let's discuss how to use a modulation envelope to modify our sound.

Below the four main envelope parameters (attack, decay, sustain, release), you'll find the input and output jacks. While the output jack is easy to understand and use, the input jack requires a little more information. All of the envelope generators in the Moog Modular require a source of input in order to work. There are many possible sources of input to use. Right-click on the input to display the different input sources, such as keyboard, sequencer, LFO, and oscillators (see Figure 9.36). By default, when working with the Blank template of the Moog Modular, the keyboard trigger is the assigned input source. This will work fine for most of our demonstrations in this chapter, but as you begin to explore the other advanced features of the Moog Modular, such as the sequencer, you may want to try different combinations.

MODULATE THE FILTER

Using the Modulation envelope to alter the filter effect of Filter 1 is a snap. Click and drag a virtual cable from the Output port of the envelope to any of the modulation inputs of the filter. After the connection is made, the next step is to assign a positive or negative value to the connection by clicking and dragging up and down on the tip of the modulation input jack.

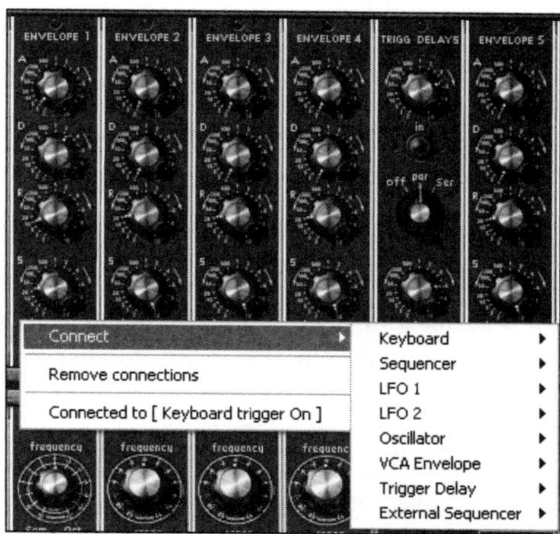

Figure 9.36

Anybody order an input source? Got your inputs right here.

Amplifier Module

The Amplifier module (a.k.a. VCA) is the final step before a signal can be heard from the Moog Modular. There are two Amplifier modules, each with its own envelope generator and panning parameters to affect the dynamics of the final signal as well as assign it to different parts of the stereo field. There are also a few additional parameters in the Amplifier module, such as:

- **Slope Time**—This parameter sets the transitional decay time of the amp envelope.
- **Slope Level**—This parameter sets the transitional decay level of the amp envelope.
- **Audio Input**—This parameter is labeled as VCO In on the graphic interface.
- **AM Input**—This input enables a unique form of modulation called *amplitude modulation.*

LFO Module

The Moog Modular provides two LFOs (see Figure 9.37). They are used to modulate specific modules of the Moog and include the following parameters:

- **Mode**—This switch works in combination with the frequency knob.
- **Frequency**—This knob sets the rate of oscillation. Note that when the Mode switch is in MIDI mode, the Tool Tip dialog for the frequency knob is read in note values rather than milliseconds.
- **Delay**—This knob determines when the LFO effect starts after a note has been triggered.

- **Fade In**—This knob creates a gradual fade-in of the LFO effect once it is started.
- **FM In**—This input is used to create a frequency modulation effect via the LFO.
- **Pulse Width In**—This input is used to create a pulse width modulation effect via the LFO.
- **Manual**—This knob determines the impulse width.
- **Outputs**—These outputs are used to determine the waveform of the LFO and where to route it. For example, you can route the sine wave output to the Modulation In of a low pass filter to modulate the filter effect.

Figure 9.37
The Moog includes two LFOs, which can be used to modulate several other parameters simultaneously.

Controlled Amplifier Module

Located directly below the strip of oscillators is the Controlled Amplifier Module section. This can be simply thought of as a mixer, since it can be used to group a series of oscillators and then route the compiled signal to one of several destinations throughout the synth interface. Refer to Figure 9.38 as we discuss the available parameters.

- **Input**—This accepts the output of any oscillator.
- **Link**—This button links two mixer channels together.
- **Soft Clip**—This is a subtle distortion effect.
- **Invert**—This button will invert the oscillator waveform.
- **Volume**—This knob adjusts the amplitude of the mixer channel.
- **Modulation In**—This input introduces amplitude modulation to the mixer channel.
- **Output**—This jack routes the output of the mixer channel to an audio input.

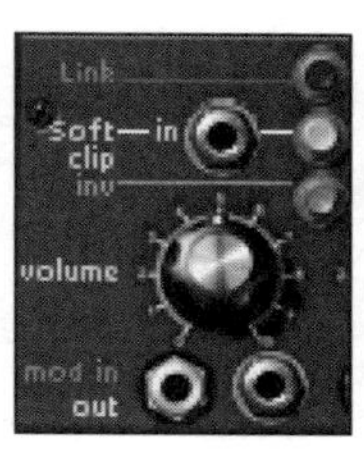

Figure 9.38
The Controlled Amplifier module is basically a hardware mixer. A special feature included here is the ability to route a single mixer output to several inputs at once.

Additional Synth Modules

In addition to the fundamental modules discussed here, the Moog Modular includes some supplementary modules to shape your sound even further. As these are discussed at great length within the manual, we'll simply list these modules to make you aware of them, so that we can get down to the programming tutorials that follow. To view any of these, simply click and hold in the Name field of any module and select any of the following:

- **Noise Generator**–This module generates either white noise or pink noise.
- **Ring Modulator**–This module multiplies two audio signals, thus creating a new signal that contains additional frequencies.
- **Envelope Follower**–This module modulates an envelope with an external signal such as a drum loop.
- **Sample and Hold**–This module generates random modulation values.

Programming the Moog Modular

As you have seen throughout this section of the chapter, the Moog Modular is a soft synth bursting at the seams with creative potential. Now that you have been introduced to its various modules and basic routing concepts, let's dig in and program a few custom sounds. Before reading the following tutorials, take a minute to initialize the Moog Modular by selecting the Blank_Synth preset (see Figure 9.39).

Programming a Bass Sound

Just as we did with the Pro-53, we'll start these programming tutorials by first designing a bass sound and then work our way up the complication ladder. Use Figure 9.40 for reference as you read the following steps:

1. Route the square wave output of Oscillator 1 to Mixer input 1.
2. Route the output of Mixer input 1 to the input of Filter 1, which is a low pass filter.
3. Route the output of Filter 1 to the input of VCA 1.

Figure 9.39

Initialize the Moog by selecting the Blank_Synth preset from the Bank drop-down menu.

Figure 9.40

We have created a simple square wave sound by routing the output of Oscillator 1 to Mixer input 1, routed that signal to Filter 1, and then completed the connection by routing the filter output to the VCA input.

Play a note on your MIDI keyboard or from the Moog Virtual Keyboard, and you should hear a simple, solid bass sound. Let's thicken up the sound a bit by making use of a second oscillator.

1. Route the sine wave output of Oscillator 2 to Mixer input 2. Make sure that the Link button is activated between these two inputs.
2. Change the octave range of Oscillator 2 to 32, which will create an ultra-low sine wave.
3. Set the frequency knob of Filter 1 to 10 o'clock, which will filter out some of the high end of the signal.

Play the sound now, and you'll certainly hear a much thicker sound than before. Now, let's assign some play parameters to the sound by switching to the Virtual Keyboard and making some adjustments. Use Figure 9.41 for reference.

1. Switch the play mode from Mono to Unisson. This performs the same function as discussed in the Pro-53, which is to double-up the voices for each oscillator in relation to the number of polyphony assigned.
2. Set the polyphony to 5 and play a note to hear the difference. It should sound big, thick, and meaty.
3. Deactivate the Legato function.
4. Activate the Glide function, which is found just to the left of the pitch wheel, and then assign a value of 25 milliseconds, which will create a sliding effect between played notes.

Figure 9.41

The Virtual Keyboard is used to assign real-time play parameters to your Moog sounds.

When you are finished, take a moment to save your new sound by clicking on the Export button and selecting Preset. A browser window will pop up, prompting you to assign a name and location to your new sound. Click Save and you're done.

Integrating the Sequence Generator

The Moog Modular sequencer generator is a fascinating and highly imaginative emulation of a classic Moog 960 sequencer. The Moog 960 sequencer is essentially an LFO that generates controlled amounts of voltage when it opens and closes, which in turn assigns a pitch to each step of a sequence.

MORE 960 INFO

While the Moog Modular manual is a good source of information, you can find much more in-depth info on the 960 sequencer at this Web site:

http://arts.ucsc.edu/ems/music/equipment/synthesizers/analog/moog/Moog.html.

In this tutorial, I will show you how to use the sequence generator along with the bass sound you just created. Switch to the synth page and follow along.

1 In the first Driver module, set the Sequencer Choice dialog to S1 to have Oscillators 1 and 2 follow the first line of the sequence generator (see Figure 9.42).

2 Next, right-click (Ctrl+click on the Mac) on the output trigger of VCA 1 and select Connections, Sequencer, Sequence Trigger (see Figure 9.43).

3 Switch to the Sequencer page and press the On button to start the sequencer.

4 Press the Off button to stop the sequencer.

Figure 9.42
Assign the Sequencer Choice dialog of the first driver to S1 to have it follow the first line of the sequence generator.

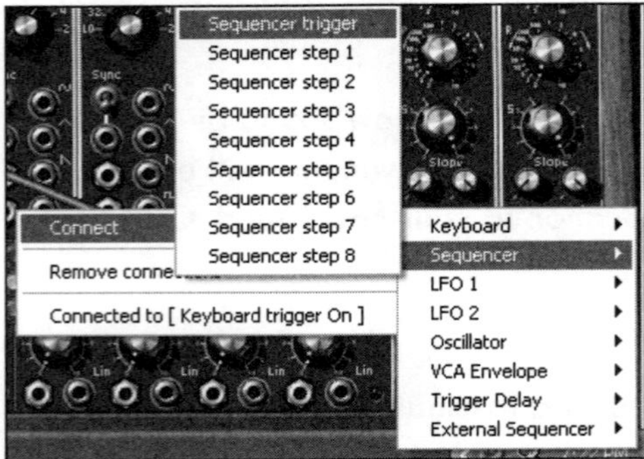

Figure 9.43
Connect the output trigger of VCA 1 to Sequence Trigger, which enables the sequence generator to trigger Oscillators 1 and 2.

If you press the On button to start the sequencer, you should hear a single pitch repetition. In order to assign new pitches to the sequence, use the Level

Output knobs along the top row of the sequencer. For example, if you wanted to create a major triad arpeggio, you could assign the following values to the Level Output knobs:

- **Knob 1**—Lowest possible value.
- **Knob 2**—Middle value.
- **Knob 3**—Highest possible value.
- **Knob 4**—Middle value.
- **Knob 5**—Lowest possible value.
- **Knob 6**—Middle value.
- **Knob 7**—Highest possible value.
- **Knob 8**—Middle value.

Finally, use the frequency knob to set the sequencer speed and the length knob to assign a sustain value to each note. Truly, there are several creative possibilities with the sequence generator. I encourage you to read through some of the sequencing tutorials to learn more about this module.

Programming a Pad/Sequence Sound

In this tutorial, we're going to get a little more complicated and program a pad sound with the Moog Modular. Unlike the sustaining pad sound that we programmed with the Pro-53, we're going to incorporate the sequence generator as a modulator to the overall sound. Be sure to initialize the synth by selecting the Blank Synth preset. Also, make sure that you switch to the Keyboard page, set the play mode to Polyphonic, assign polyphony of 8–10 note, and then finish the job by activating the Legato function.

Now we're ready to begin, so switch back to the Synth page and make the following connections.

1. Route the saw tooth output of Oscillator 1 to Mixer input 1.
2. Route the saw tooth output of Oscillator 2 to Mixer input 2.
3. Activate the first Link function and then route the first mixer output to the Filter 1 input, which should be a low pass filter.
4. Route the filter output to the first VCA input.

If you play the sound as it is, it should sound pretty plain, but that's going to change in a matter of minutes. To start, let's make some alterations to Filter 1.

Assign a low cutoff value and a moderately high resonance value. Play the sound now; it should have a nasal quality to it. In addition, you might want to alter the octave range of Oscillator 2 by switching from 16 to 8.

Now, switch to the Keyboard page and make the following adjustments to VCA envelope 1:

- **Attack**—Approx 1500ms.
- **Decay**—Approx 450ms.
- **Sustain Level**—Set to its maximum resolution.
- **Release**—Approx 1500ms.

Play the sound now, and it should gradually fade in and include a long, sustained element. Next we're going to take a different route than the typical LFO wavering sound. This time, we are going to use the sequence generator to modulate the filter as the sound plays back.

1. Navigate to the Sequencer/FX page. Right-click the On routing button of the generator and select Keyboard Trigger On (see Figure 9.44).
2. Next, right-click the Off routing button of the generator and select Keyboard Trigger Off. This will cause the sequence generator to start and stop on command when a note is either held or released.
3. Use the top row of level output knobs to write in a sequence. You might try using the sequence we created in the previous tutorial.
4. Activate MIDI Sync and use the frequency knob to assign a value of *4.
5. Navigate to the Synth page and route the output of the first sequencer row to the modulation input of Filter 1 (see Figure 9.45).
6. Increase the amount of modulation input of Oscillator 1 by clicking and dragging upward on the input jack of the modulation input (see Figure 9.46).

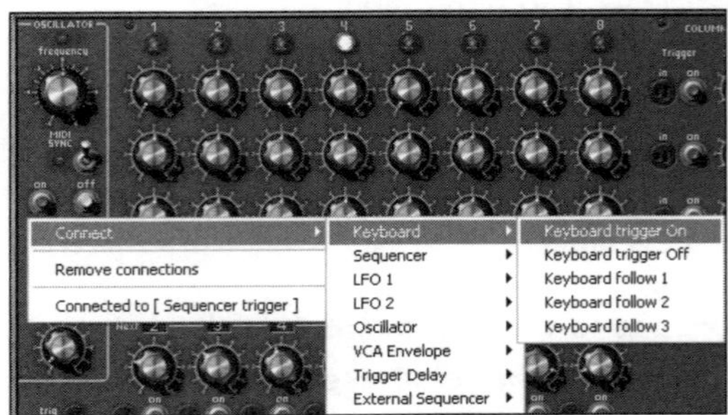

Figure 9.44
Use Keyboard Trigger On to have the sequence generator start when a key is held on the Virtual Keyboard.

Figure 9.45

The sequencer row outputs can be used to modulate different modules throughout the interface. In this case, I have routed the first row of the sequence to the modulation input of Filter 1, which will modulate the opening and closing of the filter effect.

Figure 9.46

Whenever a modulation source is routed to a modulation input, you can cut or boost the modulation effect by clicking and dragging up or down on its input jack.

Play the sound now, and you should hear a big difference. You can further enhance this effect by making a few additional adjustments to the filter parameters.

The last element you could bring to this sound would be the supplied real-time effects of the Moog Modular. For example, you could switch to the Sequence/FX page and activate the delay effect by clicking on the VCA 1 switch, followed by the MIDI Sync switch to synchronize the delay effect to the tempo of the sequence generator. At this point, it's just a matter of flavoring the sound using the various delay parameters (time, feedback, dry/wet, and so on). You could also add more depth to the sound by introducing some chorus to the mix as well. Just click on the VCA 1 switch to turn it on and make your adjustments.

10 FM Synthesis—Super Freq

Ah, the 80s—mullet haircuts, A Flock of Seagulls, films by John Hughes, and the continuing fascination of modern synth-pop made possible by the likes of Moog, Sequential Circuits, and Oberheim. Okay, maybe I was a little young to be into all that stuff, but the music of the 80s was certainly the most influential for just about any kid born in the 1970s. And within that music was the introduction of an entirely new form of popular synthesis called FM, or frequency modulation.

FM is a digital form of synthesis that can create complex sounds and aural elements with a very small number of fundamentals involved. John Chowning discovered and developed FM synthesis in 1973. He recognized that chaining two oscillators together could create realistic sounds and/or complex synthetic textures. Chowning published his findings in the *Journal of the Audio Engineering Society* in a paper titled "The Synthesis of Complex Audio Spectra by Means of Frequency Modulation." The theories and methods discussed in the paper became quite popular and set the groundwork for the FM revolution of 1983, with the introduction of the Yamaha DX7. The DX7 was a synth that didn't sport the standard sounds and fundamentals of subtractive synthesis, and it was one of the first synths to feature MIDI. It was an instant hit among synth-a-holics everywhere and was soon heard on many pop and ambient albums.

FM synthesis began to lose its popularity toward the end of the 80s, but thanks to the help of soft synths and an overwhelming interest in the virtual studio environment, FM has once again become a welcome component to electronic music. Furthermore, its implementation into popular soft synths by the likes of such companies as Native Instruments and VirSyn has realized new aural possibilities never before implemented in frequency modulation. In other words, "This ain't your daddy's FM synth!"

> **REQUIRED FM LISTENING**
> For good examples of FM-flavored music, look no further than musicians such as Depeche Mode, Yes, Pet Shop Boys, and "Mr. Synth" himself, Brian Eno. FM synthesis played a vital role in the creation of such classic albums as *People Are People* (Depeche Mode) and *Introspective* (Pet Shop Boys). Check them out on Amazon or iTunes.

Understanding FM Synthesis

Although FM synthesis might seem difficult to understand, in actuality this is far from the case. There's no doubt that the mathematical calculations behind FM synthesis are complex, but if you have a good understanding of the basics behind subtractive synthesis (see the previous chapter), then comprehending basic FM models should be a walk in the park.

FM Building Blocks—The Carrier and Modulator

As you'll recall from Chapter 9, "Subtractive Synthesis—Close Up," subtractive synthesis is accomplished by stringing together a set of modules in order to generate a signal by non-digital means. By contrast, FM is an entirely digital form of synthesis, but it still relies on a similar structure of building blocks in order to generate a signal. The only real difference between these two forms of synthesis is in how the building blocks are arranged and configured. With that understood, a basic FM model is built upon two fundamentals:

- **The Carrier**—This is thought of as the center or original frequency in FM terms. It can be comprised of any basic or complex waveform, such as a sine wave or vocal samples.
- **The Modulator**—This is the manipulating frequency in FM terms. It is routed into the input of the carrier frequency in order to merge them into a single composite waveform that contains several additional frequencies, known simply as frequency deviation.

Each of these fundamentals includes an oscillator, envelope generator, and amplifier, which are then compiled into a single "master module" known as an *operator*. Thus, operators are the main building blocks of FM synthesis. They are linked together in different combinations with the intention of generating a perceived signal. See Figure 10.1 for a visual illustration of this concept.

Algorithms

Once you understand the carrier/modulator relationship, FM synthesis really boils down to the arrangement or networking of various operators in order to construct a composite signal. The term used for these networks is *algorithm*.

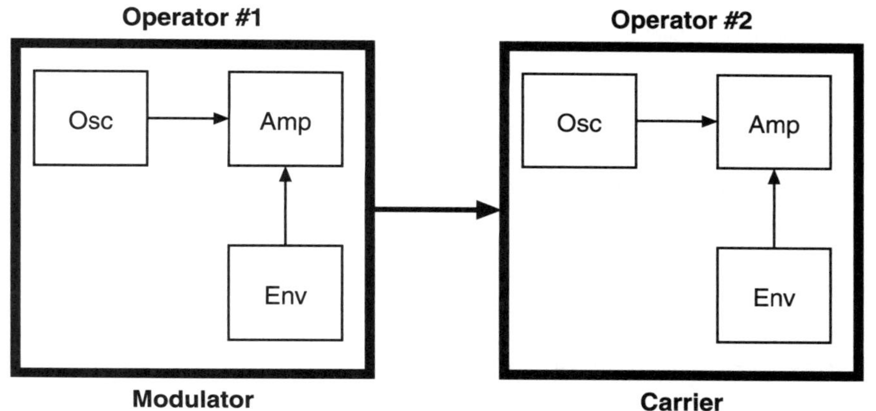

Figure 10.1
This diagram represents a very simple FM synthesis model built from two operators. The operator on the right is the carrier, which is the center frequency, while the operator on the left is the modulator. As you can see here, the audio output of the modulating operator is routed to the input of the carrying operator, which results in a new signal. The variations in the composite waveform are referred to as *frequency deviation*.

In mathematical terms, an algorithm is the step-by-step numeric process of problem solving. For example, every functioning part of your computer is algorithmically related, right down to the language code that was used to conceive and create your soft synths and samplers. By FM standards, an algorithm is a step-by-step process used to design a signal. For example, when a modulating operator is fed to a carrying operator, this would be considered a basic algorithm. A more complicated example could be several modulators fed to a single carrier in one of two ways (serial or parallel), which results in two completely different tones and textures (see Figure 10.2).

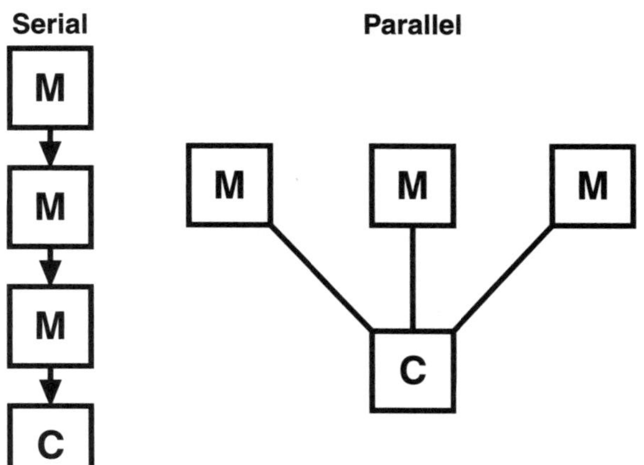

Figure 10.2
These diagrams represent two different ways to route several modulators to a single carrier. The diagram on the left is an example of a serial combination, in which the output of one modulator is fed to the input of the next and so on. The diagram on the right is an example of a parallel combination, in which the output of each modulator is fed to the carrier independently.

> **FM RADIO**
>
> Is FM synthesis related to FM radio? Sort of. Although the process of frequency modulation via radio waves is a bit different than synthesis, they both rely on the common relationship of the carrier and modulator. In FM radio, the carrier is the main transmission frequency, oscillating at an extremely high rate, rendering it usually inaudible to the human ear. The modulator is the intended audible sound source of an FM transmission, which when combined with the carrier frequency forms a composite signal. At the end of this process is the FM receiver in your car or home stereo, which decodes and separates the carrier from the modulator.

A Closer Look at FM Waveforms

Let's take a closer look at how FM properties can build complex waveforms. First, let's look at a simple FM example involving a single carrier and modulator. In Figure 10.3, I have generated a triangle waveform oscillating at a rate of 110Hz, which will be my carrier. Next, I have generated a sine wave oscillating at 10Hz, which will be my modulator (see Figure 10.4). Since the rate of the modulator is not very fast, this will produce a slight wavering (or vibrato) when combined with the triangle to give us a composite waveform as shown in Figure 10.5.

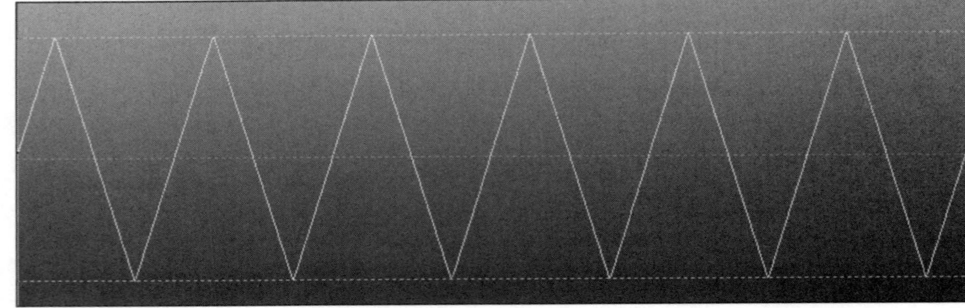

Figure 10.3

This diagram represents a triangle waveform that oscillates at 110Hz. This is our carrier.

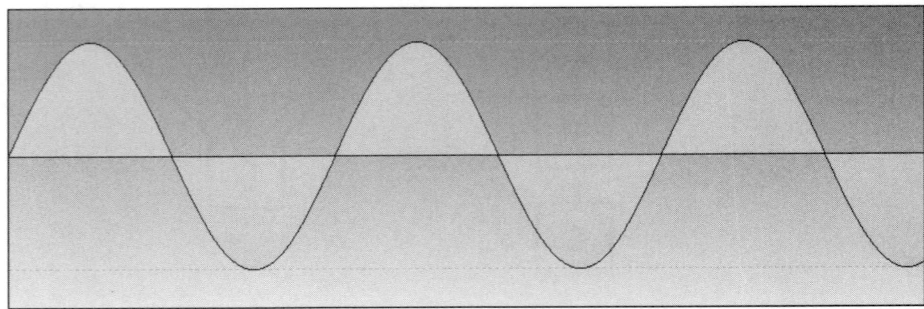

Figure 10.4

This diagram represents a sine wave oscillating at 10Hz, which will be our modulator.

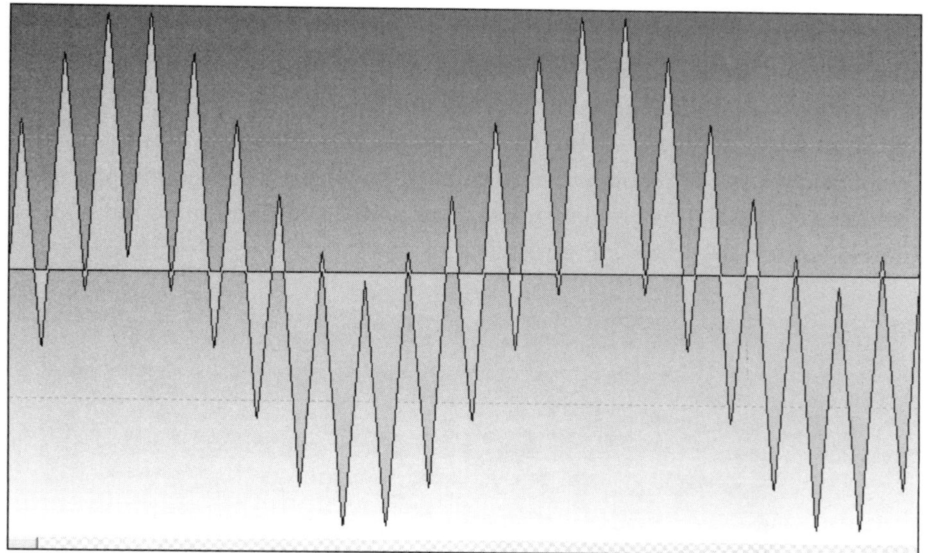

Figure 10.5

Once combined, the resulting waveform has been altered by frequency modulation, but not by much.

Now let's assign a new frequency of 100Hz to our modulator. This frequency is much closer in pitch to the carrier and, as you can see in Figure 10.6, we get a much more interesting result. New spectral content has been generated and introduced into the composite waveform.

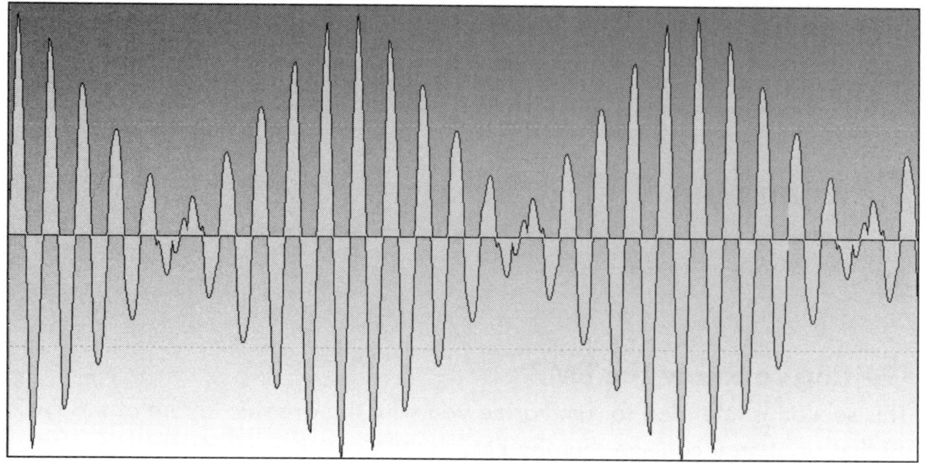

Figure 10.6

This time around, we are using the same carrier but a stronger modulator with a frequency of 100Hz, which produces a much more complex waveform.

Meet Our FM Soft Synth—The FM7

The FM7 by Native Instruments (see Figure 10.7) pays tribute to the world of FM synthesis by modeling itself after the acclaimed granddaddy of FM, the Yamaha DX7. Like the DX7, the FM7 bears a striking resemblance to its hardware relative in both look and functionality. But unlike the DX7, this soft synth contains a friendly programming interface and includes an audio input for purely twisted sound design possibilities.

Figure 10.7
The FM7 is a soft synth that is built upon the foundation of frequency modulation, but with a modern feature set made of virtual studio creativity.

> **GET THE DEMO**
> A demo version of the FM7 can be downloaded from the Native Instruments Web site at **www.native-instruments.com**.

Getting to Know the FM7

This section is intended to familiarize you with the graphic layout of the FM7. At first sight, you can see that the FM7 is split into three sections:

- The Common Parameters Strip
- The Editor
- The Virtual Keyboard

SETTING UP YOUR AUDIO/MIDI HARDWARE

If you are planning to use the FM7 in standalone mode (without a sequencer), it would be a good idea to take a minute to set up your audio and MIDI hardware. This is done by clicking on the System pull-down menu and selecting either the Audio Settings or MIDI Settings option to launch their corresponding interfaces.

In Figure 10.8, you can see that the Audio Settings page doesn't have many parameters to worry about. The In and Out ports determine which audio card will be used for routing audio in and out of the FM7, and each port includes Record Ahead/Play Ahead sliders, which adjust the latency. Once you have made your settings, click the OK button to close the interface.

The MIDI Settings page (see Figure 10.9) includes several dialogs and options, such as MIDI filtering (in and out) and assigning your MIDI hardware. Once you have made your settings, click the OK button to close the interface.

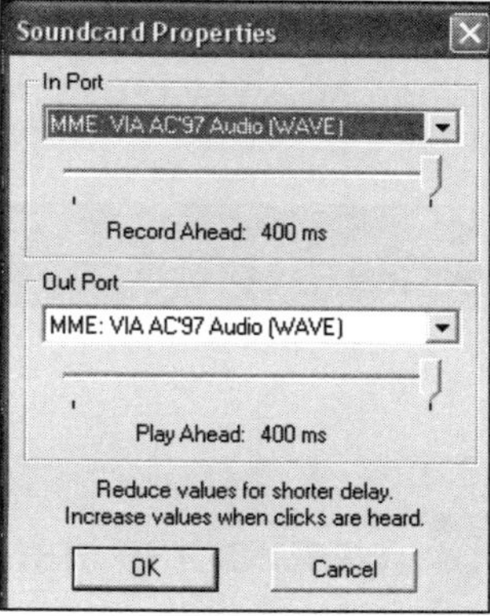

Figure 10.8
On the Audio Settings page you select an audio card to route audio in and out of the FM7. Note that I am currently using the MME (Multi Media Extension) driver of Windows XP to drive the FM7. If you have an installed audio card that supports ASIO, you can select this driver specification by selecting it from the Audio Port subdirectory of the System pull-down menu.

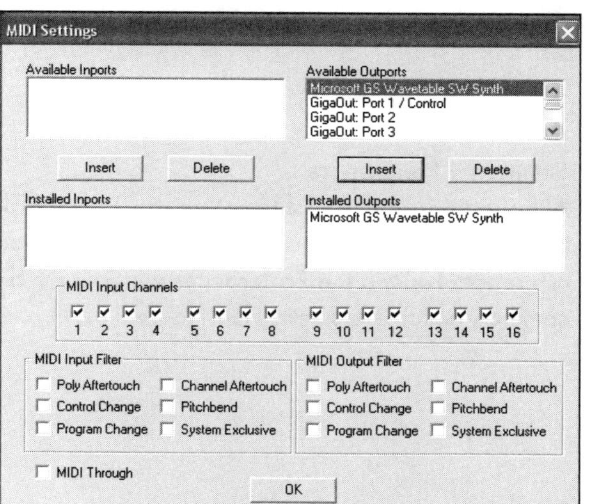

Figure 10.9
The MIDI Settings page is where you assign MIDI hardware to the inputs and outputs of the FM7. It is also where you specify which parameters will be filters when routing input or output to the FM7 interface.

USE YOUR COMPUTER KEYBOARD

A really great feature of all the Native Instruments soft synths is the ability to trigger their sounds from your computer keyboard. Use the bottom two rows of keys above the space bar to trigger the lower octaves of the FM7 and the upper keys to trigger the higher octaves. It's a real convenience, especially when you don't have a MIDI keyboard handy.

The Common Parameters Strip

As you might have guessed, the common parameters strip is where you view and edit the common or global parameters of the FM7. This can mean anything from selecting different presets to altering the appearance of the FM7. This strip is also where you can view the variations in spectrum and waveform content, which is determined by altering any parameters of an FM7 preset. In short, this is where it all begins. Use Figure 10.10 as a reference diagram as you read through the next few sections of this chapter.

Figure 10.10

The common parameters strip is used to change presets and preferences, as well as polyphony and appearance.

WEBLINK AND SERIAL INFO

As is the case with most Native Instruments soft synths, the FM7 includes a link to display basic synth information (version number, serial number) and a direct link to the Native Instruments Web site via Web browser. Click on the FM7 logo to display the basic synth information or click on the NI logo to launch your Web browser.

Setting the Preferences

Although it is not critical to set up the common preferences prior to using the FM7, it's a good idea to at least take a quick look at them for the sake of reference. Launch the Preferences window by clicking the PREF button in the common parameters strip (see Figure 10.11).

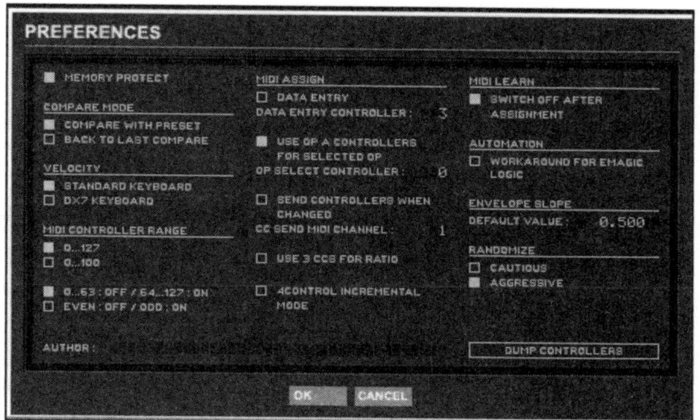

Figure 10.11

The Preferences window is where you alter the global parameters of the FM7.

As you can see, this window is split into several categories. Let's take a look.

- **Memory Protect**—When activated, this preference prevents you from accidentally overwriting any FM7 presets.
- **Compare Mode**—This category specifies how the FM7 toggles between edits made to a preset by clicking the COMP (compare) button. The COMP button shows you how the preset sounds before and after making an edit. When Compare with Preset is selected, all of the edits stored within the Edit buffer are reset to the standard preset when the COMP button is clicked. When Back to Last Compare is selected, clicking COMP restores any settings made before the COMP button is clicked.
- **Velocity**—This category allows you to use the original velocity range of the DX7 within the FM7 environment, which was 0–100. This can drastically change the brightness of any selected FM7 preset, as there are values greater than 100 in the MIDI language (0–127).
- **MIDI Controller Range**—The first option of this category assigns a value of either 0–100 or 0–127 to external MIDI controllers. The section option of this category determines the range of MIDI values that turn specific FM7 parameters on and off.
- **MIDI Assign**—This category specifies how the FM7 parameters are controlled. When the Data Entry option is activated, specific FM7 parameters are made available to be controlled via an external MIDI controller. When Use Op A Controllers for Selected Op is selected, the controls of Operator A can be used to control another operator. The final option, Send Controllers when Changed, is used to avoid any jumps in controller changes made by an external MIDI controller.
- **MIDI Learn**—When Switch Off After Assignment is selected, MIDI Learn will turn off after a specific FM7 parameter has been assigned to a MIDI controller, such as a hardware knob or slider.

- **Automation**—This parameter works around a known filter bug with earlier versions of Logic Audio.
- **Envelope Slope**—This dialog assigns an amount of slope to every new segment created within the Envelope Editor of the FM7.
- **Randomize**—This category determines the amount of randomization to use on an FM7 preset whenever the Random button is activated. When Cautious is selected, only specific parameters will be affected by the randomization effect. When Aggressive is selected, anything goes.
- **Author**—This dialog enters your name within an FM7 preset.
- **Dump Controllers**—This function sends out all programmed MIDI controller assignments to an external MIDI controller.

Once you have set your preferences, click the OK button to close the window.

Appearance Parameters

Just below the Preferences button are the appearance controls, which are used to alter the appearance of the FM7 by hiding either the editor or keyboard. To hide either interface, simply click the appropriate button once and then click it again to display it. It's very handy when you want to view the FM7 in a more compact way in order to save room on your desktop (see Figure 10.12).

Preset and Polyphony Parameters

Moving to the right, the Preset and Polyphony parameters are used to change the current preset, view its details, and assign an amount of polyphony to it. The diode display changes FM7 presets by both clicking and dragging up or down within the Preset Number dialog or clicking on the up or down arrow located at the top and bottom of the diode display.

As each new preset is selected, its name is reflected in the Preset dialog just to the right of the diode display. Just below the preset name is an information prompt, which reflects the various details that pertain to the currently selected preset. You can toggle between the various details by clicking in this dialog box. Information displayed here includes:

- **I**—This displays any information typed in the Info dialog of the FM7 Library (we'll look at this in a minute). For example, preset 001, called Exciting, has an Info dialog called Tempo Sync.
- **D**—This displays when the preset was created.
- **C**—This displays the category assigned to the FM7 preset.
- **N**—This displays the name of the preset programmer.

Figure 10.12

Now you see the editor (top), now you don't (bottom).

- **P**—This displays the currently selected parameter in the FM7 interface. Note that if you have not touched any of the FM7 parameters up to this point, then this dialog will display None.

> **EDITING PRESETS**
>
> Whenever you perform an edit to any selected FM7 preset, the FM7 will reflect this by placing a red dot in the lower-right side of the diode display in the common parameters strip.

To the right of the preset name section is the Polyphony dialog, which specifies the number of voices that can be simultaneously played from the FM7. As mentioned earlier in this chapter, the FM7 can play up to 64 voices at one time and can be changed by clicking and dragging up or down in the dialog.

> **MORE POLYPHONY—MORE CPU**
>
> As you assign more polyphony to an FM7 preset, you'll use up more of your CPU resources. If you intend to use the FM7 for percussion sounds such as a kick or snare drum, you will need only a polyphony count of 1–2 voices. If you are programming a pad sound, which involves playing several notes simultaneously, give yourself at least 8–10 voices to cover your 10 fingers.

LEDs, Spectrum, and Waveform Displays

The final part of the common parameters strip deals with the audio output of the FM7, as well as a graphical representation of the currently selected preset. There's really not that much to say about these particular displays, except that the Spectrum and Waveform displays will automatically update to reflect each new change made to an FM7 preset.

The FM7 Library

Occupying a majority of the FM7 graphic interface, the Library is used to select and manage presets and banks. Since it is the first thing you will see when first launching the FM7, this is a good time to tour this part of the interface and explain how to select and manage the provided presets (see Figure 10.13).

There are four main sections included in the Library interface:

- The Bank/Preset Listing
- The Master Control Strip
- The Randomize/Init Edit Buffer Controls
- The Detail Controls

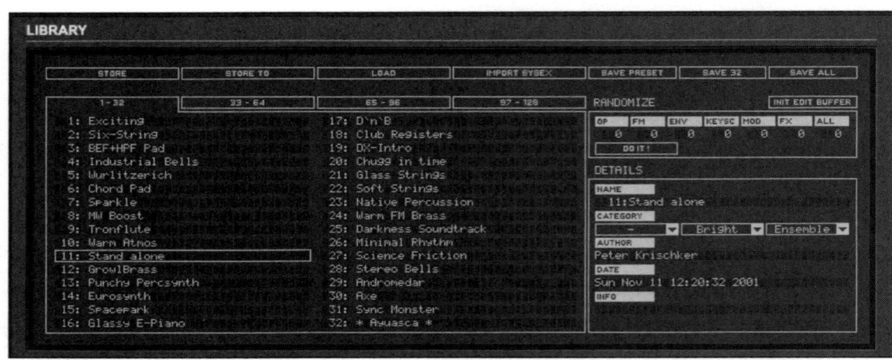

Figure 10.13
The FM7 Library is where you select and manage the supplied presets of the FM7. Additionally, you can use the Library to store your own presets with ease.

WHICH WAY TO THE LIBRARY

To get to the Library, simply click on the LIB button in the page select strip located just below the common parameters strip.

The Bank/Preset Listing

The bank/preset listing is used to list and select presets within an FM7 bank (see Figure 10.14). Each FM7 bank can hold up to 128 presets, which are selected by simply clicking on the name of the preset, at which point a green frame encompasses the preset name. Now you can press any key on the Virtual Keyboard to sample that particular preset. Furthermore, each FM7 bank is split into 4 groups of 32 presets each, and each group can be selected by simply clicking on the 1-32, 33-64, 65-96, and 97-128 buttons on the listing interface.

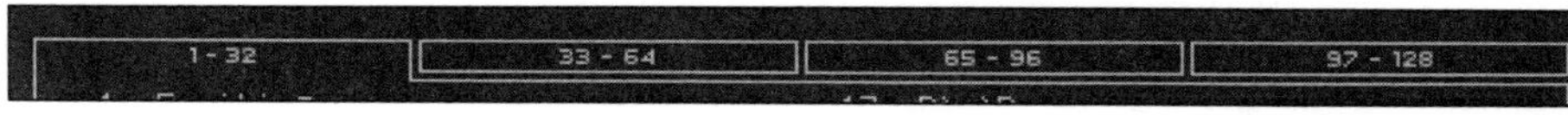

Figure 10.14

The bank/preset listing is used to select different presets within an FM7 bank.

USING MIDI FILES

One of the best ways to preview FM7 presets is to use the included MIDI file player found under the Demo Song pull-down menu. Simply select Open MIDI File and use the browser window to locate a MIDI file on your computer. Open the MIDI file, and the FM7 will immediately begin to play the file. As the file plays, use the preset listing interface to navigate through and preview each preset to find the right one for you.

The Master Control Strip

The master control strip is used to load, save, and manage your FM7 banks and presets, in addition to performing other various tasks. The main parameters of the master control strip include:

- **Store**—This parameter is used to store any edits contained within the edit buffer to the currently selected preset. Note that if Memory Protect is activated, clicking this button will bring up a pop-up window warning you that Memory Protect is still on. You can choose to save the edits and turn off Memory Protect, save the preset but not turn off Memory Protect, or just cancel the process entirely.

- **Store To**—This parameter performs the same function as Store, but Store To allows you to select a location to store the edits, rather than the currently selected preset. Click Store To and then select a preset slot to save the edits to by simply clicking once on it.
- **Load**—This parameter allows you to open individual FM7 presets (.f7p), a block of 32 presets (.f7b), or an entire bank of 128 presets (.f7a).
- **Import Sysex**—This is a special function of the FM7 that allows users of the classic Yamaha DX7, DX7II, and DX200 to import their old favorite presets via system-exclusive dump.
- **Save Preset**—This parameter saves an individual FM7 preset file (.f7p).
- **Save 32**—This parameter saves 32 FM7 presets as one chunk (.f7b). Note that the 32 presets must be currently selected in the bank/preset listing.
- **Save All**—This parameter saves all 128 FM7 presets as a bank (.f7a).

LOADING BANKS

The FM7 provides several banks that are located in the FM7 Program folder. After clicking the Load button, navigate to and open this folder, then open the Presets folder, and you'll find several banks, including the original DX7 presets, orchestral presets, and keyboard presets.

AUDIO INPUT FUN

The default FM7 bank includes three audio input examples in the 126, 127, and 128 preset slots. These are provided to familiarize you with the audio input capabilities of the FM7.

To make use of these presets, make sure that you have an audio input source from your audio card and have selected that input from the Audio Settings page.

Also, be aware that you may have to hold down a note on the Virtual Keyboard in order to hear the audio input effect.

The Randomize/Init Edit Buffer Controls

Located in the upper-right corner of the Library interface, the randomize/init edit buffer controls are used to jump-start your synthetic creativity by altering a selected preset or by wiping the slate clean in order to create a new FM7 preset from scratch (we'll be doing this at the end of the chapter). Let's discuss each of these in further detail.

The Randomize controls randomly alter various parameters of an FM7 preset. Very often, I will randomize a preset when I find that I have painted myself into a corner and need some creative help to realize a new sound or texture for a piece of music. All that is needed is to select the global parameter you wish to alter randomly (such as the envelope), assign it a numeric value by clicking and dragging up and down in the numeric dialog below, and clicking Do It. The Randomize controls are a lot of fun to use and can produce some very interesting results.

- **OP**—Randomizes the wave form, frequency ratio, and offset parameters of each operator.
- **FM**—Randomizes the FM algorithm matrix, which means it randomizes how much one operator is feeding into another.
- **ENV**—This randomly alters the envelope parameters of each operator.
- **KEYSC**— Randomizes the key scaling of each operator.
- **MOD**—This randomly alters the amount of modulation in the modulation matrix.
- **FX**— Randomly alters the parameters of the onboard real-time FX.
- **ALL**—This randomly alters all of the different Randomize categories.

The Init Edit Buffer button resets the entire FM7 interface to its default values. This is the parameter you want to use if you're planning to create a completely original preset from scratch. Just click the button once with your mouse, and you're all set to go.

The Detail Controls

The detail controls are used to view and edit preset information, such as name, date, and category. You'll recall that we looked at an abbreviated version of this earlier in the common parameters strip.

- **Name**—Type in the name of your preset here.
- **Category**—Use the provided pull-down menus to classify your preset.
- **Author**—Type in your name here.
- **Date**—Type in the creation date of the preset here.
- **Info**—Type in any important information, such as tempo sync, use with chorus, and so on.

Navigating the FM7

As you have seen over the course of the last few pages, the FM7 offers many great operational features and a fantastic selection of banks and presets to boot. But I think you'll agree that the whole point of getting a soft synth such as this one is to integrate the programming potential of FM synthesis into your music, and this is what we will concentrate on for the remainder of this chapter. For now, let's begin with navigating through the various pages of the FM7 and then move on to understanding and using the provided parameters.

To begin, you should familiarize yourself with the Page Select area, located just underneath the common parameters strip. Looking at Figure 10.15, you can see that the Page Select area includes the following parameters:

- **Operators A–Z**—These buttons select the available operators of the FM7, which is where its sound is generated. Note though that Operators X and Z are provided to alter the character of the overall signal by introducing noise and filter effects.
- **Pitch**—This button selects the Pitch page, which is used to set the pitch bend range of the FM7, as well as introduce portamento, which generates a sliding or glissando effect between notes.
- **LFO**—The LFO page provides two low frequency oscillators that modulate specific FM7 parameters.
- **Modulation**—This button selects the modulation matrix, which routes modulation to one or several different FM7 parameters. It is an intense feature, which will be explained in greater detail soon.
- **Master**—This button selects the Master page, which sets the global parameters for a selected preset.
- **Easy**—This button selects the Easy page, which is a simplified programmer for the FM7. This is a very useful feature for true beginners to FM synthesis, as it is laid out like a standard synth with no mention of operators, matrixes, and such.
- **Library**—The Library selects the different available FM7 presets.
- **Store**—This button saves the edits stored in the edit buffer to the currently selected preset. This is the same function as the Store button found on the master control strip of the Library.
- **Compare**—This button is used to toggle back and forth between a currently created edit and the one prior to it.
- **Learn**—This button assigns different MIDI controllers to specific FM7 parameters. To use this feature, just click on it and then turn a knob or push a slider on your MIDI controller to assign it.

Figure 10.15
The Page Select area navigates through the various views and parameters of the editor.

Now, let's look at the different pages of the FM7, starting with the Master page. Click the Master button and read below.

The Master Page

As you read in the previous list, the Master page is where you set and alter the global parameters of the FM7. However, this could be seen as an over-simplified explanation. You can see from Figure 10.16 that the Master page is actually split into two fundamental sections:

- The Master Parameters
- The Effect Parameters

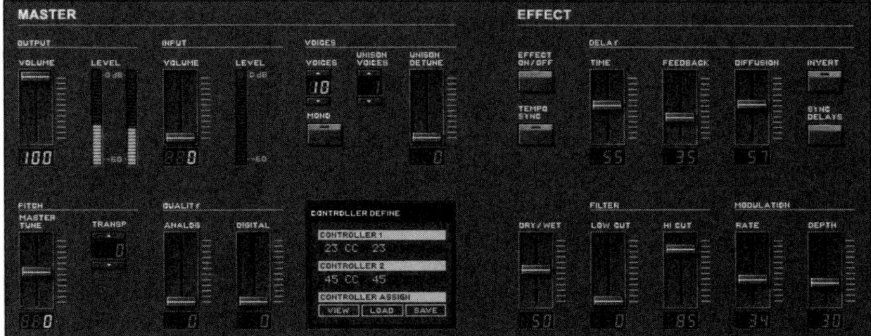

Figure 10.16
The Master page is used to set the global parameters of the FM7, including effects and polyphony.

Let's take a closer look at these two sections and discuss their purpose and functions, beginning with the master parameters.

The Master Parameters

Occupying the left side of this page, the master parameters are used to alter the global settings of a selected preset. This includes setting the amount of audio input/output, assigning a polyphony count to a preset, and altering the master pitch of a preset.

The master parameters include the following:

- **Input/Output**—These sliders assign an amount of signal input and output to the FM7.

- **Pitch**—This section manipulates the overall tuning and transposition of the FM7. The Master Tune slider adjusts the master tuning of the FM7 and has a range of -99 to +100 cents. The Transposition dialog adjusts the tuning of the FM7 in semitone increments. It has a range of +/-2 octaves.
- **Quality**—This section adjusts the aural and behavioral characteristics of the FM7. The Analog slider emulates the electronic qualities of analog gear, such as voltage and temperature irregularities, which in turn cause variations in the aural quality of the soft synth. Digital on the other hand reduces or increases the overall bit depth of the FM7. This is done to achieve a more vintage sound by operating at the same bit depth as the original DX7, which was 12 bits.
- **Voices**—This section assigns a polyphony count to a preset (which we have already discussed), but it also introduces a unique unison feature, which doubles up the number of oscillators within an FM7 preset in order to thicken up the overall signal. Use the Unison dialog to add up to 64 additional oscillators on a single patch, and then use the Unison Detune slider to the right to slightly alter the tuning of each oscillator playing in unison. This achieves a chorus-like effect.
- **Controller Define**—This section assigns external MIDI controllers to FM7 parameters by way of the modulation matrix.

The Effect Parameters

Occupying the right side of the Master page, the effect parameters are responsible for enhancing the overall FM7 signal by making use of a 4-tap stereo delay, as well as offering filter and modulation controls. Although there are a few additional filters found throughout the rest of the FM7, the purpose of these effects is to sweeten the sound just a bit before routing it to the output slider.

To activate the Effect section, click the Effect On/Off button and follow along as we discuss the various parameters pertaining to each effect, starting with the common parameters.

- **Tempo Sync**—Activating this button synchronizes the delay effect to the tempo of any incoming MIDI clock from an external source or when used within a host sequencing application like Cubase. Also note that this button also synchronizes the Modulation LFO.
- **Dry/Wet**—This slider adjusts the mix between the dry, unaffected signal and the wet or processed signal. When using the effect parameters for the first time, set this parameter to 50 for best results.

Once you have activated and adjusted these parameters, we can discuss the Delay parameters.

- **Time**—Sets the time between repeats.
- **Feedback**—This slider feeds the output back to the input of the delay, thus creating multiple repeats.
- **Diffusion**—This slider alters the character of the delay effect. At its lowest setting, diffusion sounds more like a reverb, whereas when set at its highest position, the diffusion sounds much more defined between repeats.
- **Invert**—When activated, this button alters the phase of the repeats.
- **Sync Delays**—This parameter locks the delays and modulation LFO together.

Next up is the filter, which acts a lot more like shelving EQ, cutting and/or boosting the low and high frequencies.

- **Low Cut**—This slider boosts or cuts the low frequencies of the delay repeats. At its lowest value, the low cut slider does not affect the signal, as the entire range of frequencies passes through. At its highest value, all low frequencies are cut from the delay repeats.
- **Hi Cut**—This slider boosts or cuts the high frequencies of the delay repeats. At its lowest value, the high cut slider does not affect the signal, as the entire range of frequencies passes through. At its highest value, all high frequencies are cut from the delay repeats.

The final effect available is modulation, which introduces a recurring shift to the delay repeats. This can create some wild flanging and chorus effects.

- **Rate**—This slider adjusts the speed of modulation to the delay repeats.
- **Depth**—This slider adjusts the depth or intensity of the modulation of the delay repeats.

The Easy Edit Page

For the beginner, FM synths are not all that easy to program. Although the FM7 makes the process of programming much easier to understand with its well-constructed interface, the theories behind FM sometimes get a little overwhelming, when all you're trying to do is just make a minor alteration to a preset. It could be worse. Have you ever seen the tiny diode screen on the DX7? Forget about it!

Native Instruments took this into consideration when assembling the FM7 interface and compensated by creating several algorithms of common programming functions to give you a much easier editing platform to work with, called the Easy Edit page (see Figure 10.17). Better yet, this page is useful for synthesists of every skill level. From novice to expert, the Easy Edit page offers quick and easy access to some of the most commonly used FM7 parameters. In this section, I will break this page down piece by piece to give you a better understanding of its purpose and function.

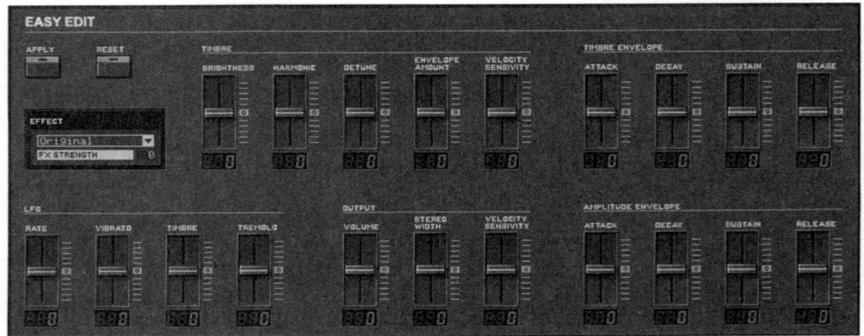

Figure 10.17

The Easy Edit page isn't just for beginners.

Main Parameters

Let's begin with the most common parameters of this interface, which are the main parameters. The main parameters are located in the upper-left corner of the Easy Edit page and contain the following controls:

- **Apply**—This button applies changes made to any of the parameters within the Easy Edit page, which are then stored in the edit buffer.
- **Reset**—Click this button to restore any edits made to the original FM7 parameters. This will not work after Apply has been selected.
- **Effect Select**—This dialog is used to select one of several real-time effects and assign it a strength value.

Timbre Parameters

To the right of the main parameters are the timbre parameters, which shape and enhance the sound of a preset with envelopes and brightness controls, in addition to velocity-themed controls. Although there are two parts to the timbre parameters (Timbre and Timbre Envelope), let's list all of the available parameters in one list. Note that these parameters are bipolar, which means that they produce numeric values above and below zero.

- **Brightness**—This slider cuts and boosts a preset's treble content.
- **Harmonic**—This slider adds and subtracts harmonics (frequencies) from the overall signal. Notice that as you alter this parameter, the spectrum and waveform displays in the upper-right corner reflect these changes.
- **Detune**—This slider alters the tuning between oscillators.
- **Envelope Amount**—This slider determines how much the timbre envelope affects the sound.
- **Velocity Sensitivity**—This slider links the timbre to the velocities at which a note is played.
- **Attack**—This slider determines how long it will take before the timbre settings reach their maximum value.
- **Decay**—This slider determines the rate of decay from the maximum to the sustain level.
- **Sustain**—This slider determines the amount of sustain time before the level of the timbre begins to drop.
- **Release**—This slider determines the amount of time before the envelope will reach a value of 0.

The LFO Parameters

The FM7 Easy page includes an LFO to modulate related Easy page parameters, including:

- **Rate**—This determines the speed of modulation.
- **Vibrato**—This slider modulates the pitch of the FM7 preset.
- **Timbre**—This slider modulates the frequency response of the timbre parameters.
- **Tremolo**—This slider modulates the overall amplitude of the FM7 preset.

The Output/Amp Envelope Parameters

Rounding out the Easy Edit page are the output and amp envelope parameters, which affect the dynamic characteristics of an FM7 preset in addition to its overall amplitude. Let's begin with the output parameters.

- **Volume**—This slider affects the overall amplitude of the FM7.

- **Stereo Width**—This slider adjusts the spread of the oscillators within the stereo field. Assigning a positive value to this slider creates a wide spread, while a negative value will box in the overall sound.
- **Velocity Sensitivity**—This slider determines how much the overall amplitude of the FM7 will be affected by varying velocities.

The amp envelope alters the dynamic character of an FM7 preset. If you want to create a preset that fades in or out slowly, you can use the attack and release parameters, respectively. As we already covered the basic amp parameters in the timbre parameters, there is no need to review them again, so it's left to your experimentation with the supplied parameters.

The Modulation Page

The Modulation page is one of the most creative points of the FM7 because it offers so many routing possibilities and a fairly easy to understand interface, although you might disagree the first time you look at it (see Figure 10.18). After I take you through the parameters of the Modulation page and a quick tutorial, I'm sure you'll change your mind.

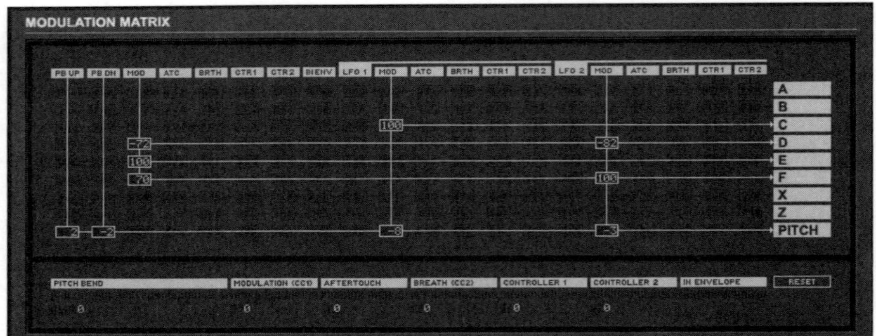

Figure 10.18
The Modulation page—Route any modulation source to any or all operators.

To begin, let's cover the basic layout of the Modulation page. The interface shown in Figure 10.18 is known as the *Modulation matrix*, with modulation sources placed in columns and destinations placed in rows. This layout enables you to send the same modulation source, such as LFO1, to all of the various FM7 operators, as well as pitch.

Since you already know the purpose of the operators, let's cover the modulation sources, which include:

- Pitch Bend Up/Down (PB UP/DN)
- Modulation Wheel (MOD)
- AfterTouch (ATC)
- Breath Controller (BRTH)
- MIDI Controller 1/2 (CTR1/2)
- Input Envelope (IN ENV)
- Main LFO1 Output (LFO1)
- LFO1 Controlled by Mod Wheel (LFO1 MOD)
- LFO1 Controlled by AfterTouch (LFO1 ATC)
- LFO1 Controlled by Breath Control (LFO1 BRTH)
- LFO1 Controlled by MIDI Control 1 (LFO1 CTRL1)
- LFO1 Controlled by MIDI Control 2 (LFO1 CTRL2)
- LFO2 Controlled by Mod Wheel (LFO2 MOD)
- LFO2 Controlled by AfterTouch (LFO2 ATC)
- LFO2 Controlled by Breath Control (LFO2 BRTH)
- LFO2 Controlled by MIDI Control 1 (LFO2 CTRL1)
- LFO2 Controlled by MIDI Control 2 (LFO2 CTRL2)

Located just below the Modulation matrix, the Modulation Monitor and Controls displays seven types of modulation information as the FM7 is played live with a keyboard or a computer mouse. Play a note on your keyboard and use either the modulation or pitch bend wheel, and you will see your real-time MIDI data displayed in its assigned spaces. Furthermore, each of these monitors includes a numeric dialog underneath, which can be used to assign a value to each monitor. Simply click and drag up or down with your mouse within each dialog. If at any point you would like to start over, just click once on the Reset button.

Assigning Modulation Sources

By now, you should have a pretty good grasp of the Modulation matrix interface, so let me show you how easy it is to assign modulation sources. First, let's locate an FM7 preset with a few active modulation routings, such as preset number 9, called Tronflute. Looking at Figure 10.19, you can see that this preset uses both LFO1 and 2, which when played create a vibrato. This is done in order to emulate the audible characteristics of an actual flute, which naturally generates vibrato with sustained notes.

Looking below the matrix, you can see that a value has been assigned to Controller 22, which is breath control. This enables you to enhance the playing characteristics of a flute even further by using an additional piece of MIDI hardware called a *breath controller*, which uses wind pressure to trigger the dynamics of the flute preset. It is a common feature to find these days on most hardware synths, but in 1983 it was a new technology. You simply blow into the breath controller while playing notes on the Virtual Keyboard, and this will enhance the attack of the flute sound. It also works well for other woodwind instrument presets, such as saxophones and clarinets.

Getting back to the matrix, let's make a few alterations to the assigned modulation sources, starting with the pitch bend parameters. As you can see, both pitch bend up and pitch bend down have assigned values of +/– 2, respectively. Let's broaden the pitch bend range by clicking and dragging upward within the numeric dialog of pitch bend up and click and drag downward within the numeric dialog of pitch bend down. This will greatly increase the pitch bend potential of the preset when using the pitch bend wheel (see Figure 10.20). Also notice that the breath noise of the Tronflute preset does not change when making pitch bend adjustments, since it is not a pitch-specific sound like a percussion preset.

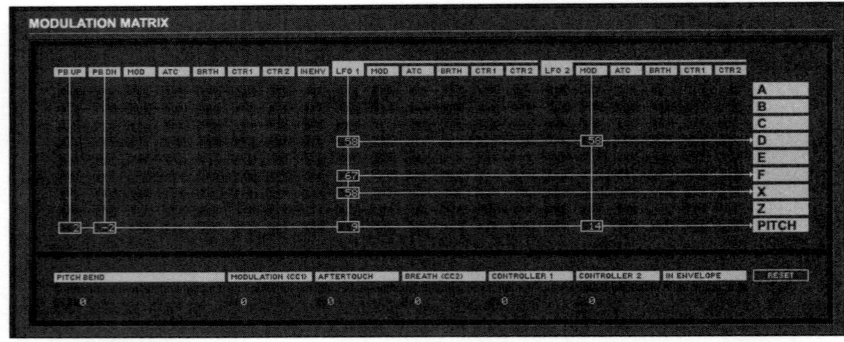

Figure 10.19
The Tronflute preset uses both LFO1 and 2 to mimic the characteristics of a flute by creating a vibrato effect.

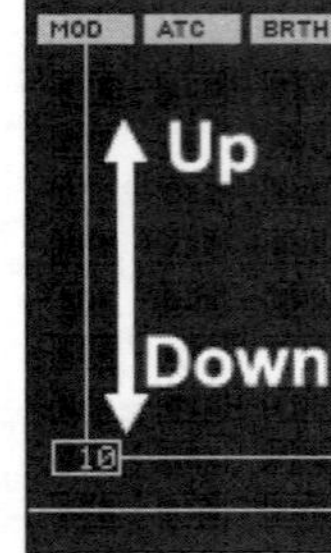

Figure 10.20
Click and drag up or down within a numeric dialog to make changes to any modulation source.

Now, let's introduce a bit of modulation wheel to Operator X, which will produce a very slight enhancement to its active filter. To do this, first locate the proper modulation source column (MOD) and then match it up with the appropriate destination row (Operator X). Now, click and drag upward within its numeric dialog and assign a value of 100. Once you are finished, play a note on your keyboard and use the modulation wheel, at which point you should hear a slight alteration to the preset filter. To remove the modulation, simply double-click on the source.

The LFO Page

No synthesizer would be complete without some kind of LFO functions, and the FM7 is no exception. The LFO page of the FM7 includes two independent LFOs, which can be used to perform one or several modulations to any active operator (see Figure 10.21).

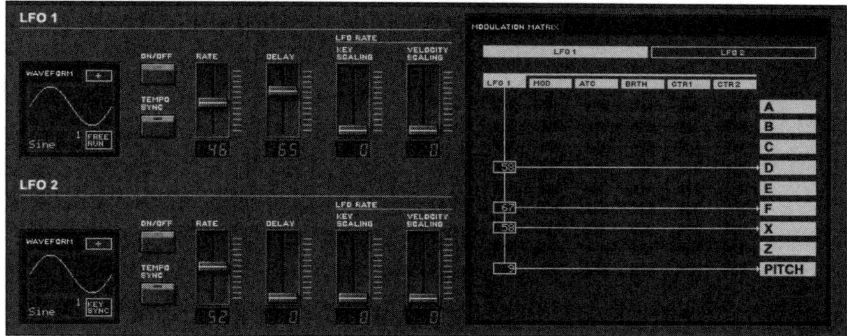

Figure 10.21
The FM7 includes two independent low frequency oscillators to modulate several FM7 operators.

The Main LFO Parameters

Let's now review the basic parameters of the LFO page. Note that LFO 1 and 2 include identical parameter sets, so there's no need to review them twice.

- **Waveform**—This dialog selects one of 33 individual waveforms. Clicking on the numeric dialog and dragging up or down can select everything from simple sine waves to customized waveforms.
- **Waveform Sign**—This parameter toggles between positive and negative polarities of an LFO waveform.

- **Free Run/Key Sync**—This dialog toggles between Free Run mode (the LFO waveform runs continuously) and Key Sync mode (the LFO resets every time a key is depressed).
- **On/Off**—This button turns the LFO section on or off.
- **Tempo Sync**—This button synchronizes the LFO to any incoming MIDI clock tempo.
- **Rate**—This slider adjusts the speed or frequency of the LFO waveform.
- **Key Scaling**—This slider alters the frequency of the LFO the higher a note is played on the keyboard.
- **Velocity Scaling**—This slider alters the frequency of the LFO according to the velocity of a played note.

The LFO Matrix

Occupying the right side of the LFO page, the LFO matrix performs the same tasks as the LFO functions of the Modulation matrix, which we looked at earlier in this chapter. You can toggle between the two LFO matrixes by clicking on their appropriate view buttons, at which time you can then proceed to assign various LFO modulation sources to one or several FM7 operators by clicking and dragging up and down. Once you have made adjustments to the LFO matrix, you can view any changes made from the LFO and Modulation pages. You can remove any assigned values to either matrix by simply double-clicking on the appropriate numeric value.

The Pitch Page

Another big plus of FM synthesis is its pitch shifting and tuning capabilities, which make it possible to play the synth in even-tempered tuning and non-standard tuning. *Even-tempered tuning* is the traditional tuning standard of music based in the Western civilization, in which an octave is evenly divided into 12 equal intervals. But as you know, the world is a big place, and it is filled with alternate tuning structures, most of which cannot be replicated easily by many forms of synthesis.

The FM7 Pitch page not only offers the ability to retune itself, but it also incorporates standard play parameters such as portamento and several modulation possibilities (see Figure 10.22).

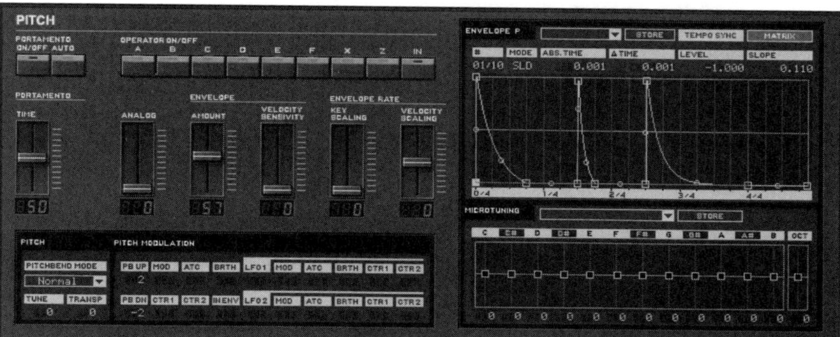

Figure 10.22
The Pitch page is used to adjust the tuning of the FM7 and uses popular play parameters such as portamento.

> **ESSENTIAL LISTENING—BEAUTY IN THE BEAST**
>
> As alternate tunings are a bit off the beaten path, it's difficult to track down relevant audio examples. But one such recording that comes to mind is *Beauty in the Beast* by synthesist/composer Wendy Carlos. Originally released in 1986, *Beauty in the Beast* was an avant-garde exploration of music compositions by way of alternate tunings. Out of print for several years, it has been recently remastered and re-released by East Side Digital with several additional features, including a "text enhanced" CD that includes a very in-depth study into the world of alternate tunings.

Portamento Parameters

The Portamento parameters can be found in the upper-left corner of the Pitch page. Portamento is a popular sliding effect used to slur between notes played on the keyboard. It's best used when playing monophonic presets, such as flutes, saxes, and trumpets. It can also be used creatively on pad sounds to create a polyphonic slide between chords.

- **Portamento On/Off**—This button activates the portamento functions.
- **Auto**—When activated, the portamento effect will be heard only when notes are played with legato (no gaps between notes).
- **Portamento Time**—This slider adjusts the slide time between each note played on the keyboard.

Envelope Parameters

Located to the right, the Envelope parameters work in combination with the pitch envelope, which we'll look at later in this chapter. As you can see, this section is divided into three sections: Analog, Envelope, and Envelope Rate.

- **Analog**—This slider introduces the tuning behaviors of a standard hardware FM synth.

- **Amount**—This slider determines how much the pitch envelope affects the pitch.
- **Velocity Sensitivity**—This slider determines how different velocity values alter the pitch.
- **Key Scaling**—This slider alters the envelope amount in relation to notes played on a MIDI keyboard.
- **Velocity Scaling**—This slider alters the envelope amount in relation to varying velocities played on a MIDI keyboard.

Pitch Bend Parameters

Located just underneath the Portamento parameters, the pitch bend parameters are used to assign specific note boundaries to the overall pitch bend potential of the FM7. At the top of this section, Pitchbend Mode offers one of four different modes, which can be selected by using the pull-down menu.

- **Normal**—Treats all notes equally.
- **Lowest**—Affects the lowest note only when several notes are held.
- **Highest**—Affects the highest note only when several notes are held.
- **Key On**—Allows the pitch bend to function with only held keys.

Underneath Pitchbend Mode, the Tune parameter adjusts the overall pitch of the FM7 by cent increments and has a range of –99 to 100 cents. Just to the right, the Transpose parameter adjusts the overall tuning of the FM7 in semitone increments and has a range of +/– two octaves.

Pitch Modulation

The Pitch Modulation matrix is a replication of the corresponding bottom row of the matrix found on the Modulation page. It functions exactly the same as the Modulation matrix, and any values assigned to the Pitch Modulation matrix will be reflected on the Modulation page.

Microtuning Parameters

The Microtuning parameters of the FM7 enable you to alter the pitch between each note on the Virtual Keyboard to make it possible to use the FM7 in unevenly tempered music. As mentioned earlier in this section, this feature is difficult to implement in most other forms of synthesis, but here it's a snap. In Figure 10.23, you can see that the main interface is subdivided into 12 individual pitch nodes, which relate to a specific key on the Virtual Keyboard. These nodes can be clicked and dragged up or down to alter their relative pitch.

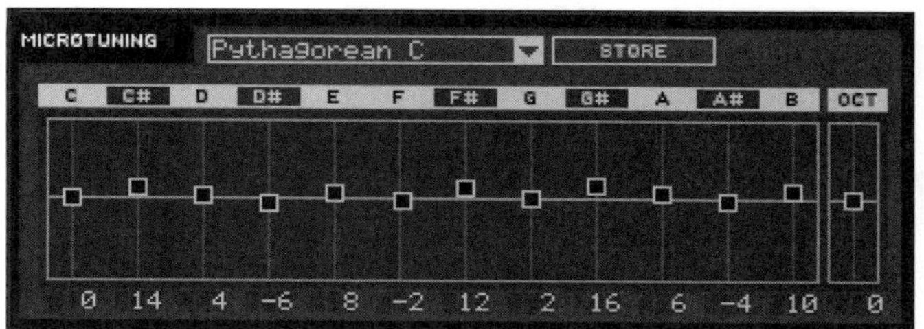

Figure 10.23
The Microtuning parameters of the Pitch page make it possible to play the FM7 with non-tempered or alternate tunings.

The Octave node functions much differently than the individual note nodes, as its purpose is to gradually sharpen or flatten the pitches of notes played on the Virtual Keyboard in relation to middle C, which remains unaffected. For example, if you assign a value of 20 to the Octave parameter, as you play higher notes on the keyboard, you will hear them gradually sharpen in pitch the further away you get from middle C. This effect really becomes apparent when you play middle C and another C note one or two octaves above middle C.

Perhaps the most helpful feature of this section is the abundance of tuning presets available in the provided pull-down menu, located just above the individual note nodes. Here you will find tuning presets that cover the globe, from the bagpipes of Scotland to the outrageous tunings of West Africa. You can also create your own tuning presets and store them by clicking the Store button just to the right.

Pitch Envelope Parameters

Just above the Microtuning parameters is the pitch envelope, which is used to alter pitch over a set period of time. Unlike the standard parameter styles of an envelope generator (such as sliders and knobs), the pitch envelope uses *breakpoints* to introduce new levels to the envelope curve. These breakpoints can then be moved up, down, left, and right to alter the attack, decay, sustain, and release. To create a breakpoint, just right-click (Ctrl+click on the Mac) along the timeline of the Pitch Envelope interface.

Let's look at an example of creating breakpoints.

1. On the Library page, click Init Edit Buffer. This will initialize the FM7 preset.
2. Select the Pitch page and increase the Envelope Amount slider, so you hear the pitch alter as you add breakpoints.
3. Right-click or Ctrl+click anywhere along the pitch envelope timeline to create a breakpoint (see Figure 10.24).

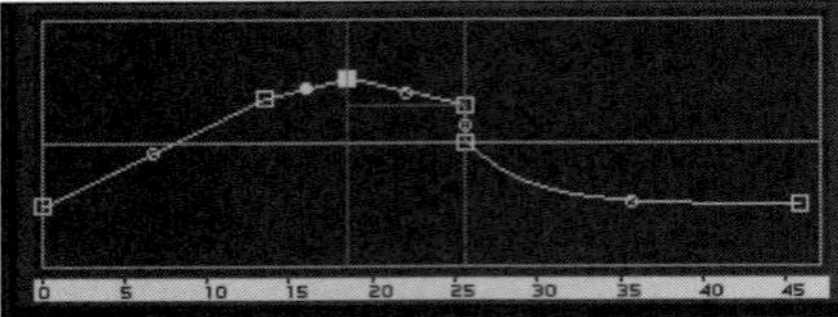

Figure 10.24
Right-click with your mouse in Windows or Ctrl+click on the Mac to create a breakpoint within the pitch envelope.

4 Click and drag the new breakpoint up or down to alter the pitch. Now play a note from the Virtual Keyboard to hear the results.

At this point, you can begin to click and drag the additional breakpoints located to the immediate left side of the pitch envelope timeline to the right in order to alter the pitch even further. When you finish, you should see something similar to Figure 10.25.

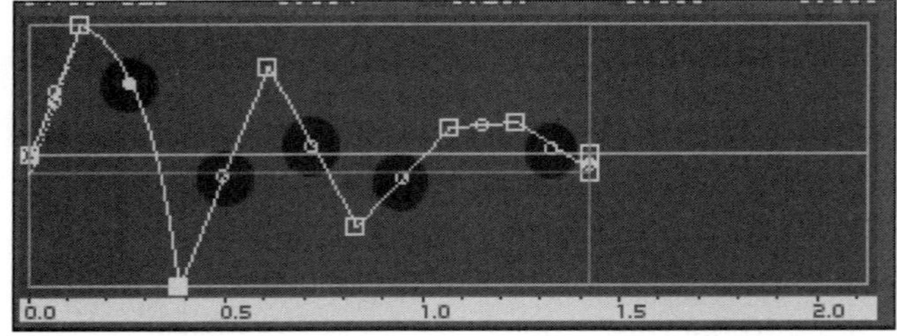

Figure 10.25
The pitch envelope now has several breakpoints. Also note the circular nodes between breakpoints, which can be clicked and dragged up or down to increase or decrease the intensity or "slope" of the envelope curve.

Looking back at the previous figure, you will now see two red vertical lines, which are used as sustain points whenever a key is depressed and held down. There are several interesting uses for this feature, especially when used in tempo with your music, but we'll hold off on this until the end of the chapter. Instead, let's acquaint ourselves with the function strip parameters.

- **Envelope Preset**—This pop-up menu supplies a long list of pitch envelope presets.
- **Store**—This button stores an envelope pattern to be used again later.
- **Tempo Sync**—This button synchronizes the pitch envelope to incoming MIDI clock signals.
- **Matrix**—This button toggles between the pitch envelope and Algorithm matrix of the FM7 operators.

THE FM ALGORITHM MATRIX

From a programming perspective, the FM7 Algorithm matrix is the most comprehensible and diverse FM programmer around (see Figure 10.26). To start, each of the operators is arranged diagonally downward from left to right, with Operators A–F as the main signal generators, Operator X as a noise generator, Operator Z as a filter, and Operator I as the audio input. Clicking on any of the operators will automatically display its graphic interface on the left side of the FM7. Right-clicking on an operator with your mouse (Ctrl+click for Mac users) will activate a selected operator. Active operators are color coded with a bright green hue, while inactive operators are grayed out.

Above, below, and to the right of every operator is a series of empty cells, which are used to route the output of a selected operator to one of several destinations within the FM7. To enter a value in any of these cells, simply click and drag up or down in the cell and choose a value between 1 and 100. As an example, let's look at the cells above, below, and to the side of Operator A (see Figure 10.27).

- **Above**—This cell feeds the output of Operator A back to its input, thus creating a feedback loop that sounds like a strong digital distortion.
- **Right**—This cell feeds the output of the preceding operator to the input of the preceding operator. In other words, route the output of Operator B to the input of Operator A.
- **Below**—This cell routes the output of an operator to the input of another operator, with the intention of using it as a modulator. For example, you can use the empty cell below Operator A to send its output to Operator B's input. Also note that an operator can be routed to any or all of the other operators in the Algorithm matrix.
- **Far Below**—At the far bottom of every operator is a cell to route its output to the main audio outputs of the FM7 and place it in the stereo field.

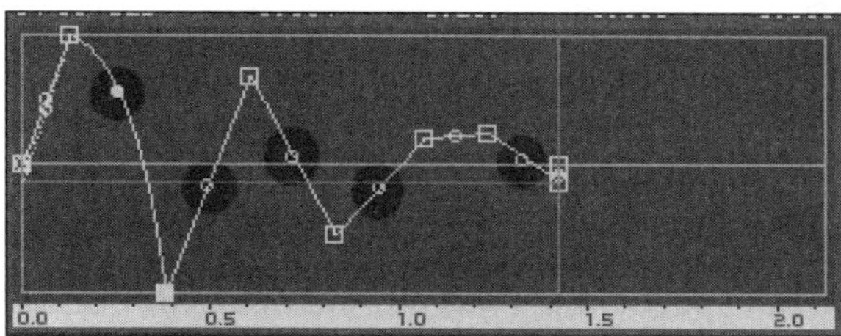

Figure 10.26
The FM7 Algorithm matrix is used to route all outputs of the operators to one or all of several possible destinations.

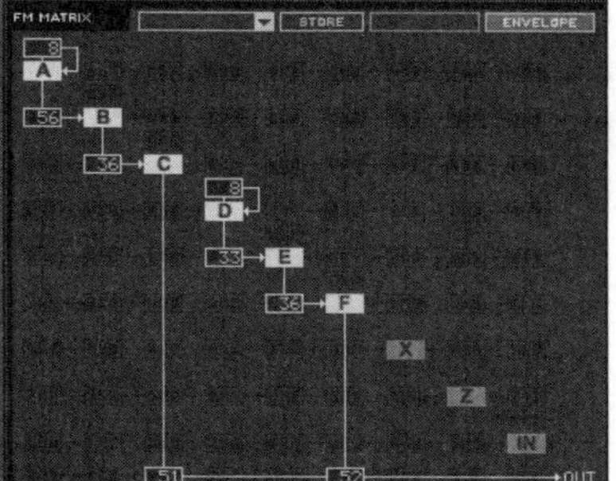

Figure 10.27
The empty cells of each operator are used to paint your synthetic masterpiece.

Located below the function strip, the envelope parameter strip alters the values of the breakpoints.

- **#**—This dialog displays the currently selected breakpoint in the envelope curve.
- **Mode**—This dialog switches between two edit options, Fix and Slide. In Slide mode, whenever a breakpoint is moved left or right, any following breakpoints to the right will move accordingly. When in Fix mode, the additional breakpoints do not move.
- **Abs. Time**—Displays the time from the beginning of the envelope to the breakpoint being edited.
- **Delta Time**—Displays the time from an edited breakpoint to the one preceding it.
- **Level**—Displays the breakpoint level.
- **Slope**—This dialog assigns an intensity or curve to the circular node between two breakpoints in an envelope curve. Click and drag up or down to alter this parameter. Also note that you can click and drag the node itself on the envelope timeline.

> **ZOOMING IN AND OUT**
>
> The pitch envelope has the ability to zoom in and out along the timeline, which comes in handy, especially when creating long, droning pad presets. To zoom in and out, use the right mouse button (or hold down the Ctrl key on the Mac) and then click and drag left and right to zoom in and out, respectively.
>
> You can also resize the timeline to display the entire envelope curve automatically by double-clicking on the timeline bar.

The Operator Pages

At the heart of the FM7 are the operator pages, which are solely responsible for generating its sound. As stated earlier in this chapter, an operator consists of an oscillator, amplifier, and envelope generator, all of which are compiled into one of several different combinations called algorithms. Over the next couple of pages, we'll discuss the various operator parameters, how they work, and how to string them together when constructing custom FM7 presets. Since Operator pages A–F have identical parameter sets, select any of these pages before continuing.

> **OPERATION: ACTIVATION**
>
> Although it's not required at this point, you could begin this section by clicking on the INIT EDIT BUFFER button in the upper-right corner of the Library page in order to clear the edit buffer. The FM7 will then disable all its operators except for Operator F. In order to use any of the other operators, you will need to reactivate them by clicking on their matching On/Off button, which is found along the operator on/off strip on the upper-left region of any operator page (see Figure 10.28).

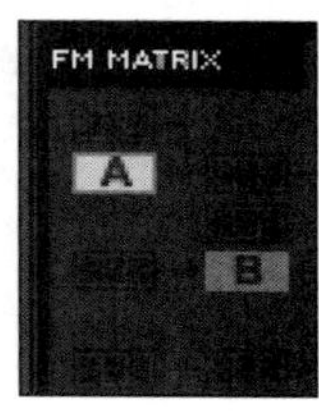

Figure 10.28
The operator on/off strip activates the signal generating operators (A–F), the effect generating operators (X, Z), and the audio input operator (I).

Operators A–F

As mentioned above, Operators A–F are the main sound sources of the FM7. Use the page select strip and click on the operator of choice to navigate between the different pages. The selected operator's graphic interface will immediately be displayed below, and its matching button in the page select strip will be color-coded red. Since Operators A–F share identical but independent parameters, we'll just look at the parameters of a single operator. Use Figure 10.29 as a reference as we review the operator parameters.

Figure 10.29
Operators A–F generate the FM7's sound.

The Copy and Paste buttons copy an operator's parameter values to a different operator. This is a good timesaver, and it makes the process of building sounds one operator at a time seamless. For example, let's assume that you have programmed Operator A to your liking and would like to duplicate its values on Operator F, with the intention of increasing its pitch by one octave. Ordinarily, you would have to reprogram Operator F one parameter at a time, but by using Copy and Paste, it's a much quicker process.

1. With Operator A selected, click on the Copy button. This will enter all of the parameter values of Operator A into the edit buffer. Also note that the Paste button LED is lit up.
2. Select Operator F from the page strip.

3 Click on the Paste button, and all Operator A values will be pasted to Operator F.

Located at the bottom left of the operator page are the Waveform Selector controls. Each operator has the ability to generate one of 32 different waveforms. This differs greatly from the old DX7, which could generate only sine waves. You can choose sine waves, square waves, saw tooth waves, and several variations based upon these fundamentals. Clicking and dragging up and down in the numeric dialog can select a new waveform, after which you can specify whether you want this waveform to run in Free Run or Key Sync mode.

- **Key Sync** mode will automatically reset the oscillator phase whenever a new note is played. This is useful when you need a group of oscillators to maintain an overall pitch while modulating.
- **Free Run** mode will not reset the oscillator phase when a new note is played.

Located to the right of the Waveform Selector, the Amplitude Modulation matrix is a replication of the matrix found on the Modulation page. It functions exactly the same as the Modulation matrix, and any values assigned to the Amplitude Modulation matrix will be reflected on the Modulation page.

After an operator's waveform has been selected, the Frequency Ratio and Offset parameters (located above) specify its overall pitch and tuning. The Frequency Ratio dialog sets the operator pitch in relation to the fundamental pitch of the actual note played on the Virtual Keyboard. The value of this dialog can be set by clicking and dragging up or down in the dialog window or by using the up/down arrow keys. Here is how the numeric values correspond to pitch:

- When set at 1.0000, the generated frequency is the same as the fundamental pitch.
- When set at 2.0000, the generated frequency will be exactly one octave higher.
- When set at 3.0000, the generated frequency will be an octave plus one fifth higher.
- When set at 4.0000, the generated frequency will be two octaves higher than the fundamental pitch.

In addition to using the Frequency Ratio dialog in exact integers, making use of the remaining decimal values leads to some very detuned and dissonant textures, which is best described by the following example:

1. Initialize the FM7 by clicking the INIT EDIT BUFFER button in the Library page.
2. Select Operator F and you'll see that its Frequency Ratio value has been set to 1.0000, which is the fundamental frequency.
3. Activate and select Operator E. Use the Output Level slider (just to the right of the Frequency Ratio parameters) to assign amplitude to it. Play the Virtual Keyboard, and you should now hear both operators. While you're at it, use the waveform selector to choose a different waveform for Operator E to make this sound a little more interesting.
4. Set the frequency ratio of Operator E to 2.0000 and play the Virtual Keyboard to hear the difference. Note that the spectrum and waveform displays in the upper-right corner of the FM7 have reflected the new harmonic content since beginning this tutorial.
5. Now use the Frequency Ratio dialog to assign decimal values to Operator E. As you make changes to this dialog, play any key on the Virtual Keyboard to hear the dissonance between the operators.

Of course, this example gets even better when using the envelope generator, but we'll get to that in the programming with FM section of this chapter. The remaining offset parameter enhances the dissonance even further by inserting separation between two operators. Use the up/down arrow keys to assign values to this dialog and listen to the results.

Now let's cover the more common parameters of the operator page, which are located to the right of the frequency ratio and offset parameters.

- **Level**—This slider sets the overall amplitude for an operator. Note that after initializing the FM7, you must assign a level to any activate operators, as they are all set to 0 with the exception of Operator F.
- **Pan**—This slider places the operator within the stereo field.
- **Velocity Sensitivity**—This slider determines how different velocity values alter the amplitude of an operator.
- **Key Scaling**—This slider alters the envelope amount in relation to notes played on a MIDI keyboard.
- **Velocity Scaling**—This slider alters the envelope amount in relation to varying velocities played on a MIDI keyboard.

Rounding out the operator interface are the envelope generator and the key scaling parameters. Note that this envelope generator functions similarly to the one found on the Pitch page. The only difference here is that the generator on the Pitch page alters the dynamics according to pitch, while the generator on the operator pages alters the dynamics according to amplitude. That said, the same parameters and rules apply here, so refer back to the Pitch page for more information.

The key scaling graph maps how the amplitude of an operator varies across the range of the Virtual Keyboard and includes the following parameters:

- **Note**—This dialog displays the MIDI note number in relation to a selected breakpoint along the key scaling graph.
- **Level**—This dialog displays the amplitude level of any selected breakpoint along the key scaling graph.
- **Slope**—This dialog assigns an intensity or curve to the circular node between two breakpoints in the key scaling envelope curve.

It uses a system of breakpoints, just like the ones found within any FM7 envelope generator. Try the following example:

1. Navigate to the circular node between the two left breakpoints and right-click (Ctrl+click for Mac users) to create a new breakpoint.
2. Click and drag the new breakpoint down until the Level dialog reads –65.
3. Click and drag the breakpoint at the far left of the key scaling graph, and then click and drag it down until the Level dialog reads –65. You should now have a key scale curve similar to that shown in Figure 10.30.
4. Play both the low and high notes of the Virtual Keyboard, and you will hear a radical difference in the oscillator's amplitude when playing the higher keys.

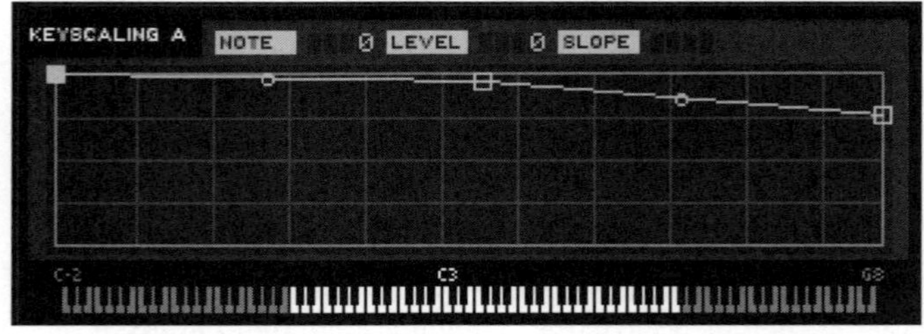

Figure 10.30
The key scaling graph is an easy way to map and modify the amplitude of an operator across the keyboard range.

Operator X

Operator X is indeed an operator in FM terms. It generates a signal and conforms to the guidelines of FM synthesis; it can be used as either a modulator or carrier. Furthermore, upon looking at Figure 10.31, you can see that it shares many similar parameters to those found on Operators A–F. However, Operator X is designed and intended to be used as a noise generator as well as a simple filter, as you will see in this section. Since there are many familiar operator parameters here, we'll just discuss those exclusive to Operator X. Let's start with the buttons and displays.

- **Page 2**—This button displays the second page of Operator X parameters.
- **Bypass**—This button bypasses Operator X entirely.
- **Saturation Curve**—This diagram displays the shape of the saturation effect created by Operator X. While it does not have any parameters of its own, its shape alters in accordance to the values set by the Saturator parameters.

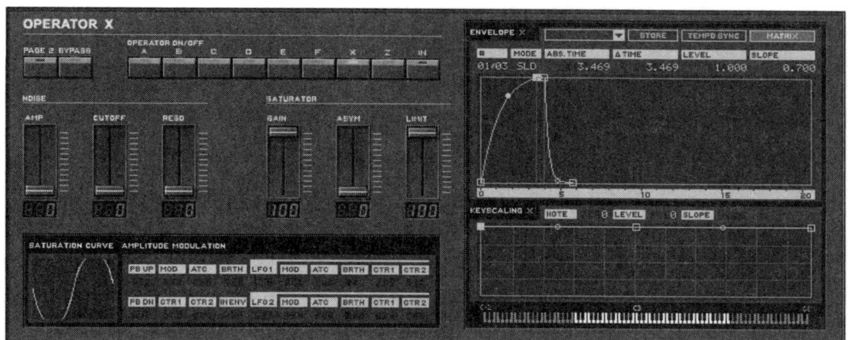

Figure 10.31

Operator X is a noise generator and filter effect that can be used as either a modulator or carrier.

Located to the right of the saturation curve, the Amplitude Modulation matrix is a replication of the Operator X row of the matrix found on the Modulation page. It functions exactly the same as the Modulation matrix, and any values assigned to the Amplitude Modulation matrix will be reflected on the Modulation page.

Operator X's common parameters are split into several sections: Noise, Saturator, Output, and Envelope Rate. Let's review these parameters starting with the first page:

- **Noise Amp**—This slider sets the noise level.
- **Noise Cutoff**—This slider controls the amount of cutoff for the low pass filter embedded within the noise generator.

- **Noise Resonance**—This slider controls the amount of resonance for the low pass filter embedded within the noise generator.
- **Saturator Gain**—This slider assigns a gain level to the saturator and directly affects the behavior of the Asy parameter.
- **Saturator Asy**—This slider alters the symmetry or regularity of the saturator.
- **Saturator Limit**—This slider is used to clip, or distort, the positive and negative parts of the preset waveform.

If you click the Page 2 button to display its parameters, you'll find that it shares the same parameters as those found on Operators A–F. But note that the Noise Level slider is viewable from Page 2 as well, making it convenient to alter the amplitude of the noise generator from either Page 1 or 2.

Operator Z

Unlike its noisy brother, Operator Z is not quite a run of the mill operator. Its job is to provide two filters for influencing the overall character of FM7 presets (see Figure 10.32). Since there are several identical parameters on the Operator Z interface, we'll skip over those and look at its unique parameters.

- **Filter Display Curve**—This diagram displays the shape and response of the filter effect.
- **Cutoff**—This slider controls the cutoff of both filters 1 and 2.
- **Resonance**—This dialog sets the amount of resonance for the filters. Either use the up/down arrows to assign a value or click and drag up and down inside the dialog with your mouse. Also note that there is a second instance of Resonance to the right, which affects filter 2.
- **Envelope Amount**—This dialog determines how much the envelope affects the filter.

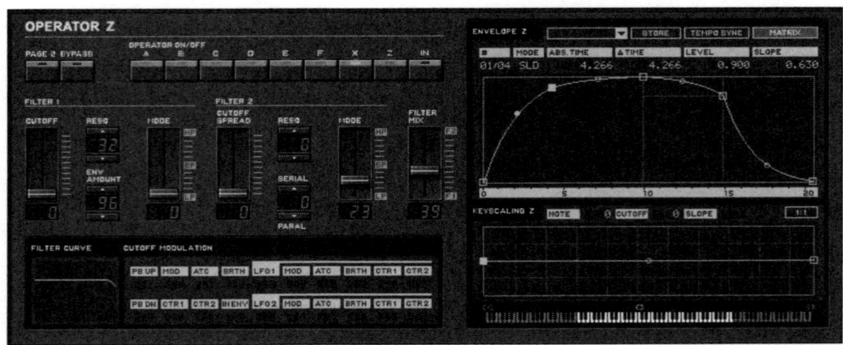

Figure 10.32
Operator Z provides two filters for shape shifting FM fun.

- **Mode**—This slider selects between one of three filter modes: low pass, band pass, and high pass.
- **Cutoff Spread**—This slider creates an offset of the cutoff values between filters 1 and 2.
- **Serial/Parallel**—This dialog toggles the two filters between Serial mode and Parallel mode (the same input feeds to both filters separately and are then mixed together).
- **Filter Mix**—This slider adjusts the mix between filters 1 and 2.

Located to the right of the Filter Curve, the Cutoff Modulation matrix is a replication of the Operator Z row of the matrix found on the Modulation page. It functions exactly the same as the Modulation matrix, and any values assigned to the Cutoff Modulation matrix will be reflected on the Modulation page.

OPERATOR I

The one operator that doesn't have its own dedicated page is Operator I, which is the audio input operator of the FM7. As previously mentioned, the FM7 is capable of receiving an audio signal and manipulating it with frequency modulation. I'll show you how routing audio to the FM7 is accomplished by selecting preset 127, named Input as Carrier, and then explain how the audio input routing is made possible by using the FM matrix as a reference guide.

As you can see from Figure 10.33, Operator F (the modulator) is active, and its output has been routed to the input Operator I (the carrier), which is then routed to the main output of the FM7. Assuming that you have set up the FM7 to receive audio input from the Audio Settings option of the System pull-down menu, you should be able to plug in a microphone and hear your voice pass through the FM7 unaffected. However, if you press and hold a key on the Virtual Keyboard and speak through the mic, you should hear a wavering vibrato sound, caused by Operator F, which is modulating your voice. You can change the vibrato rate by using the Frequency Ratio dialog, which is currently set at .0369, and you can change the shape of the vibrato by using the Waveform Selector controls.

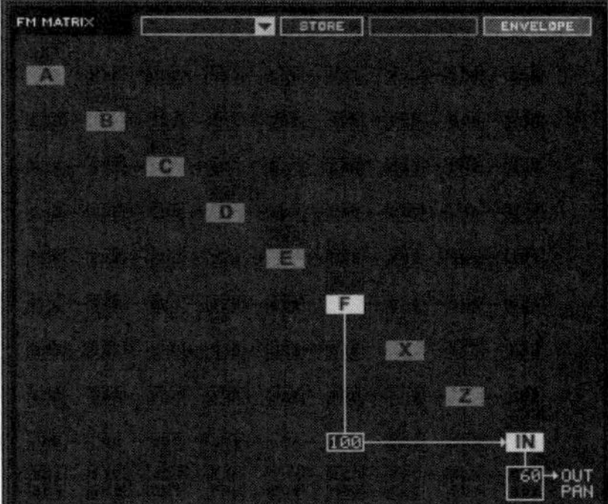

Figure 10.33

In this example of the FM Algorithm matrix, the output of the operator (the modulator) is being fed to the input of Operator I (the carrier). This enables you to use an audio signal and manipulate it via frequency modulation.

Programming with FM Synthesis

As you have read throughout the last several pages, there's a lot of programming potential embedded within FM synthesis, all of which can be easily realized with the help of a good FM soft synth. It's time to put your FM knowledge to the test and follow along as I take you through a few FM programming tutorials. Over the course of the next few pages, you'll learn how to create:

- A bass preset
- A pad preset

INITIALIZE THE FM7

Before beginning this section, take a moment to initialize the FM7 by clicking on the INIT EDIT BUFFER button in the Library page.

Programming a Bass Preset

In this first tutorial, I will take you through the steps of programming a bass preset with the FM7. Since this is a tutorial for beginners, we will use just two operators to construct this preset. If you are looking for something a little more complicated, skip over this tutorial and proceed to the next section, where you will learn how to program a pad preset, which is much more involved.

1 To start, turn off Operator F by clicking on its button in the operator on/off strip. This is more of a personal preference, since I like to begin programming with Operator A rather than F.

2 Select Operator A and activate it by clicking on its power button in the operator on/off strip. Navigate to its envelope generator and click on the Matrix button to view the Algorithm matrix (see Figure 10.34).

3 As you can see, Operator A is active but is not sending any signal to the FM7 main output, so click and drag upward in the lower-left corner cell of the matrix to send Operator A to the main output. Assign a value of 100 and press a key on the Virtual Keyboard to hear the default sine wave. We now have our fundamental frequency.

4 Activate Operator B and route its output to the FM7 main output using the same method as before, but this time assign a value of 70. This will now give us two sine waves to work with, but we're about to jazz it up a bit by having Operator A modulate Operator B. Click and drag upward in the cell just below Operator A in the matrix to route Operator A to B. Assign a value of

70 and notice that the waveform and spectrum displays of the FM7 have reflected the new spectral data created by this connection.

5 With Operator A's graphic display still active, set the Frequency Ratio dialog to .9900 and use the waveform display to select a square wave. Play the preset now, and the signal will buzz like a square wave, but it will also have a slight wavering quality to it.

6 Next, click and drag upward in the matrix cell just above Operator B to route its output directly back to its input, which creates a fantastic feedback loop. Assign a value of 40 (see Figure 10.35).

7 The last modification we'll make to Operator A is its envelope generator. Use the provided breakpoints of the generator to create a slightly slower attack to Operator A. When you're done, you should see an envelope similar to Figure 10.36.

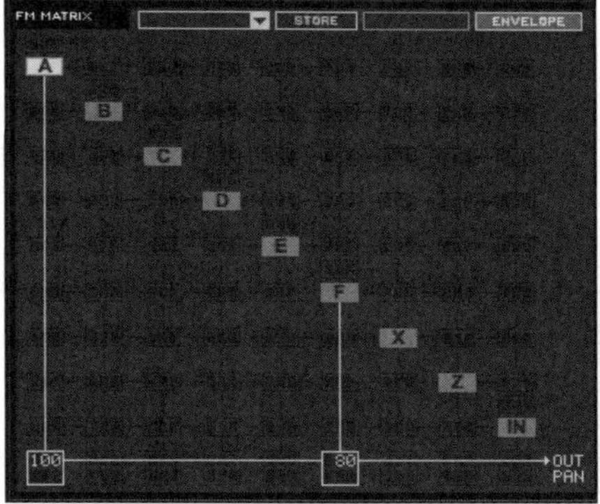

Figure 10.34
The Algorithm matrix is used to link up and configure all of the FM7 operators. Currently, you can see that an output value has been assigned to the main output with Operator A (active) and Operator F (not active).

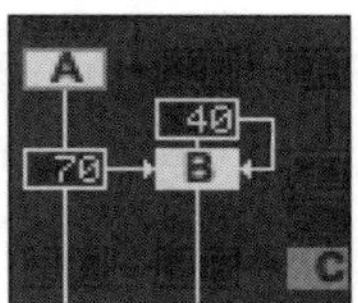

Figure 10.35
The output of an operator can be fed back to its input by using the cell directly above the operator. This is more commonly known as a feedback loop.

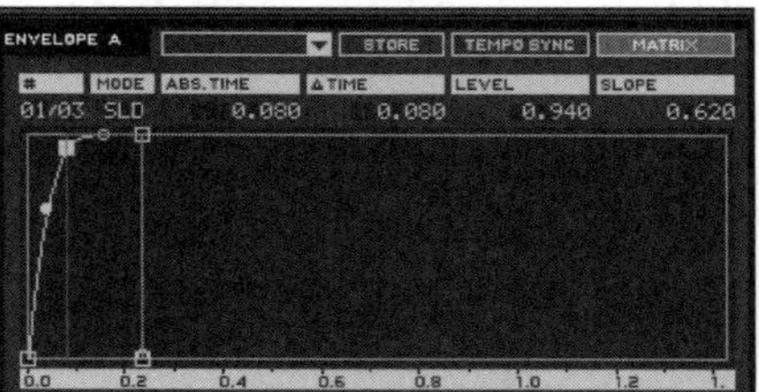

Figure 10.36
Use the breakpoints of the Operator A envelope generator to smooth out its attack.

At this point, we have created a pretty solid bass sound. Let's move on to the Pitch and Master pages.

1 Select the Pitch page and turn on the Portamento function and turn off the Auto function. Assign a Portamento value of 25 by using the Time slider just below.
2 Select the Master page and click the Mono button to place the FM7 in mono mode.
3 Use the Unison dialog to beef up the preset by assigning a value of 2, and then set the Unison Detune slider to 70. Play a note now, and it should sound much thicker and slightly detuned.
4 Activate the effects of the FM7 by clicking the Effect On/Off button.
5 Set the Delay section to the following values: Time 14, Feedback 17, Diffusion 0.
6 Set the Modulation section to the following values: Rate 1, Depth 75.

Play the FM7 now, and you should hear a big beefy-sounding bass synth. Don't forget to save your work by clicking the Store button.

DOWNLOAD THE BASS PRESET

For your convenience, I have created a bass preset based on the preceding tutorials, which you can find and download from this book's page at the Course Technology Web site: **www.courseptr.com.**

Programming a Pad Preset

Programming a pad preset is always a blast because the true synthetic nature of the FM7 shines through. In this tutorial, I am going to take you through the steps of creating a pad sound using almost all of the operators, a little filter, and a lot of tempo synced delay. Before beginning this tutorial, initialize the FM7 by clicking on the INIT EDIT BUFFER button in the Library page.

In order to make this as easy to follow as possible, I will build this preset one operator at a time, starting with Operator F.

1 Select Operator page F and use the waveform selector to choose the twentieth waveform. Use the Pan slider to assign a pan value of 70 and the Level slider to assign an output of 50.
2 Navigate to the envelope generator of Operator F, activate the Tempo Sync parameter, and create an envelope similar to the one shown in Figure 10.37.

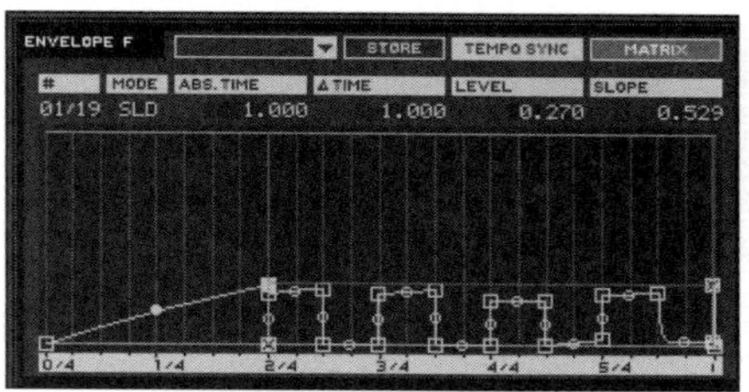

Figure 10.37

Use the Tempo Sync function of the envelope generator to create a series of breakpoints to construct an envelope similar to the one displayed here.

Next, let's introduce Operator A into the mix.

1. Select Operator page A and activate it. Use the Frequency Ratio dialog to assign a value of 3.0000.
2. Click on the Matrix button to view the Algorithm matrix and assign an output level of 40 from Operator A to the FM7 main output.
3. Use the Operator A waveform selector to choose the twentieth waveform. Use the Pan slider to assign a pan value of –70.
4. Click on the Envelope button to switch from the Algorithm matrix to the envelope generator. Click on the Preset pop-up menu and select the Same as OpF option. This will copy the envelope generator settings from Operator F to Operator A. After selecting this option, click on the Preset pop-up menu again and select Remove All Links so that you can make modifications to the envelope generator of Operator A without affecting Operator F.
5. Activate the Tempo Sync parameter and shift the breakpoints of the Operator A envelope to the right.

At this point, we have two fundamental sounds for our preset. Read on to see how to set up and use Operator B as a modulator for Operator A.

1. Select Operator page B and activate it. Use the Frequency Ratio dialog to assign a value of .0230.
2. Click on the Matrix button to view the Algorithm matrix and use the empty cell just below Operator A to route its output to Operator B by clicking and dragging up. Assign a value of 20.
3. Use the second empty cell above Operator B to route its output back to Operator A. Assign a value of 50. When you're finished, you should have a matrix configuration similar to Figure 10.38.

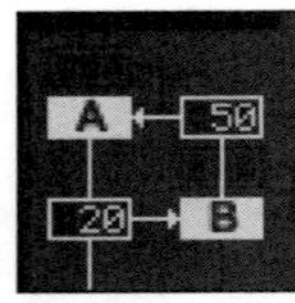

Figure 10.38
In this diagram, I have used the Algorithm matrix to send some of Operator A's output to Operator B, and I have routed Operator B's output back to Operator A to create a feedback loop of sorts.

Next, we're going to route Operator C to Operator Z to take advantage of its filters.

1 Select Operator page C and activate it. Use the Frequency Ratio dialog to assign a value of .5000.
2 Click on the Matrix button to view the Algorithm matrix and use the fifth empty cell below Operator C to route its output to Operator Z by clicking and dragging up. Assign a value of 100.
3 Use the empty cell above Operator C to route its output back to its own input. Assign a value of 40. When you're finished, you should have a matrix configuration similar to Figure 10.39.

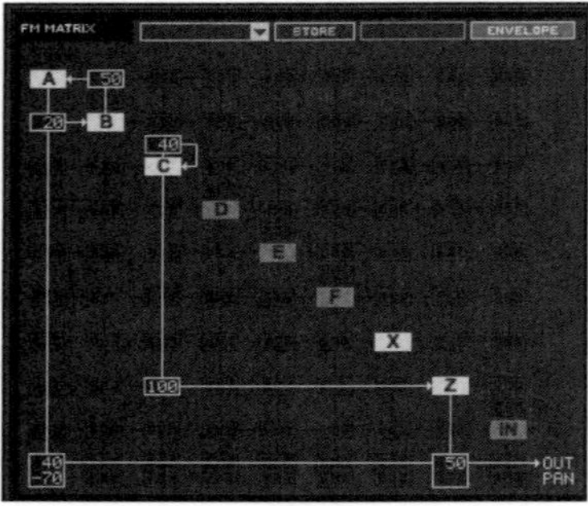

Figure 10.39
In this diagram, I have activated and routed Operator C to the input of Operator Z, but I have also routed the output of Operator C back to its own input in order to create a digital distortion.

After you have routed Operator C to Operator Z, select the Z page, activate it, and assign an output of 50 to it by way of the Algorithm matrix. Now use the following values for the Operator Z filters:

- **Filter 1 Cutoff**—11
- **Filter 1 Resonance**—100
- **Filter 1 Mode**—High Pass
- **Filter 2 Cutoff Spread**—48
- **Filter 2 Resonance**—100
- **Filter 2 Serial/Parallel**—100 (Serial)
- **Filter 2 Mode**—Band Pass
- **Filter Mix**—45

USING THE MODULATION WHEEL

Using the modulation wheel to trigger the filters of Operator Z introduces a live playing element to the pad preset, and it can be done by simply using the Cutoff Modulation **MATRIX** and assigning a positive or negative value to the MOD cell. Also note that using the Modulation page can do this.

Listening to the preset in its current configuration, it would be a good idea to bring more low frequencies to the table. Let's use Operator D to accomplish this.

1 Select Operator page D and activate it. Use the Frequency Ratio dialog to assign a value of .5000.

2 Click on the Matrix button to view the Algorithm matrix and assign an output level of 80 from Operator D to the FM7 main output.

3 Use the empty cell above Operator D to route its output back to its own input. Assign a value of 50.

4 Use the Operator D waveform selector to choose the twenty-seventh waveform.

5 Now, click on the Envelope button to view the envelope generator of Operator D. Create two breakpoints in order to create an envelope similar to the one shown in Figure 10.40.

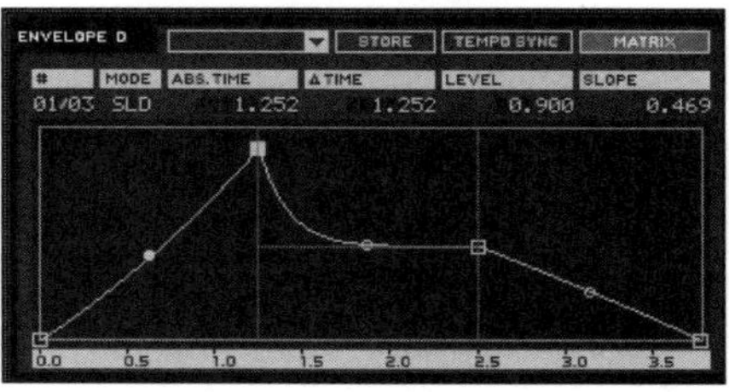

Figure 10.40

This diagram displays the envelope curve for Operator D.

Let's make this operator sound even more interesting by routing its output to Operator X, which as you'll recall is a noise generator. To do this, just click on the Matrix button and locate the empty cell that links the output of Operator D to X and then click/drag upward to assign a value of 40 to Operator X. Lastly, route the output of Operator X to the main FM7 output and assign a value of 50.

Select Operator page X, activate it, and use the following values:

- **Noise Amp**—40
- **Noise Cutoff**—75

- **Noise Resonance**—13
- **Saturator Gain**—66
- **Saturator ASYM**—22
- **Saturator Limit**—70

To finish off with Operator X, assign it to the modulation wheel by using the MOD cell of the Amplitude Modulation matrix and assign a value of 100.

Listening to the sound at this point, it sounds pretty complete on the synthetic side of things. We should finish this tutorial by using the onboard FM7 effects. Click on the Master page, activate the effects by clicking on the Effects On/Off button, and plug in the following values for the delay, filter, and modulation effects:

- **Tempo Sync**—On
- **Delay Time**—50
- **Delay Feedback**—75
- **Delay Diffusion**—10
- **Sync Delays**—On
- **Dry/Wet**—45
- **Filter Low Cut**—0
- **Filter Hi Cut**—100
- **Modulation Rate**—17
- **Modulation Depth**—38

Play the preset now, and it should sound not only interesting but soaked in real-time ambience. As a finishing touch, use the Unison dialog to assign a value of 2 to the preset, and use the Unison Detune slider to assign a value of 25.

And above all, don't forget to save your work!

DOWNLOAD THE PAD PRESET

Since this was a rather lengthy tutorial, I have created an FM7 pad preset file, which you can download from this book's page at **www.courseptr.com**. Download it, load it into the FM7, and see how well you did.

Additive Synthesis—Sine of the Times

Until recently, additive synthesis was a bit of a mystery to those of us devoted to the soft synth revolution because there were very few additive soft synth solutions, aside from certain synth ensembles embedded within Reaktor. This was due to the fact that additive synthesis requires large amounts of processing power in order to generate harmonics and manipulate them with amplitudes and envelopes. Today, this is not a problem because computers have gotten much faster and more reliable.

Additive synthesis is the most complex form of synthesis you'll find in this book, but we'll take it step by step in this chapter. To finish, we'll go through the steps of programming your own additive synth preset.

Like modular synthesis, I tend to think of additive as a "thinking man's" synth, as it requires more thought in design and use than a typical subtractive synthesizer does. Gone are the familiar parameters of resonance and cutoff, in favor of amplitudes, frequencies, and more. This is the territory of the true synth connoisseur, and this chapter will be the key to unlocking the creative potential within it.

Additive Synthesis Explained

Additive synthesis is based upon the research of Jean Baptiste Fourier, who stated that any waveform, whether simple or complex, could be broken down into a series of sine waves that oscillate at different frequencies and amplitudes (see Figure 11.1). In addition to this, each harmonic comprises several extra parameters, including envelopes and phase. In short, additive is a simple to understand but difficult to implement form of synthesis.

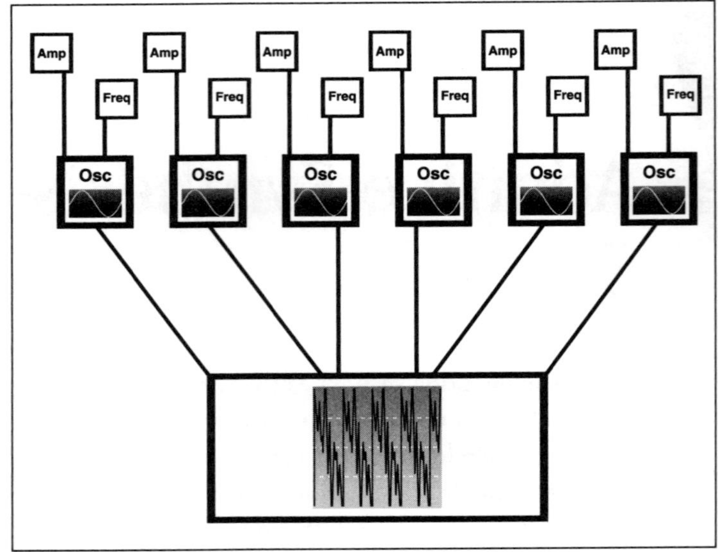

Figure 11.1
This diagram represents the basic fundamentals and structure of additive synthesis.

FFT (FAST FOURIER TRANSFORM)

One of Fourier's greatest contributions to digital audio is the Fast Fourier Transform (FFT for short) method of analyzing audio. Simply put, in audio terms it is an algorithm that solves and computes complex mathematical properties, which are then broken down to their fundamentals and represented as a sum of sines and cosines. Believe me when I tell you that you *don't* want to see the math behind this numeric beast.

Throughout this chapter, I will be using an FFT graph (supplied by Steinberg's Wavelab) to illustrate specific examples of sound analysis, and we'll then work from that graph to build new sounds with our additive synth of choice, the Cameleon 5000.

Let's begin our exploration of additive synthesis by discussing the following fundamentals:

- Harmonics (frequencies)
- Amplitudes (volume)
- Envelopes

Harmonics

In additive synthesis, harmonics are the key source of sound generation. An oscillator generating a single sine wave at an assigned frequency and amplitude represents each harmonic. As you'll recall from the synthesis fundamentals content of Chapter 8, "An Introduction to Software Synthesis," a sine wave is the simplest of all waveshapes, as it contains a single harmonic within. Yet, when combining the efforts of several oscillators generating singular sine waves at assigned frequencies and amplitudes, much more complex waveforms can be built.

To understand this ... be familiar with the *natural*
...ic with a frequency and
additional harmonics, which
...ples of the fundamental.
...c of 220Hz, which is more
...e second harmonic would
the third harmonic would be
...), and so forth. Going from
...orms, such as square waves,
... harmonic content and
...duced to the other funda-
...w of these in greater detail.

...e terms harmonics and partials to
...additive synthesis. These terms are

...al by adjusting the individ-
...en constructing complex
...2, where a harmonic
...d in frequencies and
...venth, ninth, eleventh, and
...e wave, but also notice
...monic is greatly reduced
its characteristic sound.
If the amplitude of every harmonic were equal to that of the fundamental, then the resulting waveform would not sound much like a square wave at all.

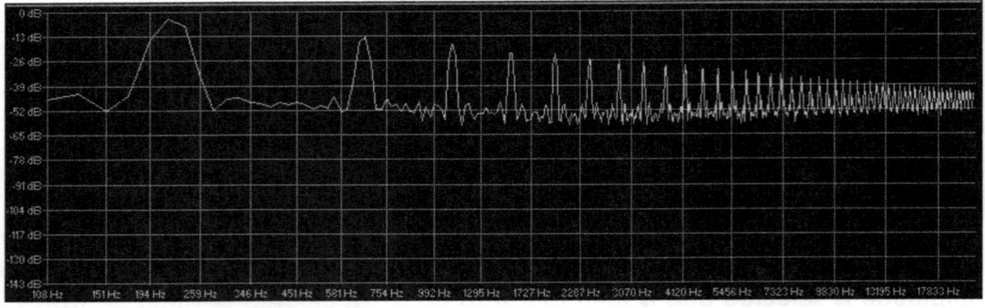

Figure 11.2
This diagram displays the harmonic breakdown of a square wave.

Envelopes

Along with harmonics and amplitudes, envelopes play a large role in additive sound shaping, as each harmonic within a sound is assigned its own attack/decay envelope. Envelopes can assign slow/fast attacks and decays to specific harmonics, which is very useful when modeling the characteristics of more complex waveforms such as those produced by guitars, pianos, or a human voice. It's also important to note that the generation of these envelopes is one of the main reasons that additive synthesis can really tax your CPU, as there are so many needed when using a large number of harmonics within a patch.

Building Waveforms, One Sine at a Time

To introduce you to additive synthesis, let's use this example to create a new but simple sound by combining three sine waves with different frequencies and amplitudes.

1. To begin, we'll need our fundamental harmonic, which is a sine wave that oscillates at a frequency of 300Hz (see Figure 11.3) and has an amplitude of 100%.
2. Next, we'll add a new harmonic that will oscillate at a third above the fundamental at 900Hz (see Figure 11.4) and has an amplitude of 50% of the fundamental.
3. Our final harmonic will oscillate a fifth above the fundamental at 1500Hz (see Figure 11.5) and has an amplitude of 25% of the fundamental.
4. When combining these three waveforms, we get a more complex waveform, as seen in Figure 11.6.

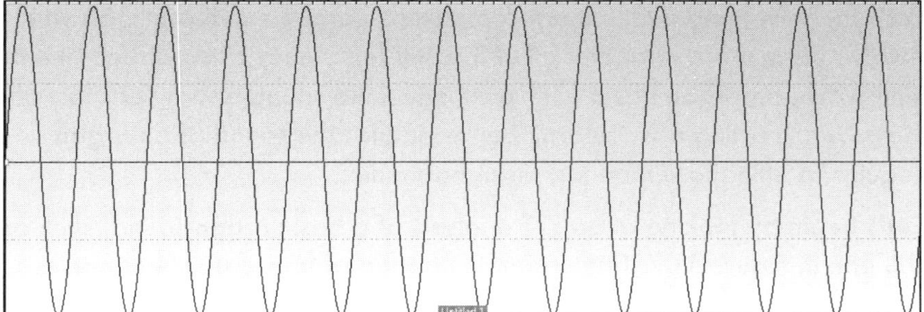

Figure 11.3

Our fundamental harmonic is a sine wave oscillating at 300Hz.

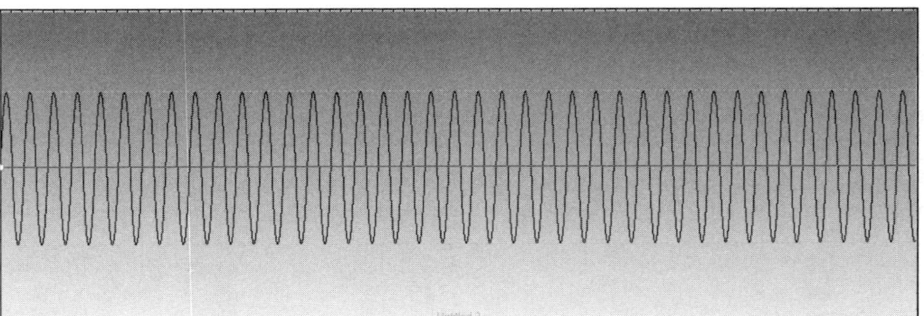

Figure 11.4

Our next harmonic

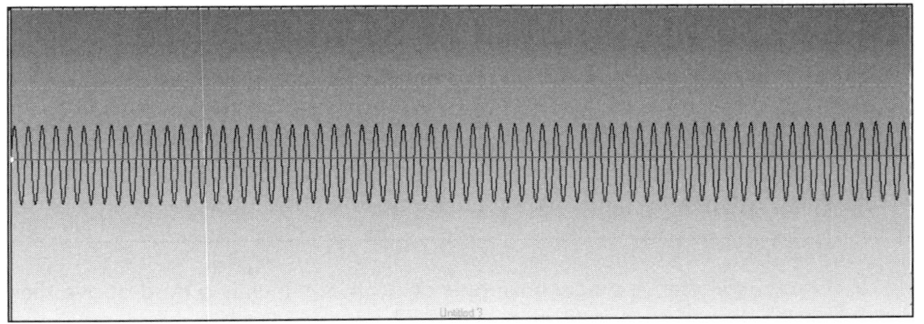

Figure 11.5

Our third and final harmonic

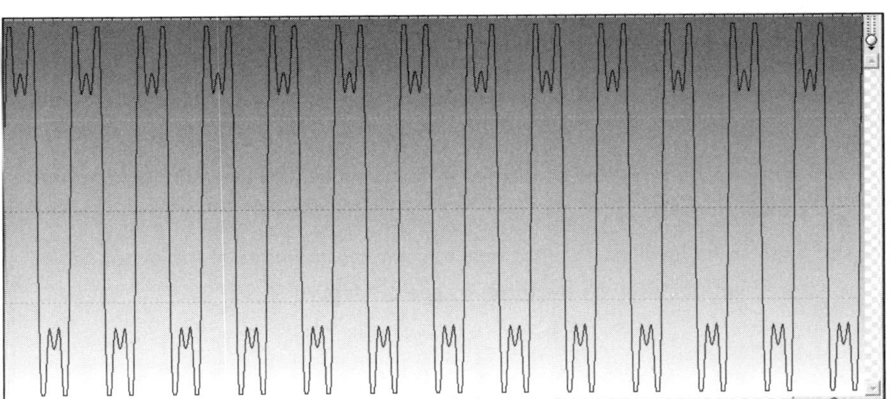

Figure 11.6

Our resulting waveform, which is composed of all three harmonics.

Let's try something a little more complex—an organ waveform. This will involve using more harmonics, but it is still fairly easy to construct. Like the sine wave, an organ has a very pure and solid sound and a very fast attack. However, creating a waveform that resembles the sound of an organ requires a little more than just three harmonics.

Let's begin by looking at an FFT analysis of a basic organ sound, such as the one in Figure 11.7. This organ has a total of four distinct harmonics, with peaks at approximately 220Hz (first), 660Hz (third), 1320Hz (sixth), 1760Hz (eighth), and 2650Hz (twelfth). In addition, we can also see that there are interesting amplitude variations in relation to each harmonic; for instance, the sixth harmonic is hotter than the third.

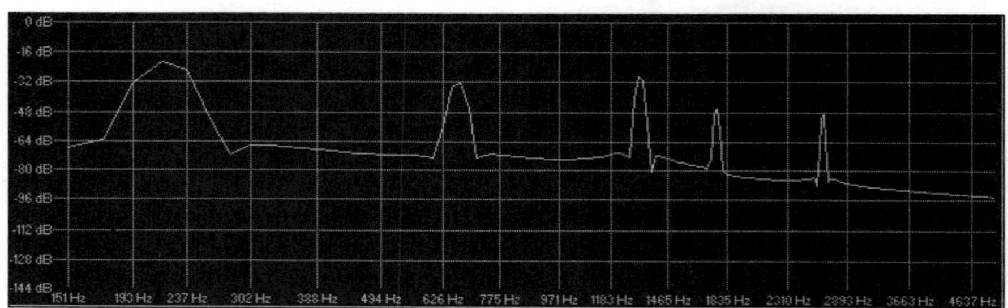

Figure 11.7
An FFT view of a basic organ sound

Using these values as a template, we can begin to construct a waveform that resembles an organ.

1. First I will need a fundamental harmonic of 220Hz at an amplitude of 100% (see Figure 11.8).
2. Next, I will create a new harmonic of 660Hz, which is a third above the fundamental (see Figure 11.9).
3. Next up is a harmonic of 1,320Hz, which is a sixth above the fundamental (see Figure 11.10).
4. Next is a harmonic of 1,760Hz, which is an eighth above the fundamental (see Figure 11.11).
5. Finally, a harmonic of 2,640Hz, which is a twelfth above the fundamental (see Figure 11.12).
6. With some level mixing that resembles the amplitudes of the organ waveform, we get a new waveform, as seen in Figure 11.13.

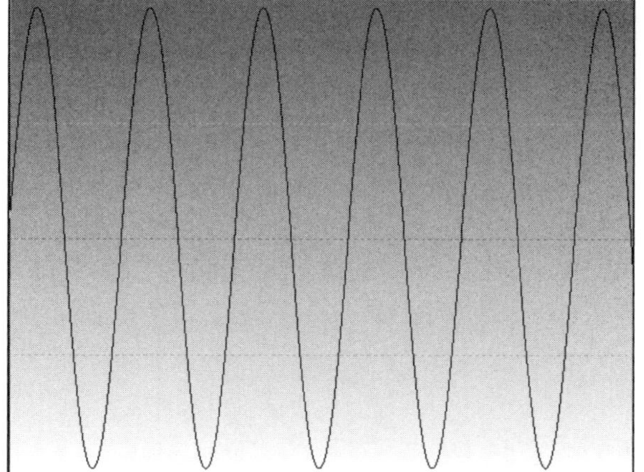

Figure 11.8
Our fundamental harmonic

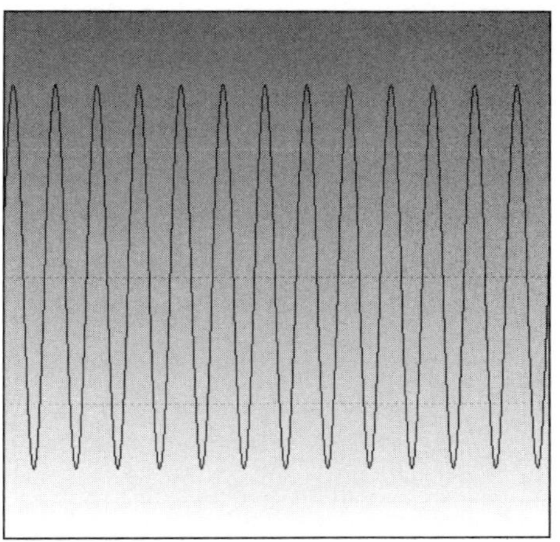

Figure 11.9
Our next harmonic

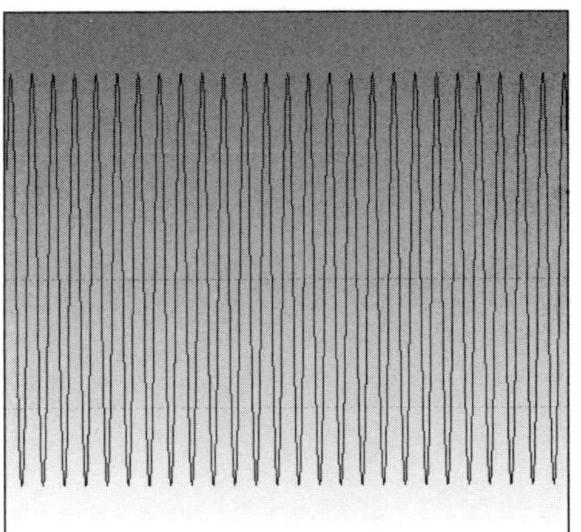

Figure 11.10
Our next harmonic

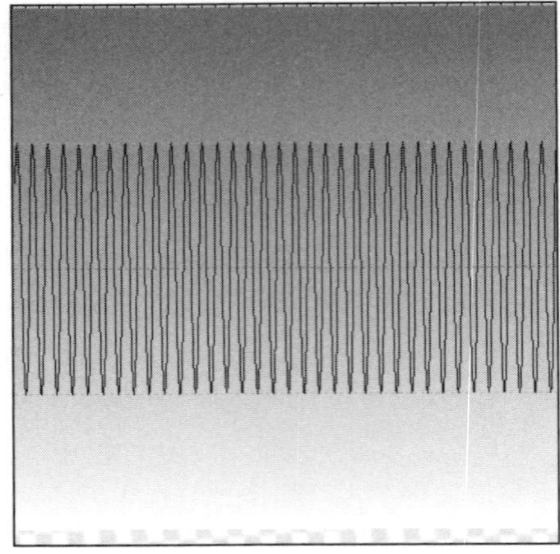

Figure 11.11
Our next harmonic

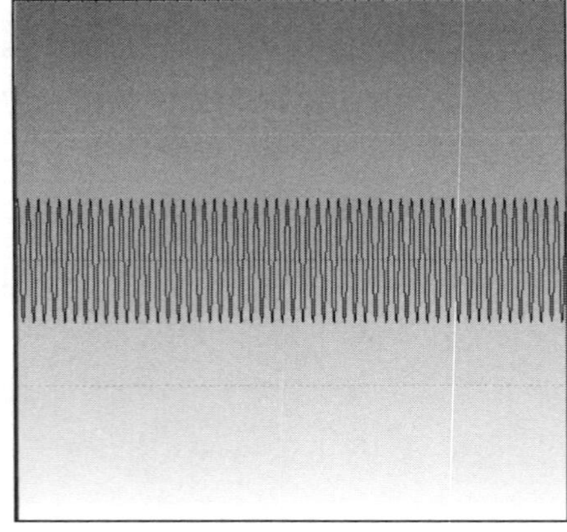

Figure 11.12
Our final harmonic of 2,640Hz

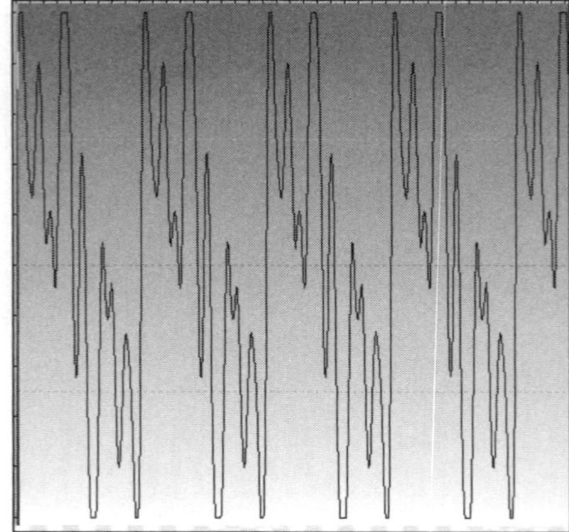

Figure 11.13
Our resulting waveform greatly resembles the original organ waveform.

ADDITIVE SYNTHESIS IN DISGUISE

Although you may not realize it, the B4 organ by Native Instruments (see Figure 11.14) is actually a relative of additive synthesis. Like additive synthesis, an organ uses a series of drawbars to introduce different frequencies and amplitudes in order to shape a new sound.

However, the B4 takes additive to a whole new level by including many additional sound design parameters, such as amp simulation, vibrato, and even a rotating Leslie cabinet.

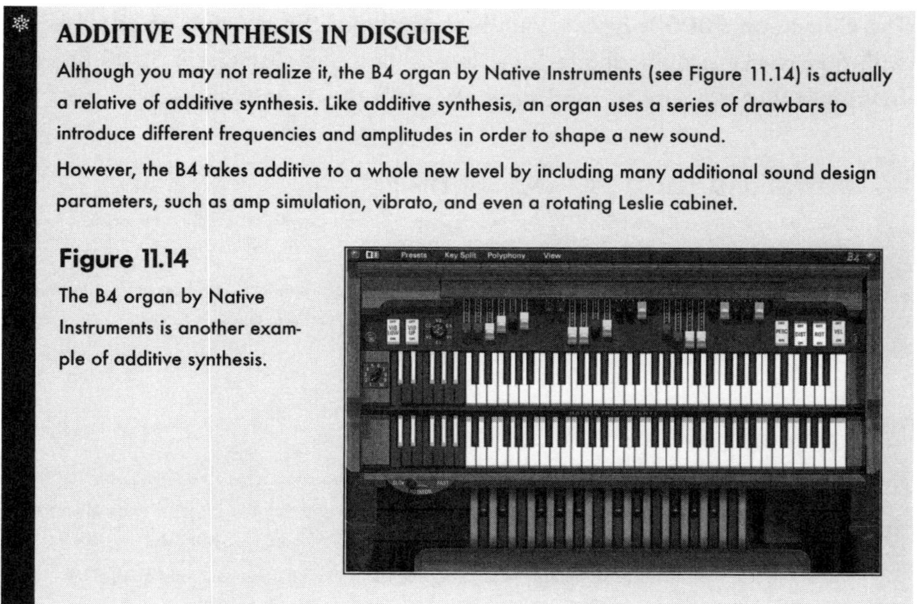

Figure 11.14
The B4 organ by Native Instruments is another example of additive synthesis.

Additive Soft Synths in Action—The Cameleon 5000

For a close-up look at additive synthesis in action, let's sample the Cameleon 5000 by Camel Audio (see Figure 11.15). With a price tag of $199, this soft synth is a great additive solution that works with any DAW application that supports audio units and VST instruments.

Figure 11.15
The Cameleon 5000 is a VST instrument and audio unit additive soft synth.

The Cameleon 5000 is a soft synth that combines the practice of additive with a retro-like graphical interface. In addition, the Cameleon 5000 has a few tricks that are sure to send synthetic chills down your spine.

DOWNLOAD THE DEMO AND SET IT UP

If you don't own the Cameleon 5000, don't despair. You can download a fully functioning demo at **www.camelaudio.com/download.htm**.

To use Cameleon 5000 with your favorite sequencer, see the procedures in Chapter 7, "Kontakt Tutorial," for setting up Kontakt and apply those instructions to the Cameleon 5000.

RESYNTHESIS

One of the latest features to come to fruition in additive soft synths such as the Cameleon 5000 and the VirSyn Cube is the implementation of *resynthesis*. Simply put, this is the process of importing a digital audio file in order to emulate that sound by way of additive synthesis.

Doesn't this sound similar to sampling? Well, the process of resynthesis is actually quite a bit different. Unlike sampling, resynthesis is a process by which a digital audio file is analyzed and broken down to its fundamentals, which would be a little like looking at it through an FFT graph. These fundamentals are then reconstructed using a combination of harmonics, amplitudes, envelopes, and a noise generator. This results in a sound that has audio characteristics similar to the original.

Of course, this is not a precise copy, as that would be more akin to sampling. Rather, resynthesis is a fascinating process of using a digital audio file as a starting point toward building a new sound.

Tour of the Cameleon 5000

In this part of the chapter, I will take you through the graphic layout and basic functionality of the Cameleon 5000. You'll soon see that it is really not all that different from any other soft synth we have seen.

Upon loading the Cameleon 5000 for the first time and launching its graphic interface, you will see that it is split into three sections:

- Preset Buttons
- Pages and Editing Parameters
- Virtual Keyboard

Presets

If you are looking to get up and running right away, then the preset section is a good place to start. The Cameleon 5000 provides many presets, which are compiled and placed into numerous banks on the left drop-down menu of the presets interface. These banks can be selected by clicking on the spin controls or just directly clicking on the bank name dialog itself (see Figure 11.16).

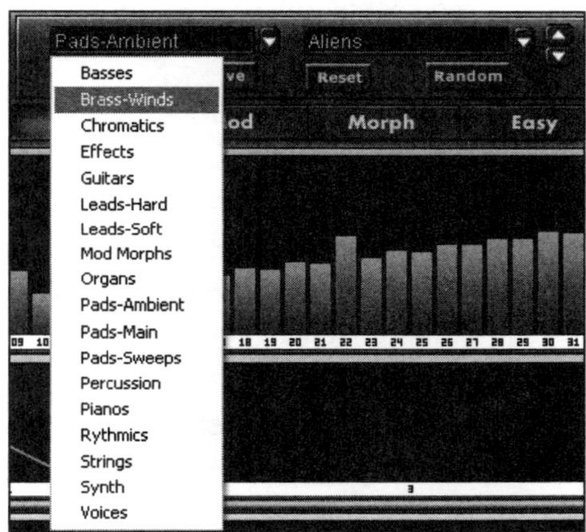

Figure 11.16
The Cameleon 5000 has a large assortment of presets to get you started on the additive path.

Once a bank has been chosen, it is simply a matter of selecting a preset on the right side of the presets interface by either using its spin controls or clicking on the name dialog.

Underneath the banks and presets are a few additional parameters:

- **Load**—This locates and loads individual presets into the Cameleon 5000.
- **Save**—This saves any new presets created in the Cameleon 5000, which are stored as .c5i files.
- **Reset**—This resets the entire soft synth to its default values. Note that this does not set all of the parameters to a value of zero as you might assume.
- **Random**—This button will place random values on just about every parameter of the Cameleon 5000.

Below the preset section are the page buttons. These are used to view and edit all the different parameters that the Cameleon 5000 has to offer.

Pages and Editing Parameters

Once a preset has been selected, the next step is to view and edit the several parameters of the Cameleon 5000. This is made possible by the Page buttons, which navigate between the different points of interest of the synth.

- **Voice Program Pages (A, B, C, D)**—These pages are for editing the individual voices of the Cameleon 5000.
- **Modulation (Mod)**—This page assigns play parameters to specific editing parameters of the Cameleon 5000. For example, you can have the modulation wheel of your MIDI keyboard affect the LFO speed or depth.
- **Morph**—This page makes the sound that you create change over time.
- **Easy**—This page offers an easy way to manipulate the global parameters of the Cameleon 5000.
- **Effects**—This page edits the parameters of the included effects, such as delay, distortion, and a very funky filter.

The Virtual Keyboard

The Virtual Keyboard is a graphical representation of a typical MIDI keyboard (see Figure 11.17). It responds graphically to any MIDI data fed to it by way of an external MIDI keyboard or by simply clicking on the keys with a mouse. Note that the Virtual Keyboard and its parameters can be accessed when viewing any page of the soft synth.

Figure 11.17
The Virtual Keyboard of the Cameleon 5000.

Aside from the keyboard itself, this section also contains a couple of tuning parameters and the Learn button.

- **Tune**—This knob controls the master tuning for the Cameleon 5000.
- **Tune Semi**—This parameter alters the master tune in semitone increments. It has a range of +/–48 semitones.
- **Learn**—This parameter assigns MIDI controllers, such as sliders and knobs, to various parameters of the Cameleon.

Exploring the Pages

Let's dig in and explore the individual pages of the interface. In this section, we'll cover:

- The Voice Program pages
- The Mod page
- The Morph page
- The Easy page
- The Effects page

The Voice Program Pages

The main course of the Cameleon is the four voice program pages, which are responsible for generating individual harmonics and amplitudes (see Figure 11.18). Additionally, each voice program page includes a noise generator. As they all contain duplicate parameters that function independently of each other, each voice program page is like having a complete additive synthesizer. In other words, you get four additive synths within one user interface.

To navigate between the four voice pages, just click on the A, B, C, or D button.

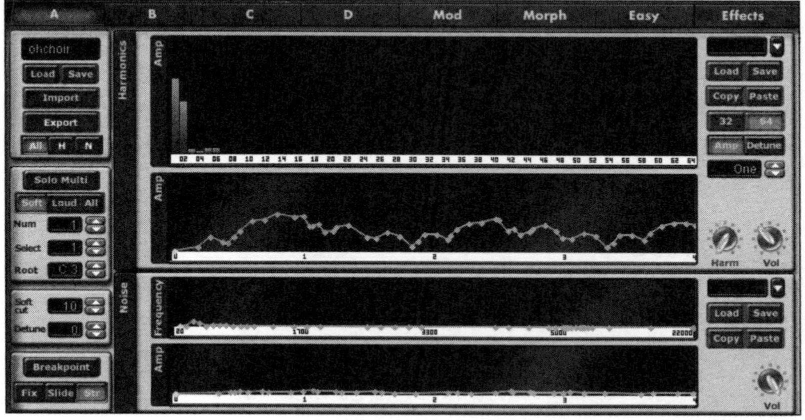

Figure 11.18

The voice program page generates harmonics and noise.

The Harmonics Section

The upper half of the voice program page is dedicated to adding and editing the harmonics of an individual voice program (see Figure 11.19).

This can be thought of as your starting place for creating your sounds. Looking at Figure 11.19, you'll see that this section is split into three subsections:

- **The First Amp**—Also called the *partial display*, it displays the introduction and amplitudes of each harmonic.
- **The Second Amp**—Also called the *breakpoint envelope*, this governs the amplitude of the entire harmonic spread over a specific amount of time.
- **Additional Parameters**—These are used to specify how many partials are used as well as other special functions. I will refer to these often throughout this section.

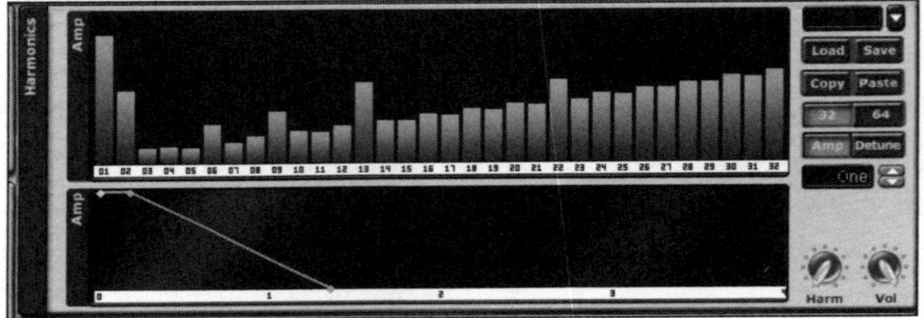

Figure 11.19
The Harmonics section of the voice program page is the first step toward designing your sounds.

The first amp (or partial display, as it will be called throughout the rest of this tutorial) displays a bar graph of 32 columns, each of which corresponds to a specific harmonic to be introduced to a signal in order to shape its timbre. Clicking and dragging up and down can adjust the volume of each harmonic. Looking at Figure 11.20, you can see that as I make changes to a harmonic, that harmonic and its volume are displayed in the upper-right corner of the interface.

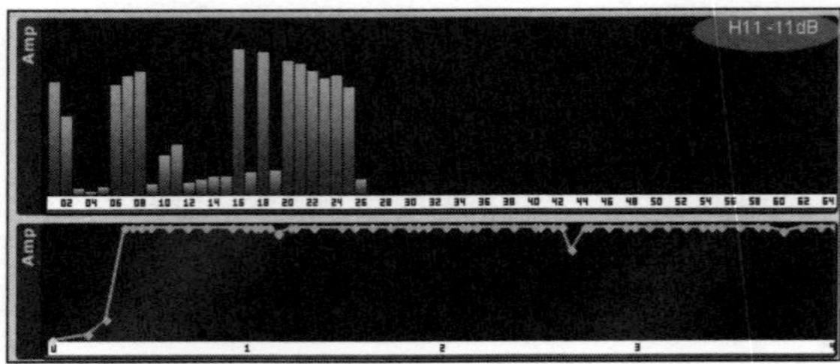

Figure 11.20
As amplitude adjustments are made to any harmonics, the number of that harmonic and its volume are displayed in the upper-right corner.

Just to the right of the partial display are nine corresponding parameters used to edit its harmonic content. These parameters include:

- **Presets**—This pop-up menu produces a list of harmonic presets that can be used as starting points for creating sounds: None, Organ, Plucked, Saw (Low Pass), Saw, Sine, Square (Low Pass), Square, and Triangle. Try auditioning each of these to familiarize yourself with the different timbres available in the Cameleon.
- **Load/Save**—These buttons are used to load and save any harmonic presets. Note that these saved files contain the .c5h file extension.
- **Copy/Paste**—These buttons are used to copy and paste any harmonic content in the partial display.
- **32/64**—These buttons are used to display either 32 or 64 harmonics in the partial display. While you will probably use the default 32 setting for a majority of this chapter, the 64 setting is fantastic for adding more harmonics to create treble heavy patches for the Cameleon.
- **Amp/Detune**—These buttons are used to toggle between the Amp mode, which enables you to edit the amplitude of each harmonic in the partial display, and the Detune mode, which makes it possible to fine-tune each harmonic in the partial display. Read the next section for more information about the Detune mode.

The second amp (or breakpoint envelope, as it will be called throughout the rest of this tutorial) is modeled after the design of a standard envelope generator; it controls the amplitude of the partial display over a specific amount of time, just as an envelope generator would on a standard oscillator-driven subtractive synth. But unlike a run-of-the-mill envelope generator, this one has much greater creative potential, thanks to Breakpoints. *Breakpoints* can be thought of as dynamic transitions in the amplitude of a sound. Using breakpoints, it is possible to create a sound that has a slow attack, at which point it fades to zero for a brief moment and then intermittently has sudden spikes in volume as it progresses onward. If you want to put breakpoints to the test, you can use up to 128 individual instances.

Assuming that you have started your sequencer application and set up the Cameleon 5000 to be used as a soft synth, let's look at an example of the breakpoint envelope:

1. Click on the Reset button, which is located at the upper-right corner of the Cameleon 5000 interface. In addition, you will need to select the None preset for the B, C, and D voice program pages so you can hear just the single voice from the A page.

2 Now, select the Organ preset from the right side of the partial display. This will load its harmonic content into the partial display and its amplitude information into the breakpoint envelope, which as you can see from Figure 11.21 has a fast attack, short decay, long sustain, and short release.
3 Click and drag the decay breakpoint to the right to prolong the decay effect.
4 Now click and drag the attack breakpoint moderately to the right to give it a slow attack. Notice that as you make the adjustments to any breakpoint, it is noted in the upper-right corner of the breakpoint envelope display.
5 With the attack set, click and drag the decay breakpoint to the left and down to create a fast decay (see Figure 11.22).
6 Now, locate an arbitrary point along the distance between the decay and sustain breakpoints and click once to create a new breakpoint. If you right-click with your mouse, you can remove the breakpoint.
7 Click and drag the new breakpoint upward to create a spike in the envelope.
8 Once you are finished, you should have an envelope that looks like Figure 11.23, and if you play back the sound, you will hear the dynamic alterations you have made to the envelope curve.

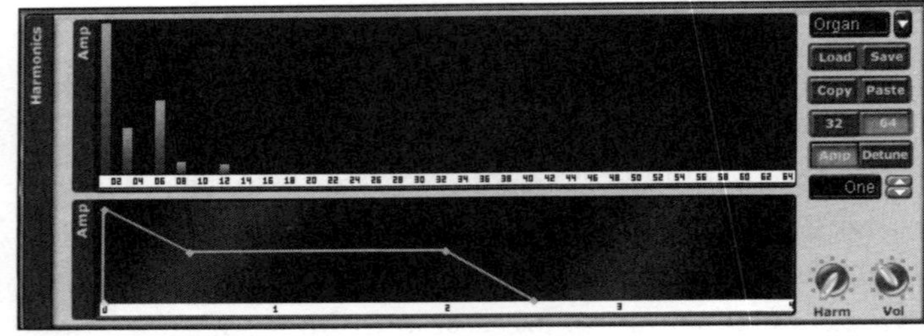

Figure 11.21

The Organ preset has a simple harmonic structure and standard envelope.

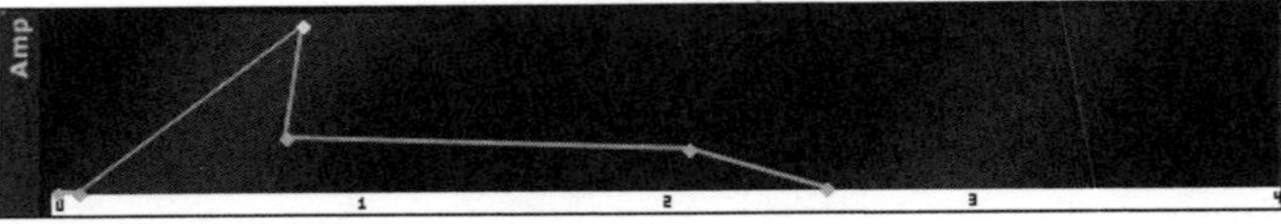

Figure 11.22

The Organ preset now has a slow attack and very abrupt decay.

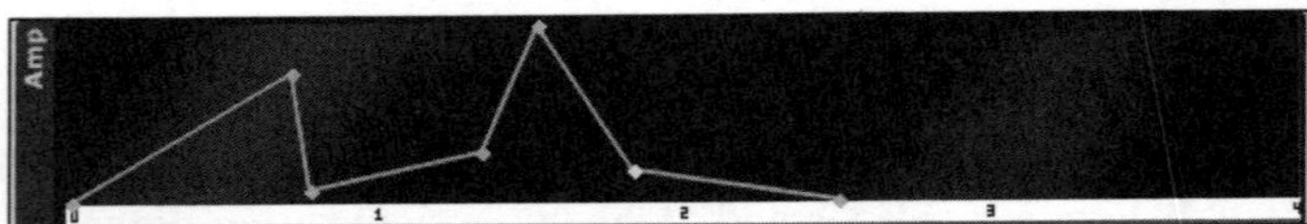

Figure 11.23

The envelope curve has now been drastically altered.

ZOOM IN—ZOOM OUT

You can zoom in or out of the breakpoint envelope by clicking and dragging up and down along the ruler strip at the bottom of its interface.

Detuning Harmonics

As mentioned earlier, the Detune mode makes it possible to fine-tune any harmonic in the partial display. Click on the Detune button to switch modes, and the partial display interface will be cut in half (see Figure 11.24). The upper half of the interface sharpens the pitch of any active harmonics, while the lower half flattens the pitch. This is done by simply clicking/dragging up and down to adjust the tuning of each harmonic.

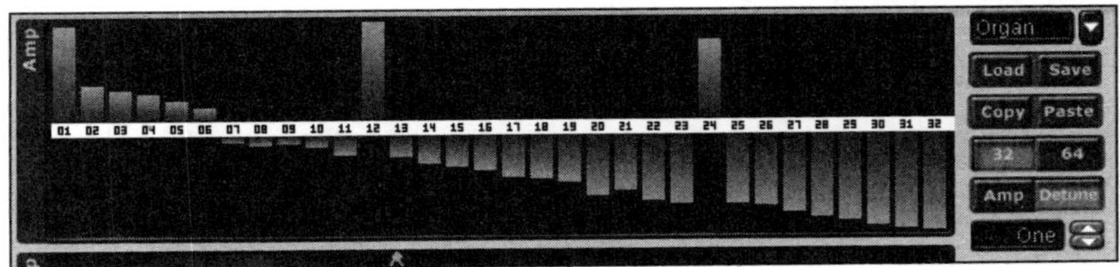

Figure 11.24

The Detune mode alters the interface of the partial display, making it possible to sharpen or flatten every harmonic.

Just below the Amp and Detune buttons is an additional interface with spin controls that allow you to decide which harmonics to detune. Clicking on the up and down spin control buttons gives you eight options, including:

- **One**—This is the default setting and adjusts the tuning of an individual harmonic.
- **Odd**—This adjusts the tuning of the odd-numbered harmonics.
- **Even**—This adjusts the tuning of the even-numbered harmonics.
- **Fifths**—This adjusts the tuning of every fifth harmonic (5,10,15,20).
- **Octaves**—This adjusts the tuning of every octave harmonic (1, 2, 4, 8, 16, 32).
- **Bright**—This adjusts the tuning to create a dark to bright transition.
- **Dark**—This adjusts the tuning to create a bright to dark transition.
- **All**—This adjusts the tuning of every harmonic simultaneously.

Just below the detune presets is the Harmonize knob, which overrides and mixes between the detune settings and the natural tunings of the Cameleon 5000. The Volume knob controls the master volume of the partial display.

The Noise Section

The lower half of the voice program page is the noise generator (see Figure 11.25). This section introduces white noise to your signal and uses similar controls to that of the partial display to shape the noise.

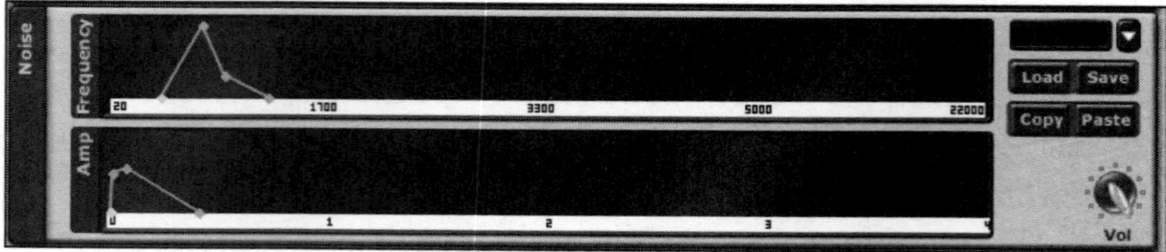

Figure 11.25
The lower half of the voice program page is the noise generator, which has a frequency range of 20Hz to 22,000Hz.

The upper half of the noise interface is the frequency envelope. This section shapes the overall frequency spectrum of white noise by introducing breakpoints to cut or boost specific noise frequencies. It has a range of 20Hz to 22,000Hz, and up to 118 individual breakpoints can be created along the envelope.

To the right of the frequency envelope are six familiar parameters that perform the same procedures as the parameters above. They include:

- **Presets**—This pop-up menu produces a list of noise presets that include Breath Hard, Breath Light, Key Hit Hard, Key Hit Light, Key Hit Medium, None, and White Noise.
- **Load/Save**—These buttons are used to load and save any noise presets. Note that these saved files contain the .c5n file extension.
- **Copy/Paste**—These buttons are used to copy and paste any noise content.
- **Volume**—This knob controls the volume of the Noise section.

DOWN WITH HARMONICS, UP WITH NOISE

Before proceeding, you might want to remove the Harmonic section completely from the mix so that you can hear the full effect of the Noise section as we make adjustments to it. Just turn down the Volume knob for the Harmonic section.

The lower half of the Noise section is the amp envelope. This works just like the envelope of the upper half of this page, in that it cuts and boosts the amplitudes of any active noise frequencies.

Now, let's get a taste of noise by following along with this quick tutorial:

1 Select the White preset from the right side of the interface. This will provide a good strong signal to shape. Play any key on the Virtual Keyboard of the Cameleon 5000, and you will hear it loud and clear. Keep in mind that since white noise is not pitch specific, you will not hear pitch differences across the keyboard.
2 Click and drag any frequency breakpoint upward to boost the frequency. Play a note on your keyboard to hear the difference.
3 Click and drag the release breakpoint of the amp envelope to the right to extend the release time. Play a note on your keyboard to hear the difference.

How do you use a noise generator like this effectively? My best advice is to preview Cameleon patches that feature the Noise section and make a few customizations to it to hear the effect.

BREAKPOINT MODE VERSUS OVERALL MODE

There are two edit modes embedded within the voice program page: Overall mode and Breakpoint mode. Overall mode is selected by default whenever the Cameleon 5000 is first loaded into the sequencer. When this mode is active, all the breakpoints are simultaneously selected, meaning that what's presented in the partial display is a summary of the harmonic content of a voice program.

The Breakpoint mode (which is activated by clicking on the Breakpoint button in the lower-left corner of the interface) presents a real-time display of the harmonic content of the voice program whenever a breakpoint is selected by clicking on it. This depicts a more graphic representation of the harmonic content within a voice program over time. Follow this example.

1 Assuming that you are in Overall mode, click on any breakpoint in either the Harmonic or Noise section. Notice that as you do, no graphic changes occur throughout the voice program.
2 Now, click on the Breakpoint button to switch to Breakpoint mode and click on a breakpoint in the Harmonic section. Notice as you do, the partial display refreshes to present the harmonic content of the voice program at the current time selected by the breakpoint. This lets you see how a sound in the Cameleon 5000 changes over time.

Although this is just a brief introduction to the Overall versus Breakpoint mode discussion, you should probe deeper to see how cool this really is.

Additional Parameters

The left column of the voice program page contains some additional parameters to drive some of the most impressive features of the Cameleon 5000, such as resynthesis, multisampling, and velocity layers. Let's take a look at these parameters.

- **Load**—This loads a voice program containing both harmonic and noise data into the page.
- **Save**—This saves a voice program, which includes harmonic and noise data.
- **Import**—This imports the WAV/AIFF digital audio and BMP picture formatted files into the voice program page to be analyzed and resynthesized.
- **Export**—This exports the current voice program as a bitmap. Just below are three export choices: All, Harmonics, and Noise.
- **Solo Multi**—This button isolates one of eight multisamples embedded within a voice program. If this function is not familiar to you, we will cover it in the next section.
- **Soft/Loud/All**—These buttons edit one or both velocity layers embedded within a voice program.
- **Num**—This specifies how many multisamples are to be included within a voice program.
- **Select**—This selects any active multisamples within a voice program.
- **Root**—This function automatically detects the root pitch of an imported WAV or AIFF file. Spin controls to the right are used to fine-tune this parameter.
- **Soft Cut**—This applies a gentle low pass filter when low velocity MIDI notes are received.
- **Detune**—This sharpens and flattens the pitch of the Cameleon 5000.
- **Breakpoint**—This button toggles the Cameleon 5000 between Overall mode and Breakpoint mode. Movement behaviors of the breakpoints are governed by the Fix, Slide, and Str modes.
- **Fix**—When this mode is selected, only one breakpoint may be altered at a time.
- **Slide**—When this mode is selected, any forward/backward breakpoint movements alter related breakpoints within the envelope in relation to time.
- **Str**—When this mode is selected, any forward/backward breakpoint movements alter the entire envelope.

IMPORTING BITMAPS

The Cameleon's method of importing a bitmap and converting it into an audio signal is impressive. Similar in nature to importing digital audio, the Cameleon treats a bitmap in the same way; it analyzes the entire digital picture and then graphs the elements of that picture against an X/Y axis (see Figure 11.26). The X-axis is read from left to right and generates an envelope for the voice program, which includes breakpoints. The Y-axis is read from top to bottom and generates the harmonic content for the voice program.

To really put this idea into perspective, try this example:

1. Press the Reset button so that you are working with a clean slate.
2. Click on the Import button and navigate to the Cameleon 5000 Data folder. Inside you will find a Bitmap folder, which contains several pictures to choose from. Select one and import it.
3. Once the bitmap has been analyzed and imported, the Cameleon 5000 will generate harmonic and envelope content.

If you have a desktop publishing application such as Fireworks or Photoshop, you can create your own bitmaps to generate voice programs.

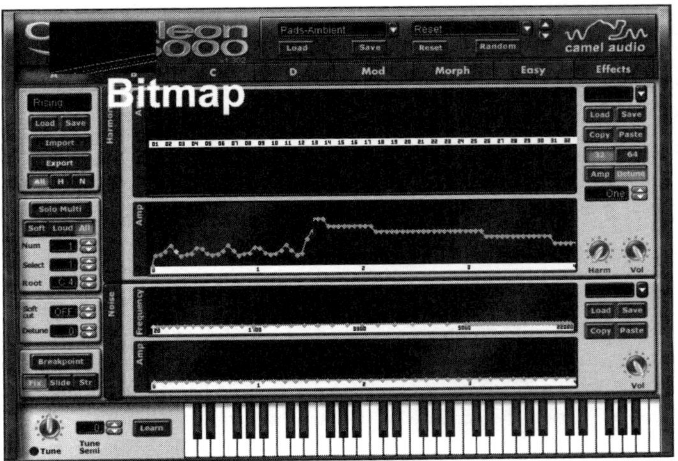

Figure 11.26
When a bitmap is imported into the Cameleon 5000, it is analyzed as a graph, in which the X-axis (horizontal) is treated as "time" for creating breakpoints and the Y-axis (vertical) is treated as harmonics.

Multisampling and Velocity Layers

The Cameleon 5000's multisampling and velocity layering features are modeled after those found in popular software samplers such as GigaStudio and Kontakt. Like a sampler, the Cameleon has the ability to import multiple samples and map them across its Virtual Keyboard per voice program page. In addition, the Cameleon can import these samples at different velocities to make the voice program more dynamic. Let's see these features in action, beginning with Multisampling.

For this example, I will import two separate samples to demonstrate the Multisampling capabilities of the Cameleon 5000.

1. Begin by clicking the Reset button in the upper-right corner of the interface.
2. Check to make sure that the All button is activated. It's located just below the Solo Multi button.
3. Use the Num spin controls to increase the number of multisamples to 2.
4. Now make sure that the Select display (located just below the Num controls) is set to 1. This means that you are going to import your first multisample.
5. Click on the Import button, locate a WAV or AIFF file, and import it.
6. Once imported, the Root display will try to guess the root note of the sample. If it is not correct, then use the spin controls to alter the root note.
7. Next, go back to the Select display and change its value to 2. This allows you to import your second multisample.
8. Repeat Steps 5 and 6 to import the next multisample.

Of course, this is just a brief demonstration on how to use the multisampling function of the Cameleon 5000. It takes a lot of time and patience to really bring out the beauty of this feature. Near the end of this chapter, I will demonstrate some creative uses for this function.

Now let's demonstrate the velocity layering feature.

1. Click on the Reset button to reset the Cameleon 5000 interface.
2. Click on the Soft button, located just below the Solo Multi button.
3. Now import a WAV or AIFF audio file into the Cameleon 5000 by using the Import button. Just keep in mind that this digital audio file should contain a low velocity value for best results.
4. Once the audio file is imported, click on the Loud button.
5. Now import another WAV or AIFF file into the Cameleon 5000 by using the Import button. For best results, use a sample with a good amount of velocity.

After you are finished, play the voice program with different velocities from your MIDI keyboard. You should hear the Cameleon 5000 switch between samples according to how hard the note is played.

The Mod Page

As if virtual synths couldn't get any cooler, the Mod page routes MIDI events (*sources*) to various parameters (*targets*) in the Cameleon interface (see Figure 11.27). For example, you could use this page to assign the modulation wheel on your MIDI keyboard to modulate the filter cutoff parameter of the filter effect on the Effects page, essentially creating a filter sweep.

Figure 11.27
Target: Originality is the name of the game when it comes to the Mod page.

Let's have a look at the different parameters of the Mod page.

- **Source**—This menu specifies a MIDI event to be used as a source of modulation. There are many standard possibilities here, such as velocity and aftertouch. But there are also some more inventive possibilities, such as LFO 1 and 2. There are over 120 individual sources, which can be viewed and selected by clicking/dragging up and down the pop-up list.
- **Target**—This menu details which Cameleon parameter is to be modulated by the chosen source. A click on this pop-up menu will display a list that includes everything from effect to morph parameters. There are over 50 individual targets, which can be viewed and selected by clicking/dragging up and down the pop-up list.
- **Low/High**—These sliders are used to assign a range to the modulation target.

There are some additional parameters in the lower half of the Mod page.

- **Pitch Bend Range**—This assigns an amount of pitch bend range in relation to the pitch bend wheel of your MIDI keyboard. It has a two-octave range.
- **LFO 1/2**—These LFOs are provided to be used as modulation sources, as noted earlier. Three different waveforms are provided, in addition to a tempo-controlled speed knob that is read in note values.

- **Mod Envelope**—This envelope is provided to be used as a modulation source. Simply select it from the Source pop-up menu and assign it to the filter effect or the Formant filter to hear it in action.

The Morph Page

The Morph page is used to program audible transitions called morphs between the parameters of each Cameleon 5000 voice program page (see Figure 11.28). These make the creative potential of additive synthesis really shine through—you can program transitions from a pad, to a sequence, to an organ, to basses or guitars. This is just a simplified definition of morphing, but I think you can see the potential for this feature.

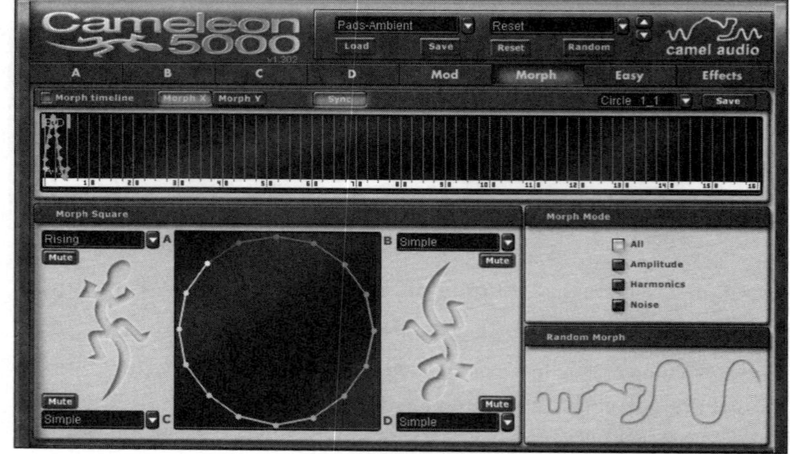

Figure 11.28

The Morph page programs morphs between voice program parameters.

The Morph Timeline

The top of the Morph page, called the *Morph Timeline*, establishes a timed pattern between the different transitions of each voice program, which is the same function as an envelope. Looking at Figure 11.29, you can see that the top half of the timeline is labeled B-D, which means that the upper portion of the timeline is directly related to voice programs B and D. Likewise, the lower half of the timeline is dedicated to voice programs A and C. This is a result of viewing the Morph Timeline with the Morph X parameter active, which is directly related to the horizontal axis of the Morph Square (see Figure 11.30). Confused? Try the following example:

1 Click the Reset button in the upper-right corner of the Morph page to start off clean.

2 Next, click on the Morph Timeline button located in the upper-left corner to activate this function.

3 At this point, you should see a basic timeline with two breakpoints. Right-click to delete the right breakpoint, which should leave you with just a single breakpoint.

4 Look at the Morph Square below, and you will now see a white dot in the center of the interface, which means that there is no morphing between voice programs.

5 Now, click/drag the breakpoint on the Morph Timeline upward and then release the mouse. Look again at the Morph Square; the white dot should now be located hard left, which is the X, or horizontal, axis.

6 Next click on the Morph Y parameter to switch from horizontal view to vertical view. Once you activate this parameter, look at the top and bottom of the timeline, and you will see that the top half is assigned to voice program A and B, while the bottom half is dedicated to C and D.

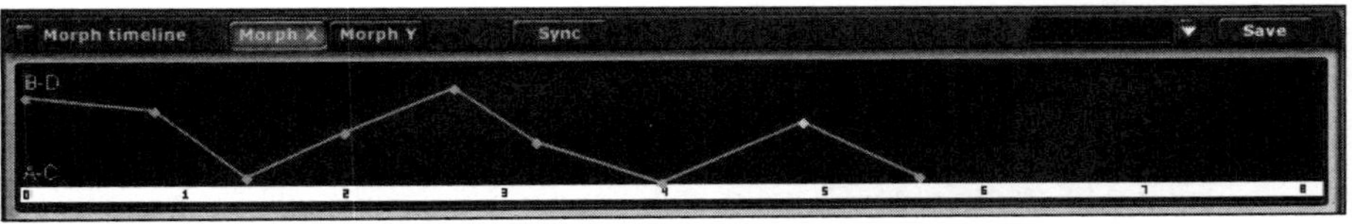

Figure 11.29
The Morph Timeline assigns a transition time between each voice program page.

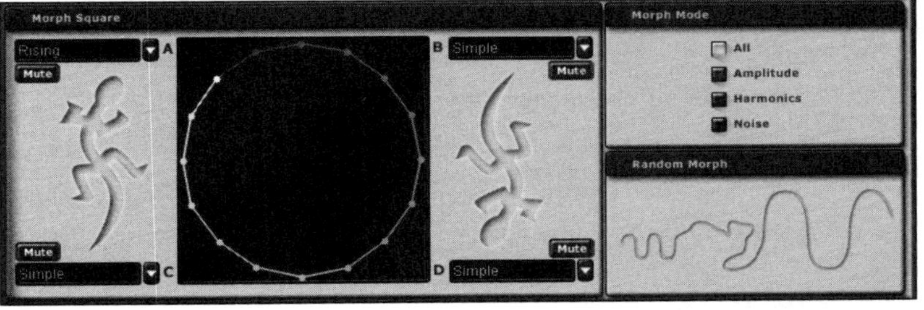

Figure 11.30
The Morph Square is directly connected to the Morph Timeline.

Now, let's list the main parameters of the Morph Timeline.

- **Morph Timeline**—This is the power button of the entire Morph page.
- **Morph X**—When this is selected, any edits to the timeline are reflected horizontally in the Morph Square below.
- **Morph Y**—When this is selected, any edits to the timeline are reflected vertically in the Morph Square below.
- **Sync**—This parameter synchronizes the timeline to the tempo of your sequencer.

- **Presets**—This pop-up menu selects different morphing presets, which affect the timeline and the Morph Square.
- **Save**—This saves any morphing presets.

The Morph Square

The lower-left portion of the Morph page, called the Morph Square, performs two functions:

- Select, change, and mute the different active voice programs within a Cameleon preset.
- Transition or morph between the audible characteristics of each voice program within a Cameleon preset.

As mentioned before, the Morph Square is directly related to the timeline above, so let's see how this works using the following example.

1. Click the Reset button to start completely from scratch. Play any note from the Virtual Keyboard and you should just hear a sine wave.
2. Activate the timeline by clicking on the Morph Timeline button in the upper-left corner of the page.
3. Now, use the preset pop-up menus of each voice program in the Morph Square to create a new basic sound. For example, you might try a combination of bass, brass/winds, effects, and chromatics.
4. Click and drag one of the breakpoints in the Morph Square to the bottom right (voice program D) of the interface. Once finished, this should be reflected in the timeline above (see Figure 11.31).
5. Play the sound now, and you should hear a transition or morph to the preset loaded into voice program D. If the transition is not occurring fast enough, make alterations to the timeline to quicken the pace of transition.

The Morph Mode

Let's go over the main parameters of the Morph page, starting with the Morph mode. This section of the page assigns the morph effect to alter the various parameters of the voice program page, which includes:

- **All**—When selected, the morph effect will alter all of the common parameters of the voice program page. This parameter is reflected in the Morph Square as a white dot.

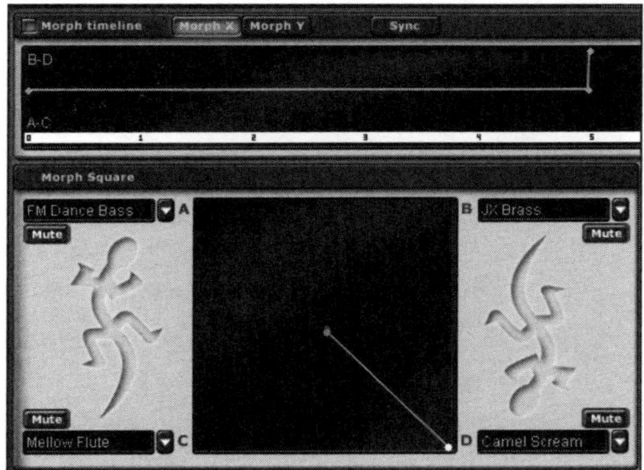

Figure 11.31

Any changes made to the Morph Square are reflected in the timeline.

- **Amplitude**—When selected, the morph effect will alter the Amp section of the voice program page. This parameter is reflected in the Morph Square as a green dot.
- **Harmonics**—When selected, the morph effect will alter the harmonics of the voice program page. This parameter is reflected in the Morph Square as a red dot.
- **Noise**—When selected, the morph effect will alter the noise generators of the voice program page. This parameter is reflected in the Morph Square as a blue dot.

Random Morph

Just below is the Random Morph section. This generates random values for the entire Morph page. Click within the camel outline in the interface, and you will see all of the parameters of the Morph page change accordingly.

> **MORPHING SUCCESS**
>
> Truly, the Morph page is an invaluable addition to the Cameleon 5000, but it takes a lot of practice to master. We've covered it pretty well throughout this section, but a better understanding of its potential can be found by using the morph presets at the top of the timeline. Try some of the easy presets found in the Hits directory, which are simple in design and use. After you have a better understanding, give the presets in the Circle directory a try for morphing fun.

The Easy Page

The Easy page is provided for those of us (like me) who want to trick out the Cameleon quickly and with ease (see Figure 11.32). It is also used to optimize the performance of the Cameleon in your computer.

- **Timbre**—This section affects the harmonic quality of a Cameleon patch by adjusting the brightness or brilliance of the signal. This section is also used to govern the mix of harmonics and noise generator.
- **LFO**—When activated, this section introduces a low frequency oscillator into the mix, which can be used to effect the pitch and amplitude of the Cameleon sound. The parameters include the waveform selector (sine, saw tooth, square), rate (tempo-synced), pitch, and amp.
- **Voices**—This section alters the three Ps: polyphony, partials, and portamento. The polyphony display assigns the total number of playable voices; partials limit the total number of partials or harmonics in a preset; the Portamento knob creates a slur or sliding sound between played notes. Note that if you are running out of CPU power, reducing the number of partials and voices can help optimize your performance.
- **Amplitude Envelope**—This section acts as a master envelope for the amplifier, which adjusts the dynamics of the overall sound. Also important to note is the Loop button, which is discussed in greater detail in the following Note.
- **Output**—This section affects the master output of the Cameleon. Included are Master Volume, Stereo Width, and Velocity Sensitivity.
- **Random Easy**—This assigns random values to the parameters of the Timbre, LFO, and Amplitude Envelope sections. This does not affect the Voices and Output sections.

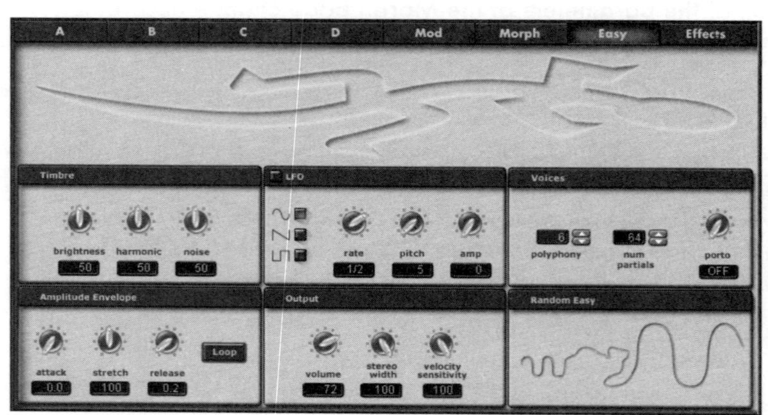

Figure 11.32

The Easy page is self explanatory, offering an easy way to manipulate and optimize the Cameleon.

LOOP MODE

The Loop button activates a very interesting and useful loop mode, which creates infinitely sustaining loops for as long as a MIDI note is held. Click once to activate it and then switch to any of the voice program pages. There you will see a pair of markers in the amp envelope; these markers are the left and right loop points (see Figure 11.33). They can be moved from left to right at will by simply clicking and dragging them with your mouse. Furthermore, if you select the Morph page, you will also see a pair of loop points there.

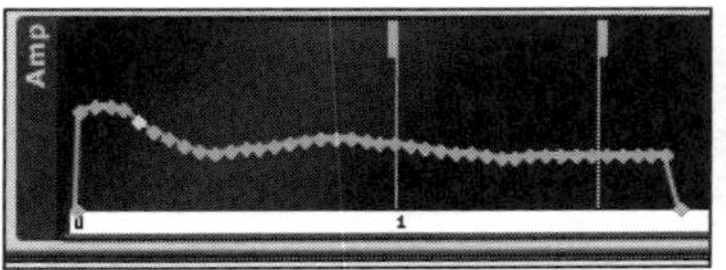

Figure 11.33
Activating the Loop mode will drop a pair of markers into each voice program page (left) and the Morph page (right) to compose sustaining loops of additive synthesis.

The Effects Page

The last page we'll explore is the Effects page (see Figure 11.34). Click once on this page to display its graphic interface. Click on the dark red LED buttons at the upper-right corner of the effect to activate it.

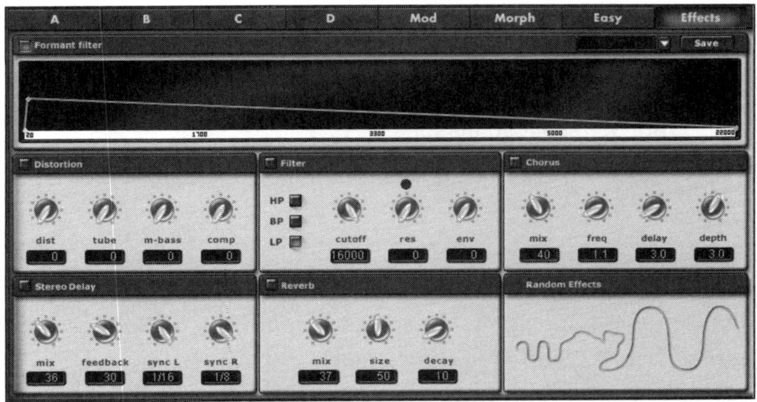

Figure 11.34
The Effects page includes many real-time effects that are CPU efficient and full of creative potential.

THESE EFFECTS ARE GLOBAL

All the effects on this page are global, which means that they alter the characteristics of the sound you create in the Cameleon. Unless otherwise specified by a manufacturer, this is the case for other soft synths that include effects.

The Formant Filter

At the top of the Effects page is the formant filter, which is basically a fancy graphic equalizer. A graphic equalizer comprises a series of filters, each of which will cut or boost a specific center frequency and frequency range. Up to 128 different breakpoints can be created by clicking anywhere within the Formant Filter interface. Clicking and dragging the created bands up or down will boost or cut the filters (see Figure 11.35).

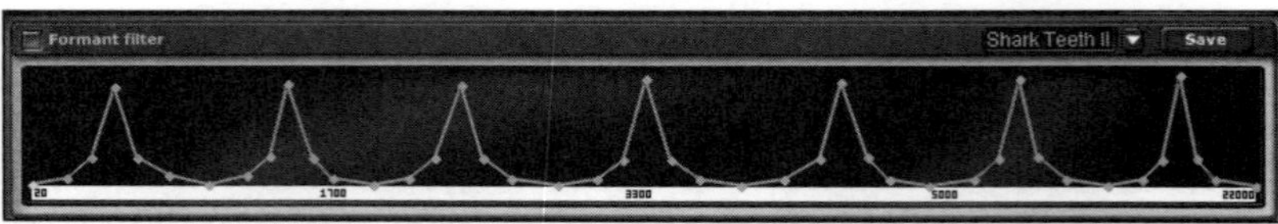

Figure 11.35

It's very easy to shape your sound by using the formant filter. Note the preset pop-up menu in the upper-right corner of this interface.

Distortion

The distortion effect adds overdrive to your synth sound. Although there are numerous uses for it, a distortion is a perfect processor to place on a bass synth or possibly percussion, making it ideal for hard-core industrial music.

Distortion includes four main parameters.

- **Dist**—Assigns the amount of distortion.
- **Tube**—This parameter creates a warm saturation effect, which sounds similar to a tube-driven amplifier.
- **M-Bass**—This parameter introduces a low frequency augmentation to the signal to beef up the tone.
- **Comp**—This parameter creates a very basic compression effect.

Filter

The filter shapes a sound by cutting or boosting specific bandwidths within the frequency spectrum. When used creatively, a filter can create sweeping effects heard so often in dance music.

The filter includes the following parameters.

- **Filter Modes**—There are three filter modes in this section. The high pass filter allows high frequencies to pass while cutting the lows. The band pass cuts both the high and low frequencies, while letting the mid-frequencies pass. The low pass filter allows low frequencies to pass while cutting the high end.

- **Cutoff**—This parameter specifies where the filter will function within the frequency spectrum.
- **Resonance**—This parameter emphasizes the frequencies set by the Cutoff knob, which thins out the sound.
- **Env**—This parameter alters the sensitivity of the filter by modulating the cutoff parameter.

> **GET PHAT**
>
> Just above the Resonance knob is an additional button, which places the filter in Phat mode. When in Phat mode, the filter produces a warmer-sounding effect while also teasing it with some additional distortion.

Chorus

Chorus doubles the original signal and slightly detunes it, which will result in a thick, dense sound. It's a popular effect for stringed instruments and pads.

Chorus includes the following parameters.

- **Mix**—This parameter shifts between the dry, or unprocessed, signal and the wet, or processed, signal.
- **Freq**—This parameter controls the rate of the chorus.
- **Delay**—This parameter sets the length of delay before the chorus takes effect.
- **Depth**—This parameter assigns the amount of depth or intensity of the chorus.

Stereo Delay

A delay takes a phrase and repeats it over and over again. In this case, the stereo delay provides two separate tempo-driven delays, one on each side of the stereo field.

Stereo delay includes the following parameters.

- **Mix**—This parameter shifts between the dry signal and the wet signal.
- **Feedback**—This parameter controls the number of times a processed phrase is repeated.
- **Sync L/Sync R**—These parameters adjust the delay between repeats. Since stereo delay is tempo specific, these values are displayed in notes rather than numbers.

Reverb

The reverb effect introduces ambience to a signal by placing it in a space that is defined by size and decay.

- **Mix**—This parameter shifts between the dry signal and the wet signal.
- **Size**—This parameter sets the size of the room, which affects the character of the reverb effect. It is very common to use a small room with percussion sounds, while pads and FX sounds get the large room treatment.
- **Decay**—This parameter sets the length of time before the reverb effect fades out.

THE RANDOM EFFECT

In the lower-right corner of the Effects page is the random effects function. Click anywhere within the Camel Audio logo and this will generate random values for all of the effects in this page, with the exception of the formant filter (see Figure 11.36).

Note that this randomize differs from the Random button at the top of the Cameleon interface. That particular Random button will assign random values to the entire interface, including the Effects page.

The Random buttons are a useful feature. There have been many times when I have found myself painted into a corner while designing synth sounds and have ended up with sounds that were a little bland. Using the random effects function can sometimes help by providing another avenue I may not have thought of before.

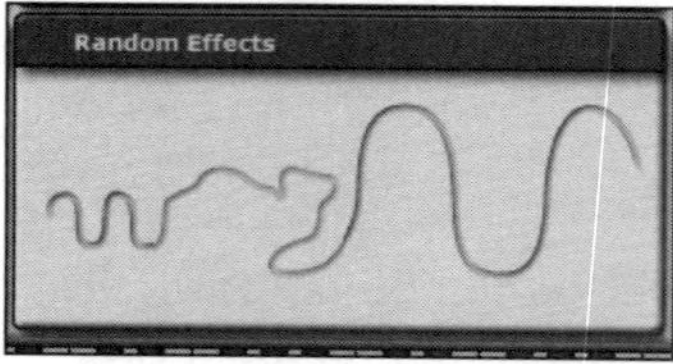

Figure 11.36
The Random Effects button randomizes all of the values in the Effects page, with the exception of the formant filter.

FUN WITH MODULATION

If you are looking for a way to channel your imagination with sound design, you might consider assigning assorted effect parameters to different MIDI events, such as the modulation wheel or aftertouch. These can all be made possible by visiting the Mod page.

Programming Additive Sounds

At long last, it's time to put your additive know-how to the test by designing your own presets. We'll continue to use the Cameleon 5000 as our soft synth of choice, but the sounds that I will be designing throughout this section can be duplicated with most other additive synthesizers that sport similar features, such as the CUBE by VirSyn (see Figure 11.37).

Figure 11.37
The CUBE by VirSyn Software is another additive soft synth that includes several features similar to those of the Cameleon 5000, including morphing and resynthesis.

Programming a Bass Sound

Let's first use the Cameleon to program a good solid bass. First, press the Reset button in the upper-right corner to start from scratch.

1. Select voice program A and choose the Sine preset in the upper-right corner of the partial display. This will create a single sine wave.
2. Use the envelope generator below to create a very fast attack, a short decay/sustain, and a very quick release. When you are finished, the partial display and envelope generator should look a lot like Figure 11.38.
3. In order to make this bass as clean as possible, select the None preset from the noise generator below. This will remove any noise from the signal.

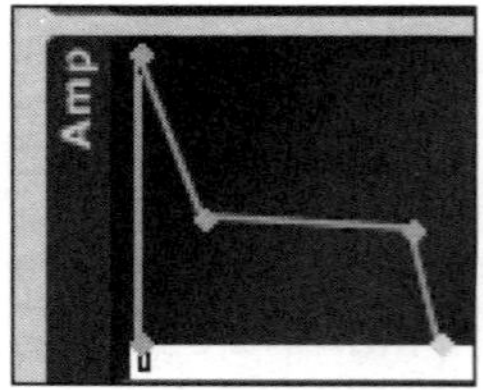

Figure 11.38

Since the bass is part of the rhythm section, it's important to keep it tight and punchy sounding. This can be done by creating a short attack, followed by a fast decay, sustain, and release.

Listening to the preset at this point, it sounds very minimal and not all that interesting, so let's activate another voice program and continue building our sound.

1. Click on the Morph page and activate the Morph Timeline. This will activate the remaining three voice program pages. However, since we are building this preset one voice program at a time, it would be a good idea to mute voice programs C and D by clicking the appropriate Mute buttons in the Morph Square. Once this is done, play a note from the Virtual Keyboard, and you should now hear only voice programs A and B.
2. Select voice program B and select the Plucked preset from the right side of the partial display. This will introduce a percussive element to the sound.
3. Click on the Detune button of the partial display to make some tuning adjustments to the individual harmonics. The idea here is to create a minor tuning adjustment to this preset to create a slight wavering sound between the two voice programs. Looking at Figure 11.39, you can see that I have made some very small adjustments to the second, third, fourth, and fifth harmonics. The trick to remember here is that a bass sound establishes rhythm and a low-end melodic structure, so you don't want to overdo it with detuning the harmonics. Instead, just flavor it with dissonance.
4. Moving downward, use the KeyHitH preset of the noise generator of voice program B to add a little percussive noise to the sound.

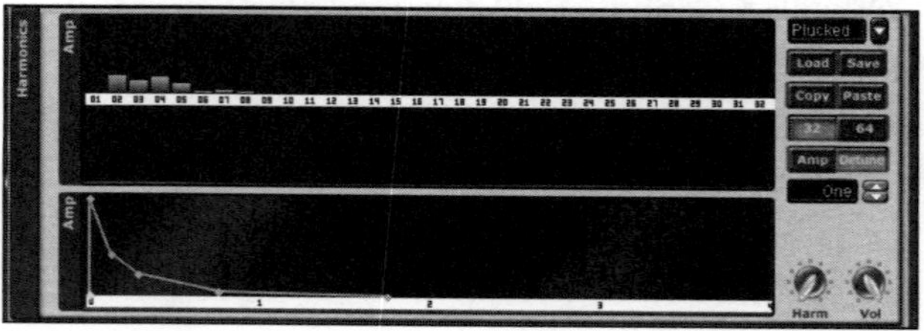

Figure 11.39

Use the Detune function to offset the tuning of a few harmonics, creating a wavering effect between the two voice programs.

The next element we're going to introduce is a morphing effect, to create a fast transition from voice program A to B.

1 Click on the Morph page. Looking at the Morph Timeline, you should see a single breakpoint. Click and drag this breakpoint down to the bottom start point of the timeline. This will allow only voice program A to be heard.
2 Next, click anywhere in the upper portion of the Morph Timeline to create a new breakpoint. We'll use this to create our transition.
3 Click and drag the new breakpoint to the left until it just about reaches the beginning of the timeline. Release the mouse and you should wind up with a transition that looks like Figure 11.40.

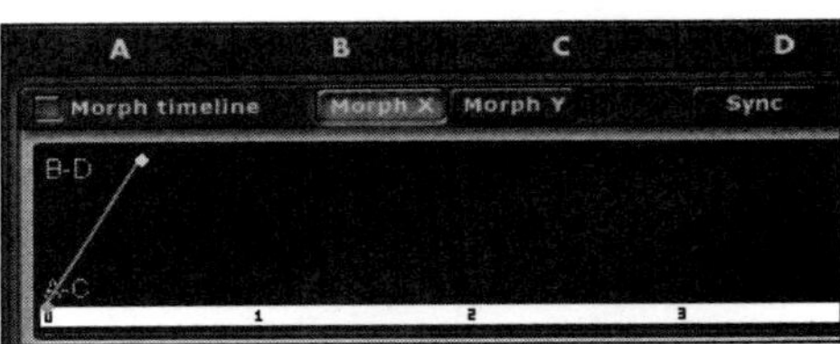

Figure 11.40
Create a new breakpoint and then click and drag it to the left to create a quick transition time.

Play the sound now, and it should sound quite a bit different. Let's wrap things up and use some effects to enhance the timbre of the bass.

1 Select the Effects page.
2 Add some chorus to the bass sound by clicking on its power button. Try adjusting the supplied parameters to enhance the detuned sound slightly and creating a doubling effect. For example, you could use the following values: Mix 68, Freq 2.1, Delay 0, and Depth 3.7.
3 Activate the filter, select the Low Pass (LP) mode, and set the Cutoff parameter to 484 and Resonance to 28. This will make the signal's texture sound a little muddy, but you will also hear a slight bell tone as well.

If you want to get a little more creative, try using the random effect parameter, or assign your modulation wheel to the filter cutoff parameter to give you real-time control from your MIDI keyboard.

SAVE YOUR WORK

Make sure that you periodically save your preset by clicking on the Save button at the top of the interface. You will then need to select a location to save it, give it a name, and finish it off by clicking the Save button to safeguard your preset.

Programming a Pad Sound

Now let's use the Cameleon to program a simple but effective pad sound. A pad sound is used mainly to fill the empty space in a mix with ambience by playing long, sustained chords. As luck would have it, the Cameleon 5000 is a fantastic soft synth to accomplish everything ambient. So, load an instance of the Cameleon 5000, press the Reset button, and follow along.

1. Select voice program A and draw in a simple harmonic pattern by clicking and dragging your mouse from left to right. When finished, you should have something resembling Figure 11.41.
2. Make some adjustments to the amp envelope of voice program A. Click and drag the decay parameter to the right to create a slow attack (see Figure 11.42).
3. Next, select the White Noise preset from the Noise Generator section. Manipulate the amp envelope of the noise generator to create a slow attack, but keep the amplitude of the noise generator down.

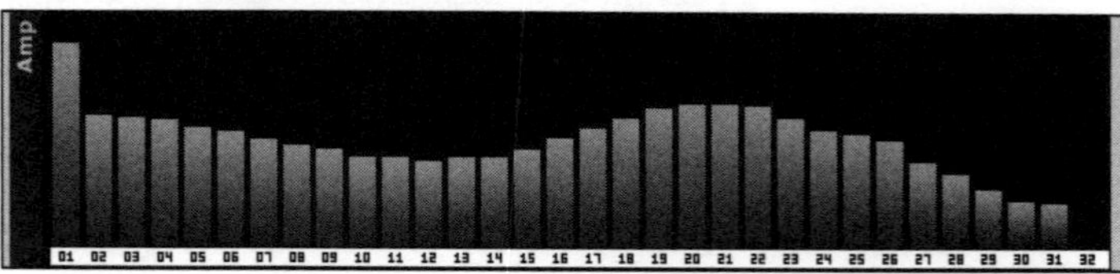

Figure 11.41
Select voice program A and draw in a harmonic pattern as shown. Play a note from the Virtual Keyboard and you should hear a nasal sound.

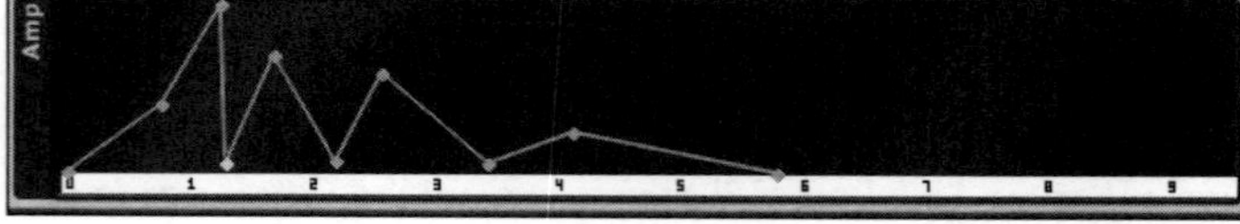

Figure 11.42
Now manipulate the breakpoints of the amp envelope in order to create a slow attack and long release. Feel free to insert a few extra breakpoints to create a few amplitude spikes.

At this point, we have a good, basic pad sound, so we'll push forward and add some effects. If this is your first time using this page, try clicking the Random Effects button in the lower-right corner of the interface to see and hear what kind of results are possible. As a finishing touch, make sure the distortion effect is turned on as well as the filter, because we're going to use those particular effects on the Mod page.

1 Click on the first Source pull-down menu and select Envelope. This will link the envelope of the Mod page to whatever target you choose.

2 Click on the first Target pull-down menu and select Filter Cutoff. This will link the Mod page envelope to the filter cutoff parameter of the Effects page.

3 Now use the breakpoints of the Mod page envelope to create a customized envelope curve (see Figure 11.43). Play the sound now and you should hear the envelope modulate the filter cutoff.

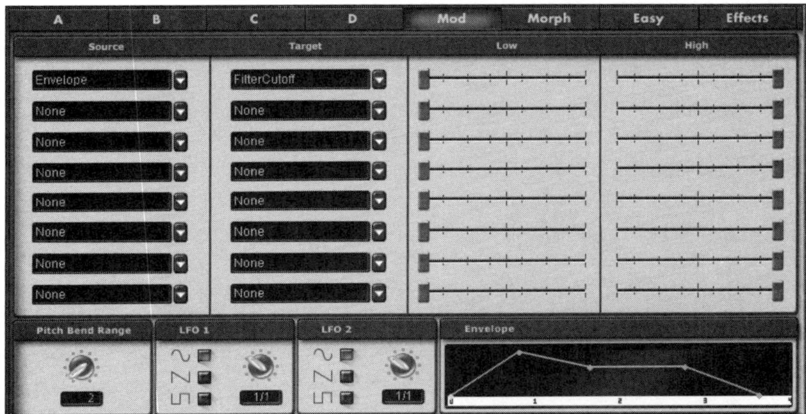

Figure 11.43

Use the Mod page envelope to create a curve that will modulate the filter cutoff of the filter of the Effects page.

12 RAM Synthesis

Introduced at the beginning of the soft synth revolution in the late 90s, RAM (random access memory) -based soft synths offered musicians a compelling alternative to using external drum machines and other hardware synths, which derived their sounds from onboard memory chips called ROM (read-only memory). Unlike samplers, ROM-based hardware synths (or ROMplers for short) offered musicians a solid selection of sounds that could not be edited in the same way as a sampler's sound set could, aside from basic synth parameters (filters, envelopes). RAM-based soft synths are closely related to ROMplers, as they too cannot manipulate any loaded sounds, apart from provided synth parameters. But unlike ROMplers, a RAM-based soft synth has the ability to change its sound sets by unloading and loading a new sound set into its RAM. Basically, what you hear is what you get. For a lot of musicians, this is a great thing, as most of them have little or no interest in tweaking sounds. They're just interested in plugging in, turning on, and writing music without hesitation.

RAM Synthesis Explained

RAM-based soft synthesis is fairly simple to understand. Unlike complex synthesis types such as subtractive and additive in which physical modeling generates a sound, a RAM-based soft synth generates its sounds by storing and playing back samples via your computer's installed RAM. Though this might at first sound similar to samplers such as Kontakt or GigaStudio, it's not exactly the same.

As you'll recall from our discussion of Kontakt and GigaStudio, with those samplers, the computer's RAM plays a much smaller role in the generation of sounds. In the case of RAM synthesis, a very small portion of a sample is stored in RAM, and the rest of the sample is played back (or *streamed*) from the computer's hard drive. This makes it possible to play large, sustaining samples because there is virtually no limit to your computer's playback capacity via hard drive.

In the case of RAM-based synthesis, an entire sample or compilation of samples is loaded into the RAM exclusively. This of course presents a strict limitation to how much sample data a RAM-based soft synth can load and play back. Now you can see why back in Chapter 2, "Configuring a Soft Synth Studio," I recommended installing as much RAM as you could afford.

What does RAM-based soft synthesis offer as benefits to a computer musician? For starters, several RAM-based soft synths offer a compelling number of world-class sounds and samples that are optimized for RAM storage, thus giving you a large library of loops, drum samples, and other instruments. Secondly, since there is virtually no physical modeling involved in RAM-based soft synths (aside from their standard synth parameters such as envelopes and filters), they are far less taxing on your computer's CPU, giving you the ability to activate and use more plug-ins within your DAW system.

Meet Our Synth—SampleTank 2 Free

There are several RAM-based soft synths on the market today with content ranging from beats and treats (Spectrasonics Stylus) to synthetic landscapes (Steinberg Hypersonic) and ethnic textures (Sound Burst Ethnosphere). However, among all of these RAM soft synths, IK Multimedia's SampleTank 2 best represents this genre by pairing an easy to understand 16-part multitimbral interface with a killer feature set (see Figure 12.1). That and the fact that the company provides a light version of the software free of charge make it the best candidate for this chapter.

GET SAMPLETANK 2 FREE

Go to the SampleTank Web site at **www.sampletank.com**. There you'll find a link to download the latest free version of SampleTank 2. Note that after installing it on your computer and running it for the first time, you will need to register it in order to unlock its entire feature set. If your studio computer has a direct connection to the Internet, this will only take a couple of minutes to complete. After that, you're all set.

Figure 12.1

Wow, the best things in life *are* free. SampleTank 2 Free, that is.

> **NOT A SAMPLER**
>
> Although the name might suggest it, SampleTank is *not* actually a sampler like GigaStudio. It is simply a sample playback device. It does have the ability to import digital audio files and Akai-formatted samples, but it cannot actually sample audio itself.

Tour of SampleTank 2 Free

Assuming that you have properly installed SampleTank 2, we're ready to begin our tour of its graphic interface. But before doing this, we should take a quick moment to discuss installing sounds, which are simply known as *instruments*. The free version of SampleTank does not include any installed instruments with the initial downloadable file. This is done to keep the file size small so that it can download quickly.

Free instruments for SampleTank can be found by browsing the SampleTank Web site (**www.sampletank.com**). You should see a short list of Web links to three free instrument files (see Figure 12.2). Download these files, decompress them, and then move the individual instrument folders into the SampleTank Free Instruments folder, which is located within the SampleTank 2 Free Program folder. After doing this, launch your sequencing application (Cubase, SONAR, Pro Tools), activate SampleTank 2, and launch its graphic interface. As you can see in Figure 12.3, the installed instruments are now listed on the right side of the interface.

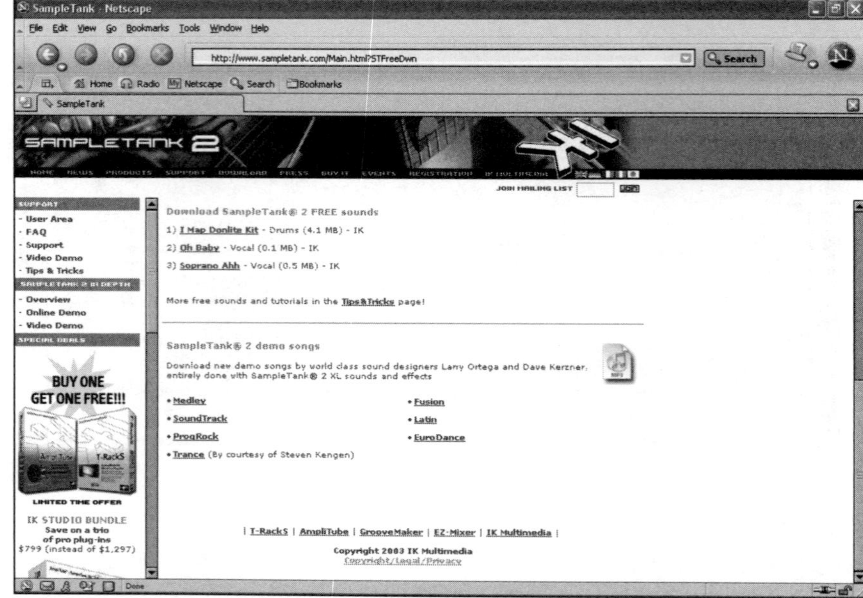

Figure 12.2

IK provides a few initial free instruments to get you started. See the Tips & Tricks page of the SampleTank Web site to find more free instruments.

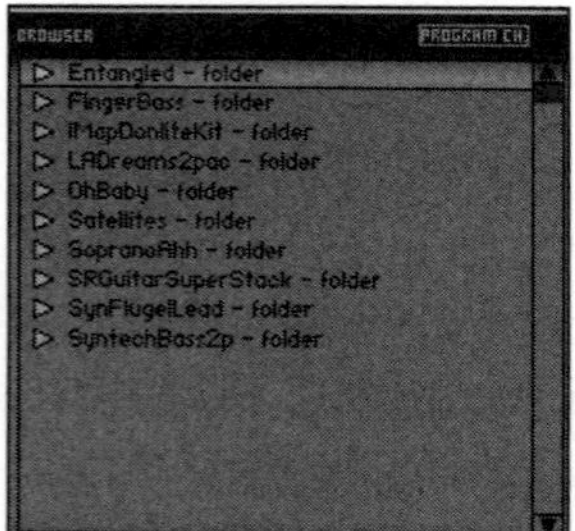

Figure 12.3

The instruments have been downloaded and installed and can now be seen and used in SampleTank 2.

We're now ready to begin our tour of SampleTank 2. Looking back at Figure 12.1, you can see that the SampleTank interface is divided into three sections.

- Parts, Mixing, and Browser
- Editor
- Mini Keyboard

Let's discuss each section.

Parts, Mixing, and the Browser

Occupying the upper half of the SampleTank interface is the Parts, Mixing, and Browser section. This is where you will locate, load, and mix all of

SampleTank's 16 parts. A *part* is simply an individual SampleTank channel. Over the next few pages, we'll discuss the basic procedures for loading and mixing instruments by providing some easy to follow tutorials.

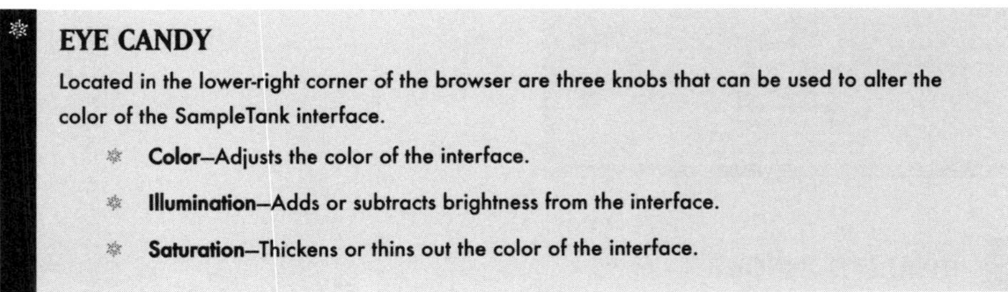

EYE CANDY

Located in the lower-right corner of the browser are three knobs that can be used to alter the color of the SampleTank interface.

- **Color**—Adjusts the color of the interface.
- **Illumination**—Adds or subtracts brightness from the interface.
- **Saturation**—Thickens or thins out the color of the interface.

Loading Instruments

To load an instrument into SampleTank, navigate to the browser column where all of your available instrument folders are listed. Note that all of the listed instrument folders include a collapsible/expandable arrow to the left, which comes into play when you decide which instrument to load. For this example, let's select the first instrument folder in this list, called Entangled, and load it into the first part.

1 Click once on the instrument folder to select it.
2 Now click on its corresponding arrow to expand it. This will display the actual instrument file within the folder.
3 Finish by double-clicking on the instrument to load it into the first part. This will take anywhere between 1 and 5 seconds, depending on how large the instrument is (see Figure 12.4).

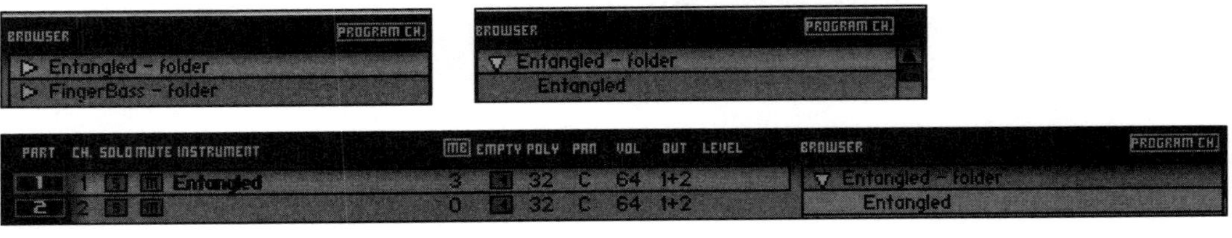

Figure 12.4

Loading an instrument into SampleTank is done by first selecting the instrument folder (upper left), then expanding its view (upper right), and finally double-clicking on the instrument to load it into a part (bottom).

To *unload* an instrument from a part, simply click on the part's Empty button, upon which a pop-up window will appear to verify the unloading of the instrument (see Figure 12.5). Click OK to unload it.

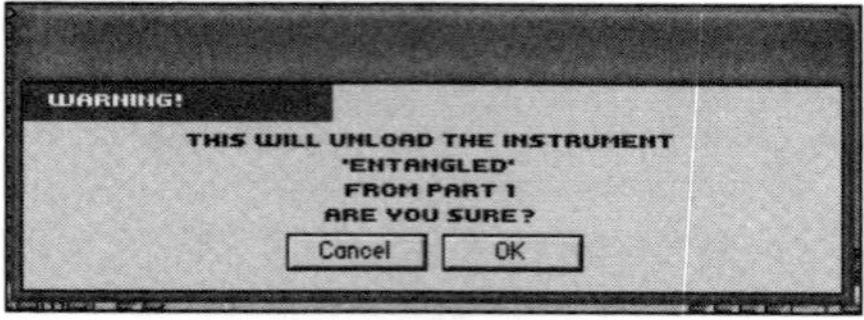

Figure 12.5
After clicking on a part's Empty button, a new pop-up window will open to verify your choice.

DISABLED IMPORT

Note that the free version of SampleTank does not import Akai or audio files into the interface. You must own the full version in order to take advantage of this feature. They can't give you everything for free, can they?

Visit **www.sampletank.com** for more information.

Working with Parts

Once an instrument has been loaded into one of SampleTank's 16 parts, its mixing and play parameters can be altered in the Mix section (see Figure 12.6).

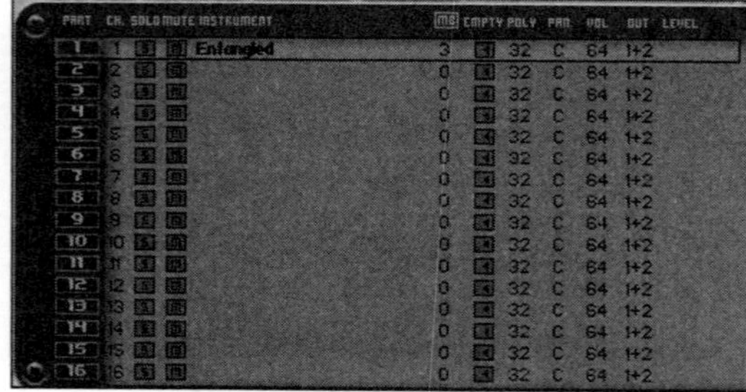

Figure 12.6
The Mix section alters the mixing and play parameters of any loaded SampleTank instrument.

The available parameters include:

- **Mute**—Silences a selected instrument from the entire SampleTank mix.
- **Solo**—Isolates a selected instrument from the entire SampleTank mix by muting the other instruments.
- **Instrument**—Lists the name of the loaded instrument.

- **Memory**—Displays the amount of RAM used by a loaded instrument.
- **Empty**—Unloads a selected instrument from a part.
- **Polyphony**—Sets the amount of polyphony for a loaded instrument.
- **Pan**—Places an instrument in the stereo field.
- **Volume**—Alters the amplitude of a loaded instrument.
- **Output**—Routes a selected instrument to one of SampleTank's outputs. Click and drag up and down to select the output.
- **Level**—Displays the volume output of an instrument when triggered.

Searching for Instruments

SampleTank's search engine is useful for locating a particular instrument or instrument classification with keywords (see Figure 12.7). These keywords are programmed into the instrument by the programmer in order to make the keyword search as thorough as possible. Furthermore, you can add your own supplementary keywords and save them to the instrument for future searches.

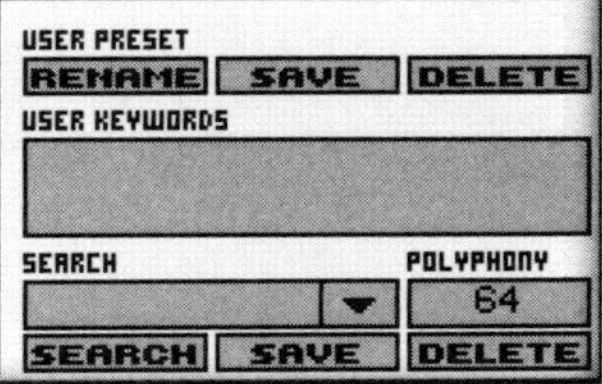

Figure 12.7
Can't find all of your bass sounds? Use the SampleTank search engine to locate them.

Let's look at an example of using the search engine by using it to locate a bass instrument.

1. Click in the Search dialog and a pop-up window will appear, prompting you to type in a keyword. For this example, I'll type in "bass" (see Figure 12.8).
2. Click on the OK button, and SampleTank should immediately list the available instruments in the browser that match the entered keyword.
3. Double-click on the appropriate instrument to load it into an empty part.

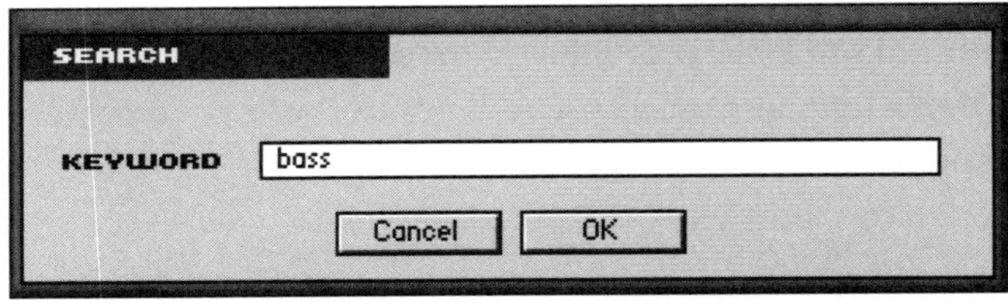

Figure 12.8
Click on the Search dialog to type in your keyword.

Now let's learn how to add your own keyword to an instrument. Note that the instrument must first be loaded into a part.

1. With the bass instrument still loaded into a part, click in the User Keywords dialog, which will open a new pop-up window into which you can type your own keywords.
2. For this example, I will type in my name and click OK (see Figure 12.9).
3. Now click on the Empty button to unload the instrument.
4. Click in the Search dialog and type in the keyword you just entered.
5. Click OK, and the bass instrument should immediately appear in the browser column.
6. Double-click on the instrument to load it into a part, and you should see the new keyword displayed in the User Keywords dialog.

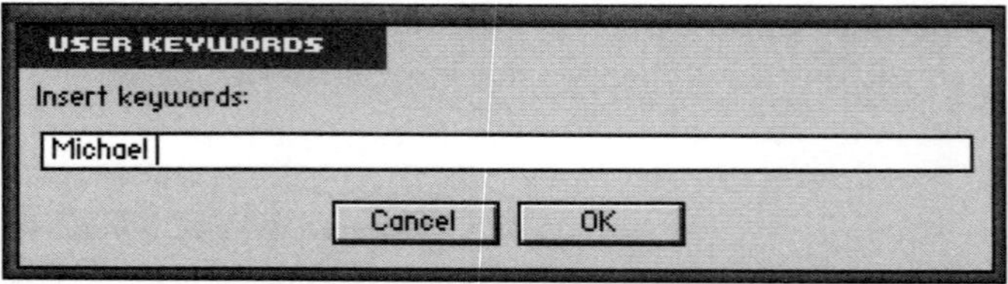

Figure 12.9
With an instrument loaded into a part and selected, clicking on the User Keywords dialog will open a new pop-up window to enter your own custom keywords. I'll type in my name.

The Editor

After an instrument has been selected and loaded into one of SampleTank's 16 parts, it's up to the editor to alter its characteristics by making use of provided synth parameters (envelopes, filters, LFOs) and up to four real-time effects. The editor is also responsible for governing the global parameters of SampleTank parts, including pan and volume.

Macro Parameters

The Macro parameters are essentially shortcuts to specific parameters within an active SampleTank instrument. Looking at Figure 12.10, you can see that the loaded drum kit's Macro parameters are linked to the individual amplitudes of the kick, snare, hi-hat, and cymbals. As you browse through other SampleTank instruments, you'll notice these parameters' assignments change.

Figure 12.10
The Macro parameters are linked to selected amplitude, envelope, or filter parameters embedded within an instrument.

Synth-Sampler Parameters

The Synth-Sampler parameters can perform several editing tasks to a loaded instrument (see Figure 12.11). With this section of the editor, it's possible to activate filters, LFOs, or envelopes to enhance the instrument's traits. Use any of the seven buttons presented in the upper portion of this interface to activate and edit its related parameters.

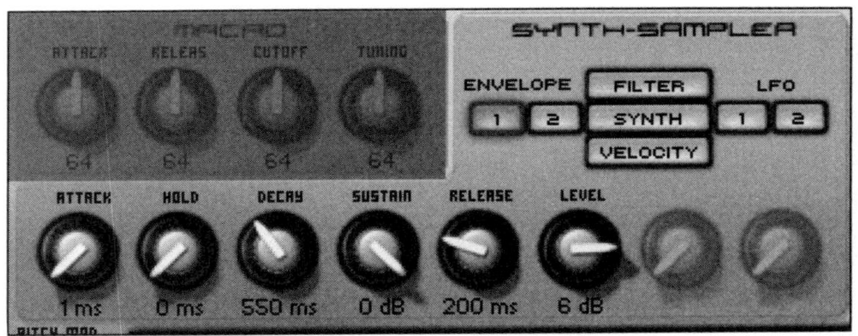

Figure 12.11
The Synth-Sampler parameters include LFOs, filters, and envelopes.

- **Envelope 1**—Attack, Hold, Decay, Sustain, Release, and Level.
- **Envelope 2**—Attack, Hold, Decay, Sustain, Release, Filter, and Pitch.
- **Filter**—Filter Type (Low Pass, Band Pass, High Pass), Filter Slope or Intensity (6dB, 12dB, 24dB), Cutoff Frequency, and Resonance.
- **Synth**—Synth Engine Type (Resampling, Pitch Shift/Time Stretch, STRETCH). Note that each synth engine includes its own set of parameters. For example, the Resampling mode includes the Pitch, Fine, and Bender (pitch bend wheel) parameters.
- **Velocity**—Curve, Amp, Filter, Pitch, Resonance, LFO Depth 1, and Envelope 2 Sustain.
- **LFO 1**—Wave, Speed, Depth, Delay, Level, Pitch, Filter, and Free Run.
- **LFO 2**—Wave, Speed, Depth, Level, Pitch, Filter, and Pan.

> **SYNTH MODES**
>
> The SampleTank 2 Synth button includes three different synthesizer engines, each of which has its own purpose and strong points. Read below to get a better idea of their different qualities.
>
> - **Resampling**—This is considered to be the "default" synth engine of SampleTank 2.
> - **Pitch Shift/Time Stretch**—This synth mode time stretches samples and loops to work at virtually any tempo. It also controls the tuning of an instrument via pitch controls.
> - **STRETCH**—Also known as "SampleTank Time Resynthesis Technology," STRETCH is a unique synth engine that avoids the unreal elements or digital artifacts of acoustic instruments when excessively transposed. It can also be used to speed up or slow down sampled loops without affecting the pitch and timbre. Note that STRETCH consumes a lot more CPU power than the other synth engines, so make sure your computer is up to the task.
>
> Much more information about these three synth modes can be found on page 47 of the SampleTank free manual.

Effects

SampleTank provides five slots to activate and use several different combinations of real-time effects for each of the 16 parts within a single instance of SampleTank (see Figure 12.12). That adds up to a potential of 80 effects within one instance of the soft synth. These effects range from the commonly known effects of compressors, reverbs, and delays to the eclectic effects of phonographs and frequency modulation.

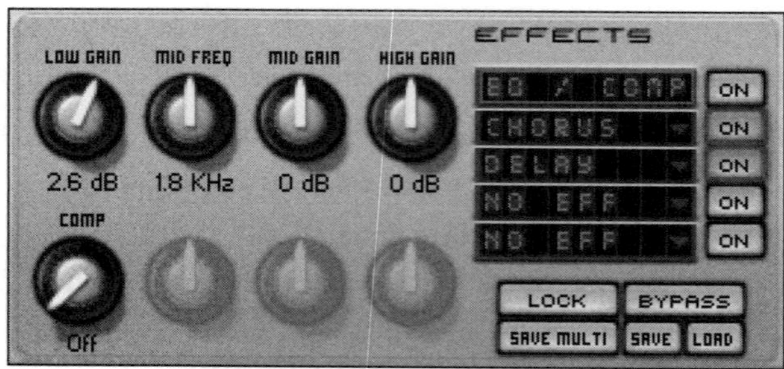

Figure 12.12
SampleTank 2 provides several real-time effects to enhance your soft synth's character.

By default, the top slot of the effects chain is permanently occupied by a combination equalizer/compressor. Click on this slot and all of its corresponding parameters will appear to the left of the effects chain. Each effect is turned on and off by using the Power button to the right of each effect slot, and a new effect can be selected for each of the four remaining slots by clicking on its corresponding arrow icon.

The available real-time effects include reverb, ambience, reverb delay, spring reverb, delay, filter, envelope filter, multi filter, wah-wah, chorus, multi-chorus, phaser, amplitude modulation, frequency modulation, flanger, envelope flanger, auto pan, tremolo, rotary speaker, lo-fi, distortion, phonograph, crusher, overdrive, preamp, tone control, cabinet, parametric EQ, channel strip, compressor, limiter, and slicer.

Portamento

In the Portamento section you can choose one of three playing modes and establish a portamento or sliding effect between played notes.

- **Portamento Time**—This knob determines the time it will take to slide from one note to the next. It has a range of 1 millisecond to 10 seconds.
- **Play Mode**—This pop-up menu selects one of three play modes: polyphonic, monophonic, and legato, which is monophonic with portamento. If you want to establish a portamento effect, you must be in the legato play mode.
- **Octave**—This pop-up menu transposes a loaded instrument in octave increments.

Loop Sync

The Loop Sync button offers a means to synchronize any loaded instruments with loops with the tempo of your sequenced song. Furthermore, the sync remains locked, no matter what tempo you choose. If you change the tempo of your song at some point, the Loop Sync function will alter the loop to fit the tempo.

An added bonus to the Loop Sync feature is its integration with the three synth modes, which were discussed earlier in this chapter.

- **Resampling**—When selected, the loop pitch will be altered in order to match the tempo.
- **Pitch Shift/Time Stretch**—When selected, the loop pitch will not be affected when altering the tempo of the loop.
- **STRETCH**—Like the previous synth mode, the loop pitch will not be affected when altering the tempo. However, unlike the previous synth mode, STRETCH works best with single instrument loops, like guitar loops or flute loops. Percussion loops can and will produce audible results that are somewhat bizarre in nature.

Pan/Volume

The Pan and Volume knobs are used to alter the panning position and amplitude levels of a single SampleTank part. Note that as you make adjustments to these parameters, their related parameters in the Part/Browser section change along with the moves.

The Mini Keyboard

New to the SampleTank 2 feature set is the inclusion of a mini keyboard, which works similarly to those found on many of the other soft synths and samplers we've looked at throughout this book (see Figure 12.13). In this case, the mini keyboard serves up a few extra surprises for your instruments.

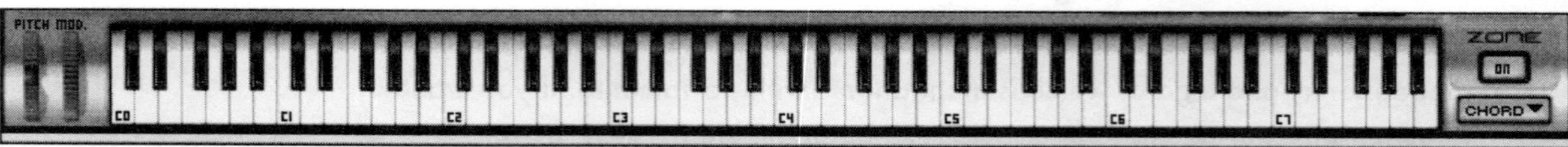

Figure 12.13

The mini keyboard triggers the samples of a loaded instrument.

Using Zones

Zones are a particularly interesting feature of SampleTank, enabling you to edit the attributes of a single sample or a small group of samples within a single instrument. For example, if you are using a drum kit instrument and would like to alter the dynamics of the snare drum, this is done with the zones functions. Click on the Zone button, and all of the loaded samples related to an instrument will be displayed in both dark and translucent pink, while the empty keys will be colored white (see Figure 12.14). Then, it's just a matter of clicking on the appropriate note along the mini keyboard and editing its individual parameters. After making your adjustments, click the Zone button again to switch back to the standard mini keyboard view.

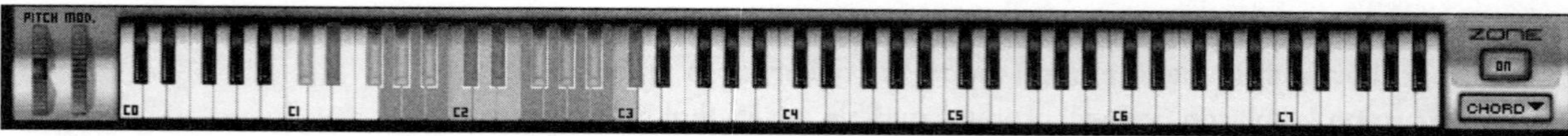

Figure 12.14

Activating the zone parameter will present all loaded samples within an instrument.

Playing Chords

At the bottom right corner of the SampleTank interface is the Chord pull-down menu. This menu lists different note intervals and chord shapes, which can be selected and then played from the mini keyboard or from an external MIDI keyboard (see Figure 12.15). This feature is very handy, especially if you don't have a MIDI keyboard available. For example, let's assume you have loaded a pad or piano instrument into SampleTank and you would like to hear a major seventh chord (a very jazzy chord), but you don't have a MIDI keyboard to trigger the four notes simultaneously. Just select the chord name and click on any note along the mini keyboard. The note that you click on will become the root of the chord, followed by the relevant notes attached to the selected chord shape.

Figure 12.15

Want to hear your instruments played as chords, but you don't have a MIDI keyboard handy? Not a problem. Just select the chord type you want and play any note on the mini keyboard to hear that chord.

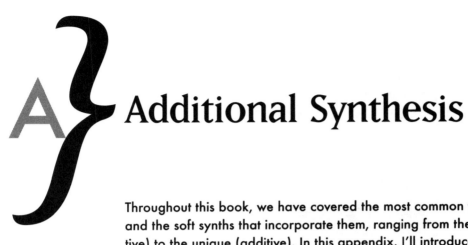

Additional Synthesis

Throughout this book, we have covered the most common types of synthesis and the soft synths that incorporate them, ranging from the familiar (subtractive) to the unique (additive). In this appendix, I'll introduce you to three more types of synthesis that are less common but with which you may wish to become more familiar.

Granular Synthesis

Granular is a unique form of synthesis that involves the fusion of small periodic bursts of sound, called *grains*. These grains can have durations of 10–50 milliseconds each on average and can originate from just about any sound source, such as samples or waveforms. Once a sequence of grains is selected, they are merged, resulting in a completely new audio event that can be further enhanced with the use of envelopes, filters, and different placements in the stereo field.

Five fundamental parameters govern granular synthesis:

- **Duration**—This determines the length of each grain.
- **Envelope Shape**—This modifies the dynamic characteristics of the composite waveform.
- **Frequency**—This determines how quickly the composite waveform repeats when looped.
- **Delay**—This assigns the amount of space between each grain.
- **Spatial Location**—This places the grains in variable locations within the stereo field.

Since there aren't a lot of soft synths that support granular synthesis, Native Instruments Reaktor 4 wins by default. Embedded within its library of *ensembles* (synthesizers), Grain States is a unique take on granular synthesis; it creates sound by using either sampled material or live input from a microphone (see Figure A.1).

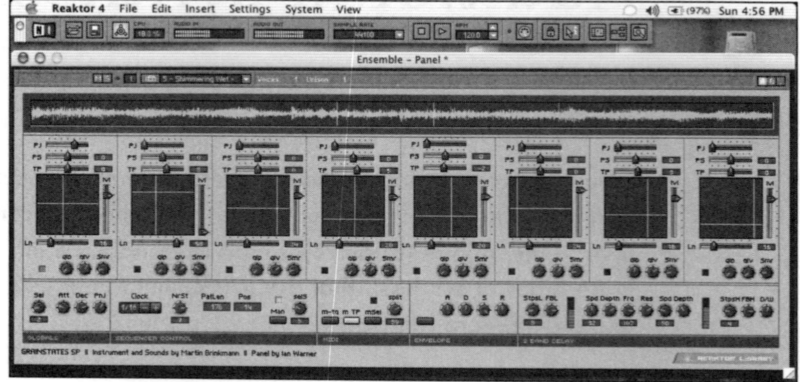

Figure A.1
The Grain States Reaktor ensemble is a synth that can use either samples or live input to generate sound.

CRYSTAL—THE GRANULAR METHOD

Although there aren't a lot of soft synths that completely support granular synthesis, there are a few that include elements of it, such as the modules in Kontakt, which we talked about in Chapter 7, "Kontakt Tutorial." Another great example of the incorporation of granular synthesis is Crystal by Green Oak (see Figure A.2). Crystal is a soft synth that primarily supports subtractive and FM synthesis, but it also includes a few sampled waveforms, which have been prepared with granular synthesis parameters.

Even better, Crystal is a free soft synth that supports MacOS9/X and Windows XP. For more information, visit the Green Oak Web site (**www.greenoak.com/vst.html**).

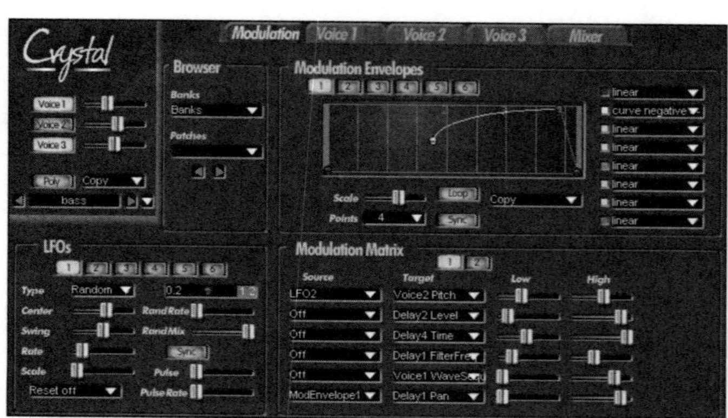

Figure A.2
Crystal by Green Oak is a soft synth that incorporates elements of granular synthesis along with subtractive and FM.

> **GRAINTABLE SYNTHESIS**
>
> Over the last few years, granular synthesis has spawned an additional form of synthesis called *Graintable*. This form of synthesis can be found only in a soft synth called the Malström by Propellerhead Software (see Figure A.3). Graintable is a merging of two forms of synthesis: granular and wavetable. Since we have already shed some light on granular, let's take a minute to discuss wavetable.
>
> Developed in the early to mid 1980s, wavetable synthesis is based on the playback of sampled waveforms. It's quite common and can be found on many standard audio cards. Wavetable synthesis possesses a few key benefits, such as the ability to sweep through the sequence of waveforms at any speed without affecting the pitch and isolating and looping specific points of the wavetable.
>
> Here's how graintable synthesis works:
>
> 1. The oscillators of the Malström play sampled sounds that have been pre-processed in a complex manner and cut into individual grains, which when compiled are called graintables.
> 2. These graintables are made up of periodic waveforms that, when combined, play back the original sounds.
> 3. At this point, the graintable is treated in the same way as a wavetable. You have the ability to sweep through the graintable and single out any nuance of the graintable that you would like to manipulate. For example, you could extract the vowel out of a voice graintable. Additionally, the graintable can be manipulated further by incorporating the ability to "shift" the frequency region or "formant" without altering the pitch, which is a granular synthesis quality.

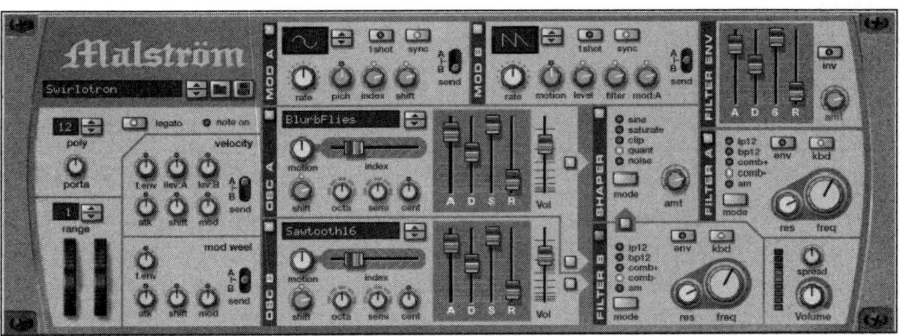

Figure A.3
The Malström by Propellerhead is found within its flagship program, Reason 2.5.

Vocal Synthesis

One of the newest forms of synthesis to come about is the *vocal synth*, which simulates the phonetic articulations of a human voice. Essentially, a vocal synth can use a library of recorded *phonemes*, which are the smallest phonetic units of a spoken language that communicate an intended meaning.

For example, the *b* of the word *bat* and the *c* of the word *cat* are both phonemes. These recorded phonemes are then converted to the synthesis engine of the vocal soft synth by way of the Fast Fourier Transform method.

One of the best examples of vocal synths is the Vocaloid Miriam by Zero-G (see Figure A.4). Based on the voice and vocal styles of Miriam Stockley (**www.miriam.co.uk**), the Vocaloid is a PC-only soft synth that works by entering lyrics and articulations such as vibrato and pitch bend. The lyrics and articulations are then processed through the Vocaloid synth engine, resulting in a vocal line that sounds incredibly realistic.

Figure A.4
The Vocaloid Miriam Virtual Vocalist is an emulation of the singing styles of Miriam Stockley (backup singer for Tina Turner, Kyle Minogue, and Adiemus).

> **HONORABLE MENTION—VIRSYN CANTOR**
>
> The Cantor by VirSyn is another example of vocal synthesis (see Figure A.5). But unlike Vocaloid, the Cantor is a lot more synthetic in texture, since it allows you to merge 120,000 phonemes with various synthesis parameters to create extremely unreal vocal lines for your music. The Cantor also supports both Mac OSX and Windows XP.
>
> For more information, visit the VirSyn Web site at **www.virsyn.com** and download the demo version.

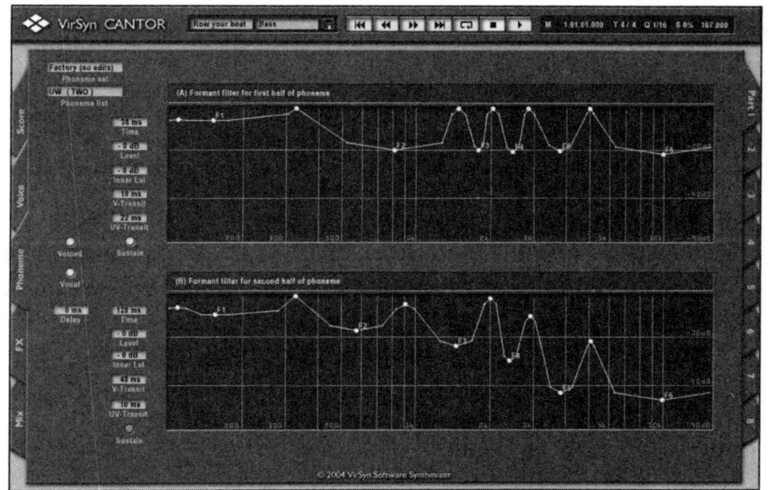

Figure A.5

The VirSyn Cantor is a vocal soft synth that combines thousands of phonemes with various synthesis parameters.

Vocoders

A vocoder (short for "voice coder") is an audio effect that uses two separate sources of input to create a new audio signal by applying the frequency bands of one signal to the other. While not really a synthesizer *per se*, the vocoder has been a highly influential sound texture used on many types of electronic music, such as "O Superman" by Laurie Anderson, "Around the World" by Daft Punk, and my favorite, "More Bounce to the Ounce" by Zapp and Roger.

The two separate audio sources that drive the vocoder are the carrier and the modulator.

The *carrier* is ideally an audio source that is constantly generating sound. For example, a good carrier could be a string pad sound playing from a subtractive synthesizer or sampler. Most importantly, a carrier must generate a perceivable pitch or frequency, as it is used to drive the modulator.

The *modulator* is typically an audio source such as a spoken voice or vocal track. Another typically used modulator is a drum loop, for creating rhythmically enhanced sounds.

Once you have these two elements, they are then routed to their appropriate vocoder inputs. The modulator is divided into a set number of bands (4, 8, 16, 32, 512, or 1024) by using band pass filters. These separate bands are then sent to an envelope follower (a device that continuously monitors and analyzes the signal levels).

Meanwhile, the carrier is processed with the same number of bands as the modulator. The same frequency ranges used in the modulator's band pass filters are also applied to the carrier. By doing this, the carrier will have the same frequency characteristics as the modulator. This means that if the modulator gets louder or more dynamic in shape, the carrier will follow and emulate this as well.

There are several virtual vocoders available on the market today, such as the Orange Vocoder by Prosoniq and the MDA Vocoder by Maxim Digital Audio. I have found that the best example of this effect can be found within the Native Instruments Vokator (see Figure A.6).

Figure A.6

The Native Instruments Vokator is a vocoding monster.

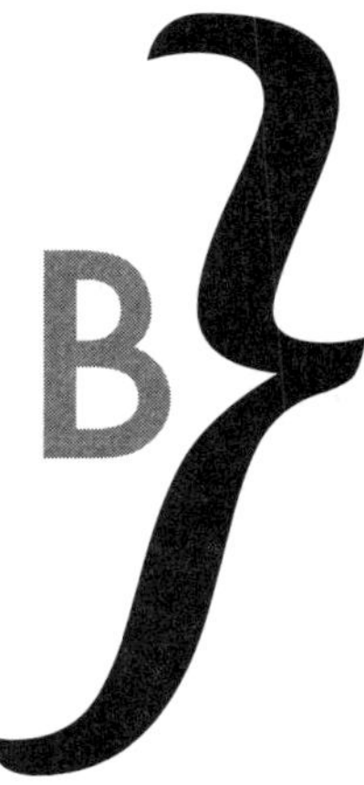

Additional Resources on the Web

Throughout this book, we have covered many aspects of software synthesis and sampling and what they can do for your music. This appendix lists some Web sites that will help you learn more about additional software and hardware and some Web resources for posting your music.

K-v-R Audio Plug-In Resources

www.kvr-vst.com

Because this book is about soft synths and samplers, it seems only right that K-v-R is mentioned first in this appendix (see Figure B.1). K-v-R is an information hub for the first and last word on soft synthesis. Its news section is updated daily, includes a soft synth database to find the right synth for you, and has an active user forum.

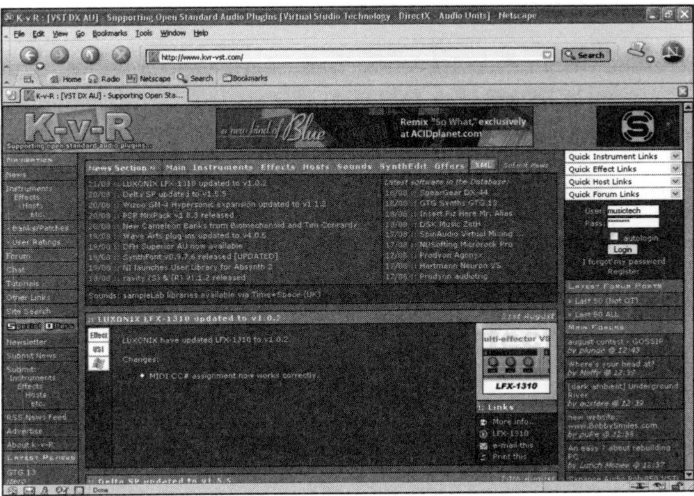

Figure B.1

The K-v-R Audio Plug-In Web site should be your first stop for information on what's hot and what's not in software synthesis.

Apple Computer

www.apple.com

If you are an avid Mac user, you probably already know about this site. Apple.com is the home page of everything that is made, created, and supported by Apple (see Figure B.2). This Web site has one of the best technical support databases around to answer just about every Apple-related question there is. There is also a comprehensive Web store to configure and build a new Mac with those hip G5 processors.

Figure B.2

Among other things, the Apple Web site has a great technical support database.

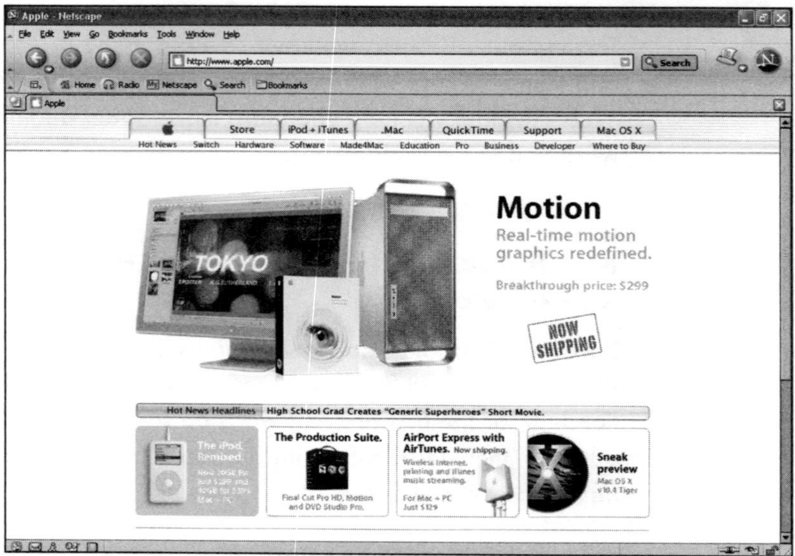

Microsoft Corporation

www.microsoft.com

For those of you on the other side of the great computer pendulum, microsoft.com is the home page for all of the programs and operating systems conceived and created by Microsoft (see Figure B.3). I use this page frequently to download new updates for Windows XP. I cannot stress enough how important it is to check frequently for security updates for your operating system, as there are so many computer viruses out there these days.

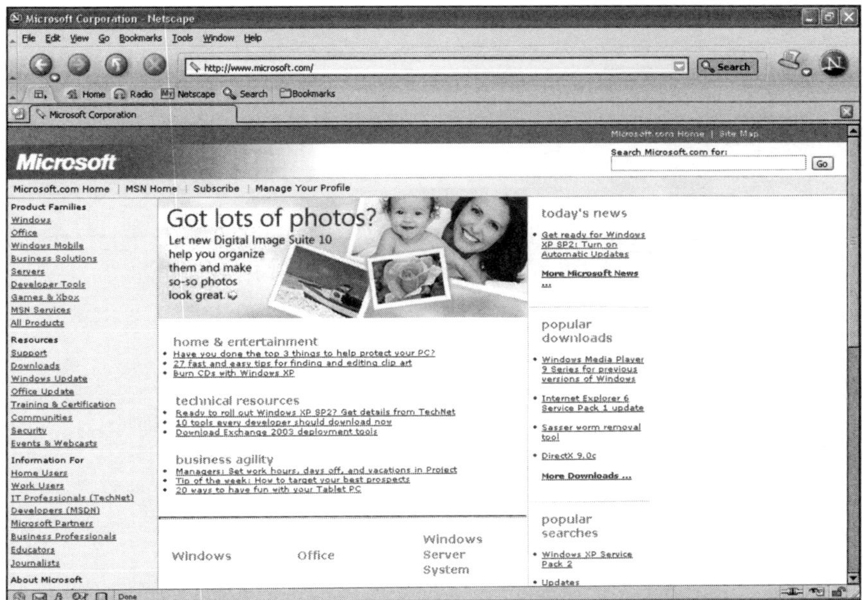

Figure B.3
The Microsoft Web site is a good source for new software updates and patches.

Harmony Central

www.harmony-central.com

Harmony Central is the ultimate musician resource on the Web, period (see Figure B.4). On this page, you'll find many informative tutorials and essays to help you better understand the technology behind these soft synths and others like it. It's also the first Web site I visit when I want to know what's new in music products. Above all, Harmony Central sports one of the most active user forums on the planet. If you can't find the answer to your question here, there might not be an answer.

Home Recording at About

www.homerecording.about.com

About.com is a Web site that I found by accident when researching the topics discussed in this book (see Figure B.5). Since then, I have come to rely on its wonderfully informative and helpful tutorials on home recording techniques and shopping guides for new studio gear.

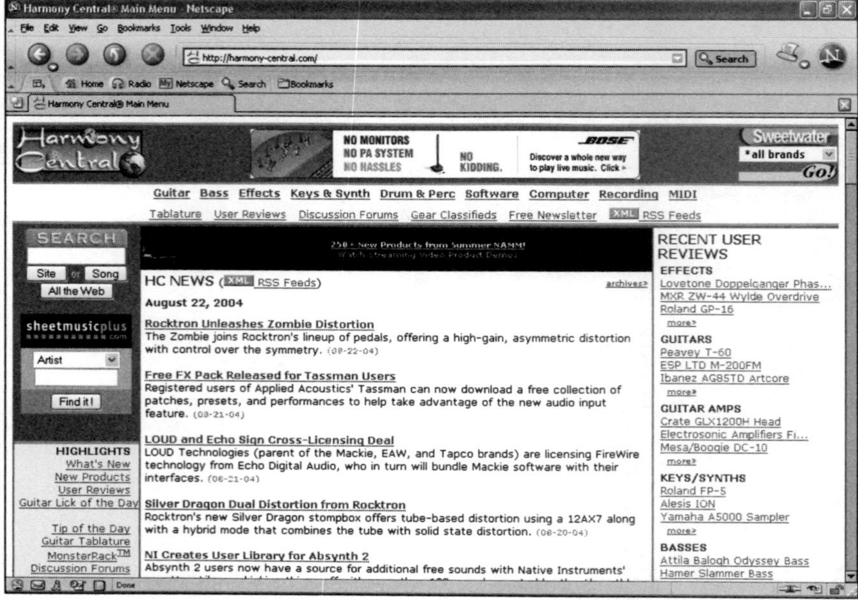

Figure B.4

The Harmony Central Web site has a very active user forum.

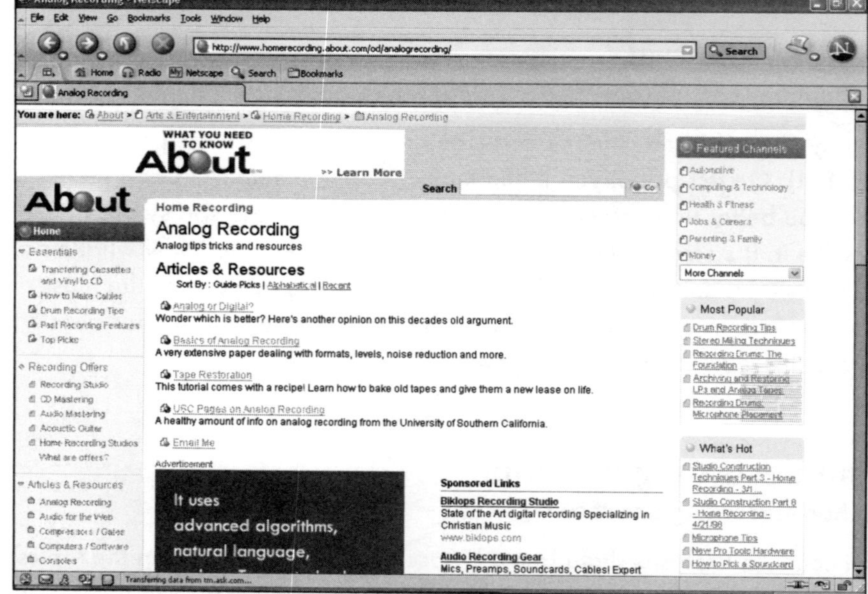

Figure B.5

The About.com Home Recording page is a great DIY resource for recording techniques.

Native Instruments

www.native-instruments.com

Where would soft synths be without Native Instruments? These guys are responsible for conceiving and creating some of the best soft synths around, most of which we've covered throughout this book (see Figure B.6). On this Web site, you'll find news items relating to the Native Instruments product line, in addition to an extremely thorough support section that will help you solve just about any technical support issue.

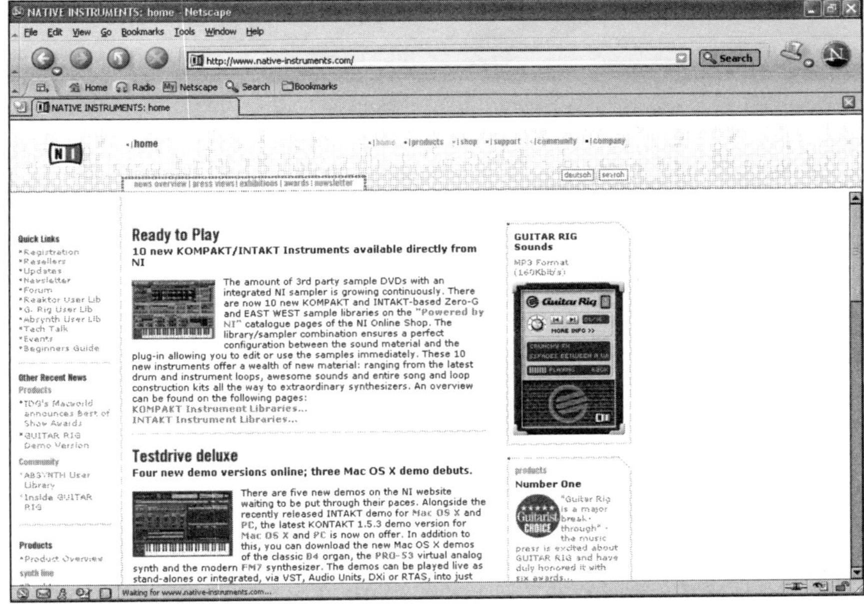

Figure B.6

The Native Instruments Web site is the place to go for everything "native."

Tascam

www.tascam.com

Tascam is the company that programs and distributes GigaStudio (see Figure B.7). On this page, you'll find updates and news items relating to GigaStudio, as well as informative articles and tutorials.

Figure B.7

The Tascam Web site is the best resource for GigaStudio updates and tutorials.

Arturia

www.arturia.com

Arturia Software programs and distributes several soft synths that emulate vintage synths such as the Moog Modular (which we looked at in Chapter 9), the Minimoog, and the Yamaha CS80. In addition, Arturia has conceived its own self-contained soft synth workstation called Storm that includes some very cool soft synths, drum machines, and samplers (see Figure B.8).

Emagic

www.emagic.de

Emagic Software is another one of the DAW biggies that has the Mac market cornered with Logic 6 (see Figure B.9). This program, although a little on the complicated side, is one of the most comprehensive music-making applications on the scene. Emagic is owned by Apple Computer, making it a powerful combination of technology and music.

Figure B.8

Arturia has a soft synth to fit every mood.

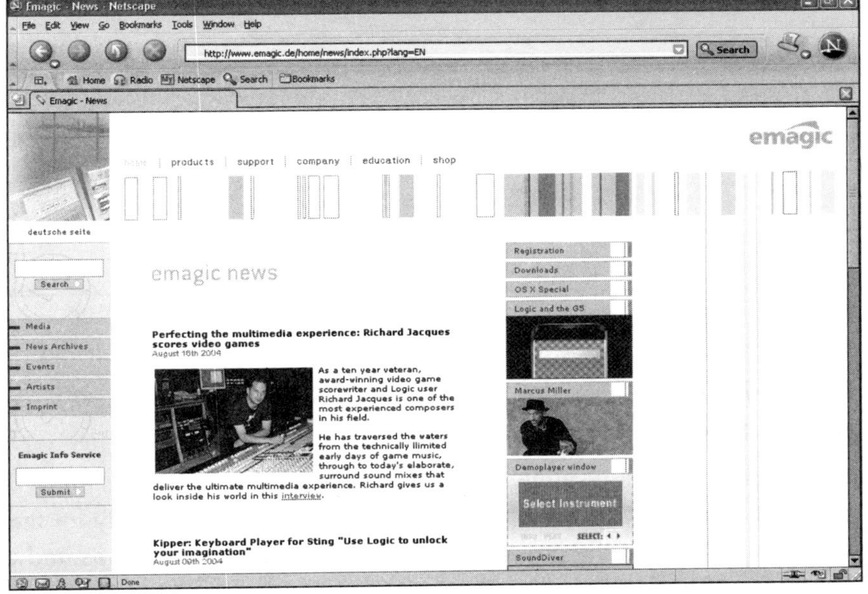

Figure B.9

The Emagic Web site provides updates to its product line and in-depth tutorials.

Digidesign

www.digidesign.com

Digidesign helped define the virtual studio by introducing its DAW application Pro Tools many years ago (see Figure B.10). To this day, Pro Tools is still used throughout the industry for post-production and song creation. Digi is also the manufacturer of some of the best-sounding hardware audio interfaces on the planet. They make hardware to match any budget and studio configuration.

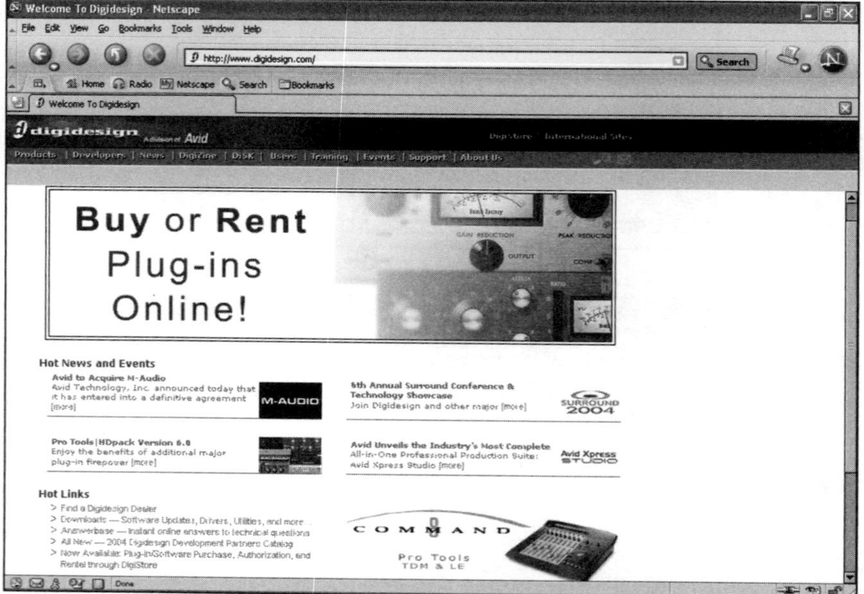

Figure B.10

The Digidesign Web site provides news, updates, and support for the various versions of Pro Tools and Digidesign hardware.

Cakewalk

www.cakewalk.com

Cakewalk's SONAR is another DAW software package that has taken the virtual studio world by storm (see Figure B.11). Made exclusively for the PC platform, SONAR is the program's program, with several features and an impressive graphical interface that meet the needs of both novice and professional musicians alike. Cakewalk also makes the Project 5 program, which makes for a good soft synth host.

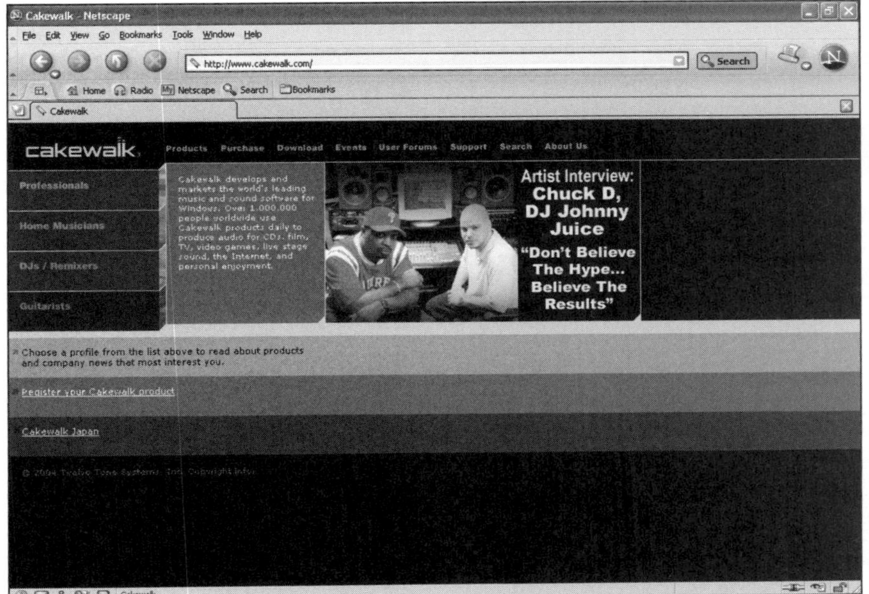

Figure B.11

The Cakewalk Web site is a well laid out Web site that provides news and updates for SONAR and Project 5.

Index

Symbols

Numbers

A

B

C

D

E

H

I

L

P

Q

R

T

W

X

Y

Z

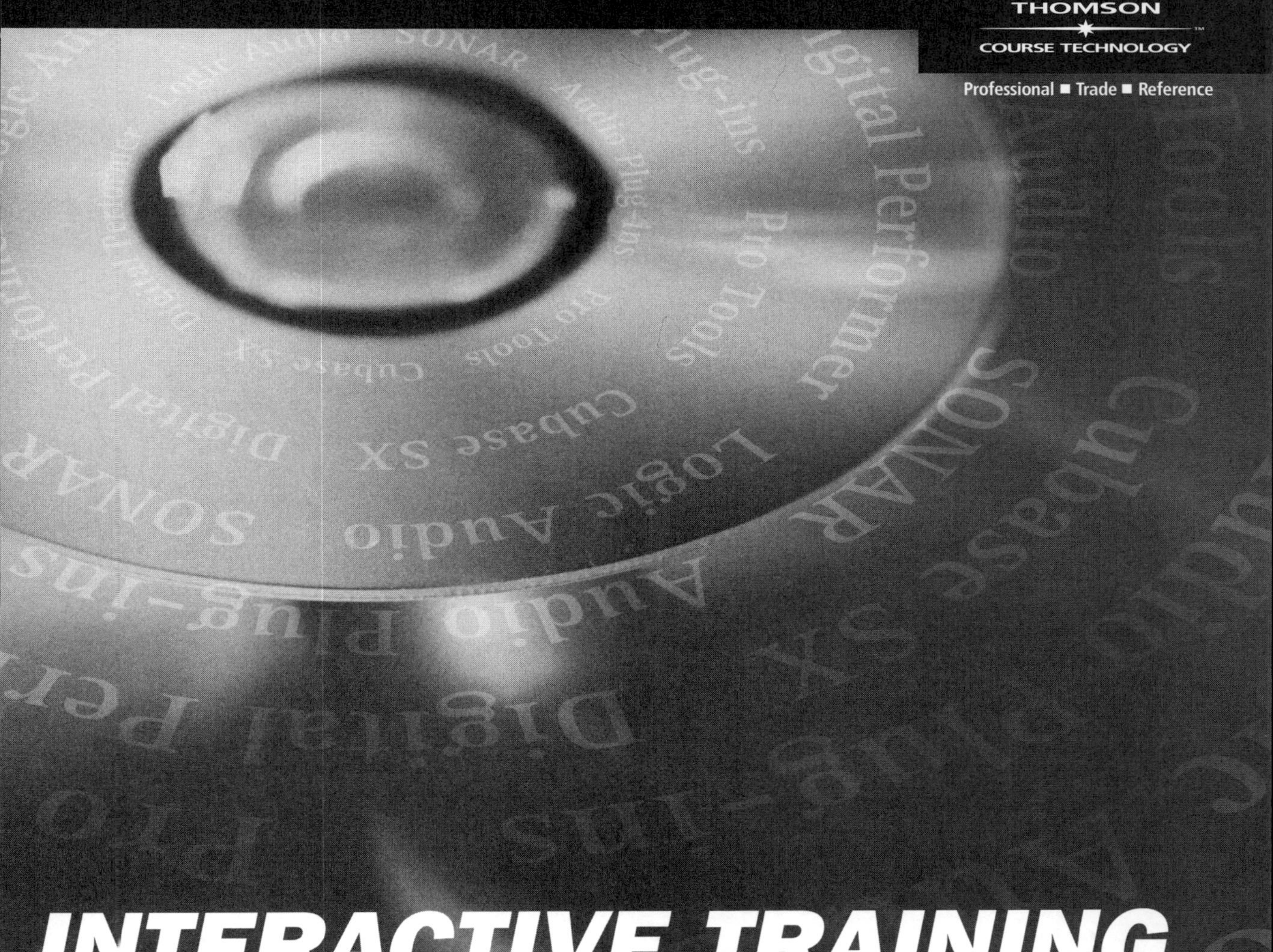